WITH GPS WAYPOINTS

Peter Vassilopoulos

· MARINAS ·

· FUEL DOCKS ·

· SUPPLY STORES ·

· GOLF COURSES ·

Books by the same author

North of Desolation Sound

Gulf Islands Cruising Guide

Western Waters Logbook

Anchorages and Marine Parks

Antiques Afloat
from the Golden Age of Boating in British Columbia

www.marineguides.com

Pacific Marine Publishing • Vancouver Canada

Pacific Marine Publishing. PO Box 1312 Stn A, Delta BC V4M 3Y8 Canada.
In the USA: PO Box 984, Point Roberts, WA. 98281-0984
Prepress graphics and typesetting Pacific Marine Publishing.
Printed in Canada.
Photographs by author unless otherwise indicated.

First Printing–August 1994. Second Printing–March 1995. Third Printing–March 1996 (Revised–2nd edition).
Fourth Printing–October 1998 (Revised–3rd edition). Fifth Printing–Dec 2000 (Revised–4th edition).
Sixth Printing–January 2003 (Revised–5th edition, with GPS Waypoints).
Seventh Printing–January 2005 (Revised–6th edition). Eighth Printing–January 2007 (Revised–7th edition).

Library and Archives Canada Cataloguing in Publication

Vassilopoulos, Peter, 1940-
Docks and Destinations / Peter Vassilopoulos. -- 7th ed.

Includes bibliographical references and index.
ISBN 978-0-919317-42-0

1. Marinas--British Columbia--Pacific Coast--Guidebooks.
2. Marinas--Washington (State)--San Juan Islands--Guidebooks. 3. Pacific Coast (B.C.)--Guidebooks. 4. San Juan Islands (Wash.)--Guidebooks. I. Title.

FC3845.P2A3 2007 387.1'5097111 C2006-906857-7

Seventh edition. Eighth printing, with new,
expanded, revised and updated information
Copies available from marine stores, marinas and book stores. Distribution enquiries to Pacific Marine Publishing Ph: 604-943-4618. email: *boating@dccnet.com*

DOCKS AND DESTINATIONS

Peter Vassilopoulos

A coastal guide to marinas, fuel and moorage facilities in the Pacific Northwest

Featuring Puget Sound and Hood Canal, the San Juan Islands, the Gulf Islands, Desolation Sound and North of Cape Caution to Ketchikan, Alaska. Plus the west coast of Vancouver Island

WITH GPS WAYPOINTS

Includes the San Juan Islands, the Strait of Georgia, the Lower Mainland, Howe Sound, the Sunshine Coast, Desolation Sound, Johnstone Strait, the Broughton Islands, Alert Bay area, Rivers Inlet to Prince Rupert, Vancouver Island–Quatsino Sound to Sooke, Juan de Fuca Strait, Admiralty Inlet, Hood Canal, Puget Sound.

Cover: Princess Louisa Inlet's dock at the fabulous Chatterbox Falls.

The author's detailed guides to the coast's more popular areas include lots of information about route planning, waterways, marinas and anchorages.

Preface

This guide covers marinas and docks with and without services. Use it whenever approaching any of the ports in order to know what dock layout and services are available. Mariners have found it particularly useful for planning and telephoning ahead for reservations. Please refer to **Anchorages and Marine Parks** for comprehensive coverage of the anchorages and marine parks on the BC coast and in the San Juan Islands. For more detailed information on popular areas covered by this guide refer to the author's **Gulf Islands Cruising Guide** and **North of Desolation Sound** (pictured above).

Boat owners are kindly asked to observe proper etiquette on the water and at the various marinas and other facilities. At some places there are severe water shortages and mariners are requested to use available water with discretion. Garbage cannot be disposed of easily at most island locations and mariners are asked to not leave their garbage at the docks. Expectations by mariners of the marina operators can sometimes be unreasonable. Please consider the difficulties under which people on the coast have to function. Their season is extremely short—about two and a half months to possibly three months of the summer holidays. They have to make a living and cover their annual costs in those short months. They have to bring in supplies, groceries and building materials from varying and often long distances.

There are many competent people working at marinas but staff who assist for summer are not always experienced and it is difficult for them to know the specific preferences of individual arriving boat operators. The facilities found along the more remote parts of the coast are usually very small businesses and mariners arriving in need of moorage and supplies are more than welcome, giving the operators an opportunity also to meet people and communicate on a friendly, personal level.

Boating friends and acquaintances have yet again offered advice on what to include and change in this new edition. I thank them for their input and have used some of their suggestions. Note that reference to water availability at marinas has been included mostly in areas where water is likely to be scarce. GPS readings have been taken with great care while visiting the various reference points. Others were referenced by using state of the art GPS equipment. Please use discretion when referencing the coordinates provided. Great care has been taken in publishing them but we cannot accept responsibility for typographic or other errors made in the process of transposing them.

I also thank the following for their help: My wife Carla, Robin Battley, Walter and Rita Lee, Henry and Jeanne Karcz, Heinz Bold, Chris and Sue Fraser, Duncan and Justin and Rosemary Taylor, Robert Hale and those fellow boat owners who have told me or reminded me about places I may otherwise have missed. Thanks also to Pacific Yachting Magazine, Waggoner, Boat Journal, Nor'Westing, Northwest Yachting, 48° North, Latitudes and Attitudes, local newspapers and others which have had kind reviews on the previous editions. Thanks to the many readers of the previous editions who reported back to me with information on changes and variations at coastal facilities.

GPS References

***Kevin Monahan** of **Shipwrite Productions** and author of the book,* **GPS–Instant Navigation**, *has kindly written the following about the use of the GPS coordinates in this guide:*

Latitude and Longitude—It's not quite that simple

Boaters using a modern GPS receiver can probably determine their position more accurately than was possible even for map-makers until just a few years ago. An unassisted GPS can now resolve a position to within 10 to 15 meters, 95% of the time. As a result, your GPS may be more accurate than your chart. As if this wasn't enough, the chart may also be drawn to a different horizontal datum than is used in your GPS, resulting in errors of up to 200 meters in Northern BC.

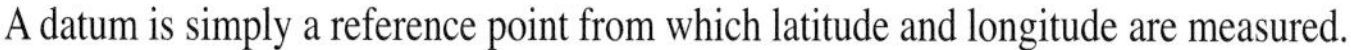

A datum is simply a reference point from which latitude and longitude are measured.

In 1927, map-makers in North America established the first truly continental datum at Meade's Ranch in Kansas. This datum was known as North American Datum 1927 (NAD27).

By 1983, using satellite telemetry data scientists had learned enough about the shape of the earth, that they were able to accurately model the surface of the earth. This allowed a new horizontal datum to be developed in North America—(NAD1983)—a datum that did not depend on any physical reference point.

When charts were drawn to the new datum, cartographers discovered that the positions of geographic features on older charts could not be reconciled with their positions on new charts—the lines of latitude and longitude on the older charts were in the wrong places. In many areas of the continent, these differences are minimal—just a few meters—but in northern B.C. and Alaska, the difference between NAD27 and NAD83 is over 200 meters.

Now that world-wide satellite positioning is available, GPS uses a truly universal chart datum—World Geodetic Survey 1984 (WGS84). In North America, WGS84 is equivalent to NAD83.

So much for the idea that latitude and longitude are absolute. Any one location can be represented by different lat/long co-ordinates, depending on the datum that is used. So in order to accurately identify a position, you must know not only the latitude and longitude, but the horizontal datum used as well.

The positions of the various docks etc. in this book have been taken directly from a Garmin GPS set to the WGS84 Horizontal Datum.

In general, it is best to match the datum your GPS reads out to the datum of the chart you are using. Thus if you are working with a chart drawn to NAD27, you should set your GPS to the same datum. Every chart should incorporate a Horizontal Datum note describing the datum used in that particular chart and the corrections to be applied to convert to NAD83 (or NAD27 as the case may be).

Boaters using electronic navigation systems with electronic charts will find that all their electronic charts have been compensated to read out in NAD83, and should simply ensure that their GPS is set to NAD83 at all times.

However, if you are using paper charts drawn to NAD27 and have set your GPS to the same datum, the latitudes and longitudes in this book will not match the positions on the chart, nor will they match the readings on your GPS. The only way to resolve this is to convert the latitudes and longitudes using the conversion factors in the Horizontal Datum note.

–Kevin Monahan

For more information on GPS and Horizontal Datums, visit www.shipwrite.bc.ca

---

In producing this latest edition of **Docks and Destinations** it is my sincerest hope that you will use it to expand your boating horizons in finding new and interesting destinations and convenient and safe overnight moorage. Like its companion guide, **Anchorages and Marine Parks**, it is designed to provide guidance but not to remove the joy of exploring for yourself. It is intended to encourage you to moor at a marina and go exploring ashore where walking the local roads and trails provides a good exercise break. Thanks to my wife Carla for assisting me in contacting marinas by boat, phone, email and fax for verification of the new information gathered for this edition. Thanks also to the marinas themselves for checking, verifying and providing information. A special thanks to Norman Elliot, Robin Battley, Sharon Allman and Iz Goto and others who supplied photographs and details for diagrams. And to Heinz Bold who flew me over some areas covered by aerial pictures.

BC is abundantly blessed with magnificent landscapes, waterfalls, mountain peaks and deep waterways. The use of photographs and other illustrations helps reveal the charm of the islands and inside passages of the area known as the Pacific Northwest. The best descriptions have been coined in the names of some coastal places such as Pleasant Harbor, God's Pocket, Minstrel Island, Bones Bay, Telegraph Cove, Kingcome, Ocean Falls and many others.

–Peter Vassilopoulos

Justin Taylor photo

Above: Downtown Vancouver has marinas which cater to visiting yachts. The harbour is protected from severe weather throughout most of summer and the marinas are just a short walk into the city centre. Several restaurants located on the waterfront will cater to you right at your boat. Venture on through the harbour to the waters of Indian Arm, as remote as any you will find farther up the coast towards Alaska. Or pull into False Creek where marinas and anchorage are available and where you can easily go ashore and visit the renown tourist attractions at Granville Island (three hour stopping is permitted at the docks pictured above).

Marinas–Guest Moorage

NOTE: GOLF COURSES are listed on marina pages by name and phone number. Carry your equipment aboard.

Guest Docks and Marinas

From Olympia to Ketchikan

The format of this book takes the reader in a south to north progression from one dock to the next, beginning in the San Juan Islands and terminating at Ketchikan, southeast Alaska. Vancouver Island west coast information is arranged from north to south. It concludes by continuing south from Juan de Fuca Strait to Olympia. The intention is to provide a logical sequence of references to fuel stops and overnight moorage en route to a final destination.

Information accompanying the graphics and photographs is up to date but constant changes are being made at various marinas. From season to season mostly small changes occur at marinas, however this book is revised and updated periodically depending on the frequency and extent to which coastal facilities are altered or improved.

Helpful Information

Many Pacific Northwest marinas are exclusively operated for privately owned pleasure boats. Here boats are stored and maintained throughout the year. As the dawn breaks each year on a new spring and the chill of winter is diminished, owners and yacht club members take to scrubbing and polishing their boats in preparation for a colourful sailpast followed by as many boating weekends and prolonged periods away as possible. Cruising to general destinations such as the the San Juans, the Gulf Islands or Desolation Sound is the trend. Frequently there are no specific plans for overnight moorage other than a vague intention to stop if there is suitable anchorage or moorage at one of several possible overnight shelters. With ever increasing numbers of boats converging on popular destinations, it is becoming essential that reservations for moorage be made in advance.

This guide is intended to help mariners decide where to stop in safe, sheltered moorage overnight and where services, needed by the boat owners or their crews, can be readily acquired. To this end it provides phone numbers, details of marina facilities, fuel stops and other pertinent information.

Heading Out

Yachts bound for the northwest inside passage from exposed Pacific coastal routes each summer appreciate the relative comfort once inside Juan de Fuca Strait. They, and Puget Sound and Lake Washington boat owners, however, may still be faced with current and tide rips off Whidbey Island. Some face the challenge of locking through the Hiram M. Chittenden locks, while La Conner mariners contend with strong tidal currents through the Swinomish Canal. Victoria and vicinity mariners require a passage around an often rough and tide-ripped Trial Islands and up through a sometimes testy Haro Strait before they reach the more placid waters off Sidney. Fortunately most Victoria residents can take one look out to sea and determine the ease of passage. Checking with the tide and current tables is always sound logic to ensure a comfortable beginning of a cruise.

Sidney and Saanich Inlet mariners are in much the same position, but they have the advantage of being where they are going without even leaving the dock (that is–practically in the heart of the Gulf Islands). And the same applies to Maple Bay, Ladysmith and Nanaimo. Mariners in these areas have enviably easy access for extended seasonal periods to the anchorages and marinas of the Gulf Islands but often look farther afield for their major trips. Their favoured distant destinations include Desolation Sound and beyond. At Nanaimo, locals and visiting mariners alike, may await the slack at Dodd Narrows before venturing south into the islands, or may stay at the docks while seas off Entrance Island settle after a storm before crossing the Strait to Vancouver, the Sunshine Coast or en route north.

Vessels at marinas on the Sunshine Coast or at places north of Nanaimo are already part way to cruising in Desolation Sound and beyond. Check your marine charts for area WG and call to ensure that no military exercises are in progress before crossing this part of the Strait of Georgia.

Mariners on the Vancouver side of the Strait of Georgia may spend days monitoring weather forecasts prior to a major trip, and certainly will listen to the reports on VHF prior to any other departure. Wind and wave height is of utmost interest, tidal changes and currents can be critical and even openings of fishing to the commercial industry can affect one's plans to set off on a voyage. Vessels leaving Vancouver and Port Moody are subject to the currents under Lions Gate bridge and Second Narrows.

Leaving False Creek is quite straight forward and bumpy conditions off Stanley Park are the quick

The lightship at the entrance to the Fraser Riveer. It is a beacon for mariners travelling north from the San Juan Islands to Vancouver or the Sunshine Coast. River outflow causes turbulence at times. Be cautious.

indicator that worse stuff lies ahead, usually beginning at Point Atkinson. Boats departing Richmond and running down the North Arm of the Fraser may reach open water before determining that it was not such a good idea to leave the dock.

Most vessels from Vancouver and Richmond areas have Howe Sound as their playground. The facilities in Howe Sound are among the best on the coast and yachtsmen find satisfaction in spending time at places on Bowen Island or at Gibsons. Out of Surrey or Delta the Gulf Islands are closer than Howe Sound, and mariners mooring their boats at Ladner, Crescent Beach or Point Roberts can be in the midst of the Gulf Islands in less than an hour (a little longer in a sail boat or displacement trawler).

Leaving the Fraser River is one of the biggest challenges on the west coast. (Returning is another.) A receding tide near low water, especially against a west or northwesterly moderate breeze (don't even think about a strong wind or worse) can be dangerous in the extreme. Refer to the government publication on Weather and Thompson's **Oceanology** for interesting information about current, wind and wave patterns at the river mouth. Bear in mind that while the weather report covers Sand Heads windspeeds it does not always provide wave height at the river mouth, a sadly lacking service, especially considering the dangerous nature of the seas at that point. You can always turn back and wait at Steveston for improved conditions or return to your marina.

Leaving Crescent Beach is straight forward enough except that it is a long run across an open bay before entering the Strait. Point Roberts is well located for quick, visual assessment of conditions in the Strait and close enough to the San Juan and Gulf islands that a crossing of the Strait is quick enough even for slower travelling vessels. But it is very exposed to bad weather conditions for a return trip and mariners should carefully determine what they can expect off Point Roberts before leaving the safety of a comfortable mooring on the other side.

Boats cruising to Canada out of other Washington ports have some extra distance to travel through US waters to reach their Canadian destinations. Many simply stay in the San Juan Islands, which have numerous well run marinas and boating facilities. Vessels passing through en route to Canada have to be mindful of wind and tidal conditions at several passages, but with careful weather monitoring the trip can be most pleasant.

Canadians travelling to the San Juans and Puget Sound should know where they are headed and check the route before leaving. Watch for obvious current-swept waterways and consult the tide and current tables. When cruising any unknown waters check what other boats are doing. If there are no other boats about be particularly cautious and double check the current predictions and weather reports.

Vessels travelling across the border, unless they have a US cruising pass and/or subscribe to *Canpass* or *Nexus* must stop at a customs dock for clearance and should carry their clearance reporting number for checking back into their home country. It is mandatory for vessels crossing the border either way to clear customs. Vessels may be stopped by the RCMP in Canadian waters and fined for not having a customs clearance number, even if just passing through with 'Right of Passage.'

Marina Etiquette

Some homes at marinas are more than just your average bungalow. There is bound to be a helipad on the yacht too.

Marinas are a home away from home. When you tie up to a dock at a private marina you are in effect stopping in to visit other boat owners and the owners and operators of the marina. What you do and how you operate your vessel says a lot about you and a lot about your experience as a mariner. Your reception from marina managers and fellow boat owners will be determined by the impression you create from the moment you nudge your boat up to the dock.

Some boat owners, and often this applies to novices, don't really care how they are perceived by others. Those same people also tend to not learn from their errors. For mariners who wish to fit in, be they newcomers or old hands, here are some basic tips, but first, take the mandatory boating course and obtain your operator's proficiency certificate.

During the peak months of summer telephone ahead for reservations. Remember changes are being made constantly and you can expect to find new additions at some docks, name and phone number changes, different regulations, revised services and other variances from the information contained in this guide. Please note the changes for your own convenience.

Before you arrive at a marina ensure you are not passing other installations at speed. Slow down well before you reach the dock. Sitting at a dock in West Sound in the San Juans once I saw a large boat come by at full speed leaving a wash in excess of two feet that caused some damage at the dock. He was heading for a club dock at the head of the bay and had totally ignored the existence of the marina tucked in behind the island to his starboard. That same week I saw a similar sized vessel do the same thing entering Bedwell Bay.

Before you enter the marina establish exactly where your assigned slip is. In many marinas you can call on VHF for slip assignment. The dock photographs and diagrams in this book should help you easily locate the slip or general area of the slip to which you have been assigned. As you approach your slip note effects of current and wind and plan your docking manoeuvres accordingly. It's always easiest to angle in towards the dock against the flow of water or direction of the wind. If you are backing your boat into a tight slip it is even more essential that you are aware of these conditions. Have your crew at the ready and prepared for landing.

Play it the way the pros do. They attach a line to a centre cleat and hold the end coiled in one hand as they step ashore. Snubbing the line to a cleat on the dock when the boat is close to that cleat will keep it there and prevent the bow or stern from breaking away and swinging out, as often occurs when only a line at the bow or the stern is used. Have fenders down at a height compatible with the height of the docks and positioned one ahead of the centre cleat and one near the stern. Once the boat is stopped the skipper can casually step ashore, secure the bow and stern lines and adjust fenders at leisure.

Crew: Other people may offer assistance. Usually they expect to be handed a line and all too often when they take it they totally destroy your docking plan. This is usually done by yarding on the bow line, bringing the bow in too close to the dock disabling you from handling the stern. You don't have to pass them a line. Do so if absolutely necessary or when the skipper has the boat docked. No harm saying to a person "Here is the line, please just hold it" or have two docksiders haul in bow and stern simultaneously. Don't try to look as though you are proficient if you cannot pull it off. You are better off to say to anyone watching as you are approaching your slip that you are new at this and would appreciate some experienced help in docking. You'll be surprised how readily people will come to

Right, top to bottom: The friendly wharfinger at Salt Spring Island steps aboard our boat to chat for a minute while collecting mooring fees. Make your stops at marinas pleasant by asking for information about local facilities and services. At Bedwell Bay, tending the fuel dock is just part of running a marina. Visiting author Bob Hale is pleased to find new facilities at Big Bay on Stuart Island. Docks and Destinations publishing associate Carla examines a weather reporting receiver alongside a Port Angeles marina–the weather at the press of a button.

your aid and how pleasant they will be when you are up front about your docking abilities.

Docking is just the beginning. You will not enamour yourself or your crew to anyone at the dock if you yell, either at them or at your crew. At many marinas there are full-time personnel employed to assist boaters docking. They are not always the most experienced but as long as you follow some of the above advice their assistance will enable you to perform a good landing.

If you are docking parallel to a long open dock, tie up your boat in such a way that you allow maximum room for the next boat coming in. If you have a dinghy in the water tuck it in under the bow of your boat while you are not using it in order that you leave room for the next boat.

Anchoring off and going ashore to visit a marina and its facilities, perhaps to have a meal, a snack or browse for some souvenir is a common practice during summer. Also common is the individual who goes ashore only to drop off a huge bag of garbage. On small, remote islands, this is a major problem. If you are a mooring guest you may do well to assess how convenient it is to leave garbage behind, even though some places have disposal bins. If you know you are continuing to a mainland facility soon, save the garbage for that stop. The same applies to water. If you are travelling to an island with limited water resources fill up before going there and use water sparingly. Do not use scarce, island water to wash your boat.

Some boat owners have been known to tie up at a marina for long periods during the day, fill up with water, perhaps use the facilities such as shower and laundry and then take off and anchor across the bay for the night. There are times when such use of moorage has denied a prospective overnight moorage customer space to tie up. Marinas have a very limited season in which to prosper and mariners who cause lost overnight moorage will not be appreciated.

Most marina operators will be happy to have you stop for a short period if you don't plan to spend the night. Some have a charge per hour. Others, like public docks, allow two hours free and then an overnight charge is levied. If you make use of marinas and their services as a paying guest you will help ensure their survival for the future.

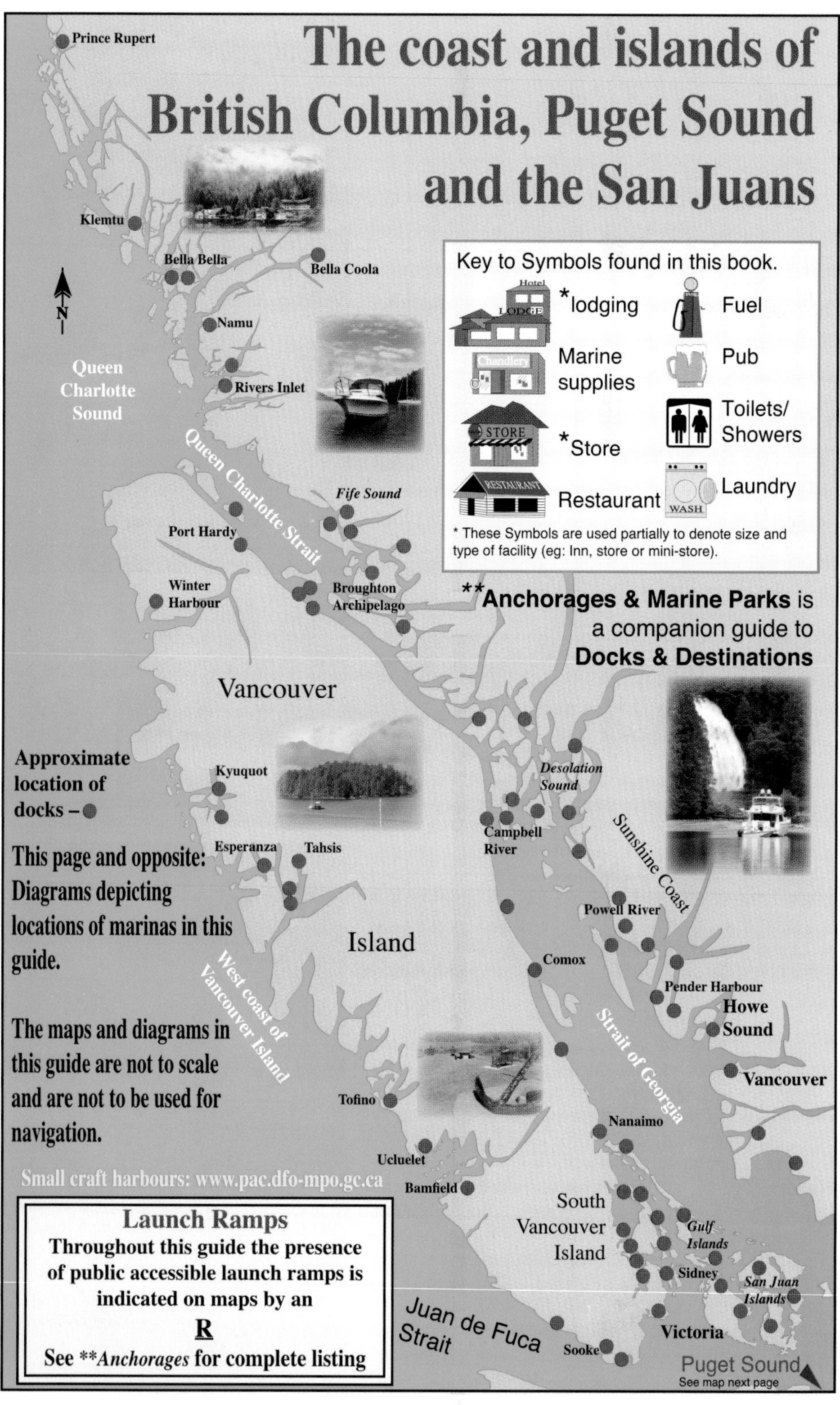
The coast and islands of British Columbia, Puget Sound and the San Juans
Key to Symbols found in this book.
*lodging
Fuel
Marine supplies
Pub
Toilets/ Showers
*Store
Laundry
Restaurant
* These Symbols are used partially to denote size and type of facility (eg: Inn, store or mini-store).
**Anchorages & Marine Parks is a companion guide to Docks & Destinations
Approximate location of docks –
This page and opposite: Diagrams depicting locations of marinas in this guide.
The maps and diagrams in this guide are not to scale and are not to be used for navigation.
Small craft harbours: www.pac.dfo-mpo.gc.ca
Launch Ramps
Throughout this guide the presence of public accessible launch ramps is indicated on maps by an
R
See **Anchorages for complete listing
Prince Rupert
Klemtu
Bella Bella
Bella Coola
Namu
Rivers Inlet
Queen Charlotte Sound
Queen Charlotte Strait
Fife Sound
Port Hardy
Winter Harbour
Broughton Archipelago
Vancouver
Island
Kyuquot
Esperanza
Tahsis
Desolation Sound
Campbell River
Sunshine Coast
Powell River
Comox
Pender Harbour
Howe Sound
Vancouver
West coast of Vancouver Island
Strait of Georgia
Tofino
Nanaimo
Ucluelet
Bamfield
South Vancouver Island
Gulf Islands
Sidney
San Juan Islands
Juan de Fuca Strait
Victoria
Sooke
Puget Sound
See map next page

Not for Navigation
Big Bay
Surge Narrows
Refuge Cove
Heriot Bay
Gorge Harbour
Campbell River
Lund
Desolation Sound
Powell River
N

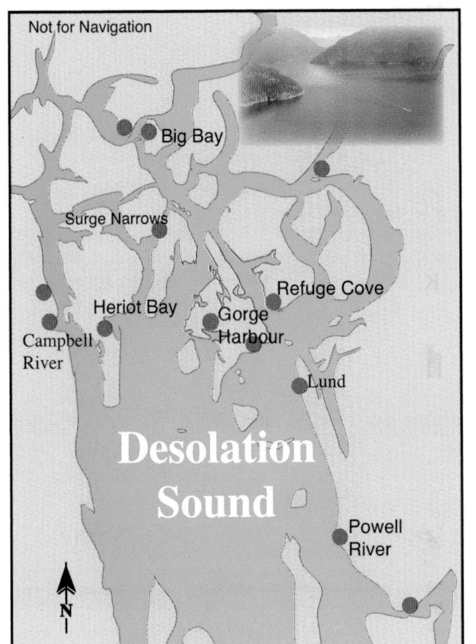

For more indepth information on the Gulf Islands and the Broughtons see the author's guides: ***Gulf Islands Cruising Guide*** and ***North of Desolation Sound***

Popular Destinations

The areas shown on these pages depict where most cruising activity takes place during the summer boating season.

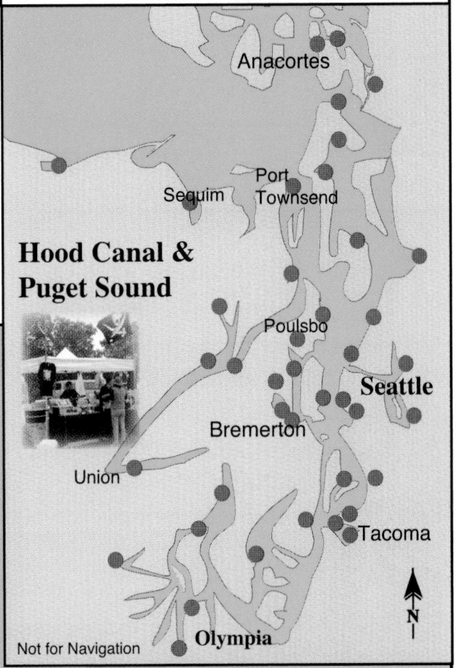

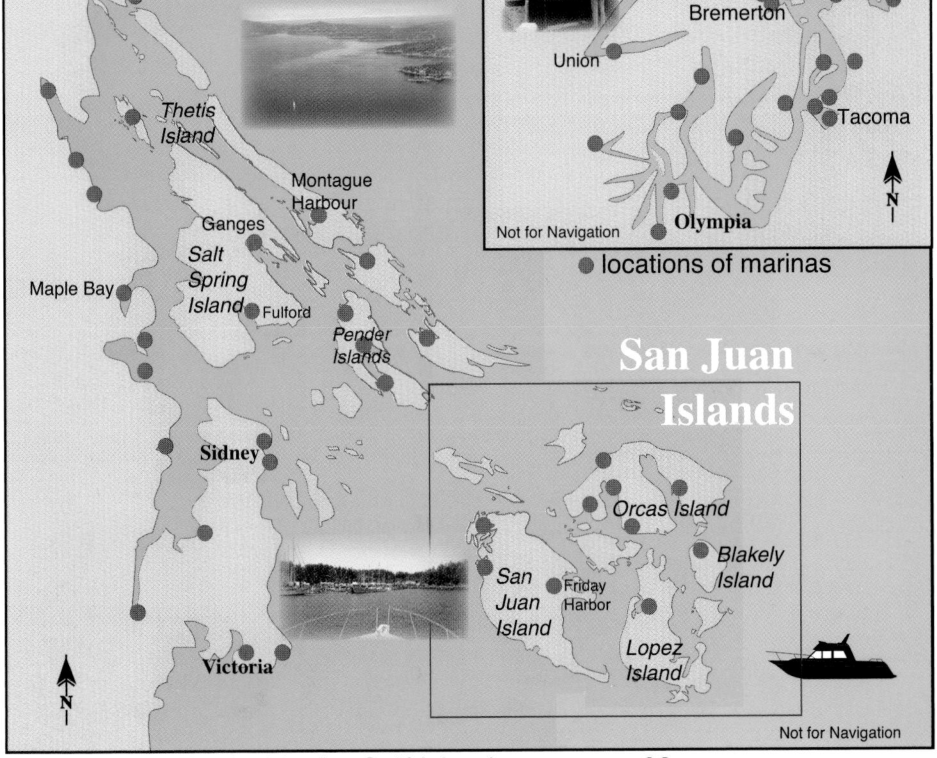

Anacortes
Sequim
Port Townsend
Hood Canal & Puget Sound
Poulsbo
Seattle
Bremerton
Union
Tacoma
N
Not for Navigation
Olympia

Nanaimo
Gulf Islands
Thetis Island
Montague Harbour
Ganges
Salt Spring Island
Maple Bay
Fulford
Pender Islands
locations of marinas
San Juan Islands
Sidney
Orcas Island
Blakely Island
San Juan Island
Friday Harbor
Lopez Island
Victoria
N
Not for Navigation

For fuel in the Gulf Islands see page 62.

Above: The marina at Roche Harbor.
Left: Whale sighting are common nearby–the farther north the bigger the whales, it seems. This was sighted off the southern tip of Alaska. Photo taken by Carla Vassilopoulos aboard a small inflatable boat.
Below: The classic Orcas Hotel overlooks the local San Juan Islands ferry terminal.

San Juan Islands

Section 1

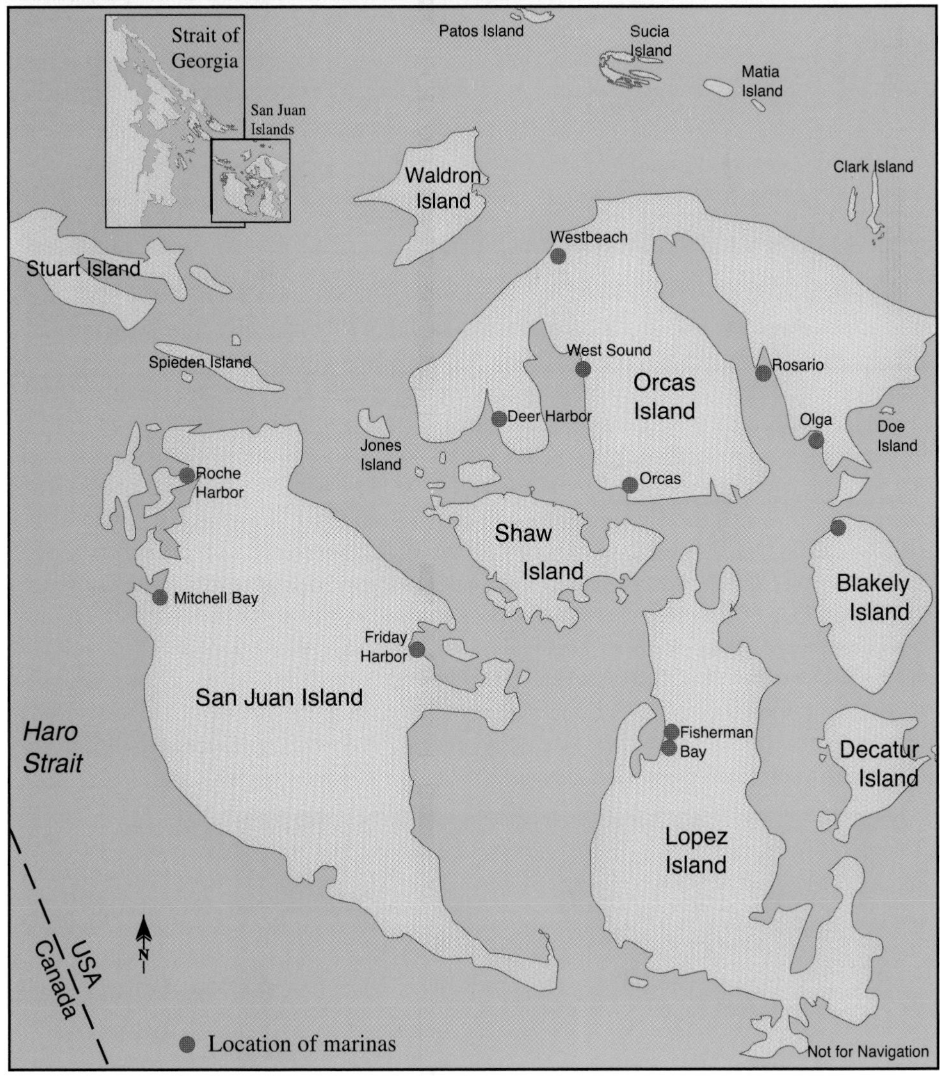

Journeying into the San Juans mariners have the pick of some outstanding marinas, fine restaurants, well-stocked marine, grocery and hardware stores as well as arts and gifts centres. There are fast food places, ice cream vendors, pubs, hotels, good accommodations and rustic bed and breakfast places. There are walking and hiking trails and roads as well as car, bicycle and motor scooter rentals. Some stops include dining at places such fine restaurants or quaint delicatessens for a good bowl of soup, a sandwich, salad or dessert. At Friday Harbour there is such a wide choice of

restaurants as well as other stores it would take an entire vacation to enjoy the place to its fullest. The annual Jazz Festival on the last weekend in July is a busy time so get in early or keep away if you want to avoid crowds. A more tranquil place may be Fisherman Bay with its good anchorage and marinas, nearby Lopez Village and pleasant dining facilities. Roche Harbor is a busy customs port and attracts some of the larger cruising yachts to its busy marina. It's a place to visit if you like to look longingly at some of those mega vessels that frequent and even monopolize it. The Hotel De Haro usually has fine dining and it's entertaining to watch the evening color ceremony at sundown. Fascinating history of the islands include the early explorations of the Spanish, the presence of the English and the famous Pig War which nearly led to an international confrontation between the British and Americans. One of the more charming remnants of recent history of the islands is Rosario Resort on Orcas Island. A stop at this facility will provide sheltered moorage as well as a chance to acquaint yourself with its splendid history.

A short or long stay in the San Juans can provide a complete vacation, and many Canadians make the trip once in a while just as their American counterparts are steaming through the San Juans en route to the Canadian Gulf Islands and points beyond.

Above left and opposite right: Friday Harbor. Opposite page: The dock at Sucia Island. It is busy in summertime but during fair weather there is also lots of good anchorage in the bay. Left: Rosario Resort on Orcas Island.

The San Juans include a number of smaller islands. The moorage in these islands is associated with marine parks and not included in this book. But there are some facilities such as the two docks at Sucia Island. They are located in Fossil Bay. The one shown below is the dock of choice due to its greater protection from prevailing winds. The other is set deeper into the bay, to the south west. They fill up fast, as do all popular destinations in summer. Please refer to the author's companion book Anchorages and Marine Parks.

Roche Harbor

48° 36.550' N
123° 09.228' W

Roche Harbor Resort & Marina

Kevin Carlton
248 Reuben Memorial Dr
PO Box 4001, Roche Harbor WA 98250
Ph: 360-378-2155 Fax: 360-378-9800
Toll Free: 1-800-451-8910
marina@rocheharbor.com
www.rocheharbor.com

Chart 18421, 18433 **VHF 78A**

Marina services:
Moorage. 377 permanent and transient slips to about 180 feet. **Pumpout** facilities.
Power at docks: 30, 50, 100 amps.
Fuel: Gas, diesel. Propane. Oil.
Snack bar, restaurant.

Customer services:
Showers, laundry, washrooms.
Public phones ashore. Phone hook up.
Walking: Road access walking, cycling.

Adjacent and nearby: Store–groceries, a wide range of provisions. Hotel, fine dining, accommodations. Gifts. Clothing, apparel, gifts, ice, fishing tackle, licences, marine supplies. Moped rentals. Horse riding. Hiking trails. Boat rentals, kayaks. Good fishing nearby. Pool and tennis courts. Nature sculpture park. Jazz festival late July–call for information. Fourth of July celebrations and fireworks. Color ceremony each sunset. Coffee wagon.
All facilities open March through October. Moorage and basic facilities open year round–partial during winter. Launch ramp nearby. Taxi or bus service to island centres and ferry to Anacortes. Airfield.

San Juan Golf and Country Club 360-378-2254

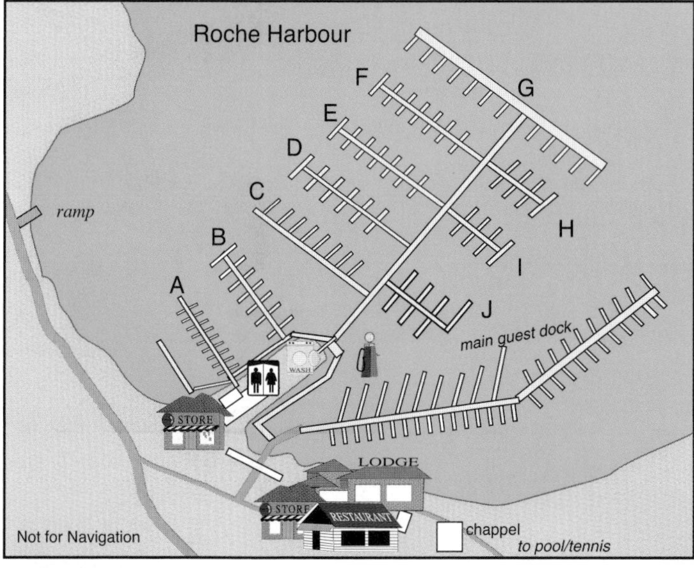

Below, left: Facilities at Roche Harbor include the well stocked store whose name commemorates the historic Lime Stone company for which Roche Harbour was founded. Below: The marina provides lots of moorage. Opposite, bottom: The very busy dock manager organizes slips and boat movement.

Hotel de Haro is the historic landmark at this famous harbor. It is a magnificent building exemplifying the type of construction and opulence of its day. There is a lot to see and do at Roche Harbor. Attend the sundown striking of the colors ceremony.

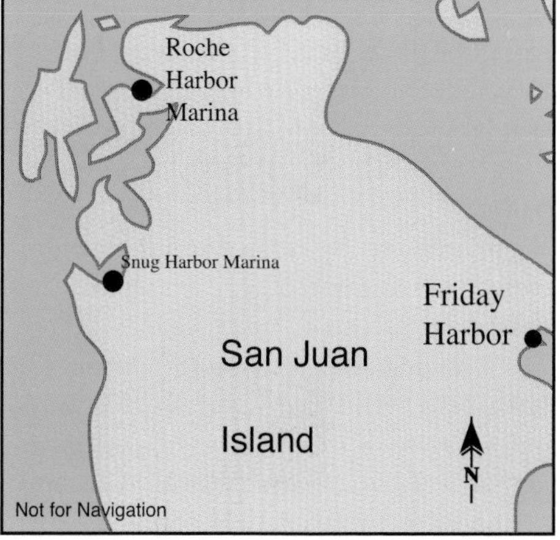

The resort is a museum in its own right, its buildings dating back to 1886. It was founded in conjunction with the adjacent lime kiln and barrel manufacturing company.

A beautifully landscaped harbor village is being developed adjacent to the marina.

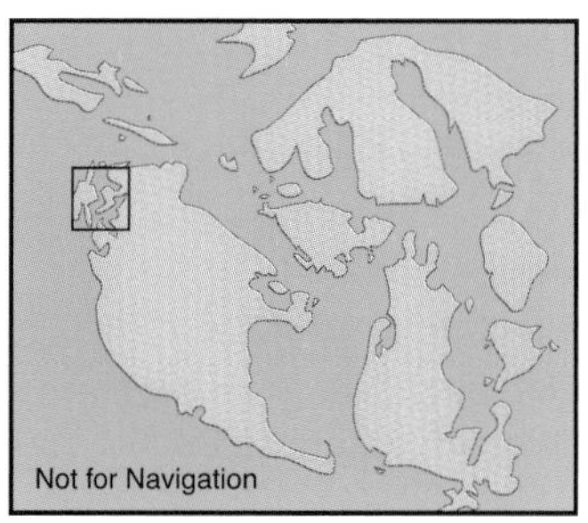

Friday Harbor

48° 32.386' N
123° 00.827' W

Port of Friday Harbor

Tami Hayes (Harbormaster)
204 Front St
PO Box 889
Friday Harbour WA 98250-0889
Ph: 360-378-2688 Fax: 360-378-6114
tamih@portfridayharbor.org
www.portfridayharbor.org

Charts 18434, 18421, Waterproof #43
VHF 66A

Marina services:
Moorage. Guest and permanent moorage with over 110 slips.
Power at docks: 30, 50, 100 amp.
Launch ramp. Internet access.
Fuel dock adjacent: Gas, diesel, propane.

Customer services:
Pumpout boat. Garbage disposal. Recycling.
Laundry, showers, ice, bait.
Pharmacies and other necessities.
Scuba diving arrangements and charters–ask at nearby dive store or marina for details.

Walking: Road access walking, cycling, car and scooter rentals.

Entertainment:
Regular annual music festival late July, Pig War Barbecue in June. Many other events.

Nearby facilities:
Nearby churches: multi-denominational. Public phones ashore. Ferry to Anacortes. Marine stores–charts, marine hardware, supplies, books, fishing licences, tackle, etc. Post office, liquor, restaurants, banks, accommodations, pubs and grocery and specialty stores. Golf, cinema, airport.

Note:
When arriving at Friday Harbor from Canadian waters first check in at the customs dock on the breakwater.
The flag up means the office on the dock is open. Down means you can check in at the office ashore or by telephone if that office is closed. Then proceed to Dock A for slip assignment or call on VHF 66A.

San Juan Golf & Country Club 360-378-2254

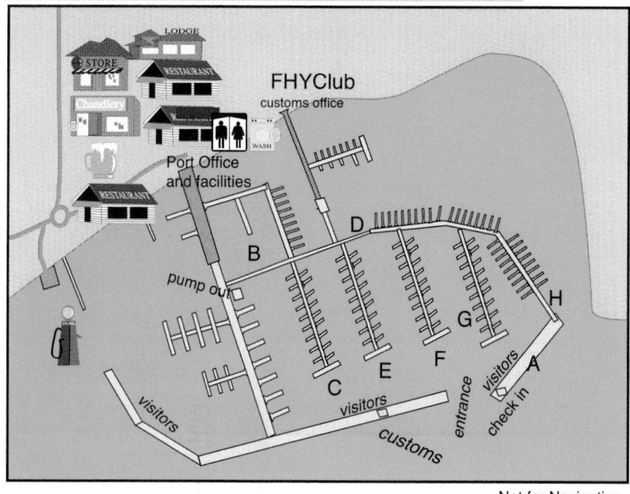

Not for Navigation

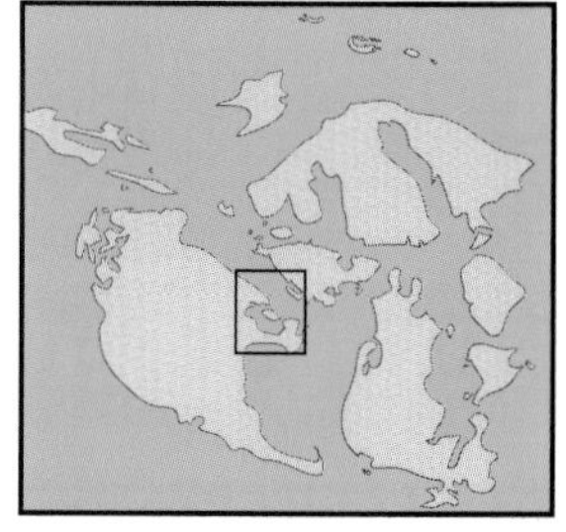

Major Customs Port of Entry:
Toll Free: 1-800-562-5943
For PIN number holders only.

Friday Harbor

This large marina is one of the busiest in the Pacific Northwest. It is a major customs stop entering United States waters for Canadian boat operators and one of the major centres for returning American mariners. Located on the east side of San Juan Island it competes with Roche Harbor as a customs stop but the two are vastly different. Friday Harbor has a large town comprising everything from city hall to cinema, supermarkets to specialty shops, hardware store, marine chandleries and a wide variety of restaurants, pubs and bistros. As a major ferry landing, Friday Harbor sees the coming and going of a vast number of people: islanders, cyclists coming to visit, campers, boaters and fly-in sightseers. During summer crowds of boaters flock to the town for the major event of the year, the Summer Jazz Festival. A Pig War barbecue is held in June.

For the boat owner there is fuel, moorage, water, showers, laundry, 30 amp electrical service and all the amenities one could imagine necessary for a major stopover. There are two anchorages in the immediate proximity of the huge marina, one adjacent to the north west marina entrance and the other out in the middle of the harbor.

Snug Harbor

Snug Harbor Marina Resort

Glenn Kalmus
1997 Mitchell Bay Rd
Friday Harbor WA 98250-8507
Ph: 360-378-4762 Fax: 360-378-8859
Chart: Waterproof #43. 18421, 18433
sneakaway@snugresort.com
www.snugresort.com

Marina services:
Moorage. Guest moorage 50'.
Reservations suggested.
Power: 30 amp.
Fuel: Gas. Repairs. Marine supplies.
Customer services: Garbage bins.
Shower, laundry, washrooms.
General store, groceries, provisions, charts, books, clothing, gifts, hardware, marine, fishing equipment. Restaurant–seasonal grill.
Public phones ashore.
Road access walking.
Adjacent Facilities: Accommodations. Ten self-contained, fully equipped bungalows. RV park. Launch ramp. Scuba charters, whale watching. Shuttle service in summer.
Note: Rocks in entrance. Channel to left. Depth 3' at zero tides.
Use large scale chart or Waterproof #43 for navigating inside Henry Island.
Nearest customs at Roche Harbor.

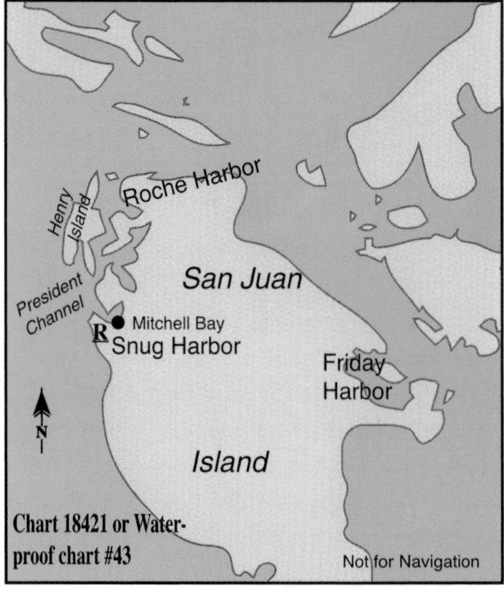

Snug Harbor Marina in Mitchell Bay is protected from the open waters of Haro Strait by a shallow entrance and drying reef. The channel at zero tides drops to three feet. The bay lies south of Roche Harbor. It is also a good anchorage.

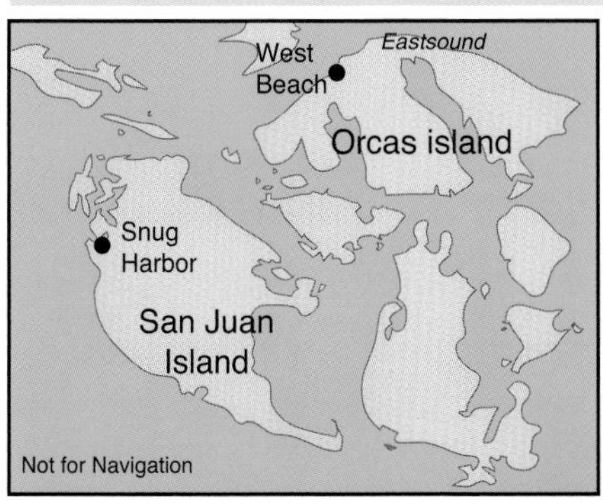

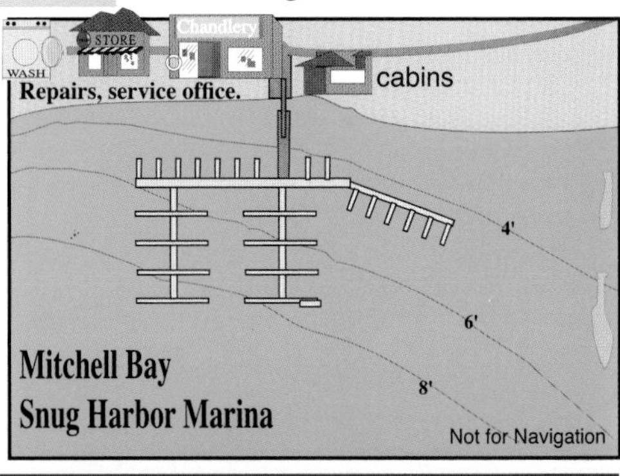

Orcas Island

Charts 18432, 18433, 18421

West Beach Resort

Jamie Hance
190 Waterfront Way
Eastsound WA 98245
Ph: 360-376-2240 Fax: 360-376-4746
Toll free: 1-877-937-8224
vacation@westbeachresort.com
www.westbeachresort.com

48° 41.268' N
122° 57.783' W

Marina services:
Moorage. Transient boats to 26'. About 700' dock space. 10 mooring buoys–seasonal.
Fuel: Gas. Propane, ice.

Customer services: Internet access. Fish cleaning facility. **Showers, laundry, washrooms.** Resort. Store, coffee shop. Espresso, charts, books, gifts, fishing tackle, bait. Kayak tours. Walking–road access. Playground. Good scuba diving, whale watching in the nearby waters.
Adjacent Facilities: Accommodations. 18 self-contained, fully equipped bungalows. RV park. Scuba airfills. Public phone. Launch ramp–guests only (fee includes parking for trailers). Shopping at Eastsound.

Below: Travelling around Orcas Island on motor scooters enabled us to visit some of the marinas by land–just for a different perspective. Carla rides past madrona trees lining the road near the entrance to West Bay Marina.

Deer Harbor

48° 37.186' N
123° 00.114' W

Deer Harbor Marina

Marc Broman
5164 Deer Harbor Rd
PO Box 344 Deer Harbor WA 98243.
Ph: 360-376-3037 Fax: 360-376-6091
info@bellportgroup.com
www.bellportgroup.com

Chart 18434 VHF 78A

Marina services:
Moorage. Transient and permanent. 110 slips. **Power** at docks: 30 amp. Pumpout service.
Fuel: Gas, diesel. Garbage disposal.
Customer services: Store–groceries, deli and provisions. Barbecue area. Accommodations. **Showers, laundry, washrooms**. Ice. Public phones ashore. ATM. Internet access. Road access walking, cycling.
Entertainment:
Heated swimming pool and spa. Small boat rentals, whale watching tours, kayaking, sunset cruises and fishing charters.
Adjacent facilities: Store–gifts, postcards, clothing. Haulout nearby. Deer Harbor Restaurant–elegant dining. Shuttle to Eastsound, Golf Course, ferries. Taxi service to island centres and ferry to Anacortes. Seaplane service to Seatac. There is a small beach alongside the marina.

Note:
• Passage through Pole Pass requires careful navigation in sometimes strong tidal currents. Be cautious of the rocky shoreline.
• Clear customs for USA destinations at Roche Harbor or Friday Harbor.

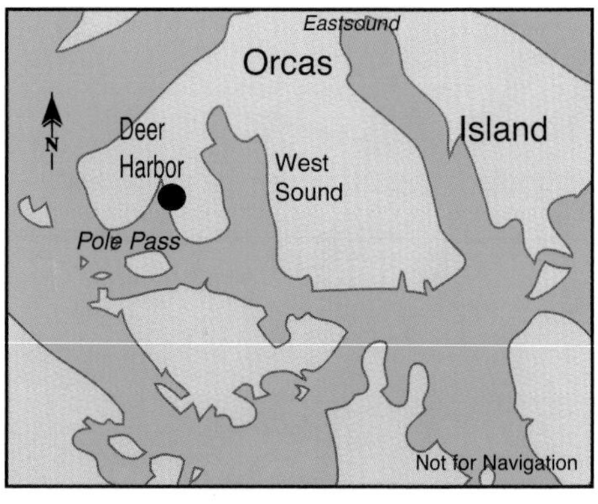

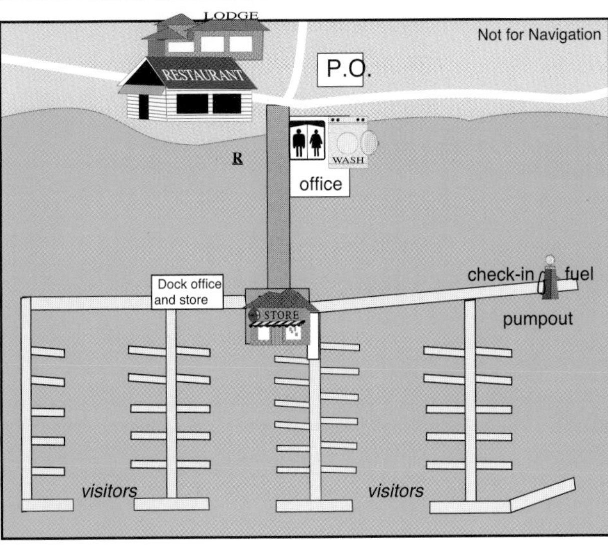

This is a busy marina in summer. It is designed and operated for visitors and has amenities for boaters on the move. Inset shows docks off season. Opposite page: Check-in and fuel dock at Deer Harbor.

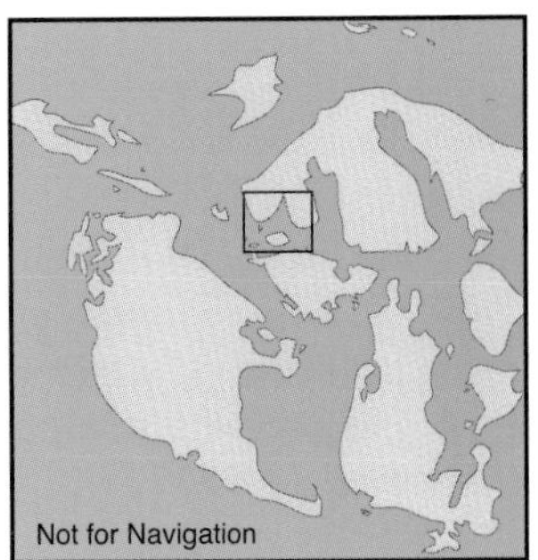

Deer Harbor

This cosy corner of Orcas Island is a pleasant stopover at docks that face a semi-protected open bay. Most wind conditions do not bother boats at the marina but a southerly or south westerly wind may cause a bit of movement, especially off season. In season many boats visit the docks to stay overnight and enjoy excellent cuisine at nearby restaurants. The marina offers fuel, water, showers, ice, snacks and groceries. A resort located just across the road offers accommodations and spa amentities.

48° 37.765' N 123° 57.631' W

West Sound

West Sound Marina

Betsy Wareham
525 Deer Harbor Rd,
PO Box 119
Orcas Island WA 98280-0119
Ph: 360-376-2314 Fax: 360-376-4634
Chart 18421, 18434
VHF 16

Hazard: Island reef off Picnic Island near the guest dock. See photo above.

Marina services:
Moorage. Some 300' of guest moorage. **Power** at docks: 30 amp. Pumpout. Garbage disposal. **Showers, washrooms.**
Fuel: Gas, diesel, oils, propane.
Customer services:
Major repair yard.Marine ways. 30 ton hoist. Complete marine chandlery. Fishing supplies. Ice. Public phone. Road access walking, cycling.
Nearby: Delicatessen–light meals.
Bed and Breakfast establishments.
Taxi service to island centers and ferry to Anacortes. Orcas Island Yacht Club. Small public dock at the head of the bay.

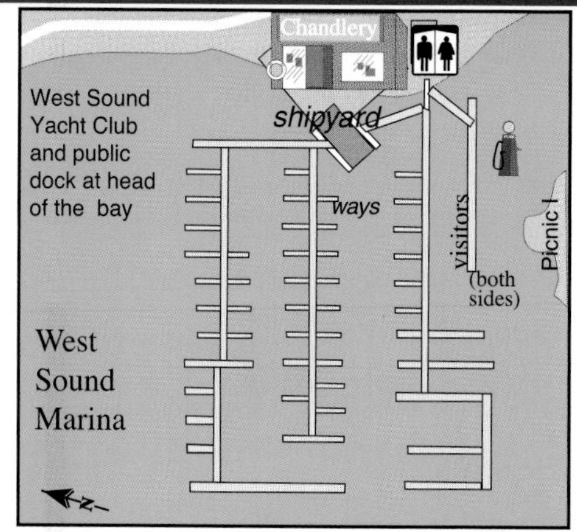

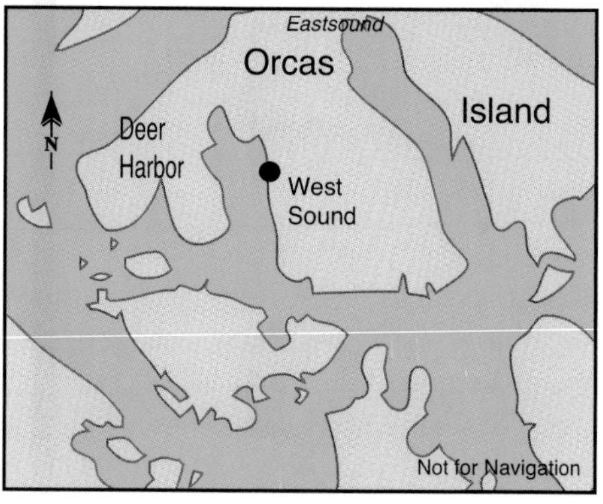

West Sound

This protected moorage is largely for long term resident boats. However, it has an excellent marine service facility with 30 ton travel lift and comprehensive repair services. It has a well stocked marine store and the buildings ashore include a large, modern, heated bay where refinishing and mechanical work can be done in any weather conditions. The facility caters to all of the San Juan Islands with a 24 hour emergency service. Transient moorage accommodates a number of boats on a 250 foot finger that is an extension of the fuel dock. Gas and diesel are available and are generally priced competitively with fuel at places such as Friday Harbor. It has a pump-out station. The facility is owned and operated by Betsy Wareham. The chandlery offers brand name outboard products, fishing gear, propane, ice and a wide variety of marine supplies. On one visit, a short walk up the road took us to a deli which served light meals at lunchtime.

An island shuttle service every two hours is available for transportation to other parts of Orcas Island such as Orcas ferry landing or the town of Eastsound.

Note:
Clear customs for USA destinations at Roche Harbor or Friday Harbor.

Note the docks at the head of the bay. One is the yacht club and the other a public dock.

48° 35.782' 122° 56.610' W

Orcas Landing

8368 Orcas Rd
PO Box 96, Orcas WA 98280-0200
Ph: 360-376-4389
Chart 18430, 18434, 18421
Time limit: 30 minutes. VHF 66A

There are stores and facilities ashore. Ice. Public phones. Road access walking and cycling. Sightseeing by bicycle is popular. Stores include liquor, groceries, gifts, clothing, art, souvenirs and refreshments. Orcas Hotel is located nearby. Shuttle service to island centers. The ferry to Anacortes is immediately alongside the landing. Be mindful of the wash created by ferries and passing vessels when tying up.

Orcas Island landing

A quaint village at the ferry landing serves the community on Orcas Island. It has an historic hotel (photo page 14) as a focal point. The Orcas Island Hotel has

Above: At Orcas Landing, store and the grocery store building beyond. Centre: Car show at Eastsound.

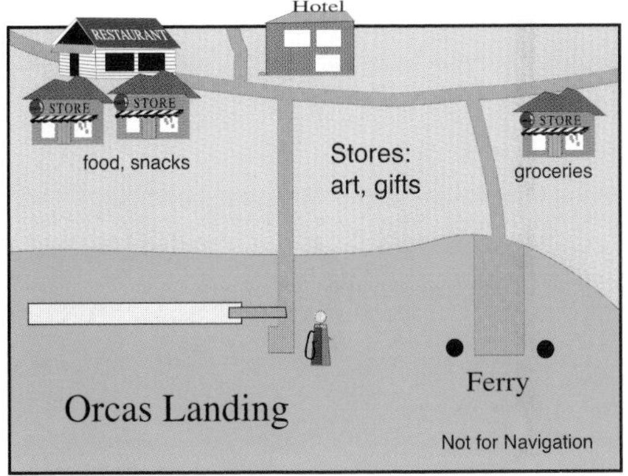

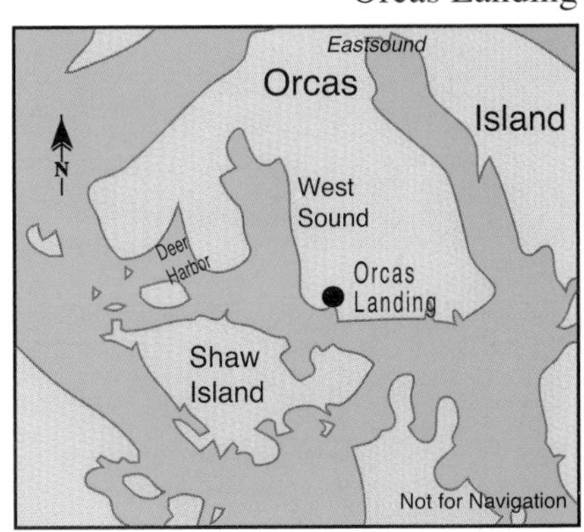

rooms and pub and restaurant, the latter of which is reputed to serve excellent meals. Through the week food is served at the pub or at the pub's outdoor terrace area. The dock at Orcas is for transient mariners only. It is long and accessible both sides although the shoreward side has a narrow entrance and if a boat is tied up at the end entry for anything but a small boat would be tight. There is a 30 minute limit to stays at the dock. On shore there is are gift and craft stores and a grocery store which has a wide selection of wares.

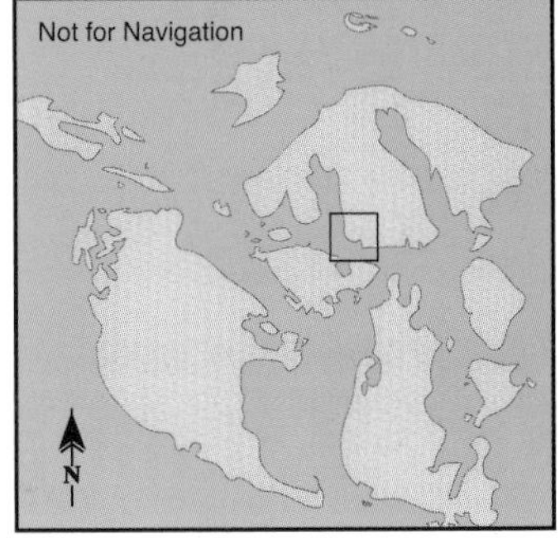

Below: The small craft dock at Orcas Landing–stops limited to 30 minutes. Opposite: The ferry at Orcas Island. The dock for small craft can be seen to port of the vessel.

The settlement is popular among transient mariners and land based visitors alike. Summer sees thousands of cyclists, campers and motorists arriving on the island in a constant stream off the ferries. At Orcas it is a common sight for crowds of vacationers to be lining up for their trip home mingling with those just arriving as they flood into the hotel, souvenir stores, grocery store, fast food restaurant, ice cream store or other facilities.

East Sound

48° 38.748' N
122° 52.208' W

Rosario Resort Marina

Gary Joseph (Harbormaster)
1400 Rosario Rd (Orcas Island)
Eastsound WA 98245-8570
Ph: 360-376-2222
Fax: 360-376-3038
Chart 18421, 18430, 18434
harbormaster@rosarioresort.com
www.rosarioresort.com

Marina services: Fuel. Gas and diesel.
Moorage. Summer April 1 to September 30. In winter the marina remains open and managed by part time staff.
Power at docks: 30 amp.
Customer services: Laundry, showers, ice. The marina is part of a large resort complex. Hotel, pub, spa, pool (indoor and outdoor), retaurants–fine dining or casual. Gift shop. Accommodations and all hotel services (including room service). Playgrounds.
Nearby church. Public phones ashore.
Garbage bins.
Recycling. Grocery store.
Road and trail access walking. Car rentals.
Entertainment: Regular live music, organ recitals in the historic mansion. Slides and

VHF 78A

Rosario history narration–year round, call for times. Golf nearby. Kayak tours. Air tours. Whale watching. Fishing charters.
Hazard: Water depth–shoals towards the end of the south channel in the marina.
Note: Reservations recommended for marina or resort. **Mooring buoys** and anchoring landing fee includes passes to spa and pools.
Nearby: Visitors by boat to **Eastsound** may tie up at the small dock near the town.

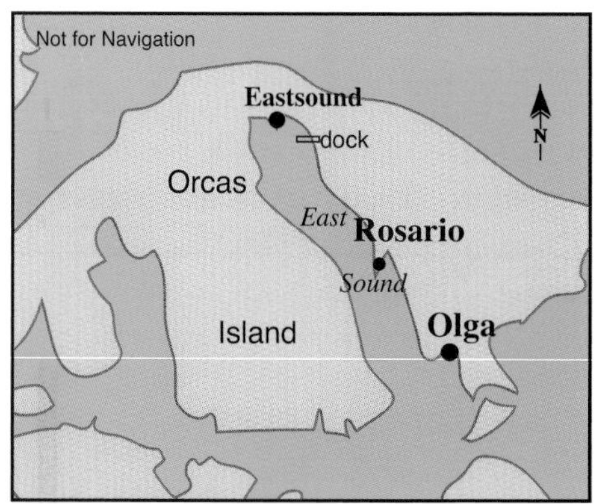

Rosario Resort

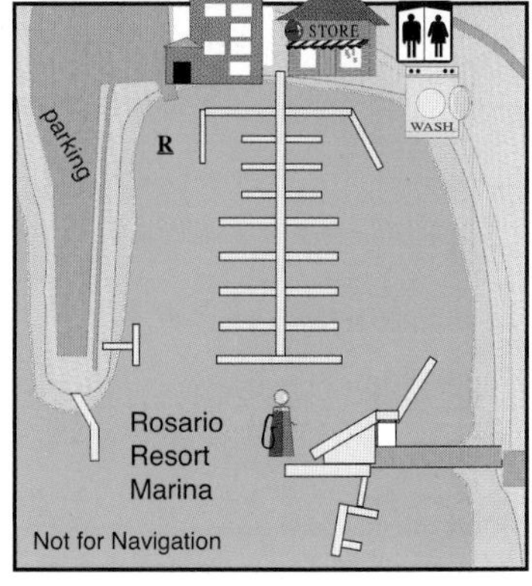

There is sheltered moorage at the docks behind the breakwater. Mooring buoys are not necessarily sheltered from the wind and waves that blow up from the southeast in East Sound some afternoons. The hotel is a feature of the San Juan Islands with a colourful history and excellent restaurant. Facilities include water, showers, store and a swimming pool with hot tubs.

Robert Moran, who built Rosario Resort after retiring in 1904, was a former shipbuilder in Seattle. He used shipbuilding methods and materials in the construction of the mansion. The building's walls are made of 12 inch concrete and the roof is sheathed in copper. Windows are 7/8 inch plate glass and many sections of the interior are panelled in mahogany.

One of the resort's major features is the Kimball pipe organ, said to be the largest installed in a private residence in the United States. The mansion was listed in the National Register of Historic Places in 1979. The estate was sold in 1938 and the new owners created the resort in 1960.

Rosario is the closest sheltered marina for accessing Eastsound, a bustling village that attracts many visitors annually, mostly by ferry via Orcas. There are restaurants, stores, banks, post office, medical clinic, movie theater, pharmacy, churches, galleries and many other facilities. Eastsound airport provides tours for visitors wanting a lofty look at the islands.

The town of **Olga** (photos at top of page) has a quaint village store and community docks. Stop and dine at the local cafe and art gallery restaurant.

A sign on the dock reads: "Dock maintained with community labor and moorage fees collected after 6 pm." It is exposed and not recommended for overnight unless you are certain of favourable weather. Olga is exposed to southeast or southwest winds.

Opposite: The Rosario docks (top) are protected behind a breakwater with a fuel dock at the entrance. The mansion, (inset), looks over the sweep of East Sound. Top: The historic old Olga store. Right: The landing at Olga.

Blakely Island

48° 35.157' N
122° 49.231' W

Blakely Island General Store and Marina

Ken Parker
1 Marina Rd
Blakely Island WA 98222
Ph: 360-375-6121 Fax: 360-375-6141
info@ blakelymarina.com
www.rockisland.com/~blakely/

Chart 18430 **VHF 66A**

Marina services:

Moorage. Guest moorage–25 slips, year round. **Fuel:** Gas, diesel (Saturdays in off season). **Power** at docks: 30 amp.

Customer services:

Showers, laundry, washrooms.

Wi-fi Internet access. Store. Provisions. Groceries. Clothing, gifts. Tackle, bait. Fishing and marine supplies. Ice. Groceries, old-time soda fountain, espresso. Store open May 15 to September 15. Garbage disposal for marina guests.

Nearby facilities: Post office, restaurant, liquor store at Orcas Ferry Landing.

Note:

Entrance depth to 8' at zero tides.
Fuel dock accessible either side.
Covered docks at entrance are private.
Clear customs for USA destinations at Roche Harbor or Friday Harbor.

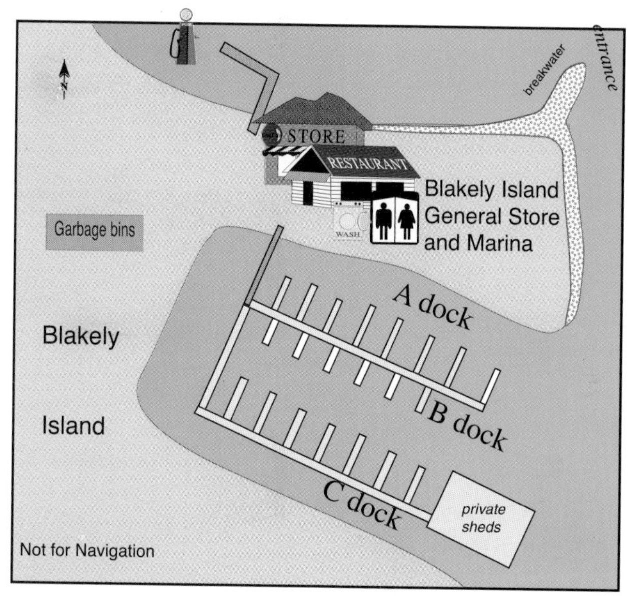

Entrance: pass the small breakwater to your starboard. The entrance is narrow and shallow at low tide. The level of the water drops to 8 feet but it is an easy passage.

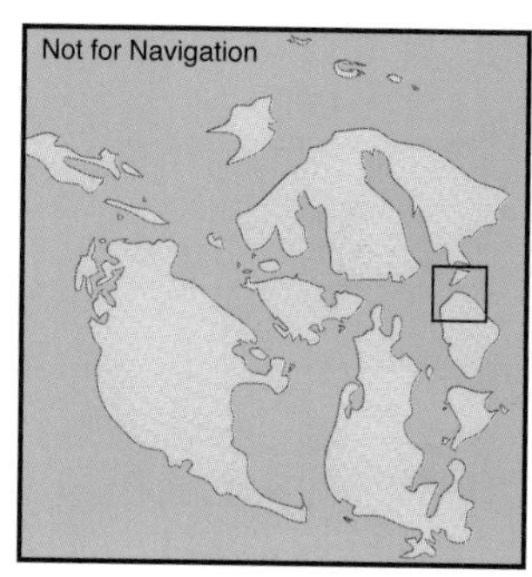

Opposite and left: Blakely Island Marina showing the store and fuel dock. There is a patio out front. It faces the open passage and overlooks the entrance. Bottom: The fuel dock is accessible from either side.

Blakely Marina

There is no access to the rest of the island, which is privately owned. The marina has facilities for guest boats and a sheltered bay where a number of boats can moor. Access is limited to higher tides for deep draft vessels. The depth through the channel is 8' at zero tides. A current runs past the entrance. This is a beautifully landscaped island and although most of it is private the scenery is enjoyable from the marina or the patio ashore.

48° 30.848' N
122° 54.936' W

IMC

Entrance
48° 31.580' N
122° 55.267' W

Fisherman Bay

Chart 18434

Islands Marine Center

Ron Meng **VHF 69**
2793 Fisherman Bay Rd
PO Box 88, Lopez Island WA 98261-0088
Ph: 360-468-3377 Fax: 360-468-2283
imc@rockisland.com
www.islandsmarinecenter.com

Marina services:
Moorage. Guest moorage on the south side of marina. About 1000'. Wireless internet access. **Power:** 20, 30 amp.
Customer services:
Showers, washrooms.
Yacht sales and service. Various makes of marine engines and boating equipment. Marine chandlery, hardware, charts, clothing, gifts, electronics, fishing tackle and information. Ice. Road access walking, cycling. Rental apartments available.
Entertainment: Golf nearby. Picnic and barbecue area. Bicycle rentals. Wine tasting at nearby vineyards.
Adjacent facilities: Lopez Islander Resort and restaurant next door. **Fuel:** at Lopez Islander Resort. Boatyard. Repairs and service. Haulouts. 15 ton travel lift and launch ramp.
Lopez Village is less than one mile away. Stores–groceries, provisions, inn, meals, accommodations. Farmers market on Saturdays in summer. Skateboard park. Community center.
Note: Customs Port of Entry at Friday Harbor or Roche Harbor.

Below: The marinas and anchorage in Fisherman Bay. The bay opens off San Juan Channel.

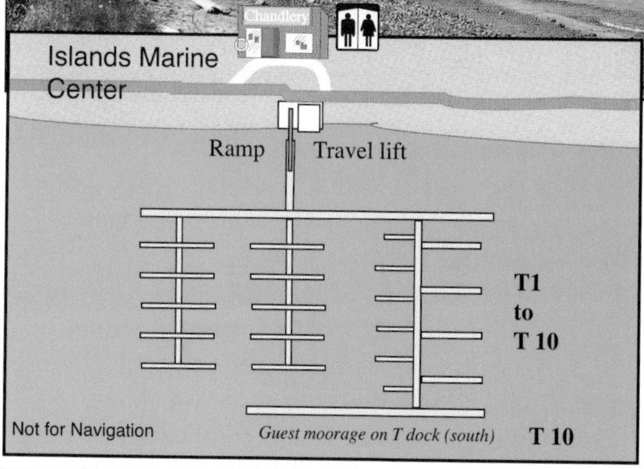

Lopez Island Golf Club 360-468-2679

Chandlery

Islands Marine Center

Ramp

Travel lift

T1 to T 10

Not for Navigation

Guest moorage on T dock (south)

T 10

The entrance, above, to Fisherman Bay is narrow and shallow, but deep enough for a safe passage for most craft at low tides.

Hazard: Be cautious, the shallowest water at the entrance has only five feet of depth at zero tide. Follow all the markers carefully.

A sign on marker number five reminds mariners to round marker eight inside the bay leaving it to starboard. It is located not far from the outer floats of Islands Marine Center shown in the distance and to the right in the aerial photographs on the opposite page.

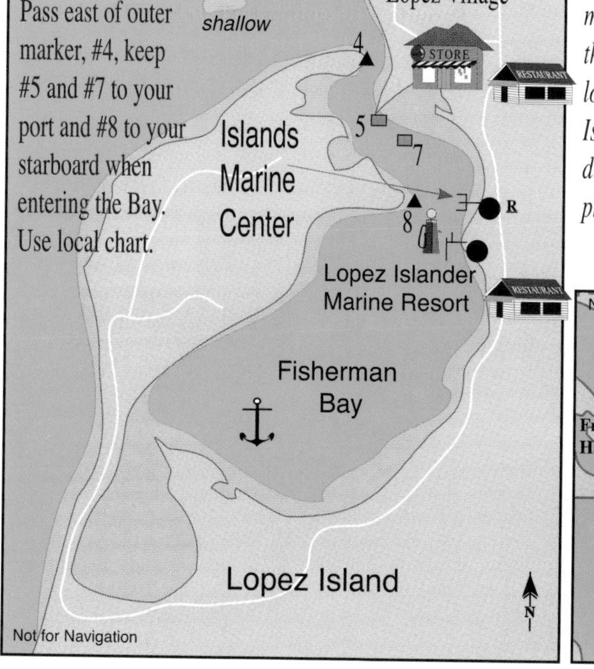

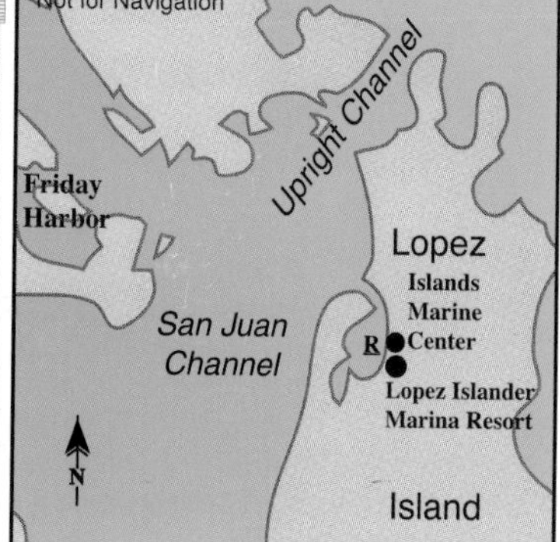

Lopez Islander Resort & Marina

Bill & Earle Diller. Kathy Casey.
2864 Fisherman Bay Rd
PO Box 459 Lopez Island WA 98261-0088
Ph: 360-468-2233 Fax: 360-468-3382
Dock: 360-468-3383
li@rockisland.com
www.lopezislander.com
Charts 18421, 18430, 18434 VHF 78A
Marina services:
Moorage. Guest mooring–about 64 slips. Reservations suggested.
Power: 30, 50 amp.
Fuel: Gas, diesel. Sea plane float for float planes that call at the marina.
Customer services:
Showers, laundry, washrooms. Internet access. Store on dock, groceries, provisions, charts, clothing, gifts, books, bread, fishing tackle. Ice. Playground. Courtesy phone on dock.
Hotel accommodation–28 rooms. Swimming pool. Hot tub. Conference and banquet facilities. Salmon fishing and scuba diving charters. Wildlife & whale watching. Restaurant lounge Ph: 360-468-2234. Patio service. Espresso bar. Dockside welcome package June to September.
Walking: Road access walking, cycling.
Entertainment: Golf nearby. Hot tub. Bicycle and kayak rentals and guides.
Adjacent facilities: Lopez Village less than one mile. Stores, arts and crafts, churches, accommodations. 5 miles to ferry service.

Not for Navigation
Lopez Village
shallow
4
5
7
8
IMC
Fisherman Bay
Lopez Islander Resort & Marina
Anchoring
N

Above: At Lopez Village–the village inn.
Top: View from IMC Marina. Lopez Islander Resort and Marina is the facility on the left of the two marinas in the top photo on the opposite page.

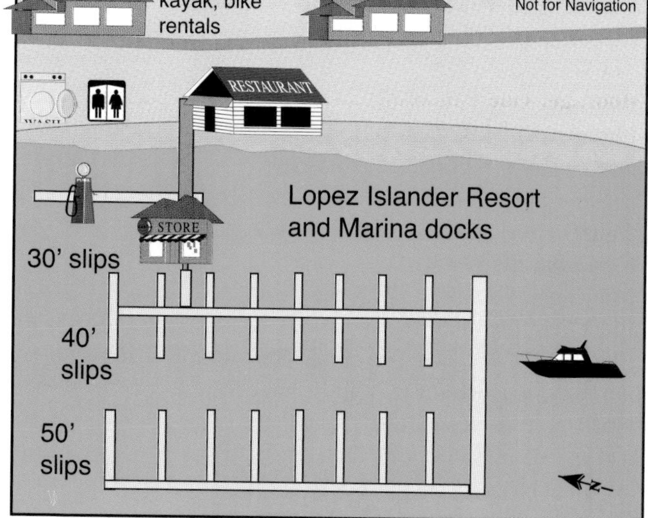

Lopez Island Winery 360-468-3644, is open to the public and wine tasting is available April to mid December, Fridays and Saturdays from 12 noon to 5pm. The vineyards are a short distance beyond the Lopez Island village and a reasonable walk or a quick drive away. Lopez wines are made from local Madeleine Angevine, Siegerrebe and from Yakima Valley Chardonnay and Cabernet Sauvignon/Merlot.
Lopez Island is one of the easiest islands in the San Juans for cycling. Bicycle rentals are available adjacent to Lopez Islander Resort and Islands Marine Center. An extensive road system allows wide exploration of the many interesting things to see and do on the island.

Right: The fuel dock at Lopez Islander Resort with Island Marine Center beyond.

Point Roberts Marina

Traveling South?
See Section 8 for marinas
from Blaine to Olympia.

Point Roberts

48° 58.333' N
123° 03.817' W

Point Roberts Marina

Allan Sharp
713 Simundson Dr
Point Roberts WA 98281
Phone: 360-945-2255 Fax: 360-945-0927
prmarina@pointrobertsmarina.com
www.pointrobertsmarina.com

Charts Cdn: 3492, 3463. US: 18421

Customer Services:

Moorage 24' to 125'. 220' guest dock.
Fuel: Gas, diesel, propane.
Power: 20, 30, 50, 100 amp, **Showers, laundry, washrooms.** Public phones. Internet access. Restaurant. Chandlery, bait, tackle, fishing licences, repairs, service. Two pumpouts at guest and fuel docks. Workyard. Haulouts–35 ton travel lift, monorail sling hoist–small boats to 4,000 lbs.
US Port of Entry. Customs.
Mostly for permanent moorage.
There is lots of space for visiting vessels at the long finger in the entrance channel as well as other slips. Championship golf course. Air park nearby.

VHF 16 switch to 66A

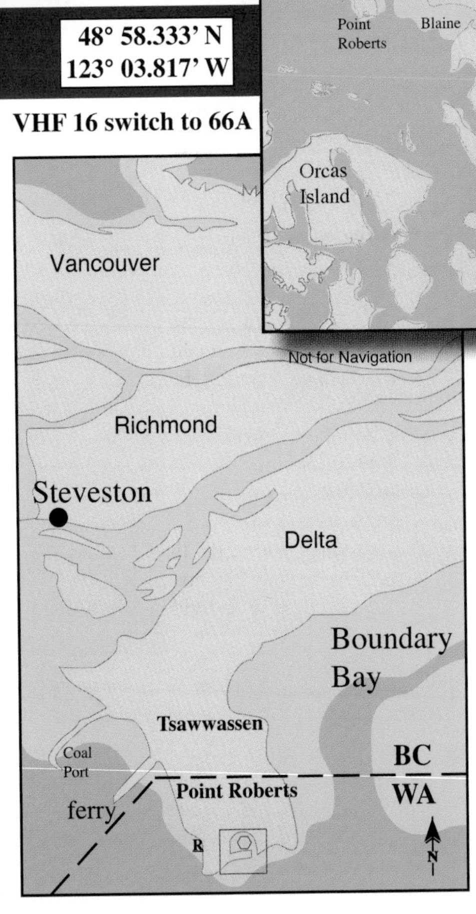

Point Roberts Golf and Country Club 360-945-4653

Although this marina is not in the San Juan Islands, it is very near. Access to it from the islands is closest from Sucia Island. It is a large centre for repairs and provides a good stop for access to the British Columbia mainland. In the photo, opposite, beyond the marina can be seen the island ferry landing and the coal port. Customs requires reporting when landing from Canadian ports. Point Roberts is on the tip of a peninsula which is attached to the BC mainland. A nearby border crossing by land takes you into Greater Vancouver.

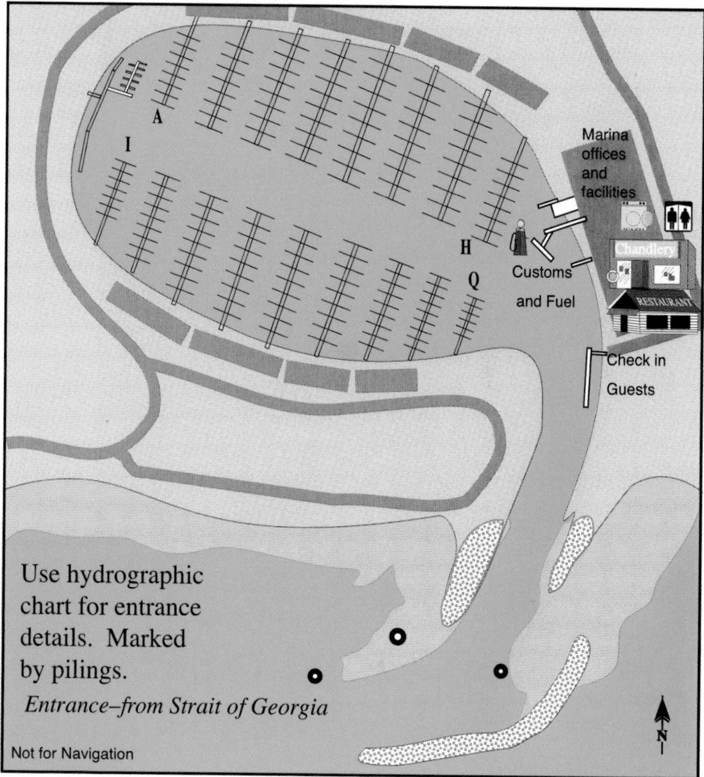

Coastal Marine Parks

see also ***Anchorages and Marine Parks***

Marine Parks in the San Juan Islands and British Columbia offer tranquil and delightful moorage. They have been established for use by the general public and attract hikers, back-packers, cyclists, RV campers and mariners. Many parks have picnic and overnight camp sites with trails and beaches. Some have docks adequate to moor dinghies only, some to moor a number of small to medium sized craft and others none at all. Most have mooring buoys for safe overnight mooring. Flat fees are levied for use of docks or mooring buoys. These change periodically but at present they are about $10 per mooring buoy per night, for boats under 45 feet, and the charges usually apply afer 1 pm in the San Juans and after 6 pm in Canada.

The authorities ask that parks be respected and kept clean. Garbage should not be disposed of unless there is a specific disposal station. Sewage should not be discharged in marine park anchorages and noise should be limited to daylight hours. There are marine park hosts at some Marine Parks and in BC their presence will be indicated by the flying of a BC Parks Marine Park Host burgee. The host is usually a member of a power squadron, a yacht club, a sailing association or is an individual who has volunteered to assist visitors.

In Washington State it is possible to purchase an annual moorage permit which allows use of mooring buoys and docks at the various locations throughout the year without further fee. Fees are in effect year round at some facilities while at others only between May and September. In the San Juan Islands these include Sucia Island, Stuart Island, Jones Island, James Island and Matia Island.

For more information on marine parks in US waters contact Washington State Parks Headquarters at 360-902-8844 or *www.parks.wa.gov/boating/*
In Canada, 2930 Trans Canada Hwy, Victoria BC V9B 5T9 Ph: 250-387-4363.
www.britishcolumbia.com/parks *www.bcparks.com*

Vancouver Island

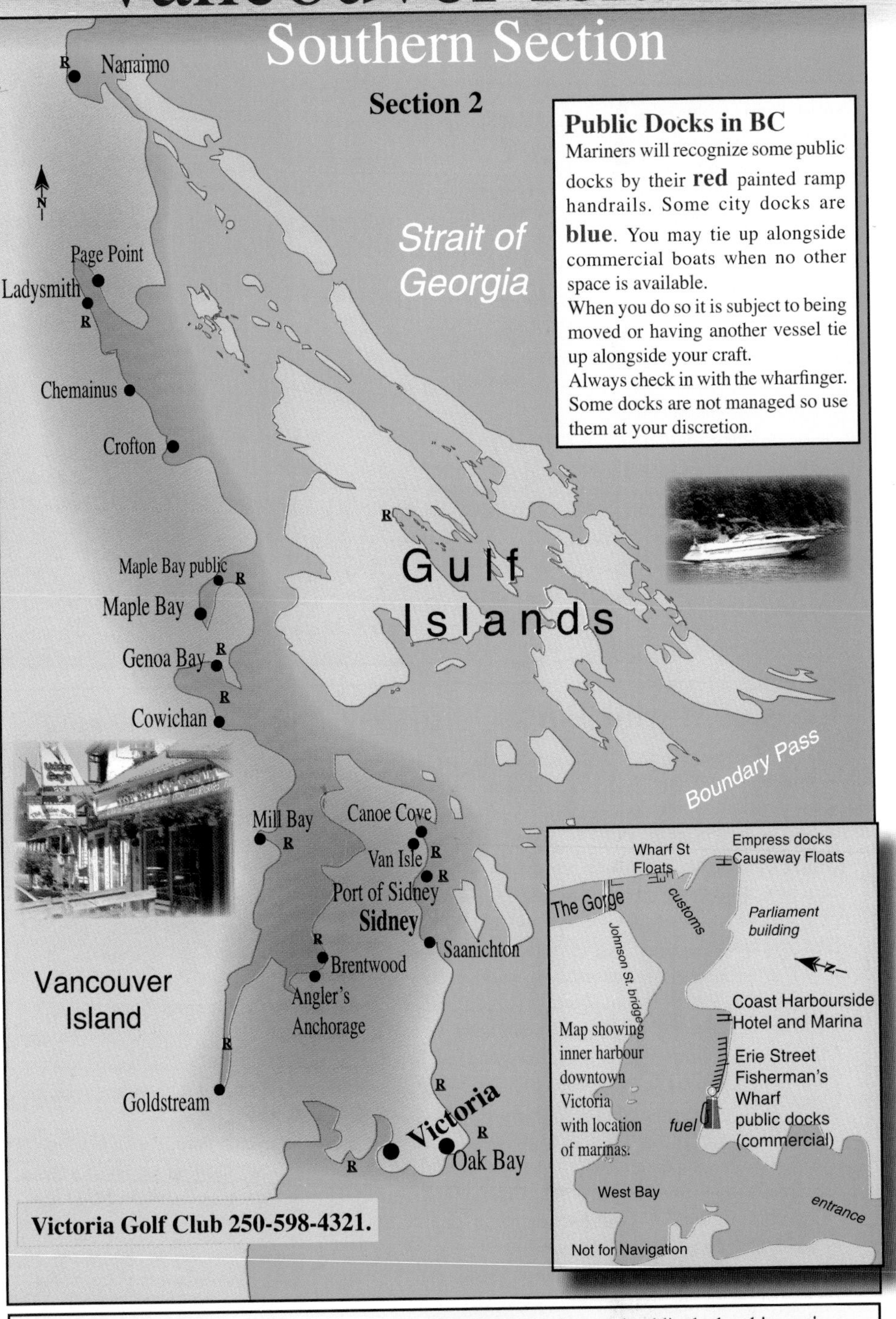

Public Docks in BC

Mariners will recognize some public docks by their **red** painted ramp handrails. Some city docks are **blue**. You may tie up alongside commercial boats when no other space is available.
When you do so it is subject to being moved or having another vessel tie up alongside your craft.
Always check in with the wharfinger. Some docks are not managed so use them at your discretion.

● Marina locations
R Launch Ramps

Map shows marinas and public docks, this section.
Not to be used for navigation.

Uplands Golf Course 250-592-7313

Coast Marina
48° 25.420' N
123° 22.788' W

More golf courses near the city–ask at marinas

Left: Docks at the Coast Harbourside Victoria Hotel and Marina.

Victoria

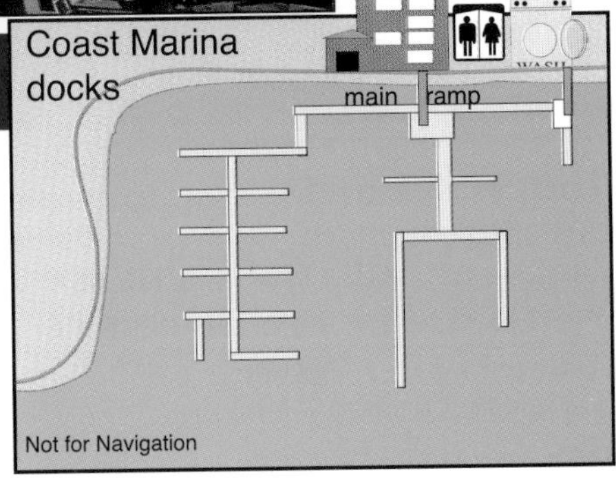

The Coast Victoria Harbourside Hotel and Marina.

Gail Windle **VHF 66A**
146 Kingston St, Victoria BC V8V 1V4
Ph: 250-360-1211 Fax: 250-360-1418
victoriamarina@coasthotels.com
www.coasthotels.com

Charts 3412, 3440, 3461, 3462, 3313
Fuel: (at adjacent fuel dock) gas, diesel.
Marina Services: Moorage. Visitors welcome. Reserve in summer. **Water** at dock. **Power:** 30, 50 amp. Pumpout. **Garbage disposal. Showers, washrooms.** Pool, spa, sauna at hotel included in moorage. Award winning restaurant in hotel. Concierge service available to marina guests. Whale watching tours and other attractions.
Complimentary shuttle from the hotel to downtown Victoria.

There are many reasons to put into Victoria. It is a major customs port with a customs dock alongside the large public marina on Wharf Street. Another public dock with limited space on either side of a single slip is located just before the Johnson Street bridge. Additional moorage under the same control as the Wharf Street dock is located right in front of the Empress Hotel.

Good moorage is also available at Coast Harbourside Victoria Hotel and Marina. Beyond the Johnson Street bridge is The Gorge, and if you are ever in Victoria a slow cruise up there in your runabout or dinghy can make for a pleasant excursion.

Diagrams pages 40 & 43.

Victoria's Empress (Causeway) floats in front of the Empress Hotel.

Wharf Street Marina

Empress Floats.

203-468 Belleville St
Victoria BC V8V 1W9 VHF 66A
Ph: 250-383-8326 Fax: 250-383-8306
Toll free 1-877-783-8300
manager@victoriaharbour.org
www.victoriaharbour.org

Charts 3313, 3440, 3412, 3461, 3462

Marina services: Transient moorage–reservations for boats over 65'. **Power:** 20, 30 amps. **Laundry, showers, washrooms.** Garbage disposal. **Internet access.**

Caution: Adjacent Seaplane landing area. Check chart for caution areas. Enter and exit along yellow buoys–see diagram page 43.

Customer services: Customs/phone. Nearby city downtown within walking distance. Hotel Empress across the street.

Entertainment:
Downtown Victoria. Walking–promenade.

Adjacent or nearby services:
Ferries, seaplane services. Hospital, banks, bank machines, car rentals, post office, swimming pool, telephone, taxi service. Museums. Summer entertainment on the promenade and in the city. This is a busy marina.

Additional moorage is available at the Wharf Street Marina.

Note: Rafting is permitted at public docks. There is no moorage available at the Fisherman's Wharf. Visiting vessels should try local marinas.

The Victoria Public Docks are all run by the Greater Victoria Harbour Authority.

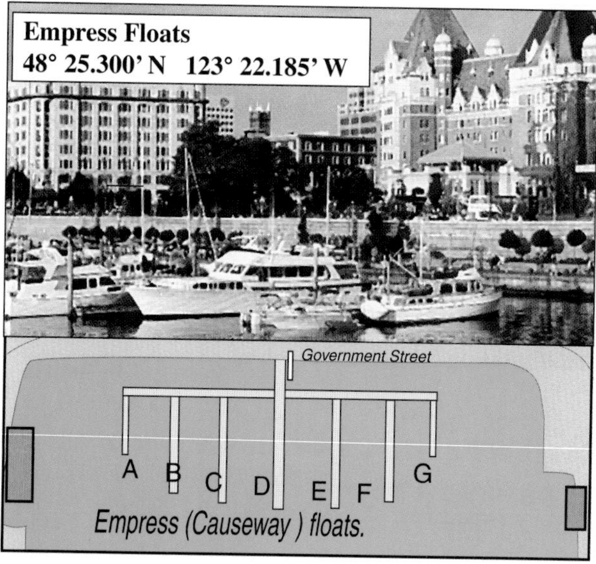

The Empress (Causeway) floats are located in front of the Empress Hotel.

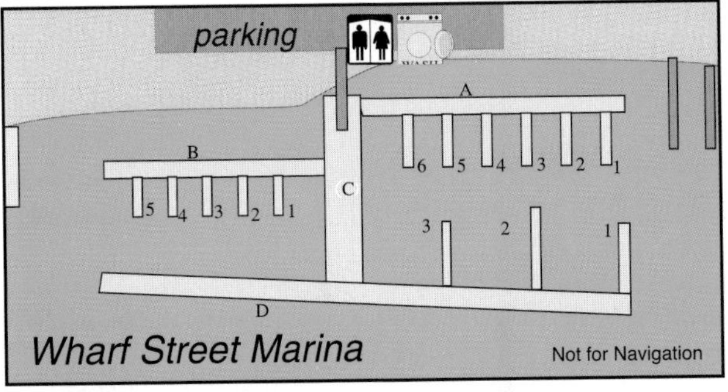

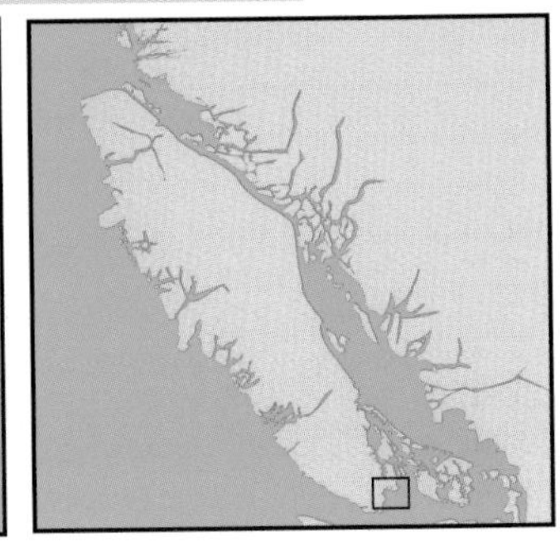

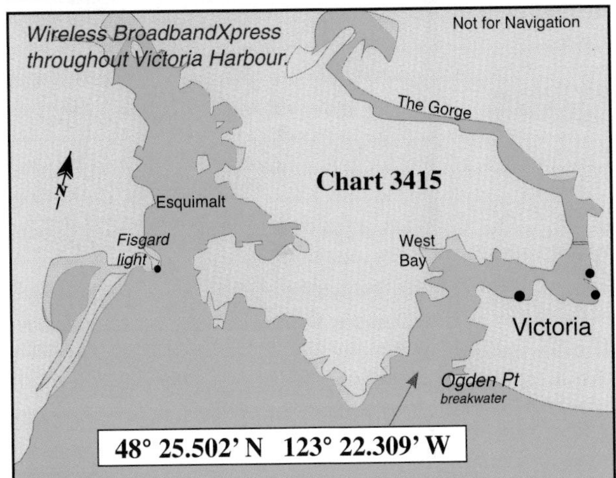

Opposite page: The docks at Wharf Street are probably the first place most mariners look for moorage. The alternative is in front of the Empress Hotel or at Coast Harbourside Marina near Fisherman's Wharf.

The diagram left shows Victoria Harbour in relation to the adjacent Esquimalt Harbour where dock facilities are occupied by the Canadian military.

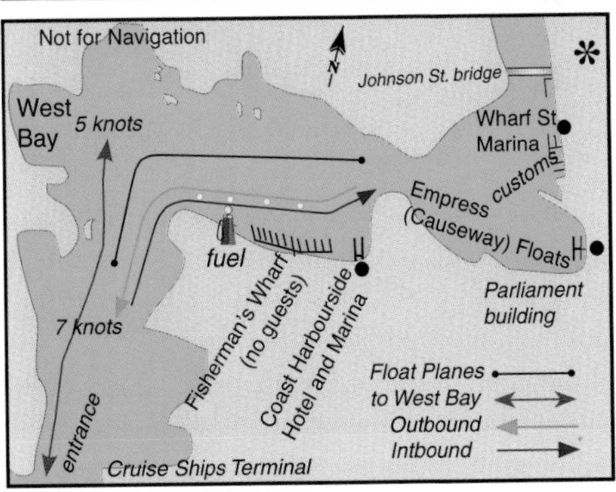

Caution: Seaplane landing area on approaches to Victoria Inner Harbour. Follow the yellow markers in and out of the harbour. See diagram left.

Wharf Street Marina.

203-468 Belleville St
Victoria BC V8V 1W9 VHF 66A
Ph: 250-383-8326 Fax: 250-383-8306
Toll free 1-877-783-8300
gvha@victoriaharbour.org
www.victoriaharbour.org
Charts 3313, 3412, 3440, 3461/2
Marina services:
Moorage: Transient moorage.
Resevations taken for boats 65' and over.
Rafting is permitted.
Power: 20, 30, 50 amp.
Laundry, showers, washrooms.
Garbage disposal.
Customer services:
Customs phone.
Nearby city downtown within walking distance. Hotels nearby. Walking–seawall and promenade.
Entertainment:
Downtown Victoria, Old City and China-town. Scuba diving at the Breakwater.
Adjacent or nearby services:
Ferries, seaplane services, customs. Hospital, banks, bank machines, car rentals, post office, swimming pool, public pay phone, taxi service. Museums.

Above: The marina and adjacent anchorage at Oak Bay. Anchoring is not recommended. Below: Fisherman's Wharf in Victoria has no space for visitors.

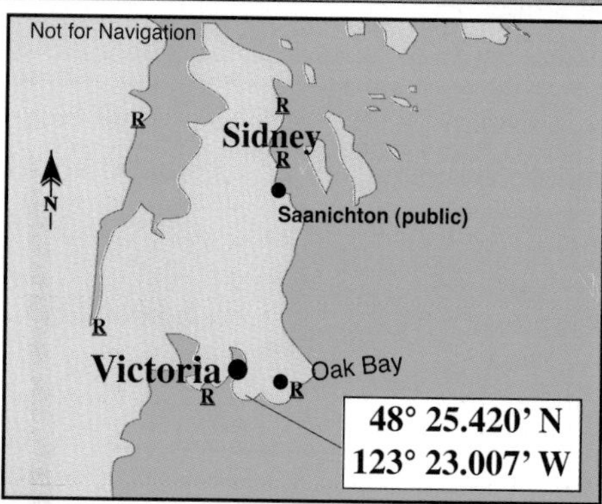

Vancouver Island South

Victoria Golf Club 250-598-4321.
Uplands Golf Course 250-592-7313

Oak Bay Marina opens off Baynes Channel in the lee of Discovery Island. Watch for Lewis Reef on the northbound approaches to the entrance.

48° 25.431' N 123° 17.897' W

Oak Bay Marina

Manager Jill Smillie
1327 Beach Dr
Victoria BC V8S 2N4 VHF 66A
Ph: 250-598-3369 Fax: 250-598-1361
Tollfree 10800-663-7090
jill_smillie@obmg.com
www.obmg.com
Charts 3313, 3440, 3424, 3462

Hazard: Rocky entrance. Shoals and shallows–marked with buoys. Consult charts.

Marina services:
Fuel: Gas, diesel at marina fuel dock. Mechanic and services available.
Moorage: Permanent moorage and some overnight slips. Reserve in summer.
Power: 15, 30 amp.
Laundry, showers, washrooms.
Customer services: Customs/phone. Chandlery. Tackle shop. Gift shops. Restaurant, coffee bar.
Nearby village–Oak Bay Avenue 6–8 blocks. Walking on road and beach front.

Going North–from Victoria

The fabled Gulf Islands are steeped in history and folklore and there are books on many subjects dealing with these fascinating islands as well as the San Juans. As you make passage along the east shore of Vancouver Island, stopping possibly in Victoria or Sidney to clear customs, you unfold places of interest and people of charm and character that will please you.

You may prefer to tie up at a dock and take in the local facilities. Victoria has the charm of British styled stores, pubs and restaurants. British imports are the speciality and if the atmosphere of old England does not strike you immediately go and reserve afternoon tea at the Empress Hotel. Tourists flock to Victoria each summer and the attractions include the Royal BC Museum, parliament buildings, wax museum, undersea gardens, scenic London-bus tours and much more. Try also the Port of Sidney, Canoe Cove or Van Isle Marina. All three have good restaurants including places where you can sit and take in the magnificent crimson summer sunsets. Consider the fine restaurants at Tsehum Harbour, the quaint pub at Canoe Cove or any of a variety in Sidney including those at the waterfront. In Saanich Inlet stop at Anglers Anchorage Marina or Brentwood Bay Lodge and Spa and take your dinghy around to Butchart Gardens for a day of strolling in one of the most magnificent masterpieces of landscaping anywhere. Pull into Mill Bay and walk up to the local shopping centre for some tasty cappuccino or shopping at the well-stocked Thrifty Store. Continue up the coast through Genoa Bay for a safe overnight stop and fine dining, or visit Maple Bay for good moorage and a sumptuous meal at the marina restaurant.

In the Victoria Harbour moorage options include the Empress floats in front of the Empress Hotel (seen in the photo left) and the Parliament buildings (above). This location gives the visiting mariner the opportunity to see the best of the city. Victoria boasts one of the top tourism billings in Canada, with its very British atmosphere highlighted by pedigree pubs, London open-top buses and High Tea at the Empress Hotel.

Port Sidney

48° 39.104' N
123° 23.491' W

Port Sidney Marina

9835 Seaport Place
Sidney BC V8L 4X3 VHF 66A
Ph: 250-655-3711 Fax: 250-655-3771
lcurrie@portsidney.com
www.portsidney.com
Charts 3313, 3476, 3441, 3462
Marina services:
Fuel not available. Fuel docks at Tsehum Harbour and Canoe Cove (nearby, north) Mechanic and services available from local and nearby marine operators. Marine stores in uptown Sidney.
Moorage: 300–400 slips. Permanent moorage and plenty of overnight slips. Reserve in summer. Excellent moorage. Dockominium ownership resales. Pumpout.
Power at docks: 15, 20, 30, 50 amp.
Laundry, showers, washrooms.
Activities dock–reserve for group private functions. **Interenet access.**

Nearby:
Post office, general stores, books, charts, fishing licences, tackle, bait, fresh produce, groceries, bakery, hardware, dry cleaning, liquor, pharmacy, clothing, gift stores, churches all within walking distance.
Numerous restaurants, coffee shops, bistros and cafes.
Walking trails or road access.
Some beachfront walks.
Town streets and waterfront roads allow views while walking.
Kayak and other small craft rentals available. Scuba diving arrangements and charters, whale watching–ask marina for details.
Water taxi service to other marinas.
International airport nearby.

Entertainment:
Nearby historic Butchart Gardens.
(Sidney Museum summer hours–7 days per week. Features whales with murals and other historic exhibits–closed during construction).
Golf, tennis and other recreation nearby.

Saanichton, Sidney

Public dock
Charts 3313, 3441, 3462
Manager • Float length 10 m
Lights • This dock is located South of Sidney–Restaurants, shops, medical centre, churches are not within walking distance–they are located in Sidney. Ferries at and north of Sidney to BC mainland and US ports.

Piers Is
ferries
Coal Is
Tsehum Harbour
R
Sidney
Port of Sidney
Saanichton
R
Not for Navigation

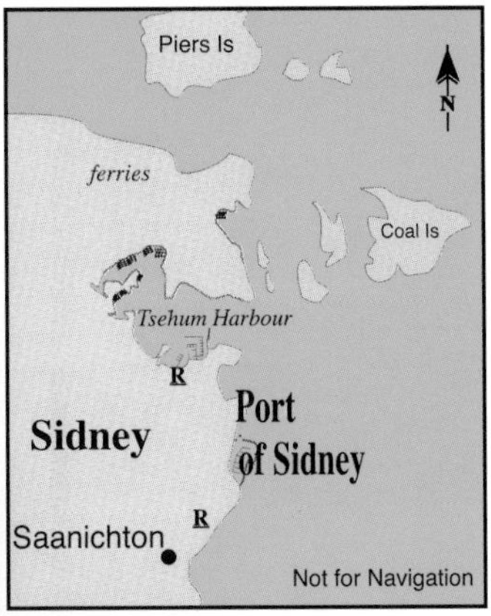

The Port Sidney Marina attracts many boaters from BC and Washington. It is a busy customs port and allows access to the many shops and services in the town.

Inside the store/office at Port Sidney Marina

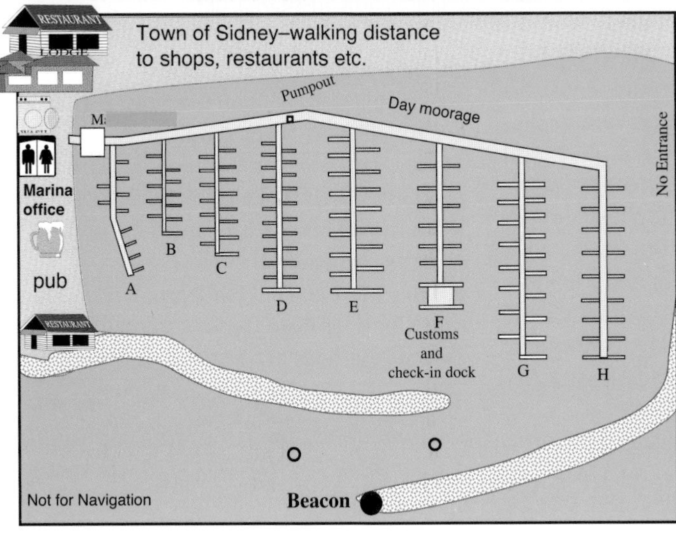

The aerial photograph above and the diagram left show the magnitude of the marina and the layout of the docks. Note: Even slip numbers on northwest side of slips. Odd numbers on southeast side. Do NOT use the opening at the north side of the marina. There are rocks and reefs and only a few locals know the route and tides for that opening.

Photo courtesy of Van Isle Marina

Tsehum Harbour

VHF 66A

Van Isle Marina

Greg Dickinson
2320 Harbour Rd
Sidney BC V8L 2P6
Ph: 250-656-1138
Fax: 250-656-0182
info@vanislemarina.com
www.vanislemarina.com

Hazard–Rocks inside marked by beacons.

Enter from around the breakwater to Tsehum Harbour. Designated marina for courtesy customs clearance. Customs dock.

Marina services:

Laundry, showers, washrooms. Visitors check in at the fuel dock. Reservations suggested. **Fuel**: Gas, diesel, stove oil. Outboard mix. Pumpout. **Power**: 15, 30, 50, 100 amp. 120, 208 volt available. Public phone–ashore and on the docks. Marine store on fuel dock 250-656-1138. Waste oil disposal, holding tanks pumpout. Ice. Charts, fishing tackle, licences, bait, life jackets etc. Mechanic and services available from local and nearby marine operators and facilities.

Philbrooks shipyard is located adjacent to the marina complex. Dining at Dock 503 waterfront cafe. Yacht sales and service in marina complex. Philbrooks Shipyard adjacent: Haulouts. Boatlift railway 150 tons or 120 feet. Docks can accommodate craft to 300+ feet. Large permanent marina with many overnight mooring slips. Many facilities ashore.

Nearby fine restaurants open 7 days a week. Nearby churches. Walking trails or road access. Some beachfront walks. Views from town streets and waterfront roads.

Entertainment:

Cablevision available. TV and telephone hook-ups. Scuba diving arrangements and charters–ask marina for details.

Nearby historic Butchart Gardens. Bus, taxi and rentals plus water shuttle to downtown Sidney, easy access to Victoria, airport, ferries. Golf, tennis and other recreation nearby. Walk Roberts Bay Bird Sanctuary nearby.

Nearby facilities:

All Bay Marine, The Boat Yard, Jensen Marine. Compass Rose Books, Tanners Books. Tsehum Harbour public dock nearby.

Above: Van Isle Marina. The fuel and Customs docks are in the left foreground. A new dock has been added alongside the breakwater.

Looking northwards over Tsehum Harbour. The fuel dock at Van Isle Marina can be seen in the lower centre of the photograph. Westport Marina, upper right of bay, also offers some transient moorage.

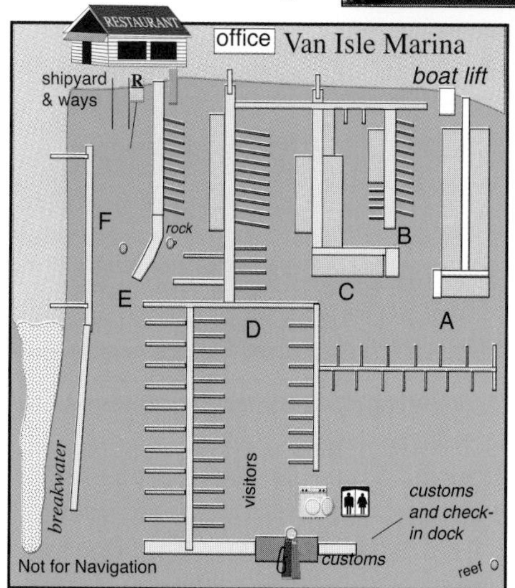

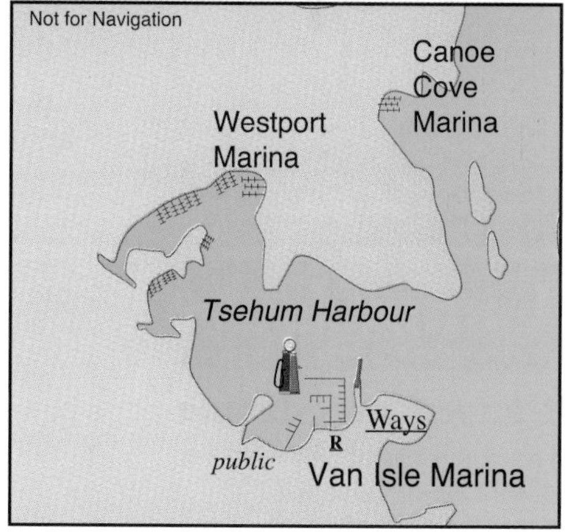

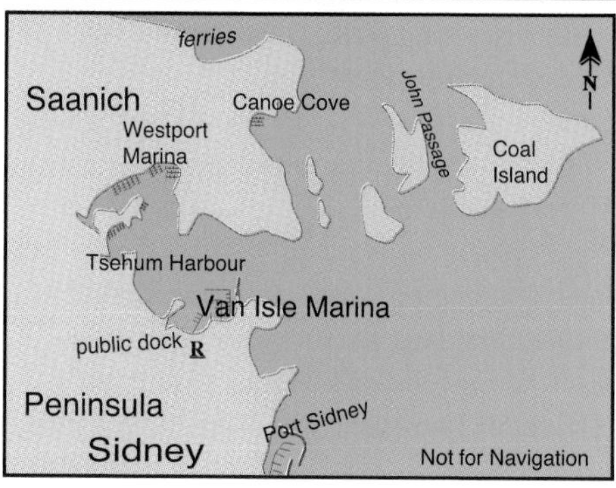

Tsehum Harbour
(Shoal Harbour Public)
Sidney, Vancouver Island.
Public dock
Charts 3310, 3476, 3441.
Managed • Float length: 318 m
Ramp • Breakwater • Garbage • Waste oil disposal • Parking • Water • Lights • Power • Telephone • Washrooms • Adjacent marinas, restaurants, chandlery, haul outs, marine repairs and full shipyard services.

Westport Marina

Division of Thunderbird Marine Corp
Manager: Ken Gowan
2075 Tryon Rd
Sidney BC V8L 3X9
Phone: 250-656-2832 Fax: 259-655-1981
westport@thunderbirdmarine.com
www.thunderbirdmarine.com
Charts 3476, 3313

Marina services: Limited guest moorage, reservations required. **Power:** 15, 30-amp, snack bar, washrooms, showers, garbage disposal, marine/fishing supplies, ice, 50-ton travel lift (max. 70'), marine repair services, marine mechanic.

Nearby facilities: Restaurants, grocery store, marine chandlery, liquor store, playground, hiking trails.

Canoe Cove

Charts 3313, 3476, 3441, 3462
VHF 66A

48° 40.966' N
123° 24.025' W

Canoe Cove Marina

General manager: Don Prittie
2300 Canoe Cove Rd
Sidney BC V8L 3X9
Ph: 250-656-5566
Fax: 250-655-7197
Service department Ph: 250-656-5515
wharfaget@canoecovemarina.com
www.canoecovemarina.com

Customs services.
Designated marina for courtesy customs clearance on dock C.

Hazard: Rocks in north entrance marked by poles. Narrow waterway to fuel dock. Go Slow. Use right-of-way.

Marina services:
Fuel: Gas. Diesel. Stove oil. Propane. Ice.
Marine chandlery: Charts, fishing tackle, licences, bait, life jackets etc.
Full service boatyard including mechanical, shipwrights, electrical, rigging, fibreglass and upholstery shops.
Haulouts. 35 ton travel lift. 65 ton ways.
Moorage: Large permanent marina with limited overnight moorage slips. Reserve.
Power at docks: 15, 30 amp.
Laundry, showers, washrooms.
Customer services:
Customs dock. Coffee shop. Artist studio. Walking neighbourhood roadways.
Entertainment:
Nearby historic Butchart Gardens. Bus, taxi and rentals plus water shuttle to downtown Sidney, road access to Victoria, airport. Golf, tennis and other recreation nearby.
Adjacent facilities: The Stonehouse Pub open 7 days a week.
Nearby: BC Ferries Swartz Bay to Vancouver and Gulf Islands.
Churches in Sidney and nearby.

Approaching Canoe Cove from Swartz Bay.

Ardmore Golf Course 250-656-4621

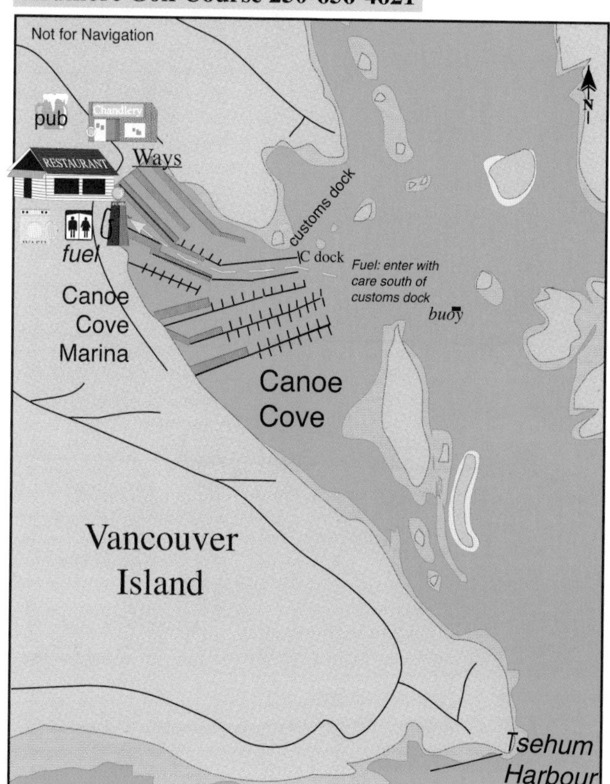

Glen Meadows Golf Course 250-656-3921

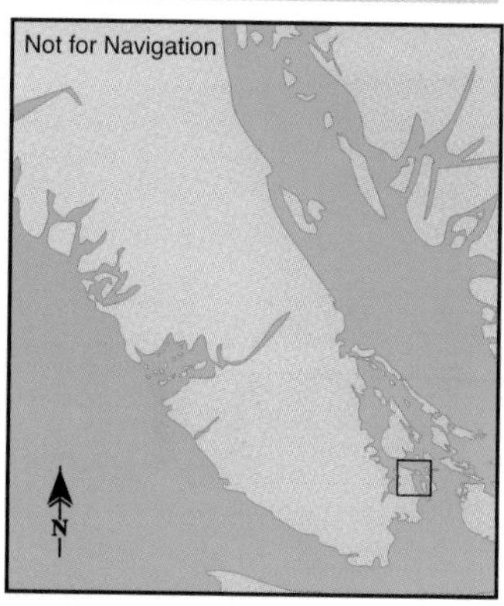

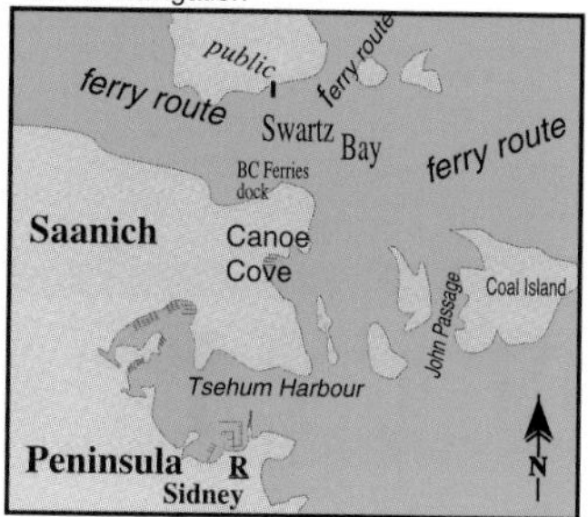

Canoe Cove Marina

This cosy marina is a classic, with many permanent resident boats and room for guests. Mariners stop in for fuel at the dock tucked away between docks C and D or to clear customs. There is a homey cafe for breakfast or lunch and early light dinner in the summer. For finer fare the Stonehouse Pub a short way behind the marina has an atmosphere that matches its good dining. Special events are celebrated at the restaurant with appropriate meals for the occasion.

The large boat yard adjacent to the marina has haulout and dry storage space and is operated by the marina. The ways will allow haulouts of larger vessels and the travel lift caters to more average sized boats. A chandlery situated near the cafe carries a wide range of items for repairs, service and annual maintenance.

The property is quite extensive with a resident artist and a well-known yacht brokerage company. Many boat owners at the marina commute by ferry from the mainland and other parts taking advantage of the marina's close proximity to some of the most favoured cruising destinations on the coast and in the nearby islands.

Piers Island, Sidney

Public dock
Charts 3313, 3476, 3462, 3441
Manager • Float length 63 metres
Used primarily by local residents.
Located opposite BC Ferries Swartz Bay terminal (Sidney). A small dock next to the ferries serves islanders.

Approaching C dock at Canoe Cove

Brentwood Bay

Charts 3313, 3441, 3462 • VHF 66A

Brentwood Bay Lodge & Spa

Harbourmaster: Matt Smiley
849 Verdier Ave
Brentwood Bay BC V8M 1C5
Ph: 250-652-3151 Fax: 250-544-2069
Toll free 1-888-544-2079
marina@brentwoodbaylodge.com
www.brentwoodbaylodge.com

Marina Entrance.

Marina services: Pumpout boat. Mechanic and services available from local and nearby marine operators. Ice.

Moorage: 50 slip marina with overnight moorage to 100 feet. Reserve.

Power at docks: 15, 30, 50 amp.

Laundry, showers, washrooms.

Customer services: Internet access.
Eco Adventure Centre. Wilderness Eco Cruises, kayaking, diving.
Shuttle to Butchart Gardens, wineries.
Two restaurants with outdoor patio–fine dining in Arbutus Grille and Wine Bar.

Casual dining in Marine Pub. Open 7 days a week. Cafe and wine and spirits shop, full service spa and outdoor heated pool and hot tub.
Public pay phones ashore.

Entertainment:
Live music on select nights. Nearby historic Butchart Gardens. (Dinghy in to small dock at Butchart Gardens). Bus, taxi and rentals to downtown Sidney, Road access to Victoria, airport, ferries. Golf, tennis and other recreation nearby. Walking trails or roads. Some beachfront walks.

Adjacent and nearby facilities:
Fuel at Mill Bay, Goldstream or Sidney.
Launch Ramp nearby on native land.

Hazard–Reef off outer dock. Keep U22 marker to starboard. Approach dock from ferry terminal. Check your chart.

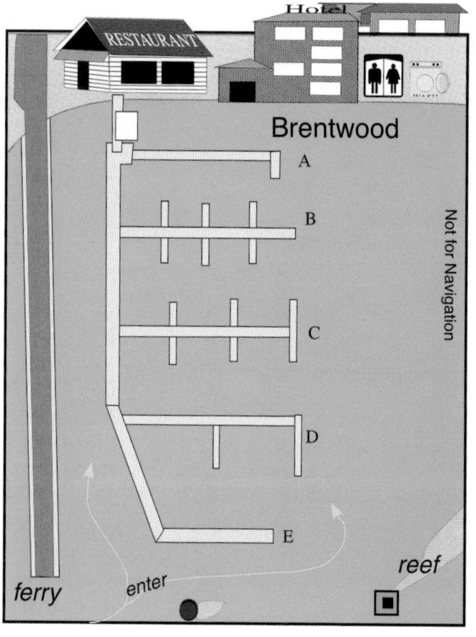

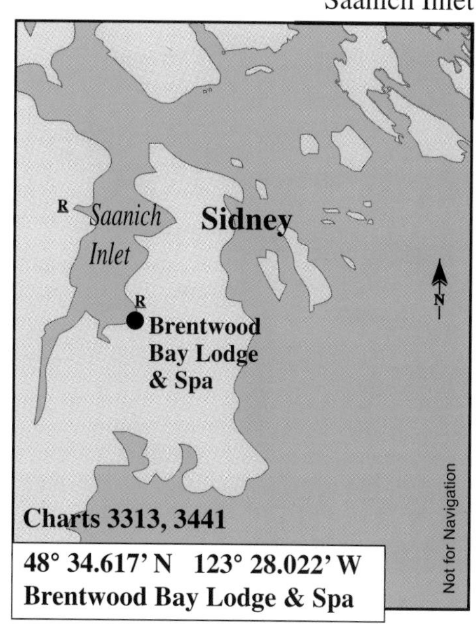

Brentwood Bay

Charts 3313, 3441

Alongside ferry dock–service to Mill Bay on opposite side of Saanich Inlet. Wharf is used by commercial traffic awaiting and offloading ferries.

Float length 22 m. Adjacent: Private marinas and nearby Anglers Anchorage Marina. Walk in adjacent park.

Opposite: Brentwood Bay Lodge and Spa marina docks and adjacent hotel spa.

Top and above left: The marina docks and the lodge with the Eco Adventure Centre building at the head of the dock.

Above right: Shipbuilding yard and dock facilities to the north of the ferry landing at Brentwood Bay.

Angler’s Anchorage Marina

Angler’s Anchorage

Charts 3313, 3441, 3462

Angler’s Anchorage Marina

Mark Tigchelaar
933 Marchant Rd
Brentwood Bay BC V8M 1B5
Ph: 250-652-3531
Fax: 250-652-9923

Canada Customs
Clear at Port Sidney Marina.

Marina Entrance:
Marina located in the south end of Brentwood Bay. Refer to chart 3313 for navigation.

Marina services:
Mechanic and services available from local and nearby marine operators. Repairs can be arranged.

Moorage:
Large marina with limited overnight moorage slips.

Power at docks: 15, 30 amp. Pumpout.

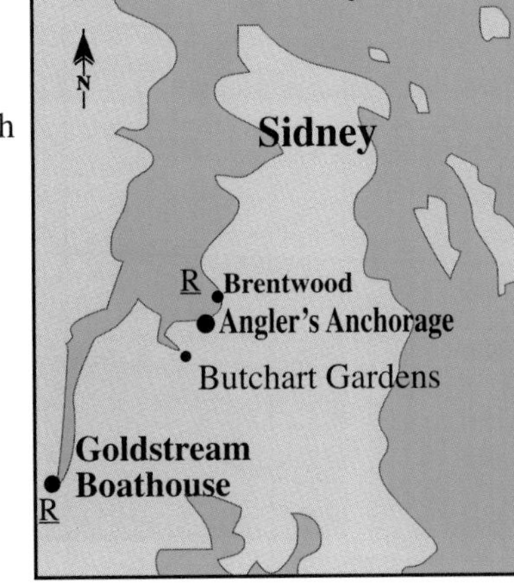

Customer services:
Laundry, showers, washrooms.
Nearby churches. Dockside marine restaurant. Public pay phones ashore.

Restaurant on site. Entertainment:
Nearby historic Butchart Gardens.
Bus, taxi and rentals to downtown Sidney, road access to Victoria, airport, ferries.
Walking trails or roads. Some beachfront walks.
Golf, tennis and other recreation nearby.

Adjacent facilities:
Brentwood Bay Lodge and Spa/Marina.
Public dock. Restaurants, shopping in nearby Brentwood Bay. Launch ramp nearby on First Nations land.

This marina is the closest facility to Butchart Gardens. Check with the marina for overnight moorage. If available, take your dinghy to the dock at the Gardens. Enquire about the ferry service.

Saanich Inlet approaches to Brentwood Bay

Photo courtesy of Butchart Gardens

Butchart Gardens

800 Benvenuto Ave
Brentwood Bay BC V8M 1J8
Toll free 1-866-652-4422
www.butchartgardens.com
Fireworks display Saturday nights in summer. Anchor out and row to dinghy dock, or anchor in Tod Inlet and watch.

Above: The dock and fuel pump at Goldstream. View looks north towards entrance of Saanich Inlet. Top: Butchart Gardens dinghy dock (on left).

Goldstream

Goldstream Boathouse

Lida Seymonsbergen
3540 Trans Canada Hwy
Victoria BC V9B 6H6
Ph: 250-478-4407 Fax: 250-478-6882
seymonsbergen@lincsat.com
Charts 3313, 3441, 3462 VHF 66A
Marina services:
Fuel: Diesel and gas. Oil filters.
Marine supplies dock.
Moorage. Transient 300' available.
Power at docks: 20, 30 amp. **Washrooms.**
Garbage disposal.
24-hour security.

Charts 3313, 3441, 3462

48° 29.907' N
123° 33.117' W

Customer services:
Road access walking. Parkland trails at adjacent Goldstream Park. Bait, ice, tackle, snacks. Public pay phones.
Entertainment:
Historic landmark boathouse.
Crab and prawn fishing. Squid spawning, salmon run.
Taxi and car rentals to downtown Victoria.
Adjacent facilities:
Launch ramp. Two-lane marine repair facility–haulouts to 50 feet.

public float

fuel dock

48° 38.987' N 123° 33.087' W

Mill Bay

Mill Bay Marina

Dockmaster: Bill Day

740 Handy Rd **VHF 66A**
Mill Bay BC V0R 2P0
Ph: 250-743-4112 Fax: 250-743-4122
Toll free 1-800-253-4112
millbaymarina@shaw.ca
www.millbaymarina.com

Marina services:
Fuel: Gas. Diesel.
Power at docks: 15 amp–multiple outlets.
Laundry, showers, washrooms.
Chandlery with marine supplies. Ice, fishing tackle, bait. Specializing in prawning, equipment and optics. Mechanic and services can be arranged. **Moorage:** 158 plus slips–permanent marina with 600' overnight moorage. Reservations suggested.
Customer services:
Rental boats. **Launch ramp** (2 ramps). Shopping centre and grocery store nearby (Thrifty) will deliver purchases to your boat. Nearby churches. Road access walking. Some nearby river and beach trails.

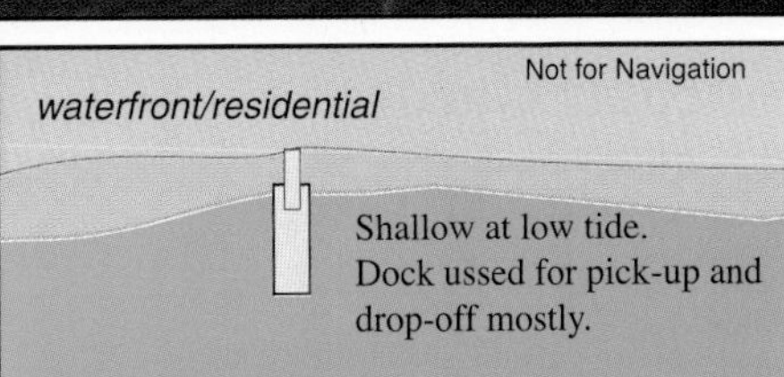

Mill Bay public dock
Manager • Float length 15 metres.

Photograph shows Mill Bay Marina. Note the two launch ramps. The one to the right is a public ramp.

Charts 3313, 3441, 3462

Thrifty Foods located just up the road.
Entertainment:
Butchart Gardens near Brentwood Bay.
Mill Bay marina is a good location for viewing seals and underwater marine life at low tide.
Bus, taxi and rentals to nearby shops or downtown Victoria.
Golf, wineries nearby.
On arrival check with fuel dock on south side of marina for moorage allocation.

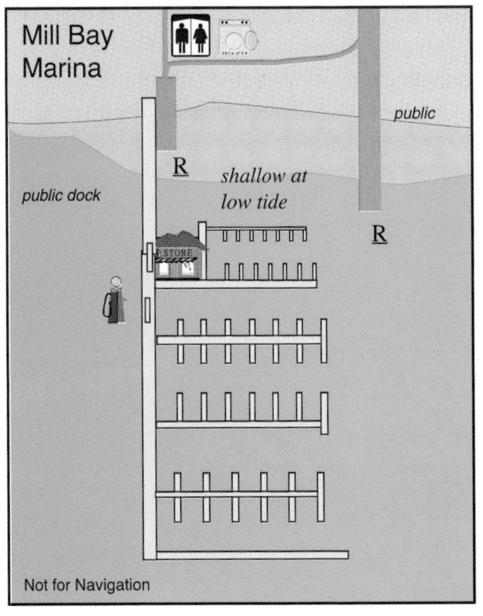

The shopping centre at Mill Bay has good grocery shopping as well as a variety of interesting stores, art centres, restaurants, espresso and coffee shops among others.

The centre is an easy walk from the marina.

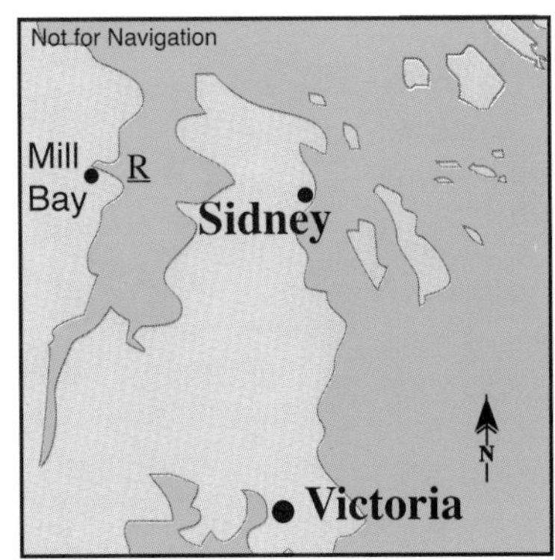

The main float to the south includes a fuel dock and overnight moorage for larger vessels. Small craft will be assigned slips inside.

Beyond Mill Bay, travelling north, there is a relatively sheltered marina at Musgrave Landing on Salt Spring Island. It's good for a short visit, or deviate to Cowichan, Genoa Bay or Maple Bay.

View west from above the public docks.

Fisherman's Wharf
48° 44.515' N
123° 36.935' W

Cowichan Bay

Charts 3313, 3478, 3441, 3462

Cowichan Bay Fishermen's Wharf

Chuck Von-Haas
1699 Cowichan Bay Rd. PO Box 52
Cowichan Bay BC V0R 1N0
Ph: 250-746-5911 Fax: 250-701-0729
Cell 250-701-2230 VHF 66A
www.haabc.com www.cbfwa@shaw.ca

Marina services:
Moorage: Overnight available–3 docks–being expanded. Rafting allowed. Check in on arrival or reserve. **Power** at docks: 20 amp. Multiple outlets. Internet access-wifi. **Showers, laundry, washrooms**.
Nearby services: Charters. Bed & breakfast. Ice, fishing tackle, licences, bait. Boat lift, liquor store, post office, bank machine, pub, hotel, restaurant, shops, swimming pool, taxi, hardware, grocery. Mechanic and marine service can be arranged. Road access walking. Some nearby river and beach trails. Launch ramp nearby.

NOTE: *Adjacent hotel dock is reserved for hotel guests only.*

Cowichan Golf and Country Club
250-746-7211 250-746-5333
Duncan Meadows 250-746-8993
Arbutus Ridge 250-743-5000
March Meadows 250-749-6241

Below: The Oceanfront Grand Resort and Marina overlooks Fishermen's Wharf and has a dock that accommmodates hotel guest boats. No entrance on the shore side of the breakwater.

Above: Waterfront homes at the west end of Cowichan's marinas. Below: Public dock on the left, and Masthead Marina and restaurant to the right.

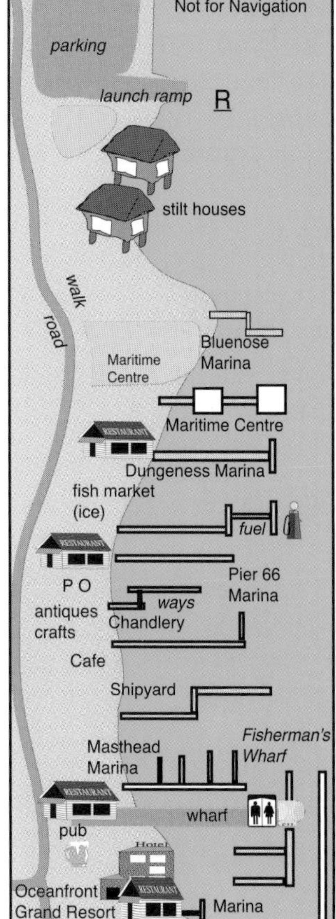

Cowichan is a working harbour. The atmosphere of the village is captivating and visitors are welcome to stop and experience its ambience. Moor at Fisherman's Wharf when the fishing fleet is away and at other marinas in the bay subject to space being available. Photo opposite page, top, shows marinas with Fisherman's Wharf in the foreground.

Inset: There is nothing like a boat in your backyard. It's on the ways at the shipyard in Cowichan.

Pier 66 Marina

Tom and Sharon Ingram
1745 Cowichan Bay Rd
Cowichan Bay BC V0R 1N0
Ph: 250-748-8444 Fax: 250-748-8444
sales@pier66marina.com

Moorage: Overnight available. Check in on arrival or reserve.

Marina services:
Fuel: Gas, diesel, premix, ice, oil, bait, licences. **Garbage disposal.** Convenience store. **Water** at dock.
Power: 15 amp. Multiple outlets.
Public pay phone. Nearby take out restaurant. Fish market. Liquor store in the grocery store at Pier 66 market.
Nearby and adjacent services: Grocery store and marine chandlery. **Showers, laundry**, charters, accommodation, boat lift, post office, bank machine, pub, liquor agency, shops, swimming pool, taxi. Mechanic & service arranged. Road access walking. Nearby river and beach trails.

Dungeness Marina

Owners: Rob & Carrie Hokanson
1759 Cowichan Bay Rd. PO Box 51
Cowichan Bay BC V0R 1N0
Ph: 250-748-6789 Fax: 250-748-9869
info@dungenessmarina.com
www.dungenessmarina.com

Marina services:
Power at docks: 30 amp. **Garbage disposal. Washrooms. Showers, laundry**. Sewage pumpout. **Moorage:** Overnight available. Check in on arrival or reserve.
Nearby: Charters. Bed & breakfast. Ice. Marine supplies, hardware, groceries, charts, tackle, boat rentals, fishing licences, bait. Liquor store, post office, bank machine, pub, restaurant, shops, taxi. Mechanic and services can be arranged. Nearby churches. Road access walking. Some nearby river and beach trails.

The Oceanfront Grand Resort and Marina faces into the open basin of Fisherman's Wharf at Cowichan.

Bluenose Marina

Jim Howard
1765 Cowichan Bay Rd
Cowichan Bay BC V0R 1N0
Ph: 250-748-2222 Fax: 250-748-8982
www.skycrane.ca
Marina services:
Power at docks: 15 amp.
Washrooms. Laundry. Shower.
Garbage disposal.
Telephone, restaurant, taxi.
Moorage: Overnight available. Check in on arrival. Anchorage in good weather.
Nearby services:
Restaurant adjacent. Shops, bakery, stores in town. Visit the adjacent Maritime Centre.

The Oceanfront Grand Resort & Marina

1681 Botwood Lane
Cowichan Bay BC V0R 1N0
Ph: 250-701-0166 Fax: 250-701-0126
Toll free 1-800-663-7898
info@thegrandresort.com
www.thegrandresort.com
Small dock in shallow water located adjacent to the public marina. Hotel overlooks docks. Photograph left.
Marina services: Moorage: Overnight available. Check in on arrival or reserve. Docks 5' at low tide.
Power at docks: 20 amp.
Hotel. Washrooms, showers.
Telephone. Cable Phones, TV hookups. Ice. Beer in the liquor store. Accommodation. Swimming Pool. Restaurant. Pub. Taxi service.
Nearby services:
Laundry, boats for rent, launching, charters. Bed & breakfast.

Cherry Point Marina

1241 Sutherland Dr
Cowichan Bay BC V0R 1N2
Ph: 250-748-0453 Fax: 250-748-0453
Not shown in diagrams. It has limited visitor moorage, mostly for smaller boats.

48° 45.468' N
123° 35.738' W

Genoa Bay

Charts 3313, 3478, 3441, 3442, 3462

Genoa Bay Marina

Will Kiedaisch, Ben Kiedaisch
5100 Genoa Bay Rd
Duncan BC V9L 5Y8
Ph: 250-746-7621 Fax: 250-746-7621
Toll free 1-800-572-6481
will@genoabaymarina.com
www.genoabaymarina.com

Marina services:
Moorage. Large marina with permanent and transient moorage.
Water at dock (please conserve).
Power at docks: 15, 30 amp.
Laundry, showers, washrooms.
Ice. Repair service available.
Customer services:
Restaurant. Licensed. Breakfast, lunch, dinner. Patio service. Barbecue area. Raven House Grill on dock in summer. Tenting. Captain Morgan's B&B for accommodations or breakfast.
General store: groceries, fishing gear, licences, fresh baked goods. Some boat supplies, books, gifts. Kayak rentals.

VHF 66A

Hazard: When entering the bay keep to port of day beacon. Avoid marked shore-side reef.

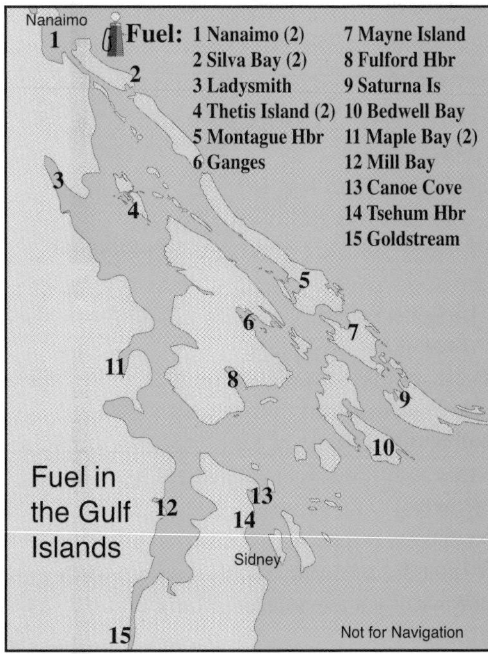

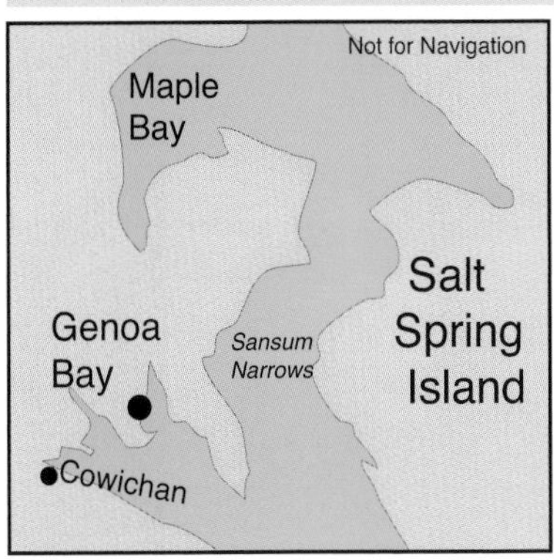

This page: A busy Genoa Bay Marina. There is a cafe on the dock in summer. Opposite: Aerial view of the marina.

Video rentals. Art gallery.
Gifts and fine art.
Public pay phones ashore.
Courtesy van available.
Entertainment:
Road access walking or cycling.
Nearby hiking trails.
Adjacent facilities:
Anchorage. Yacht Sales.
Launch ramp.

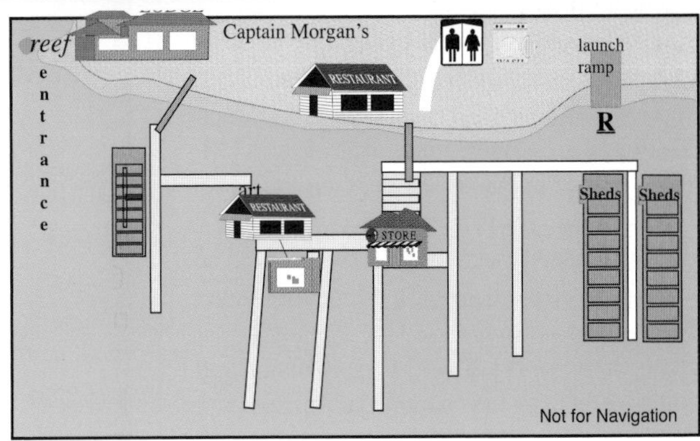

48° 47.743' N
123° 36.010' W

Maple Bay

Charts 3313, 3478, 3442, 3441, 3462

Maple Bay Marina

David and Carol Messier
6145 Genoa Bay Rd
Duncan BC V9L 5T7
Ph: 250-746-8482 Fax: 250-746-8490
Toll free 1-866-746-8482.
info@maplebaymarina.com
www.maplebaymarina.com

Marina services: **VHF 66A**

Fuel: Gas, diesel, propane. Ice.
Guest moorage, about 50 slips. Reservations suggested. Yacht enclosures (houses) for a wide range of sizes. **Power**: 15, 30, 50 amps. Garbage disposal. Recycling.
Laundry, showers, washrooms.

Customer services:
Internet access. The Shipyard Pub & Restaurant–licenced and open year round. Patio service. Breakfast served during summer. Liquor store. Beer/wine off-sales. ATM. Postage sold in marina office. General store. Coffee shop. Souvenirs.
Shipwright and mechanical services. Marine chandlery. 50 ton travel lift. Yacht brokerage. Float plane service.
Plans in the works 2006/7 for expansion and improvement to marina and facilities.

Adjacent facilities:
Bed & breakfast accommodations nearby. Golf. Adventure charters. Rental cars. Canoe and kayak rentals and guided tours.

Entertainment:
Annual classic and wooden boat festival every May long weekend. Groups and Rendezvous welcome–full use of Quarter Deck (covered picnic and BBQ area). Playground.
Road access walking or cycling trails. Beautiful landscaped gardens to walk through.

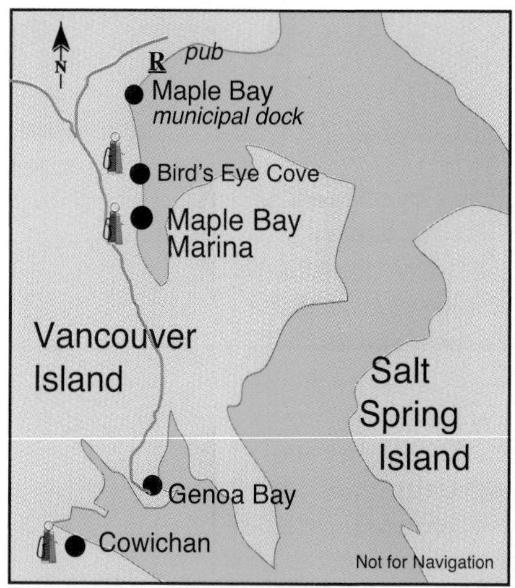

Left: The aerial view on the opposite page and this photo show the scope of dock space at Maple Bay.

Below: The Store at Maple Bay has gifts as well as light meals, snacks and ice cream.

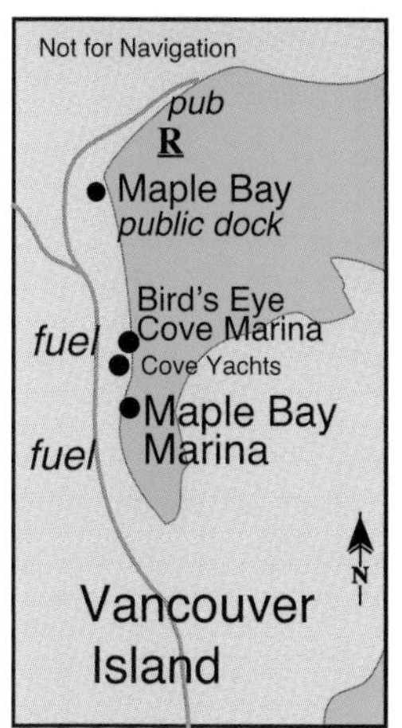

Maple Bay

Municipal dock
Manager
Harmen Bootsma
Ph: 250-246-4655
Charts 3313, 3478, 3441, 3442, 3462

- Float length 46 metres • Water
- Lights
- Public pay phone
- Launch ramp
- Restaurant.

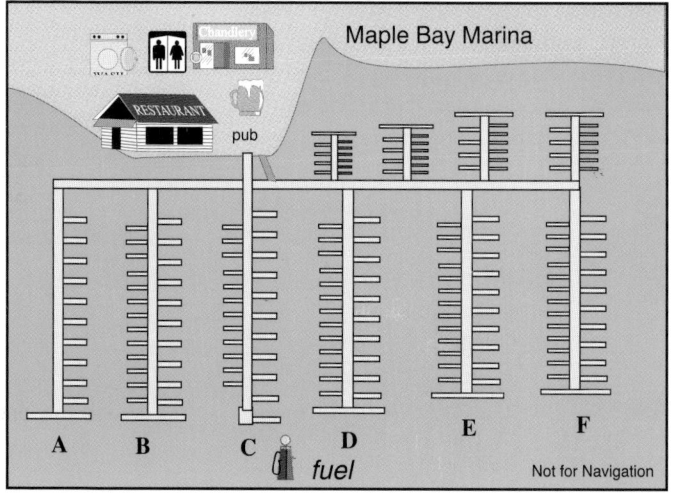

Bird's Eye Cove Marina (above and in the foreground, left) is a popular fuel stop. Service and repairs at adjacent Cove Yachts. This is a good fuel stop with a small store and available moorage. It is a short dinghy ride to the pub and public dock in Maple Bay.

Bird's Eye Cove Marina

James Marshall **VHF 66A**
6271 Genoa Bay Rd, Duncan BC V9L 5T8
Ph: 250-746-5686 Fax: 250-746-5685
dockrat@shaw.ca

Marina Services: Fuel dock–all fuels and oils. Tackle, fishing supplies, ice, snacks. **Guest moorage–**10 slips. Reservations preferred. **Power:** 15, 30 amp. **Washrooms,** garbage disposal. Yacht sales. The marina is open year round. Service and repairs adjacent at Cove Yachts. **Nearby:** Brigantine Pub–cold beer and wine store. Maple Bay Yacht Club. Golf. Access to town of Duncan.

Cove Yachts (1979) Ltd

6261 Genoa Bay Rd
Duncan BC V9L 5Y4 VHF 66A
Ph: 250-748-8136 Fax: 250-748-7916
Travel lift. Ways. Commercial and pleasure craft work. Marine supply store.

The public float at Maple Bay is in the outer bay before approaching Bird's Eye Cove. There is a fine restaurant at the head of the dock. Fuel is available at Bird's Eye Cove Marina and Maple Bay Marina. The Brigantine Pub dock is a short way to the north of these floats.

Maple Bay to Crofton, Chemainus and Ladysmith

There is sheltered moorage at Maple Bay. Two marinas and a yacht club are the major facilities in Bird's Eye Cove. Or stop at the public dock or the Brigantine Pub for off-sales, dining or refreshment. Travelling north, an overnight stop at the sheltered harbours of Crofton and Chemainus can be a memorable experience. The government docks have room for transient boats in the summer. Off season if there is no room to tie up it is possible, preferably for not too long a stay, to come alongside a docked fishing boat. Fishermen generally do not object to having a boat moored temporarily alongside them. However you may prefer to be tied directly to the dock for easier access to and from your moored boat.

At Ladysmith, within easy walking access from the government docks, one can find many store facilities and boating requirements, supplies and services and a touch of coastal history. It is an old coal mining town named for the town in South Africa which was under siege during the Boer War and relieved by the British coincidental to the founding of Ladysmith in BC. Its naming also honoured the charitable wife of Sir Harry Smith, governor of the Cape Province of South Africa.

Across the harbour the docks at Page Point Marina are most hospitable to recreational boats. During summer a steady stream of craft call at the lodge for overnight moorage, fuel and very limited supplies. Also a regular clientele check in for the sumptuous meals served at the lodge. Moorage is sheltered and the docks are available especially for visiting boats.

From Ladysmith it is easy and quick to access several outstanding destinations. Among them are Telegraph Harbour, Wallace Island, Chemainus and Pirates Cove.

Above: The pub in Maple Bay has its own dock for stops while dining.
Right: Crofton has lots of room when the fishing fleet is out, but prepare to raft to other boats. The ferry terminal is adjacent and there are stores and cafes nearby.

Public docks Crofton to Ladysmith

Crofton Municipal dock
Manager–Harmen Bootsma
• Laundry nearby • Float length 158 m
• Launch ramp • Breakwater
• Garbage • Water • Lights
• Power: 20, 30 amps.

Chemainus Municipal dock
Manager–Harmen Bootsma
• Float length 125 m • Power 30 amps
• Water • Showers • Washrooms •
• Laundry nearby.
Ph: 250-246-4655 for reservations

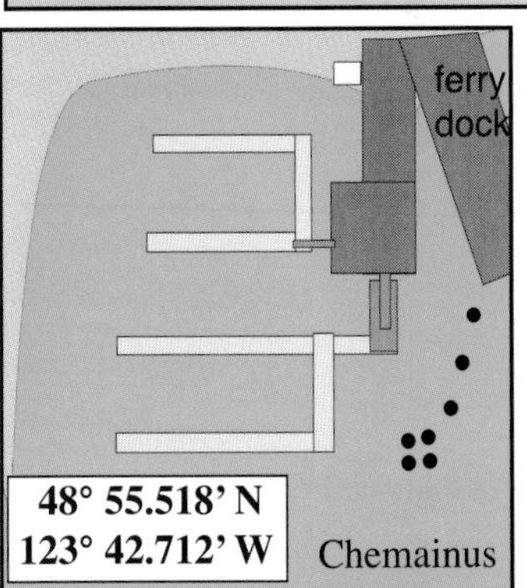

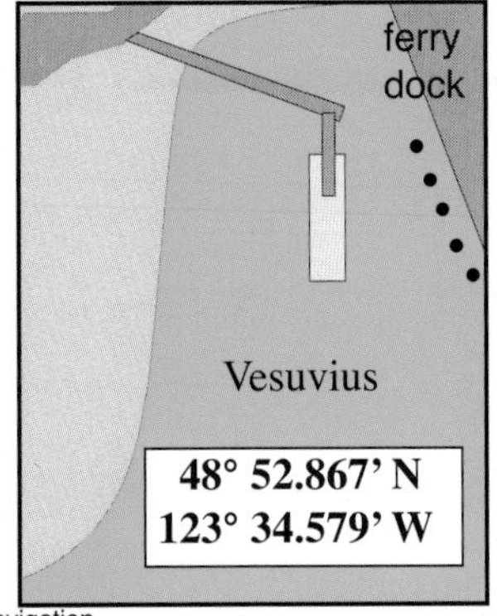

Not for Navigation

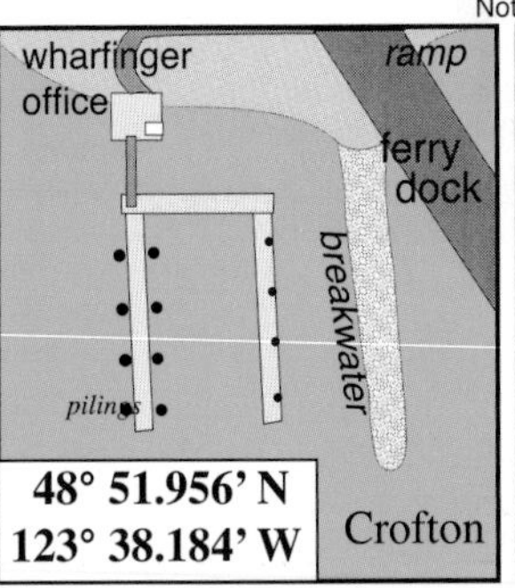

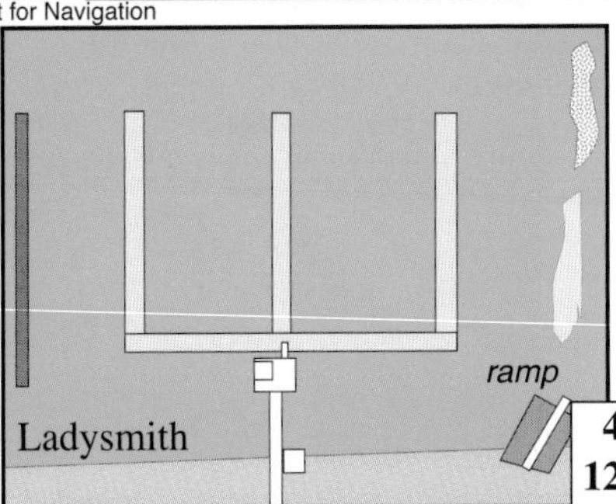

Above: The local museum at Chemainus has lots of interesting maritime, local and town history.

Cottonwood Golf Club 250-245-5157

Above: Ladysmith Harbour with the public dock to the right and the Maritime Society at centre. Opposite: Chemainus docks, expanded to accommodate more pleasure boating visitors to the town. Left: A mural at Chemainus. Below: Ladysmith public marina launching ramp.

Fisherman's Wharf

Vancouver Island
Fisherman's Wharf Association
Ph: 250-245-7511
Manager • Float length 213 m

Launch ramp • Breakwater • Grid • Garbage • Waste oil disposal •
Water • Lights • Power • Public phone •
Near uptown restaurants, shops. The Maritime Society docks are adjacent to the south.

Ladysmith Harbour

49° 00.615' N
123° 49.389' W

Page Point Inn and Marina

Lexie and Lawrence Lambert
4760 Brenton-Page Rd
Ladysmith BC V9G 1L7
Ph: 250-245-2312 Fax: 250-245-7546
Toll free 1-877-860-6866
info@pagepointmarina.com
www.pagepointmarina.com

Marina services:
Fuel: Gas. Diesel. Ice.
Marine supplies. Service available.
Garbage disposal.
Guest moorage, about 1,000 feet of space.
Power: 30, 50 amps.
Laundry, showers, washrooms.

Customer services:
Restaurant. Fine dining. Licenced.
Patio service. Fireside pub. Gift shop.
Public pay phones ashore.
Daily float plane service accessible and stops at marina for pick-up.

Charts 3313, 3475, 3443, 3463
VHF 66A

Entertainment:
B&B guests–canoes, rowboats. Sailboat rentals. Road access walking or cycling. Golf nearby, arrangements–ask at marina for details. Car rentals. Bus or boat rides can be scheduled into nearby Ladysmith.

Adjacent facilities:
Bed and breakfast accommodations at the rustic but elegant lodge. Make reservations ahead in summer months.
Short boat trip to Ladysmith–stores–stop at government dock opposite/south just inside entrance to Ladysmith harbour for access to town.

Above: Page Point Inn & Marina. The property is located on Page Point, from which it takes its name. Not to be confused with Page's Marina in Silva Bay.

Ladysmith Maritime Society

PO Box 1030 Ladysmith BC V9G 1A7
Ph: 250-616-6433

Moorage: Limited space. No reservations. Power 15, 30 amps. Call ahead to check space availability. The Society docks are located immediately to port after passing Sibell Bay to starboard. This bay is good for anchoring. It is the location of the Seattle Yacht Club station on the Dunsmuir Islands. The public docks just beyond have full facilities but can be crowded when the fishing fleet is in.

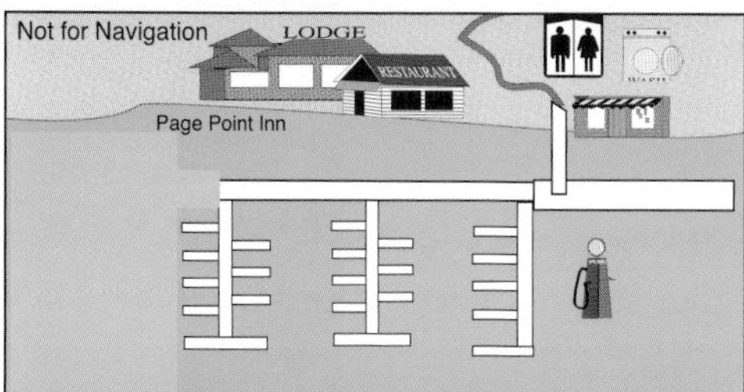

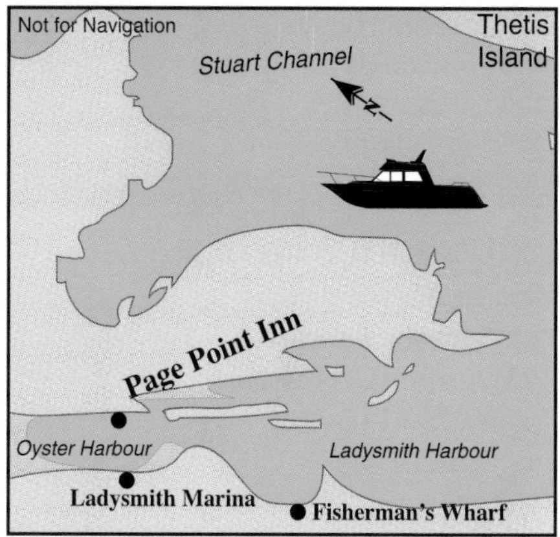

Page Point Inn and Marina offers outstanding overnight sheltered moorage, fuel, restaurant and many amenities. Fuel and some supplies are available at the dock.

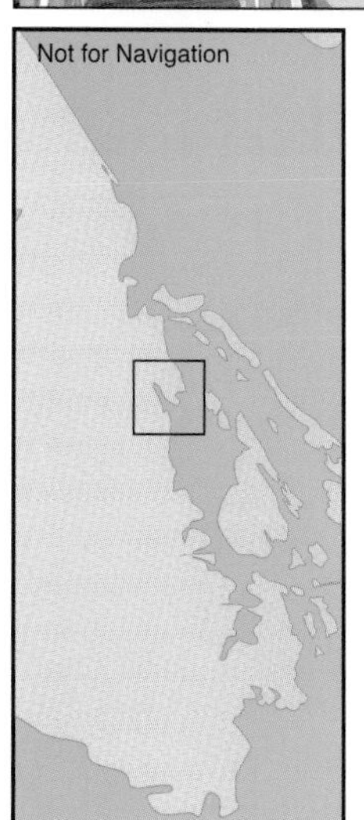

Ladysmith Marina

Page Point Inn and Marina

Ladysmith Marina
49° 00.386' N
123° 49.618' W

Ladysmith Harbour

Ladysmith Marina

Charts 3313, 3475, 3443, 3463

Manager Rob Waters
12335 Rocky Creek Rd
Ladysmith BC V9G 1K4
Phone: 250-245-4521
Fax: 250-245-4538
VHF 66A

Marina Services:
Guest moorage–reservations required. **Power** at docks: 15 amps. Garbage disposal. **Washrooms**.
Haul out and repairs, marine sales and services. Coffee shop. Boat top repairs. Welding repairs. Docking to 50 feet and marine lift to 30 feet. Parking. One kilometre uptown to city of Ladysmith.

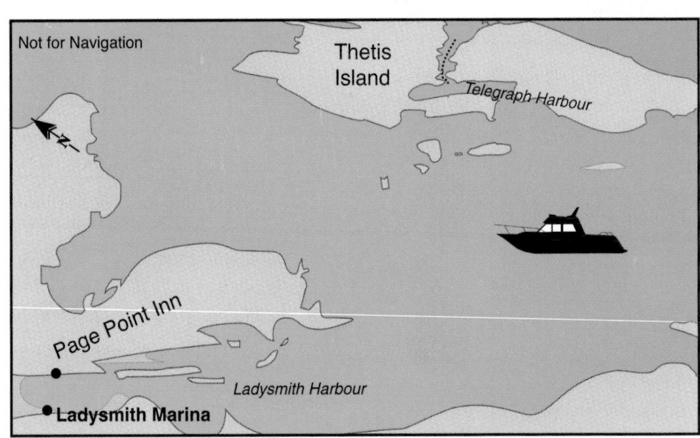

Top: Oyster Harbour marinas location at Ladysmith. Above right: The entrance to Ladysmith Harbour with the public dock and Maritime Society to left. Oyster Harbour beyond.

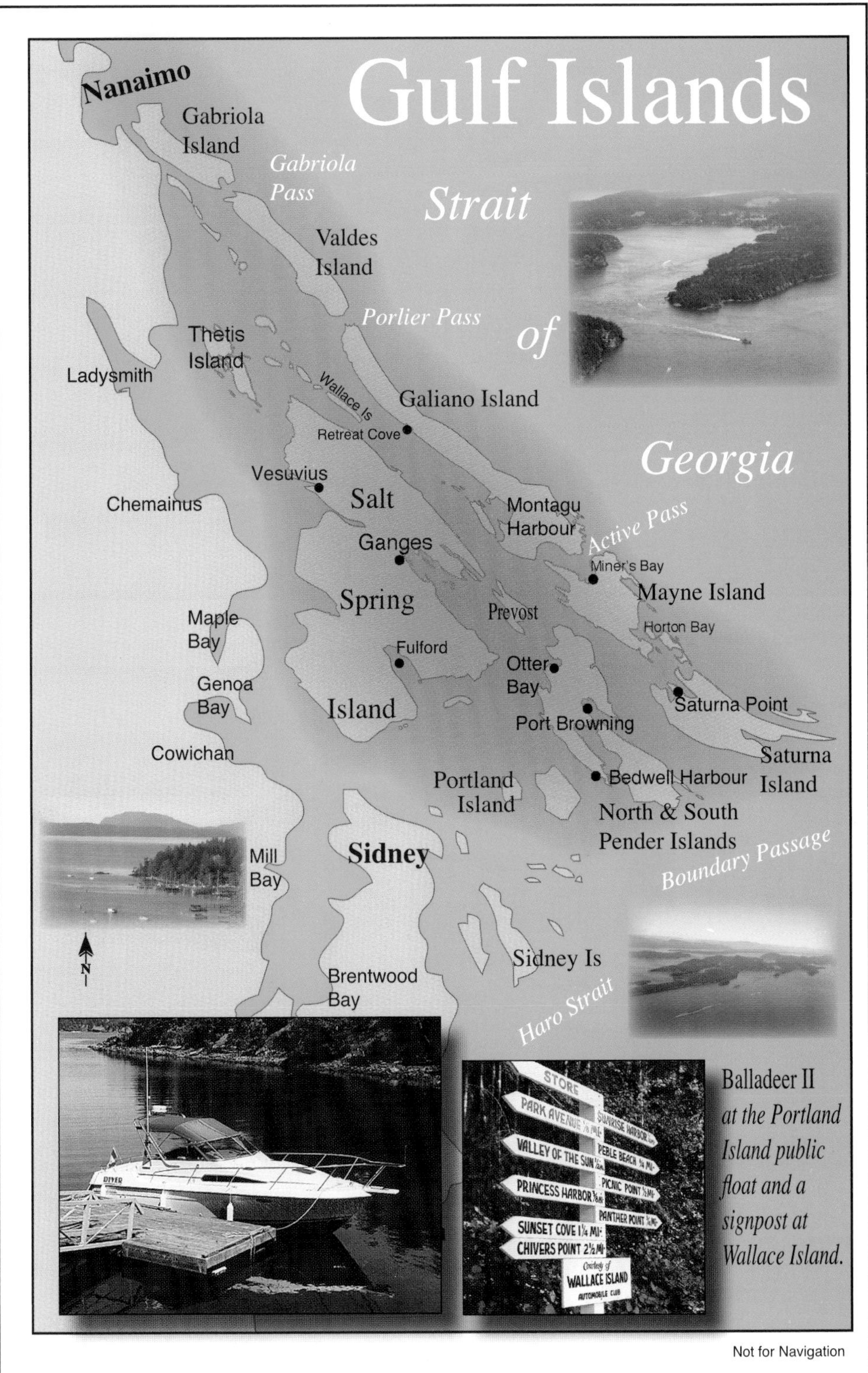

Balladeer II at the Portland Island public float and a signpost at Wallace Island.

Top: A popular event at Ganges is the Saturday morning farmers market in summer. Right: Special dock for the lamb roast at Saturna Island, a popular event every year.

The Gulf Islands offer many anchoring and mooring alternatives. The diagram on the previous page shows the main archipelago which makes up the group of islands that are most popular for overnight use. Note the cautions in the following text but always be mindful of weather conditions and forecasts.

Salt Spring Island is the largest of the Gulf Islands and has most facilities and amenities similar to mainland and Vancouver Island centres. Ganges holds an open air market every Saturday through the summer. The town is alive with vendors at the market and musicians in the local park.

One of the most popular events in the Gulf Islands is the annual lamb roast on Saturna Island. It is held on July 1st (Canada Day), when hundreds of boats will be found at anchor in Winter Harbour. A large dinghy dock is in place for the event.

Salt Spring Island

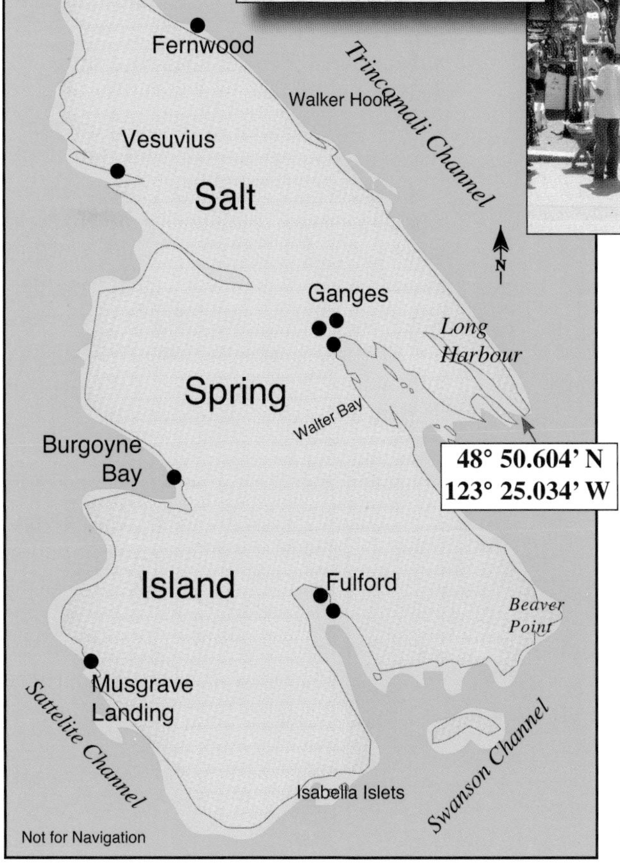

Fernwood
Trincomali Channel
Walker Hook
Vesuvius
Salt
Ganges
Long Harbour
Spring
Walter Bay
Burgoyne Bay
48° 50.604' N
123° 25.034' W
Island
Fulford
Beaver Point
Musgrave Landing
Sattelite Channel
Swanson Channel
Isabella Islets
Not for Navigation

Top: A view over Ganges, the popular Gulf Islands destination where every Saturday morning the farmers market attracts a large crowd of visiting mariners. Above: The farmers market and musicians at Ganges.

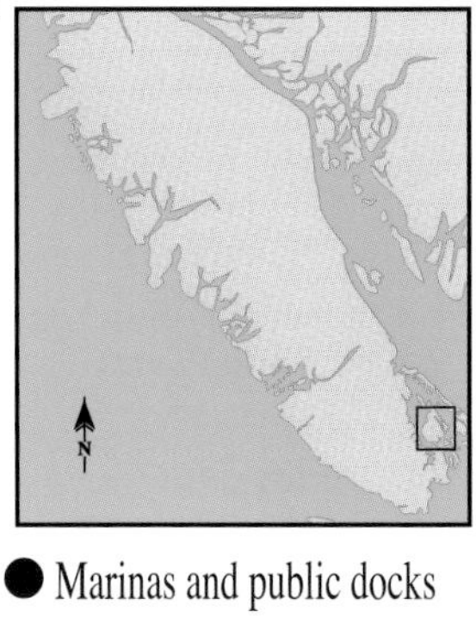

● Marinas and public docks

A view of Fulford Marina from the public dock and ferry landing.

Fulford Harbour

Charts 3313, 3478, 3441/2, 3462/3

Fulford Marina

Bill and Gay Perry
5–2810 Fulford-Ganges Rd
Salt Spring Island BC V8K 1Z2
VHF 66A
Ph: 250-653-4467 Fax: 250-653-4457
fulfordmarina@saltspring.com
www.saltspring.com/fulfordmarina

Marina services:
Moorage: Seasonal. Guest moorage April 1 to September 30 only. 600' plus 10 slips guest docks. Reservations suggested. Large breakwater float.
Fuel: Available seasonally next door at Roamers Landing. *Flag denotes open.*
Power at docks: 20, 30 amp.

Customer services:
Showers, washrooms. Laundry at Fulford Inn, about a mile away.
Entertainment:
Island tranquility. Eagles, herons, kingfishers, otters and seals. Waterfront gazebos and barbecue area. Beaches. Tennis courts.
Nearby facilities:
BC Ferries to Sidney. Government docks. Places of interest: Historic churches. Fulford settlement–gifts, art, bakery, groceries, restaurants, hotel. Walk to Drummond Park. Nearby private museum of Indian Art–Bob Akerman collection and his wife's classic doll collection. Five minutes walk to pub, beer and wine store, grocery store, coffee shop, crafts, parks, ferry. 20 minutes to lake. Salmon charters and sightseeing/eco tours.

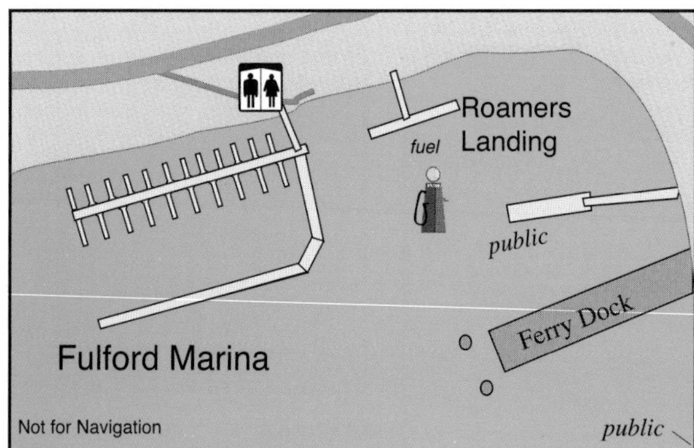

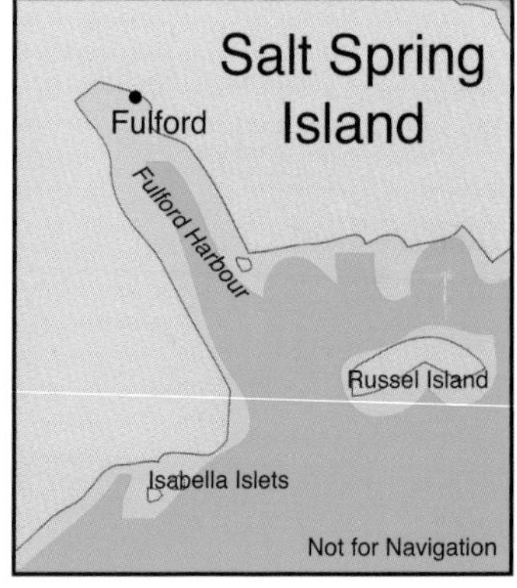

Left to right: The marina, fuel dock, public docks (middle of bay and single dock outside) and the ferry landing. Below: Cruising into the entrance to Fulford . Bottom: The public dock sometimes has space for tie up–usually rafted.

Roamer's Landing VHF 66A

Rose Marie and Peter Roemer
2850 Fulford-Ganges Rd Salt Spring Island BC V8K 1X6
Ph: 250-653-4442 or 250-653-4481
r.roamer@saltspring.com

Marina services:
Fuel stop only. Gas and diesel.
Flag up when open.

Public docks:

Fulford Harbour, Outside of breakwater. Harbour Authority of SSI.
• Float length 16 metres. Kayak rentals. Possible overnight moorage in calm conditions. Ferry to Sidney. Restaurants, shops.
Manager-Bart Terwiel Ph: 250-537-5711
Two hours free 8am to 4pm.
Charts 3313, 3478, 3441/2, 3462/3
ssha@saltspring.com

Fulford Harbour, Inner dock
Manager-Ph: 250-537-5711
• Float length 36 m • Lights • Power • Public pay phone • Limited guest space. Marina and fuel nearby.

Charts 3313, 3478, 3442, 3462

Ganges

48° 51.257' N 123° 29.835' W

Ganges Marina VHF 66A

Rick Barbieri – owner
Jim Robertson, Shirley Command – mngrs
161 Lower Ganges Rd
Ganges BC V8K 2T2
Ph: 250-537-5242 Fax: 250-538-1719
gangesmarina@shaw.ca
www.ganges-marina.com

Marina services:
Moorage: Guest moorage about 100 slips. Reservations taken.
Fuel: Gas, diesel, oils.
Power at docks: 15, 30, 50 amps.
Internet access

Customer services:
Public pay phone ashore. Marina store has some supplies. Ice.
Laundry, showers, washrooms.
Complimentary coffee, tea and muffins in the morning.
Car rentals at marina.

Top: Ganges with its marinas and anchorage.

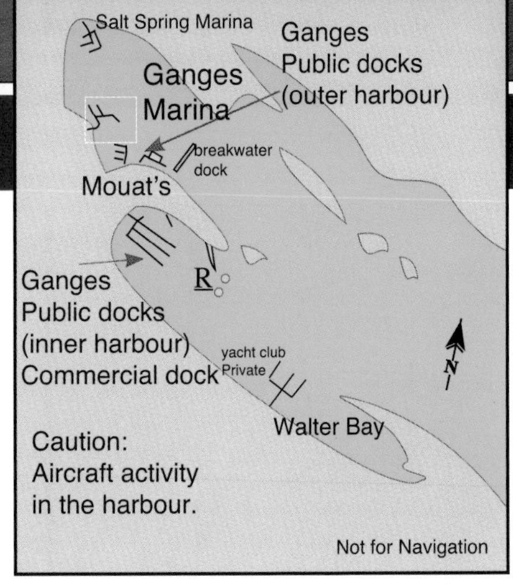

Entertainment:
Ganges Saturday morning public market. Art galleries.
Walking and cycling on island roads, some nearby waterfront and beachfront access. Playground.

Nearby:
Government docks. Shopping centre. Propane. Close to all Ganges facilities. Fresh produce. Bakeries. Thrifty Foods Ph: 250-537-1522–groceries. Restaurants. Anchorages and places of interest. Churches. Arts and crafts. Hotels, bed and breakfast. Bistros. Pubs.

Photograph above and below show Ganges Marina occupying a large portion of the bay. Ganges Marina is a popular venue for yacht club cruises and other boating rendezvous. There are patio docks as well as a room for group use. No moorage on outside of the breakwater dock.

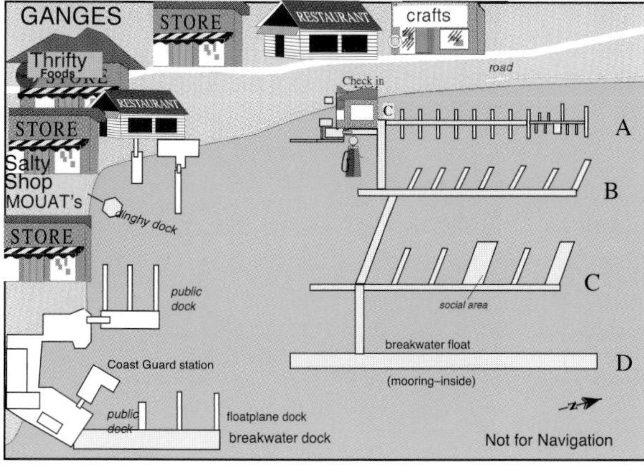

Ganges is the business centre and hub of the Gulf Islands. It is not only located on the largest of the Gulf Islands but also it has the largest population of all communities in the archipelago. Activities on Salt Spring Island as well as arts and crafts attract many visitors each summer. The morning farmers market held on the waterfront every Saturday has become a colourful attraction.

The work of local artists can be seen and bought in the several art shops and galleries in Ganges. Shopping at Mouat's historic store provides opportunity to stock up on the items you need for your boating comfort, safety and convenience.

The many other speciality, souvenir and book stores in the town will provide hours of pleasurable shopping or window shopping. And the restaurants are of a variety that will enable you to select from a wide range of menus. Hastings House, one of the top restaurants in Canada, is located in Ganges.

Gulf Islands

Salt Spring Marina

Lesley Cheeseman
124 Upper Ganges Rd
Salt Spring Island BC V8K 2S2
Ph: 250-537-5810 Fax: 250-537-5809
Toll free 1-800-334-6629
Charts 3313, 3462/3, 3478 VHF 66A

Marina services:
Moorage: About 50 slips and 380' outer dock for guests and Seattle YC outstation. Pumpout. Propane nearby.
Power: 15, 30 amp.

Customer services:
Rogue Cafe. Public pay phone ashore. Marine chandlery, fishing licences and tackle. Marine service.* Haulouts, towing. **Showers, washrooms. laundry,** souvenirs, coffee, ice, bait, fishing gear. Internet access. Budget car rentals. Shuttle to town.

Entertainment:
Ganges Saturday public market. Arts. Galleries. Scooter, kayak and boat rentals. Walking on island roads, some nearby waterfront and beachfront access.

Adjacent and nearby facilities:
Moby's Marine Pub, Rogue Cafe, historic Hastings House restaurant. Playgrounds. Shopping centre. Post office, banks, churches, groceries, restaurants, hotels, bed and breakfast. Liquor store. Auto supplies up town.

Salt Spring Marina, right, is to left in the photo above. Hastings House restaurant overlooks the anchorage.

Boat services include temporary stopping if space permits, at the government dock on the north side of the town or in the harbour. Ganges Marina and Salt Spring Marina provide overnight and extended mooring and all marina services. For groceries and supplies, Mouat's and Thrifty Foods are popular stores and there are a number of restaurants and pubs near the marinas.

Above: Restaurants overlook Ganges Harbour. Top: One of the busy stores in downtown Ganges.
Right: The market at Ganges on Saturday mornings. Local merchants and artisans conduct business from their outdoor stalls. There is live music too.
A note of caution: Walking in and around town can be pleasant, but caution should be exercised due to the heavy traffic on some of the roads and limited pedestrian sidewalks out of town.
A waterfront boardwalk has been under construction for some years but the sections have not yet been connected due to unavailability of land in one area.

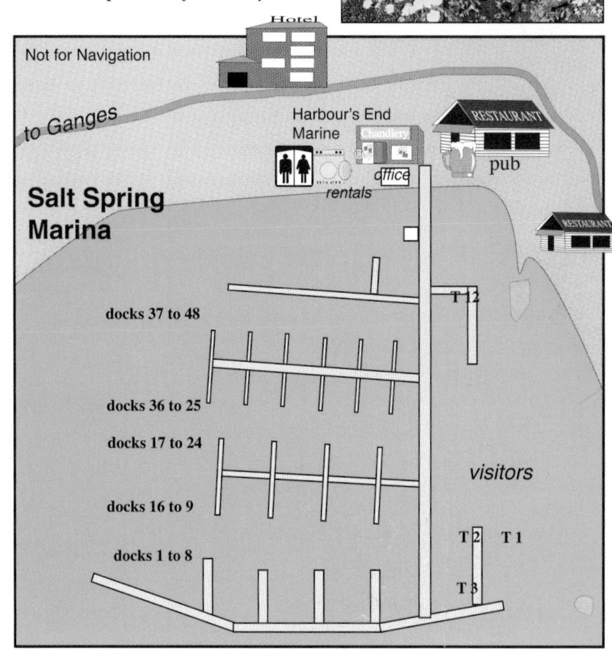

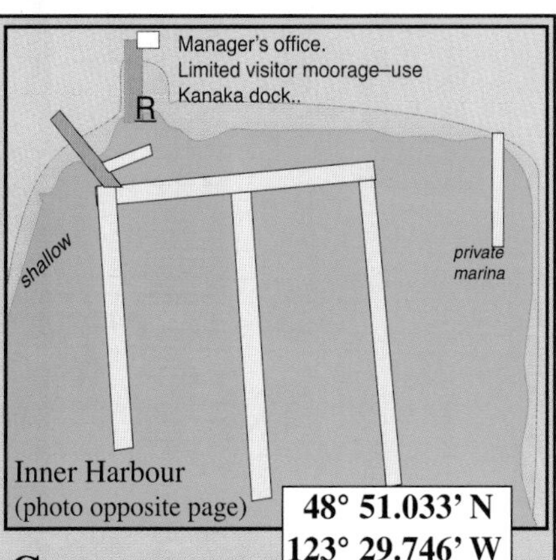

48° 51.033' N
123° 29.746' W

Ganges
Salt Spring Island
Public docks

Ph/Fax: 250-537-5711 VHF 09

Ganges Boat Harbour (Inner Harbour)

Harbour Authority of Salt Spring Island.
ssha@saltspring.com
Centennial Dock (and office) Manager • Float length 326 m • **Launch ramp** • Rock breakwater • Waste oil disposal • Water • Lights • Power • **Washroom** • **Showers** (serves all local public docks). Adjacent restaurants, shops.

Breakwater dock

Harbour Authority of Salt Spring Island. Breakwater: use inner fingers. • Aircraft Float • Water • Lights • Power: 20 amp • Pumpout station • rafting • Adjacent restaurants, shops. Fuel dock at Ganges Marina. Coast Guard dock adjacent.

(Kanaka dock–outer harbour)

Harbour Authority of Salt Spring Island. Manager–*check in at office in Inner Harbour for stays over two hours* • Two outer fingers and east side of main float for visitors • Garbage • Water • Power: 20 amp • rafting • Adjacent to restaurants and shops. School boats at inner finger. Ambulance/coast guard auxiliary adjacent.

Ph/Fax: 250-537-5711–for all public docks at Ganges.

Charts 3313, 3478, 3442, 3462

The outer harbour public docks and the Ganges town waterfront. The dinghy dock is located between the public dock in the foreground and the private dock left.

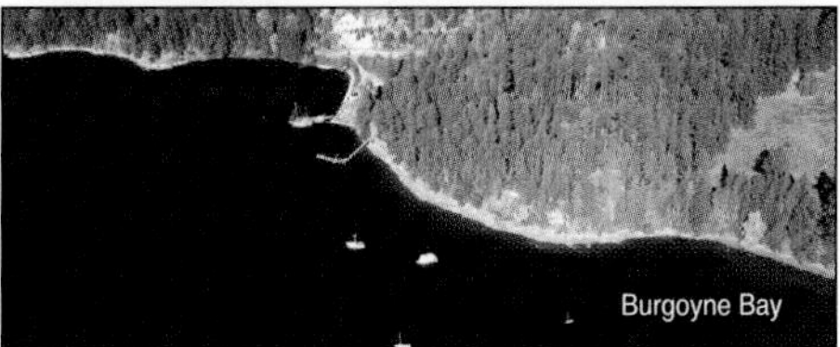

Fernwood

Capital Regional District Public dock
250-537-1638 Peter Lake-manager • Float length 12 m •
Charts 3313, 3462, 3442

Burgoyne Bay VHF 09

Salt Spring Island Public dock
Ph: 250-537-5711 • Manager • Float length 10 m • Charts 3313, 3478

Musgrave Landing, Salt Spring Island Public dock • Float length 12 m
Ph: 250-537-5711 Charts 3313, 3441/2

Top: The Inner Harbour lies behind the breakwater on the southeast side of Ganges. The small marina alongside the breakwater is private. Right: View of Ganges Harbour from above the Ganges Yacht Club at Walter Bay. The Outer Harbour is beyond the village. Ganges Marina and Salt Spring Marina can be seen beyond Grace Islet. Bottom: Moored alongside the public dock at Vesuvius.

Vesuvius Bay Public Dock

Saltspring Island Harbour Authority
Bart Terwiel
Phone/Fax: 250-537-5711
ssha@saltspring.com
Chart: 3478
Located on the northwest side of Salt Spring Island.
VHF 09
Public dock with limited space. Exposed to westerly winds and ferry wash. Rafting.

Nearby facilities: BC ferry to Crofton. Restaurant and restaurant dock to east of public dock. Taxis available for service into Ganges and other parts of Salt Spring Island.

Right and above: The floats at Port Washington will accommodate several small boats but are exposed to washes from ferries and some wind conditions. The general store has served passing vessels since the early 1900s.

Top: Looking north towards Active Pass. Port Washington opens into North Pender Island to the right.

Above: Poets Cove at Bedwell Harbour. This is a popular destination with large docks, fuel and supplies as well as a resort complex with many amenities including a pool and spa.

The Pender Islands

Photo top: Pender Canal between Port Browning and Bedwell Harbour. At Beaumont Marine Park in Bedwell Harbour there are mooring buoys in protected anchorage. For the energetic, hiking trails on Mount Norman regional park, overlooking Bedwell Harbour, are accessible.

The Pender Islands are blessed with beautiful, unspoiled and charming features and are centrally located in the Gulf Islands, providing moorage, anchorage and safe stops for all boat operators. One of the main harbours in the Penders is Bedwell Harbour with its resort, marina and adjacent anchorage.

The Pender Canal, separating South from North Pender, is a narrow passage which curves its way under a low bridge that connects the two islands. At high tide boats will clear the bridge if they are no taller than 26 feet.

Otter Bay is another of the Gulf Islands' major ports for recreational boating. It has a fully operational marina with good docks and a store that has local crafts, fine art, clothing, books, some fresh produce, canned goods and frozen foods among other items. The marina office sells fishing licences and can provide information on local island services such as mechanical, bed and breakfast and ferries schedules. A large lawn is a playing field for children and there are several picnic tables placed along the waterfront. A swimming pool has hours set aside for adult only usage. If you want a catered meal go to the nearby golf club or take in one of the local restaurants, some of whose dinners are legendary.

Bedwell Harbour

Charts 3313, 3477, 3441, 3462 VHF 66A

Poets Cove Marina & Seaside Resort at Bedwell Harbour

Director marina operations Tara Hodgins
9801 Spalding Rd
South Pender Island BC V0N 2M3
Ph: 250-629-2111 Fax: 250-629-2110
Toll free 866-888-2683 VHF 66A
marina@poetscove.com
www.poetscove.com

Customs service. Clearance by phone for all persons May 1 through Sept 30. CANPASS only Oct. 1 through April 30.

Marina services:
Fuel: Gas and diesel. Lubricants.
Moorage. Large marina with mostly transient moorage–110 slips. **Water** at dock-limited supply. **Power** at docks: 30 amp.
Laundry, showers, washrooms. Tackle shop on dock.

Customer services:
Restaurant. Pub. Breakfast, lunch, dinner. Licensed. Also patio service. Beer and wine store. Swimming pool. ATM. Lodging. Conference center/ballroom. Fitness centre. Spa, pool & hot tub. Playground. Internet access.
Store: Fresh baked goods, gifts, groceries.
Marina store: Fishing gear, licenses, bait, ice, charts, books.
Tennis racquets available. Bicycle, kayak, canoe & boat rentals. Public pay phone ashore. Garbage disposal.

Entertainment:
Road access walking or cycling. Nearby hiking trails. Live music weekends, summer. Tennis courts. Market. Seasonal barbecue.

Adjacent facilities:
Pet area. Beaumont Marine Park. Camping, hiking. Mooring buoys.
Nearby Mt. Norman is accessible by trail.

Opposite page: Poets Cove Marina at Bedwell Harbour– also pictured right and below. Below, right: Pender Canal, the narrow passage between Bedwell Bay and Port Browning, was man made to provide an alternative route between the islands. Clearance at high tide is 26 feet. At low tide the depth of water is seven feet.

This is one of the main American entrances to Canadian waters in British Columbia. It is a busy customs stop throughout the summer months June through September. Bedwell is one of the most used entry ports for vessels arriving, including returning Canadians, out of the San Juan Islands or Puget Sound. The facilities at Poets Cove have been as comprehensive as you will find anywhere in British Columbian waters.

The docks are extensive and power and water are available. Water is not for washing boats due to the relative short supply from its island source. The fuel dock serves gas and diesel and other marine products.

Showers, laundry, a general store, restaurant, snack kiosks, and a marine bar and bistro are poplar among visiting boaters. The dining room has elegant decor and fine cuisine.

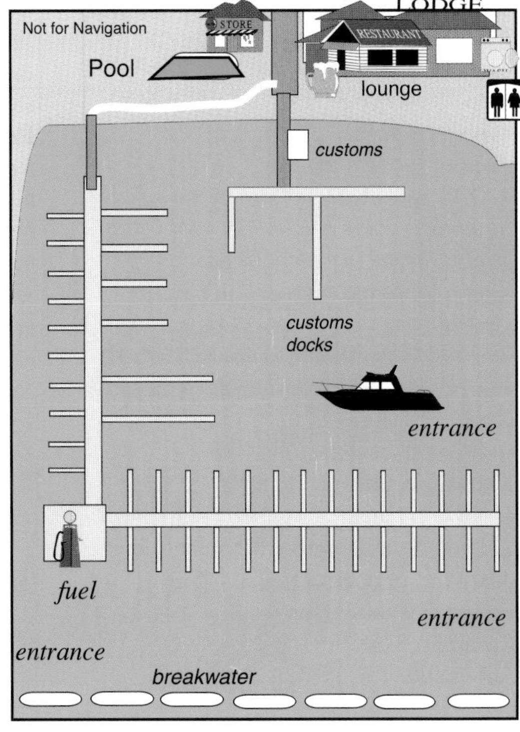

Port Browning

Marina:
48° 46.579' N 123° 16.249' W

Port Browning Marina

Lou Henshaw
4605 Oak Rd
PO Box 126, Pender Island BC V0N 2M0
Ph: 250-629-3493 Fax: 250-629-3495
info@portbrowning.com
www.portbrowning.com

Caution: Narrow, shallow Pender Canal divides the two Pender Islands. Check chart and tides.

Customs: Check in at Bedwell Harbour or Port Browning–designated Canpass reporting sites.

Marina services:
Moorage. Large marina with permanent and transient moorage. There is about 3,000 feet of docks space.
Power at docks: 15 amp.
Laundry, showers, washrooms.
Reservations advised summertime.
Garbage disposal.

Charts 3313, 3477, 3441/2 VHF 66A

Customer services:
Pub. Restaurant. Breakfast, lunch, dinner. Licensed. Also patio service.
Cold beer and wine store at marina.
Public pay phones, water taxi, tour company.
Wifi internet access.
Entertainment:
Swimming pool, large lawn, camping.
Tennis. Golf nearby.
Saturday morning early farmers' market at nearby shopping plaza and at the island community centre.

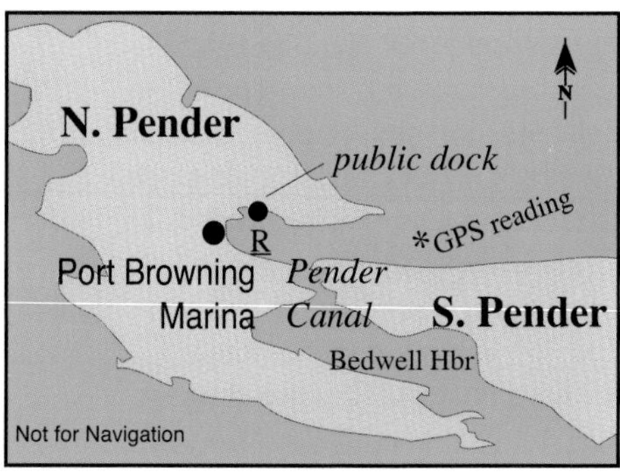

Pender Island Golf and Country Club 250-629-6659

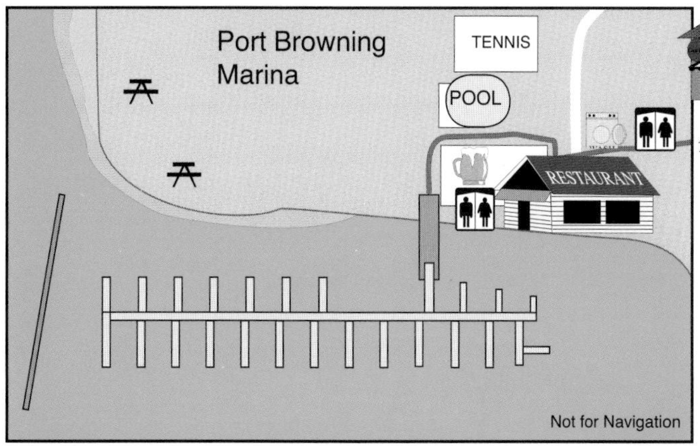

Docks and facilities at Port Browning include pub, restaurant and tennis courts.
A large expanse of lawn is used frequently in summer for yacht club or group gatherings and regular weekend camping and barbecues.

Below: Port Browning from the east. Pender Canal opens at the left.

Port Browning is the nearest marina to the North Pender Island shopping centre and supermarket. Visit the well-stocked Talisman Books and Gallery.

Road access walking or cycling. Take care walking the narrow island road.
Good beach access.

Nearby facilities:
Shopping centre nearby at town centre–five minutes walk. Wide range of services, liquor store, bank, post office, art, gifts, dairy products, bakery. Tru Value Foods supermarket. Delivery to marina possible. Pharmacy. Gas station. **Talisman Books.** Restaurants, B&Bs, accommodations on the island. Check at shopping centre. Small craft launch ramp located on the beach near the marina.
Grass air strip adjacent to shopping centre.

Browning Harbour

North Pender Island–public dock
Al Cannon–manager. Capital Regional District. Ph: 250-539-3036
Chart 3313
Float length 27 metres (blue dock)
Store, shopping complex nearby.
Port Browning Marina is located almost directly opposite.

Otter Bay

Charts 3313, 3441/2 VHF 66A

Otter Bay Marina

Chuck Spence
2311 Mackinnon Rd
North Pender Island BC V0N 2M1
Ph: 250-629-3579 Fax: 250-629-3589

Hazard:
Keep clear and east of green spar U 57.

Marina services:
Launch ramp (small craft).
Moorage. Large marina with permanent and transient moorage. About 50 slips.
Reservations advised in the summertime.
Water at dock. Use sparingly please.
Power at docks: 15, 30 amp.
Laundry, showers, washrooms.
Customer services:
Store. Gifts, bait, ice, limited groceries, charts, fishing tackle, licences and snacks.
Garbage disposal (reminder-the islands have difficulty with garbage so please avoid dropping garbage even when service is offered).
Road access walking or cycling.
Take care walking the narrow island roads.
Public pay phones ashore.
Eagles, herons, otters and seals. Bicycle, boat and kayak rentals. Playground.
Adjacent facilities:
BC Ferries dock.
Picnic tables, barbecue area.
Gazebo.
Deck on breakwater at marina.
Golf course–10 minutes walk. Club coffee shop and restaurant.
Islander Restaurant, artists' galleries nearby.
Shuttle service to shopping centre in July and August.

Otter Bay Marina is a very popular resort. Weekends in mid summer and on holidays are booked well in advance. For many years Otter Bay operated with minimal dock space and limited service. When Chuck Spence took over running the facility he and his late wife, Kay, set about enlarging the docks, replacing the buildings on shore and adding amenities to make a visit a more enjoyable experience. They achieved this and more with the provision of a swimming pool, coffee bar and store. The pool has hours set aside for adult use only which is popular among those needing to relax undisturbed while they bathe during a hot day.

Otter Bay was not always the laid back cruising destination it is today. At one time it flourished as a fishing centre featuring such establishments as cannery, saltery and reduction plant. In 1963 it took on a new life as a marina and by 1972 it had moved to the ownership of Bob and Karen Melville. After nearly 20 years they moved to the BC Interior when David Bromley bought the marina and the Spences took over managing it. The Melvilles left a legacy at Otter Bay in the way of Karen's flower and vegetable garden as well as the fruit trees that can be found on the property.

There are world class vacation cottages at Otter Bay. The property, Currents at Otter Bay, boasts 31 architect designed fully furnished fractional ownership cottages.

Crew off anchored boats are welcomed ashore–check in with the dock manager. There is a possible fee during busy periods.

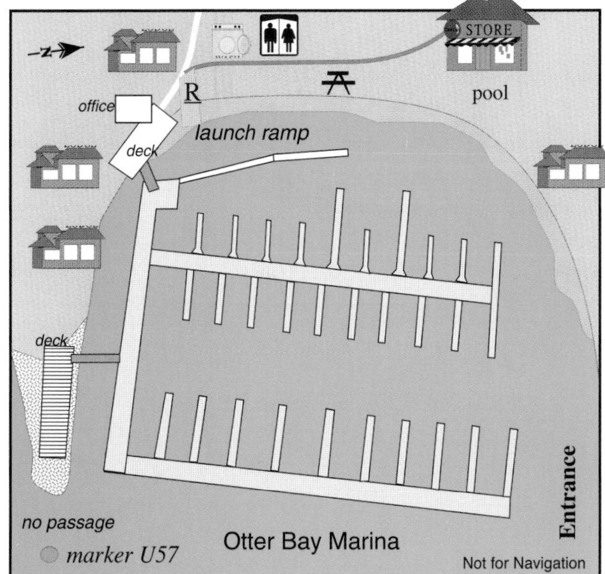

Top: Summer months at Otter Bay are busy so make reservations ahead of your arrival. Opposite: Aerial photo of the marina and a view of the store and pool.

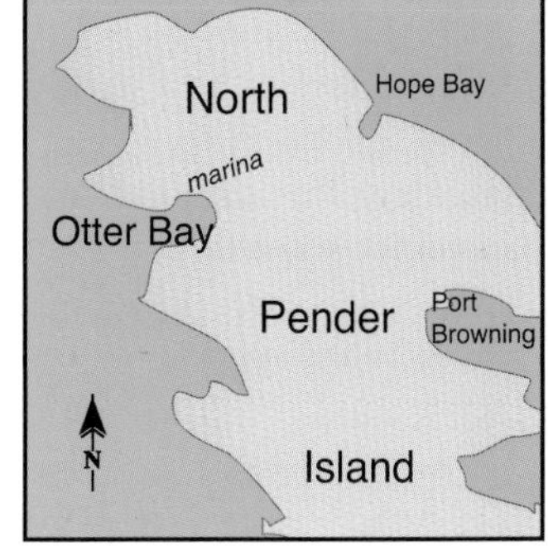

Hope Bay, restaurant, stores and public docks in Navy Channel.

Hope Bay

North Pender Island
Manager Peter Binner
Ph: 250-629-9990

48° 48.210' N
123° 16.484' W

Charts 3313, 3477, 3461, 3462, 3441/2
Public dock • Float length–69 metres • Lights • Stores, restaurant. Two-day **mooring buoys** for Hope Bay customers. Fish/crab sales at dock in summer.

Port Washington

North Pender Island Ph: 250-539-3036
Al Cannon (CRD-public dock–blue)
Charts 3313, 3442, 3462
• Float length 45 m • Aircraft float • Public pay phone ashore • Nearby arts and crafts. Walking–island roads. Coffee bar. Snacks, gifts. Fair weather moorage.

48° 48.756' N
123° 19.267' W

Left: Hope Bay–the docks and the restaurant.
Above: Port Washington–the historic store.

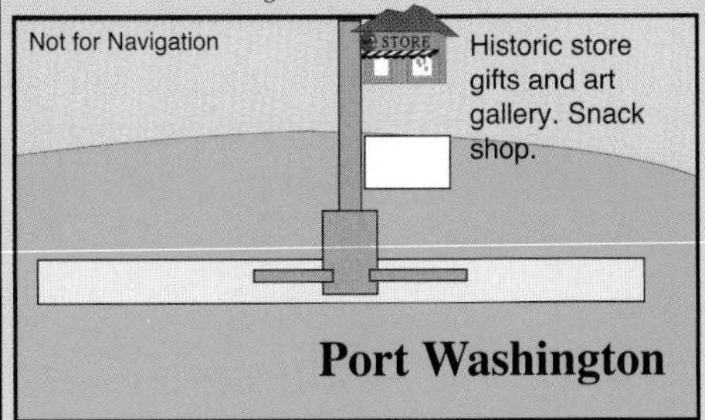

The dock at Saturna Point. Inset and bottom: The lamb barbecue July 1st each year attracts a lot of boats to Winter Cove on Saturna Island. The dinghy dock fills up as the boats arrive.

Charts 3313, 3477, 3441, 3462

Saturna Point

Saturna Point Landing

Fuel Dock, Lyall Harbour
Harbour Master Gloria Manzano
Saturna Island BC V0N 2Y0
Ph/Fax: 250-539-2480

Marina services:
Government dock. Limited space–mostly drop off/pick up. Not intended for overnight.
Fuel: Gas, diesel, outboard mix, oil.
Public pay phone.
Store and Lighthouse Pub ashore.
Adjacent:
General store: groceries, fishing tackle, hardware, licences, ice, bait. Propane available nearby.

Post office about 1 mile up the road. Also adjacent: BC Ferries. Use caution manoeuvering when ferry operating. Winter Cove anchorage, Boot Cove (poor anchorage).
Entertainment:
Saturna Lodge and Restaurant.
Vineyards on island–enquire at store.
Annual lamb barbecue July 1st at Winter Cove. Island tranquility. Eagles, herons, otters and seals.

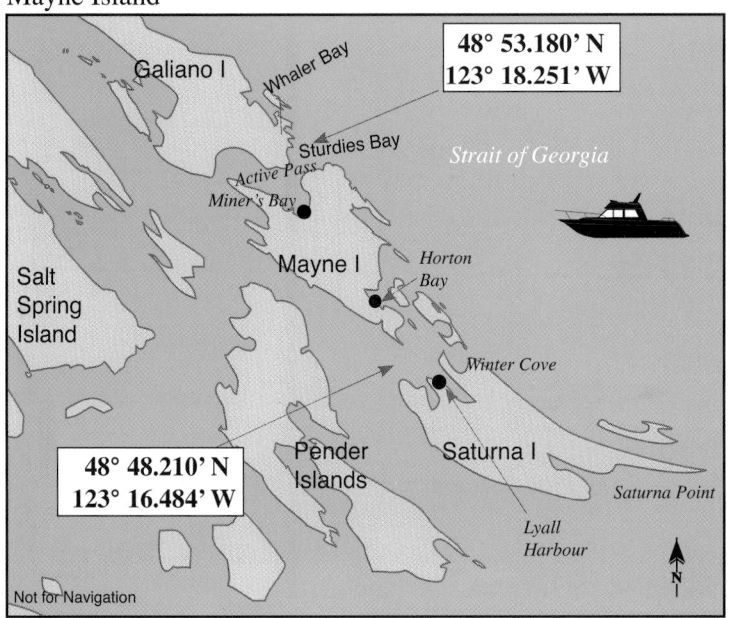

Opposite page: A ferry going through Active Pass. The dock and fuel float in Miners Bay are operated by the community. It is open seven days a week for fuel. Other marine services are available through the general store on shore. The public dock is subject to wash from passing vessels.

Charts 3313, 3473, 3442, 3462

Active Pass

In Active Pass one has to be mindful of the strong current and tide rips as well as the constantly passing ferries. Fishing in the pass, and particularly at each entrance to the pass is extremely popular and rewarding. However, here again, one should exercise caution due to the passage of ferries. Fishing vessels are obliged to move aside for approaching ferries. Common sense calls for such action to avoid collision and also to aid the ferries in their tight manoeuvering in the restrictive passage.

Left: The ferry landing and boat dock at Sturdies Bay. The float is small and is not suitable for accommodating overnight visitors. It is convenient for picking up and dropping off ferry passengers for Galiano Island.

When approaching Miner's Bay for fuel, simply steer directly towards the fuel dock. The water shallows off towards the shore but mooring buoys indicate adequate water in their vicinity. Watch for the swells created by passing ferries and other vessels and wait for them to pass before attempting to dock at the fuel dock or the government floats behind the modest wood piling breakwater.

Active Pass

Charts 3313, 3473, 3442, 3462

Miner's Bay Mayne Island

48° 51.179' N
123° 18.155' W

Public dock (blue) Ph: 250-539-3036
Manager Al Cannon • Float length 37 m
Aircraft float • Lights • (CRD managed)
Marine Services:
Fuel • gas, diesel, outboard mix.
Tackle, bait, propane. Candy, pop.
Adjacent restaurants, shops.
Small craft moorage. No water or power on docks. No laundry–No washrooms.
Taxi service. Access to settlement.
Near Ferry service–Gulf Islands to the mainland and Sidney. Groceries, stores, accommodation, churches nearby.

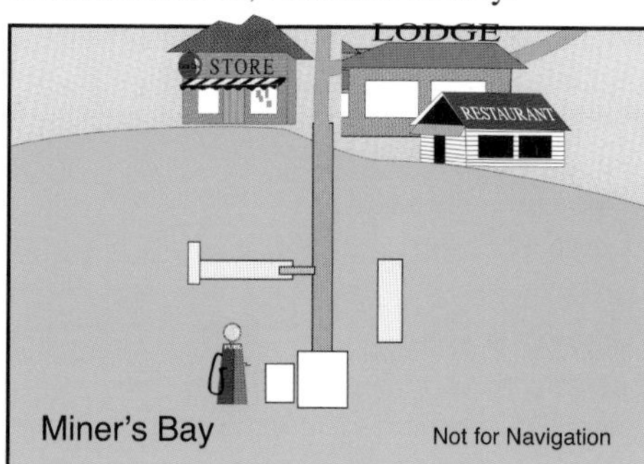

Easy walking on island roadways.
Ferry wash causes some rolling at dock.
On the opposite side of Active Pass brief stops are possible at the small dock in Sturdies Bay adjacent to the ferry landing.

Top: The dock at Miner's Bay. Inet: The fuel dock. Note the ferry passing in Active Pass. Above: Whaler Bay.

Whaler Bay

48° 53.038' N
123° 19.594' W

Public dock (Small Craft Harbours–red)
Manager Joy Wilson 250-539-5420 •
Lights • Power. No facilities.
Limited dock space. Nearby convenience store. Near ferry dock. Bakery and Deli.
Art and Soul Craft Gallery. Book store.

Montague Harbour

Charts 3473, 3313, 3442, 3462

Montague Harbour Marina

Marilyn Breeze
3451 Montague Rd,
RR 1 S-17, C-57, Galiano Island BC V0N 1P0
Ph: 250-539-5733 Fax: 250-539-3593
montaguemarina@gulfislands.com
www.montagueharbour.com
VHF 66A

Marina services:
Fuel: Gas. Diesel. Oil. Marine supplies. Open May through September–guest **moorage**. **Limited water**. **Power**: 15, 30 amp.

Customer services:
Grocery store, books, charts, clothing and gifts, fishing supplies. Harbour Grill restaurant–licensed family sundeck serving hot meals all day. No off-sales. Public pay phone. Garbage disposal (fee).

Adjacent facilities and entertainment:
Marine park at Montague Harbour. Mooring buoys and dock. Extensive walks and camp ground, beaches and picnic facilities.
Sea kayak float. Scuba diving good in Active Pass and nearby reefs. Use charter services. Golf. Floating bakery.

Public docks on Galiano:

North Galiano

Summer only. Public dock
Small Craft Harbours (red)
Ph: 250-539-5420. Joy Wilson.
Charts 3313, 3443, 3463
Float length–12 metres
Public pay phone ashore
Adjacent the old Spanish Hills Store.

Retreat Cove (photo opposite page)

Galiano Island. Public dock (blue).
Ph: 539-3036 Al Cannon (Capital Regional District). Charts 3313, 3442, 3463
Float length 24 metres.

Montague Harbour

Galiano Island Public dock (blue)
Ph: 539-3036 Al Cannon
Charts 3313, 3473, 3462
Float length 50 metres
Adjacent Montague Marina.

Sturdies Bay

Galiano Island. Public. Small Craft Harbours Ph: 250-539-5420. Joy Wilson.

Opposite: Montague Harbour on a quiet day in late summer. Trincomali Channel with Wallace Island lie beyond the harbour. Top and above: Montague Harbour Marina. To the left is the small public dock. The fuel dock is easy to access. Centre, right: Store and espresso bar overlooking the docks. Patio service at the restaurant. The marina has a well stocked store and a kayak rental office. Right: Retreat Cove public dock and anchorage on the west side of Galiano Island.

Retreat Cove

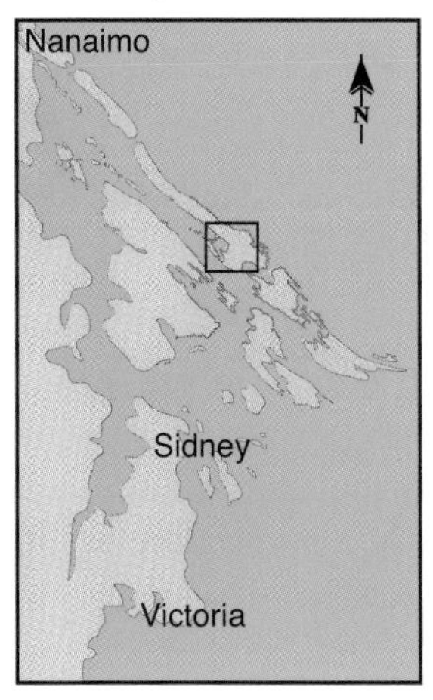

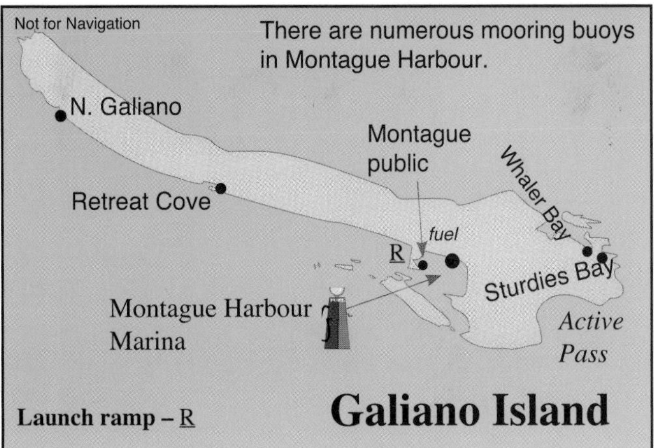

En route up the coast towards Thetis Island and its popular marinas many stop at Princess Bay on Wallace Island. Nearby is Conover Cove where you can stop at the dock and go ashore to hike the easy trails that run the length of the island.

One of the busy docks in the middle of summer at Ganges Marina on Salt Spring Island.

Bottom: At the dock in Horton Bay, Mayne Island.

Horton Bay

Mayne Island
Small Craft Harbours (red)
Ph: 250-539-5420.
Joy Wilson manager

- Float length 60 metres
- Garbage • Lights

Charts 3313, 3477, 3442, 3462
Be mindful of the currents and reef at the entrance to Horton Bay from the direction of Lyall Harbour.

Telegraph Harbour occupies a central location in the Gulf Islands. The tidal "Cut" allows limited passage between Thetis and Kuper Islands

Thetis Island

There's a waterway in the Gulf Islands that draws boats to the challenge of its shallows. One which lures sailors like the legendary sirens to an ignominious fate of running aground if not onto the rocks, to reach the prize beyond of sheltered anchorage and a fair haven from unexpected squalls and wind. The shallow, narrow passage that separates Thetis Island from Kuper is the eastern entrance to one of the most centrally located and popular anchorages in the Gulf Islands. The canal (known as 'The Cut') lets shallow draft boats through at medium to high tides and denies passage to all but the tiniest of craft at low tides. It dries at a one foot tide. But despite the quirks and whims of the famous passage, it is the waterway that experienced cruising yachtsmen associate with Telegraph Harbour. Explore the area: take a dinghy ride through "The Cut" and see the shallows for yourself before taking your boat through. The alternative route into Telegraph is around the south end of Kuper or the north of Thetis. If you are coming from a Vancouver Island base and returning to Vancouver Island after a stay at Telegraph Harbour, the passage is not an issue. But if you are crossing the Strait of Georgia and entering the Gulf Islands through Porlier Pass then the canal is the preferred way in. Choose a high tide to approach the canal or plan a longer, but pleasant detour around Thetis or Kuper.

Make reservations before arriving at a marina expecting moorage. When you arrive in Telegraph Harbour look for moorage at Thetis Island Marina or at Telegraph Harbour Marina. At the former you may look for the pub, at the latter you will want to moor quickly and head up the dock for one of

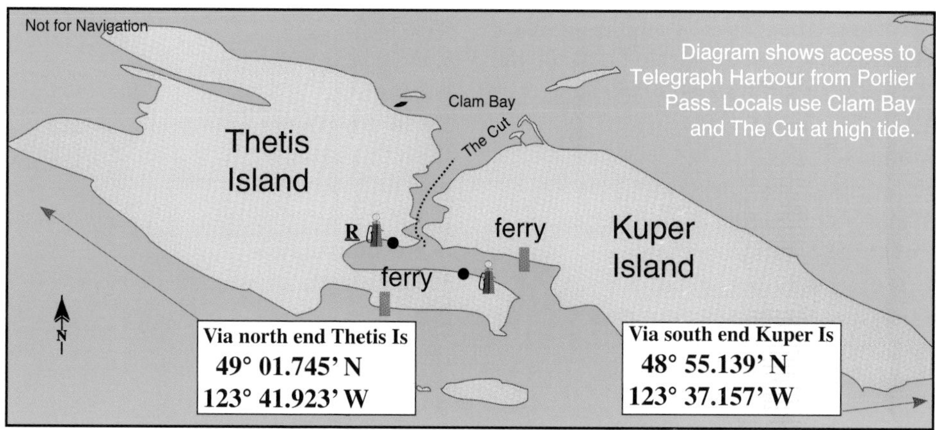

Telegraph Harbour

Gulf Islands

Telegraph Harbour Marina

Ron and Barbara Williamson
PO Box 740 Thetis Island
BC V0R 2Y0
VHF 66A
Ph: 250-246-9511 Fax: 250-246-2668
Toll free: 1-800-246-6011
sunny@telegraphharbour.com
www.telegraphharbour.com

Charts 3477, 3313, 3442, 3463

Marina services:
Moorage. About 2,500' visitor dock space. Guest moorage open Easter to Thanksgiving. Reservations suggested.
Fuel: Gas. Diesel. Oils.
Marine supplies.
Fishing gear, supplies, charts, bait, ice.
Water. Limited supply–use sparingly.
Power at docks: 15, 30 amp.
Customer services:
Laundry, showers, washrooms for overnight moored guests.
Store with groceries. Cafe and '50s style soda fountain serves pizza, salads, sandwiches, espresso–Thetis Island Pot of Gold coffee, milkshakes, sundaes, ice cream cones, produce, gifts, arts and crafts, books, snacks. Catering services available.
Boating groups book events/rendezvous. Playground. Picnic/barbecue facilities ashore. Book ahead in summer.
Nearby:
Road access walking or cycling.
Some nearby parkland and beach trails.
Public pay phones ashore.
Daily float plane service to Thetis Island with float at Thetis Marina.
Fresh roasted coffee available on island.
Entertainment:
Volleyball, shuffleboard, horseshoes.
Short ferry trip to Chemainus shops and famous murals.
Adjacent facilities:
Bed & breakfast accommodations nearby.

the delicious old fashioned milkshakes for which the marina store has become famous. Owners at Telegraph Harbour Marina are Ron and Barbara Williamson, who promise a warm welcome to all mariners.

Across the harbour, Paul Deacon and his staff at Thetis Island Marina, go to great lengths to welcome you and make you feel at home. In fact, so warm is the welcome at the two marinas at Thetis Island that we have found ourselves cancelling our continuation plans in favour of just staying around longer than planned. And extending a visit is a logical choice considering the advantages of being there. The harbour is very protected from winds and weather and moorage is sometimes available without reservations even in the busy summer period.

When rounding Thetis Island the western entrance to Telegraph Harbour is via Preedy Harbour where seals can be seen sometimes sunning themselves on the rocks just off Foster Point. Thetis Island Marina juts out into the main passage and posted signs effectively call on boats entering Telegraph Harbour to slow down. Thetis Island Marina has a pub and serves meals from a more varied menu than that at Telegraph Harbour Marina. The regular clientele at the two marinas can be quite different, naturally, the pub being typically a congregating place for those who enjoy the pub atmosphere. Telegraph Harbour

Opposite: The Cut and Telegraph Harbour Marina. Above and below: A friendly gathering place.

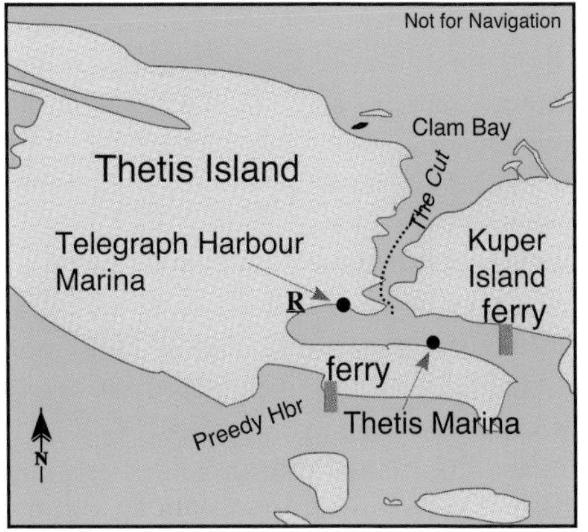

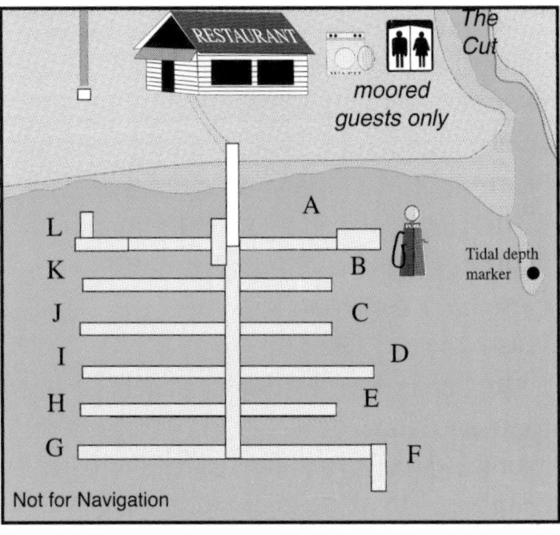

Thetis Island

Charts 3477, 3313, 3442, 3463

VHF 66A

Thetis Island Marina and Pub

Paul Deacon
General Delivery
Thetis Island BC V0R 2Y0
Ph: 250-246-3464 Fax: 250-246-1433
marina@thetisisland.com
Web: www.thetisisland.com

Marina services:

Fuel: Gas, diesel, propane.

Marine supplies, bait, charts, tide tables, ice. Liquor store.

Transient moorage. About 3,000'. Reservations suggested.

Power at docks: 15, 30 amp–multiple outlets.

Water. Limited supply–use sparingly. Outlet for 18 litre Columbia Ice water jugs.

Laundry, showers, washrooms.

Customer services:

Post Office. ATM. Store–groceries, dairy treats, ice cream, bakery products. Frozen foods, produce, gifts, books, snacks, toiletries. Restaurant/pub–meals available inside or on large sunny patio. Boating groups book weekend events/rendezvous. Playground. Swings, two horseshoe pits. Picnic/barbecue facilities ashore. Arrange/book ahead in summer.

Fresh market produce and local crafts –ask marina staff for market locations and times.

Public pay phones ashore and at fuel dock. Daily float plane service. Fresh roasted coffee available on the island.

Entertainment:

Short ferry trip to Chemainus shops and famous murals. Live entertainment in the pub on long weekends through summer months. Major sporting events available on satellite TV.

Adjacent facilities:

A variety of comfortable bed & breakfast accommodations are located nearby. Good scuba diving nearby. Nearby church.

Road access walking or cycling.

At the marina and nearby: Island arts and crafts, knitted goods.

Mount Brenton Golf Club 250-246-9322

Left: At Thetis Island Marina. The pub and restaurant are busy year round, with a patio that is particularly popular in summer.

Opposite: Aerial view of Thetis Island Marina. At Telegraph Harbour, boat rendezvous' are lots of fun. Dining on the patio. Above: Fun in the marina.

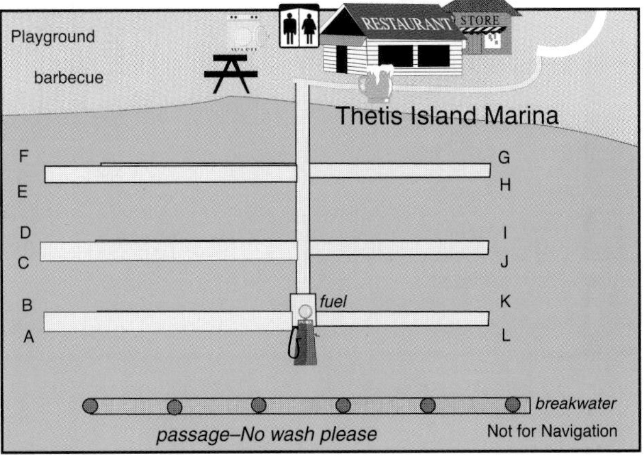

is more suitable for families and family activities. Like most of the Gulf Islands water is in short supply on Thetis and boat owners are asked to use only what they need for their fresh water tanks. Garbage is a problem for marinas but they do allow disposal of garbage by moorage customers. The Thetis Island post office and a propane filling station is located at Thetis Island Marina. The convenience stores at both marinas carry some souvenirs, charts and books as well as a selection of items for replenishment of boating supplies. Other than these stores at the two marinas there are no shops or shopping centres on the island. However, Chemainus on Vancouver Island, which is a short ferry ride away, has a selection of stores and restaurants to please everyone. It is worth the ferry ride to stroll around this artistic Vancouver Island centre. The passenger ferry leaves Thetis Island for the run across Stuart Channel eight times a day.

Not far from Telegraph Harbour Marina is a well-known supplier of fresh roasted coffee. *Pot of Gold* is open at most times to sell their rich aromatic beans or freshly ground coffee to islanders and visitors alike. Just stroll up to the entrance of their property and make your purchases at the gate stall and self-service bakery.

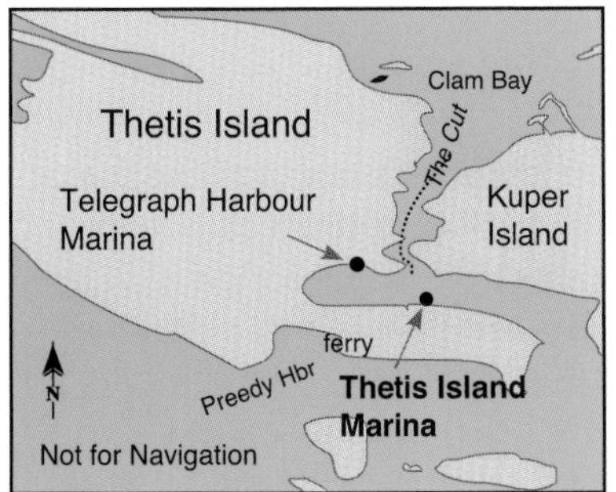

Thetis Island is known for its arts and crafts. Crafts on sale on the island represent the works of various islanders and prices are generally more favourable than those for similar items in the cities. Look for their wares and details at the two marinas.

If you enjoy strolling a walk along any of the Thetis Island roads is relaxing and easy without any significant hills and traffic. Or at low tide you can don your boating boots and go beachcombing along the dry but marshy flats of the canal and watch your fellow boat owners trying their luck in The Cut.

Gabriola Island

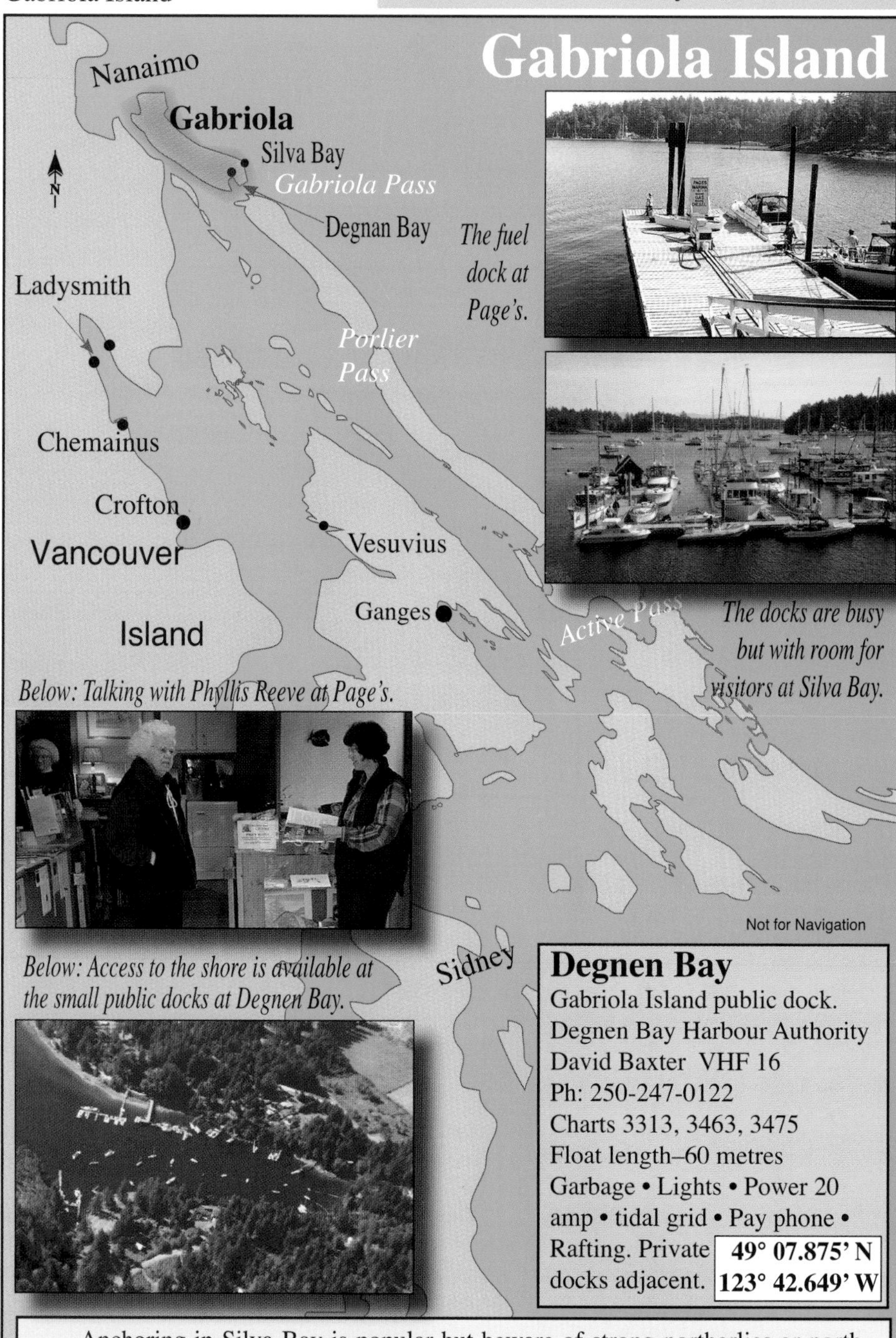

The fuel dock at Page's.

The docks are busy but with room for visitors at Silva Bay.

Below: Talking with Phyllis Reeve at Page's.

Below: Access to the shore is available at the small public docks at Degnen Bay.

Degnen Bay

Gabriola Island public dock.
Degnen Bay Harbour Authority
David Baxter VHF 16
Ph: 250-247-0122
Charts 3313, 3463, 3475
Float length–60 metres
Garbage • Lights • Power 20 amp • tidal grid • Pay phone • Rafting. Private docks adjacent.

49° 07.875' N
123° 42.649' W

Anchoring in Silva Bay is popular but beware of strong northerlies or northwesterlies that tend to howl into the bay at times causing the need for a watch during the night when anchors drag. Page's Marina, which has been around a long time, has some interesting works of art on display as well as casual supplies, books and crafts. The facility is also known as a fuel stop and transient moorage marina.

*Commodore Pass
49° 09.080' N
123° 40.962' W

Silva Bay

Charts 3475, 3313, 3443, 3463

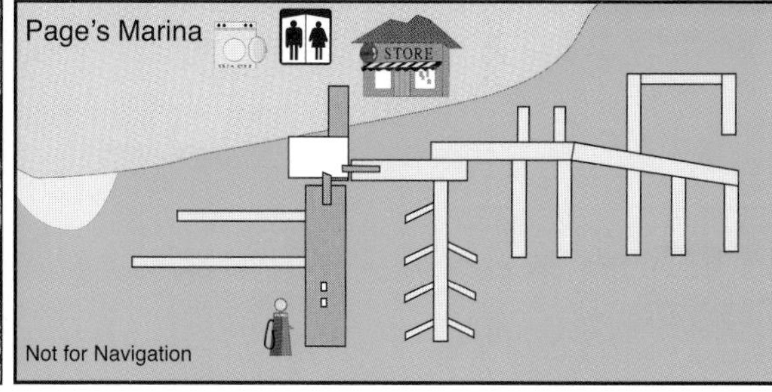

1. Page's Resort & Marina

Ted and Phyllis Reeve
3350 Coast Rd
Gabriola Island BC   V0R 1X7
Ph: 250-247-8931 Fax: 250-247-8997
Charts 3475, 3310
mail@pagesresort.com
www.pagesresort.com

Marina services:
Fuel: Gas. Diesel. Outboard oil.
Moorage mostly to 30 feet, some larger. Reservations suggested. **Water** at dock. Limited drinking supply. **Power:** 15 amp.

Customer services:
Showers, laundry, washrooms. Public pay phone. Garbage disposal.
Rental cottages. Tenting. Picnic area.
Office/store has charts, art, books, etc.

Entertainment:
Fishing charters can be arranged. Walking road access. Good scuba diving in nearby locations. Provincial park nearby.

Adjacent facilities: Mobile repairs, service, available–250-247-8385. Grocery store at Silva Bay Inn. Liquor store.
Taxi service to golf course, shopping.

Top: Page's Marina fuel dock is easy for docking. It is located at the end of the passage south of Sear Island. Watch depths at low tide and use your chart.

Commodore Pass is one of the entrance passages to Silva Bay. **Pass clear of Ship Rock in entrance.**

The Silva Bay resort and Marina (foreground) with the Royal Vancouver YC station on the opposite side of the bay. Page's at lower right.

Silva Bay

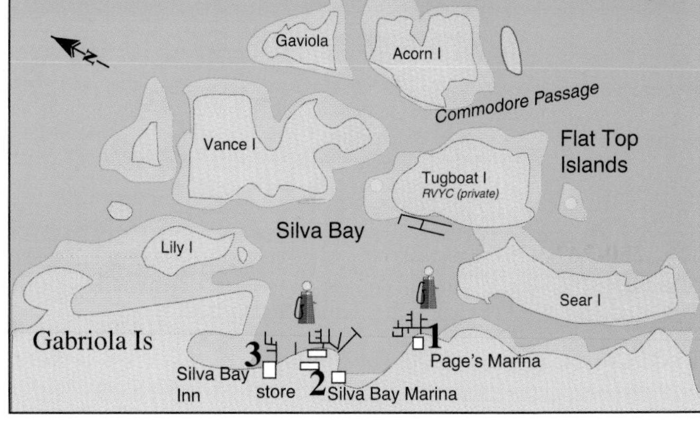

2. Silva Bay Resort and Marina

Janice Fuller
3383 South Rd **VHF 66A**
Gabriola BC V0R 1X7
Ph: 250-247-8662 Fax: 250-247-8663
Charts 3475, 3313, 3463, 3443
silvabay@canada.com
www.silvabay.com

Marina services:
Fuel: Gas. Diesel. Outboard mix. Moorage. 37 slips–reservations suggested. **Washrooms, laundry, showers**, Garbage disposal. Ways, shipyard. **Water** at dock. **Power:** 30, 50 amp. ATM, tennis courts, Sunday market, Float plane service. Golf, adventure charters. Nearby grocery store.

Customer services:
Silva Bay Bar and Grill. Liquor store.

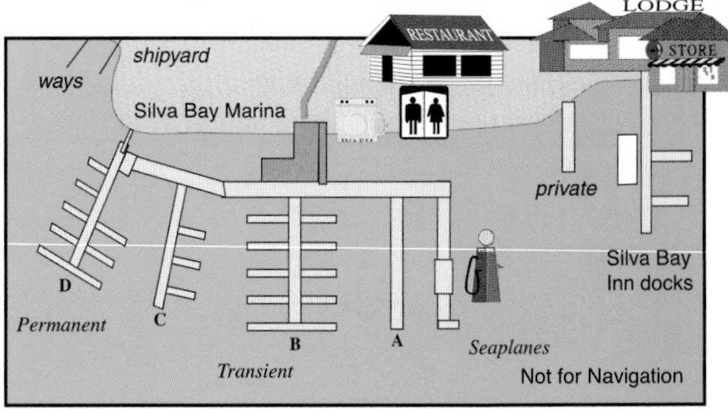

Top: The docks and restaurant at Silva Bay Marina are busy in summer.
Above left: Silva Bay Inn has been totally refurbished. Served by the small dock north of Silva Bay Marina.

3. Silva Bay Inn

3415 South Rd, Silva Bay
Gabriola BC V0R 1X7
Ph: 250-247-9351 Fax: 250-247-9094
info@silvabayinn.ca www.silvabayinn.ca

Marina services:
Dinghy dock serves customers to **G&S Quality Meats** and Silva Bay Inn.

Customer services:
Grocery store–meat, cheeses, organic fruits & veggies, ice. Inn, art store.

Charts 3475, 3313, 3443, 3463

Entertainment:
Fishing charters can be arranged.
*Good scuba diving in nearby locations.

Adjacent facilities:
Nearby restaurant, liquor store, marine mechanic, fuel.
Accommodation at Inn.
Self-contained kitchenette suites–7 units.
* DIVER Magazine: *www.divermag.com*

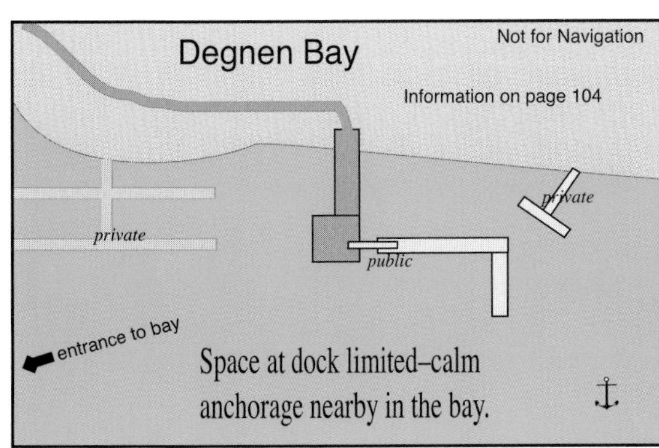

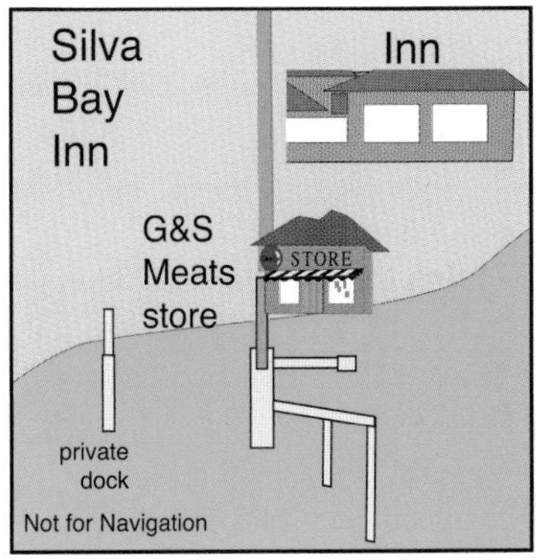

Above: Nanaimo Harbour with entrance to the visitor docks to the right–pictured here. Below: A ferry approaching the Nanaimo dock in Departure Bay. The channel inside Newcastle Island is lined with marinas.

Not for Navigation

ferries
Departure Bay

Brechin Point
49° 11.439' N
123° 56.861' W

Esso
BRECHIN POINT
MARINA
ramp
Stones Marina
Blue Peter-
haulouts, service
ANCHORAGE MARINA
Newcastle Marina
Nanaimo Harbour
City Marina
Moby Dick Oceanfront
Lodge and Marina
Channel View Marina
Nanaimo Shipyard
Townsite Marina
Nanaimo Yacht Club
Newcastle Island Passage
Newcastle Island
Oregon Rock
Mark Bay
Protection Island
Bate Point Reef
Dinghy Dock Pub
Satellite Reef
Carpenter Rock
Cameron Island
Nanaimo Boat Basin
Bastion Square
Private dock
McKay Channel
N

Marker P12
49° 10.526' N
123° 56.125' W

Boat Basin entrance
49° 10.273' N
123° 55.986' W

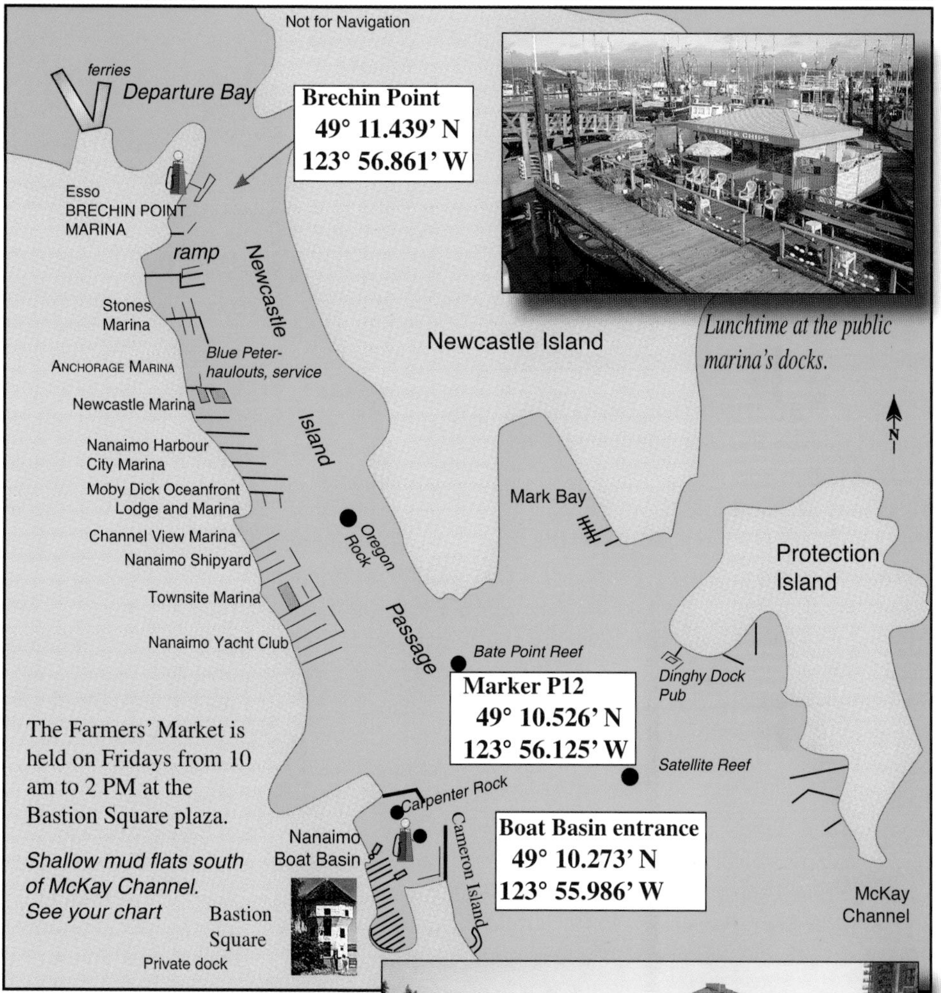

Lunchtime at the public marina's docks.

The Farmers' Market is held on Fridays from 10 am to 2 PM at the Bastion Square plaza.

Shallow mud flats south of McKay Channel. See your chart

Nanaimo

Nanaimo and its nearby islands.

Growth of the city of Nanaimo continues at a fast and furious rate. Marinas and docks are plentiful with several having been upgraded substantially but with little, if any, moorage available. The waterfront has undergone a massive face lift and new restaurants and public areas have evolved. There is a regular ferry service between Newcastle Island Marine Park and Nanaimo and a foot ferry that serves the famous Dinghy Dock Pub on Protection Island. Their docks accommodate boats but space ashore is shared with the non-boating public.

Vancouver Island

Port of Nanaimo Boat Basin

(and Cameron Island Marina) VHF 66A

David Mailloux
10 Wharf St, Nanaimo BC V9R 2X3
Ph: 250-754-5053 Fax: 250-754-4186
marina@npa.ca
www.npa.ca

Marina services: Fuel, Petro Canada: Gas, diesel, mixed gas, ice. Service available. Wi-fi Internet access.**Moorage**: Large civic marina with pleasure boat moorage in summer. In winter docks are heavily used by fishermen.

Reservations taken for 600 foot floating breakwater pier for large vessels and adjacent **Cameron Island Marina Ph: 250-755-1216** seasonal May to Sept. **Power**: 15, 20, 30, 50 and 100 amp. **Laundry, showers, washrooms.** Ice machine. Sani-station pumpout. Hydraulic crane to 1000 lb.

Customer services: Customs/phone 24 hour service. Maps, brochures, dining guide. Road access walking or cycling or vehicle rentals. Downtown Nanaimo at doorstep of marina. Grocery stores, shops. Regular scheduled float plane service to Vancouver.

Charts 3447, 3458, 3313, 3443, 3463

Entertainment:

Restaurants, pubs and theatres, arts and crafts exhibits, stores and galleries. Bathtub race every July. Many festive activities.

Fish and chips and Penny's Palapa cafes on dock. Casino nearby. DVD rentals.

Adjacent and nearby facilities:

Walkway, plaza and shops. Farmers' Market Fridays 10am to 2pm. Shipyards, ways, all marine services. Lighthouse Bistro/Pub. Newcastle Island Marine Park–docks, walking trails, camping, picnics, BC Ferries to mainland nearby. Walk on ferries to Newcastle or Protection Islands. Protection Island: Dinghy Dock Pub. Anchor off and row to dock. Visit the **Dock Shoppe** on promenade and **The Chart Shop** on Church Street.

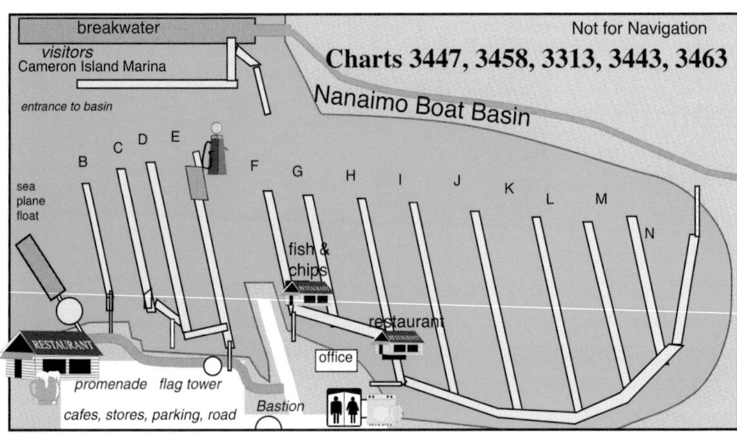

No wake speeds are enforced in the Harbour. Mind the reef and shallows in mid channel marked by a piling with a sign indicating correct passage. Avoid the mud flats to the south.

Petro Canada

Located inside Boat Basin
Ph: 250-754-7828 Gas, diesel, oil, salt water fishing licences.
Charts at The Chart shop and the Dock Shoppe

Townsite Marina

No guest moorage available
20 Townsite Rd Nanaimo BC V9R 5T2
Ph: 250-244-2920 Fax: 250-244-2970
Located adjacent Nanaimo Yacht Club.

Nanaimo Shipyard Group

1040 Stewart Ave, Nanaimo BC V9S 4C9
Ph: 250-753-1151 Fax: 250-753-2235
rvw@nanaimoshipyard.com
www.nanaimoshipyard.com
Marina services:
Haulouts. Repairs. Vessels to 200 feet.
Chandlery Ph: 250-753-1244.

Moby Dick Oceanfront Lodge & Marina

1000 Stewart Ave Nanaimo BC V9S 4C9
Ph: 250-753-7111 Fax: 250-753-4333
Toll Free: 1-800-663-2116
mobydicklodge@shaw.ca
www.mobydicklodge.com

Nanaimo Harbour City Marina

Ron and Susan Mielke
1250 Stewart Ave
Nanaimo BC V9S 4C9
Ph: 250-754-2732 Fax: 250-754-7140
info@harbourcitymarina.com
www.harbourcitymarina.com
Moorage for permanent tenants and boats in for work. Haulouts. Repairs, welding. Boatyard. Travel lift.

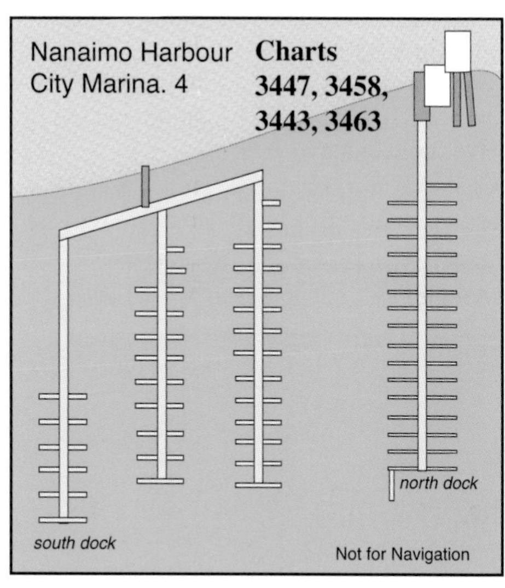

Hazard: Enter Nanaimo via south of Protection Island. From the north/Departure Bay watch correct channel when proceeding past Oregon Rock. Use passage on Newcastle Island side, indicated by the sign on the mid-channel marker.

Dinghy Dock Floating Marine Pub

8 Pirate's Lane, Protection Island BC
PO Box 771, Nanaimo BC V9R 5M2
Ph: 250-753-2373

Charts 3447, 3458, 3313, 3443, 3463

Boats anchored out call Dinghy Dock Pub on VHF 18A

Marina Services

Tie up space for restaurant/pub.
Open year round.
Showers. Pub restaurant dining. Laundry, showers, washrooms.
Walking on Protection Island. There is moorage and anchoring at Newcastle Island Marine Park nearby. The ferry between the Nanaimo Boat Basin and Protection Island leaves the docks hourly, 9:00 am to 11:00 pm. **Ferry information Ph: 250-753-8244**

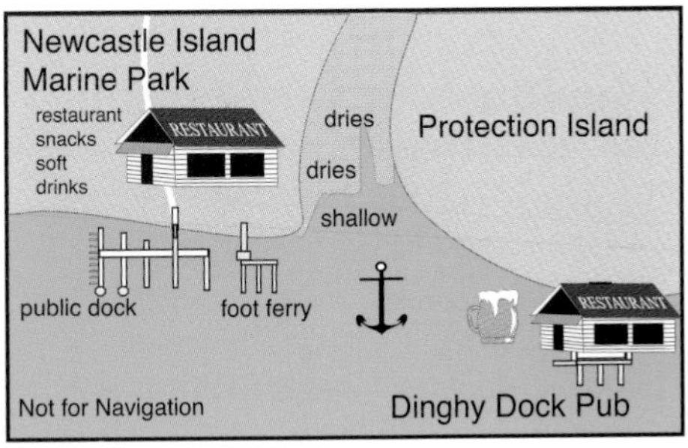

Newcastle Island Marine Park

The dock is a short distance away from the Dinghy Dock Pub. There are several slips for medium to larger sized boats as well as numerous slips for smaller boats and dinghies. Going ashore at Newcastle Island is a treat, providing lots of treed pathways for hiking, walking or cycling. An interpretive centre functions in summer for the use of students, groups and others interested in the use of the facilities. There are overnight facilities, including washrooms and a restaurant.

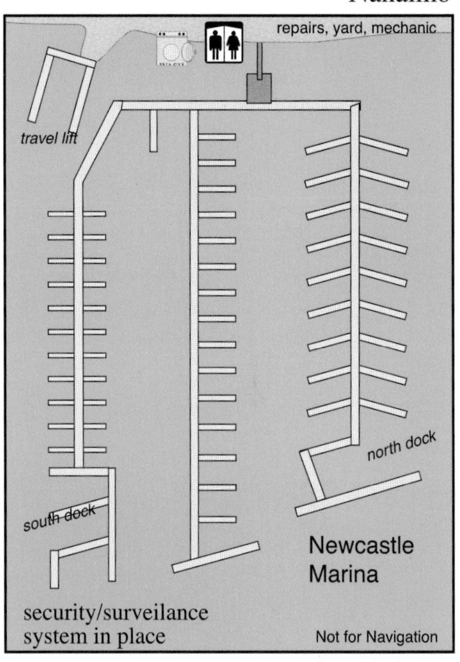

Newcastle Marina

Owner Gerald Chow
1300 Stewart Ave
Nanaimo BC V9S 4E1
Ph: 250-753-1431 Fax: 250-753-2974
Toll free 1-866-883-2628
newcastle@shaw.ca

Marina services:
Haulouts. Repairs. Welding. Yard. Storage. Mostly permanent moorage. Security/ surveillance system. **Showers, laundry, washrooms. Power:** 15 amps.
One guest dock to 35’.

Nearby facilities:
All facilities and services are available.
Road access walking or cycling.
Shipyards, all marine services.
BC Ferries to Vancouver and Galiano.
Ferry to Newcastle and Protection Islands.

Blue Peter Marine Services

1520a Stewart Avenue
Nanaimo BC V9S 4E1
Ph: 250-754-7887 Fax: 250-754-7885
Shipyards, haulouts. all marine repairs, refits and service. Chandlery adjacent. Located near launch ramp and ferries.

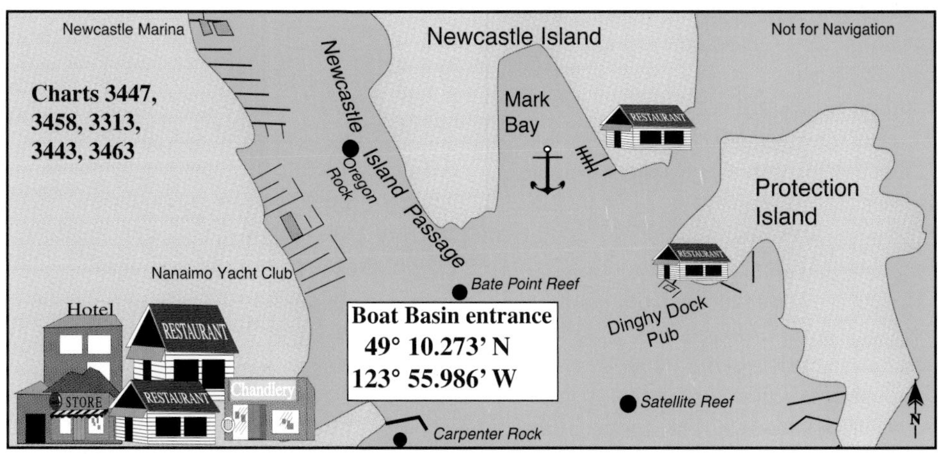

Opposite page: Dinghy Dock Pub (inset) and aerial view of its location on Protection Island.
Bottom: Newcastle Island Marine Park docks, Mark Bay anchorage and the marinas that line Newcastle Island Passage. Top, this page: Nanaimo Yacht Club and adjacent marinas.

Stones Marina & Boatyard

Carol Stone & Carol Archibald
1690 Stewart Ave
Nanaimo BC V9S 4E1
Ph: 250-753-4232 Fax 250-753-4204
email@stonesmarina.com
www.stonesmarina.com

Charts 3447, 3458, 3443, 3463

Location: next to Seaquarium, and near BC Ferries.

Launch ramp adjacent.

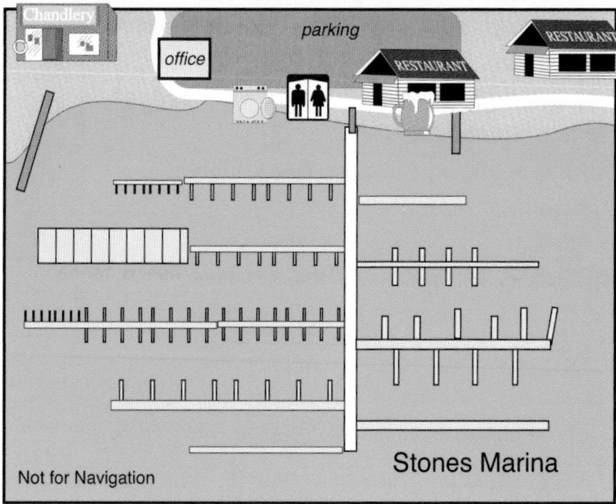

Marina services: Moorage:
About 500' guest moorage in summer months.

Power: 15, 30 amp.

Customer services:
Ice. Laundry, showers, washrooms.
Public pay phone. Garbage disposal. Store. Tackle, fishing licences, bait. Mobile LPG service. 83 ton travel lift. Large fenced boatyard. Marine sales. Two pubs, restaurants adjacent and nearby. ATM. Liquor store.

Entertainment:
Walking: Road access walking or cycling. Road or water access to ferries to Galiano Island, Newcastle and Protection Islands.

Adjacent facilities:
Muddy Waters Pub, restaurant and RV Park. Brechin Esso fuel dock and seaplane float. City of Nanaimo by road or dinghy.

Brechin Esso Fuel

1958 Zorkin Rd, Nanaimo BC V9S 5T9
Ph: 250-753-6122 Fax: 250-753-9378
Doug at 250-754-2317
Seaplanes, marina.
Fuel: Gas, diesel, oils, avgas, jet fuel.
Customs point of entry–boats and planes.

Vancouver Area

Section 3

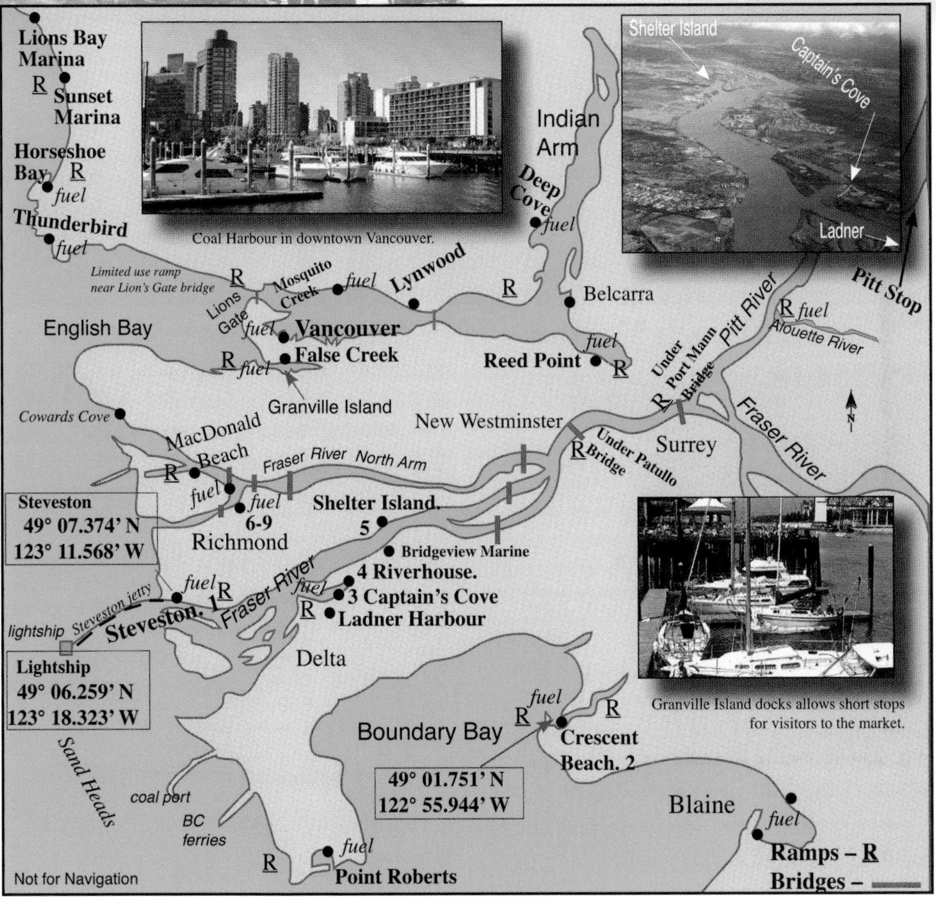

Lions Bay Marina
R
Sunset Marina
Horseshoe Bay R fuel
Thunderbird fuel
Coal Harbour in downtown Vancouver.
Limited use ramp near Lion's Gate bridge
R
Lions Gate
Mosquito Creek
fuel
Lynwood
Indian Arm
Deep Cove fuel
R
Belcarra
Shelter Island
Captain's Cove
Ladner
Pitt Stop
English Bay
fuel Vancouver
R fuel False Creek
Granville Island
fuel
Reed Point R
Under Port Mann Bridge
R
Pitt River
R fuel
Alouette River
Fraser River
Cowards Cove
MacDonald Beach
R
Fraser River North Arm
New Westminster
R Under Patullo Bridge
Surrey
N
fuel
fuel 6-9
Steveston 49° 07.374' N 123° 11.568' W
Richmond
Shelter Island. 5
Bridgeview Marine
4 Riverhouse.
3 Captain's Cove
Ladner Harbour
fuel R
Steveston jetty
lightship
Steveston. 1
Fraser River
fuel
R
Delta
Lightship 49° 06.259' N 123° 18.323' W
Granville Island docks allows short stops for visitors to the market.
Boundary Bay
fuel
R
R
Crescent Beach. 2
Sand Heads
coal port
BC ferries
49° 01.751' N 122° 55.944' W
Blaine
fuel
R
fuel
Point Roberts
Ramps – R
Bridges –
Not for Navigation

Fraser River: Use charts 3490, 3463 (South Arm) and 3491 (North Arm)

1. Steveston Harbour

Near the mouth of the south arm of the Fraser River. Steveston Harbour Authority
Ph: 604-272-5539 Fax: 604-271-6142
info@stevestonharbour.com
www.stevestonharbour.com
Charts 3490, 3463
Float length–200' transient. • Water • Parking • Lights • Waste oil disposal • Garbage • Power: 20, 30 amp • Public pay phone • Washrooms • Public fish sales float • Showers • Adjacent city restaurants, shops, marine stores, chandleries, repair facilities. Auxiliary Coast Guard. **Esso and Chevron Fuel**–two locations. Additional public docks (Paramount) for fishing and commercial vessels. 50 ton Travelift. Call for visitor dock space. **Launch ramp.**

Steveston waterfront.

Nico-wynd Golf Course 604-535-9511

Crescent Beach Marina shows the launch ramp to the right between two fingers. The fuel dock is centre foreground. Below: Crescent Beach Marina is on the Nikomekl River.

2. Crescent Beach Marina (1967) Ltd.

Carol Charles
12555 Crescent Rd
Surrey BC V4A 2V4
Ph: 604-538-9666 Fax: 604-538-7724
info@crescentbeachmarina.com
www.crescentbeachmarina.com

49° 03.367' N
123° 53.475' W

Fuel: Gas, diesel. Chandlery, bait, fishing supplies. 30-ton trailer. Haulout to 50'. **Launch ramp. Washrooms, laundry and showers.** Ice.
Guest moorage (phone for reservations). **Power:** 15, 30 amp. public pay phones. Playgrounds, golf nearby.
Entrance: Follow red right returning markers in channel through Boundary Bay.

3. Captain's Cove Marina

Elizabeth Model
6100 Ferry Rd, Ladner BC V4K 3M9
Ph: 604-946-1244 Fax: 946-1246
info@captainscovemarina.ca
www.captainscovemarina.ca

Fresh water moorage. Visitor's dock. **Water. Power:** 30 amps. **Fuel:** Gas, diesel, engine and outboard oils.
Showers, laundry, washrooms. Public pay phones. Rusty Anchor Pub. Travelift 60 tons, repairs, service, storage and workyard, power wash, painting. **Launch ramp** adjacent.

Cove Links Golf Course 604-946-1839

Crescent Beach Marina is tucked in the curve of Boundary Bay, behind the railway line.

49° 06.921' N
123° 04.933' W
Chart 3490

Above: The docks at Captain's Cove Marina. There is lots of room for visitors staying overnight and accessing the Rusty Anchor Pub restaurant and adjoining Cove Links golf course.

View of the fuel stop and visitor docks at Captain's Cove Marina in Ladner on the Fraser River.

4. River House Marina (South Arm)

5825 60th Ave, Ladner BC V4K 3E2
Ph: 604-940-4496 Fax: 604-940-7502
marina@riverhousegroup.com
www.riverhousegroup.com

Manager Walter Greene. Some guest moorage. **Water. Power**: 15, 30 amps. Garbage disposal. River House Restaurant & Marine Pub. Low bridge beyond Captain's Cove Marina. 9'9"– 21'9" tidal clearance.

The marina docks and restaurant at River House.

Most marinas in the Greater Vancouver area offering moorage for overnight customers are dedicated to providing permanent moorage. Some have many slips during summer when many of their customers' boats are away. Boat operators in transit from southern ports to places such as the Sunshine Coast and Desolation Sound should consider Vancouver's downtown area or False Creek where there are many attractions. In the Fraser River, one can cruise all the way up to Mission or turn off on the Pitt River and enjoy a splendid run into Pitt Lake.

Entering the Fraser River is safe provided you do so when winds are relatively calm and the tide is right. At about maximum low tide with a northwesterly wind you are well advised to wait. Beware of the shallows off the mouth of the river, especially if you do find yourself running into some wind and waves. It is well marked but the shallows actually extend somewhat beyond the markers, especially around the beacon to the south of the lightship.

Stopping at Steveston is a treat if you can find moorage. The variety of shops, cafes and restaurants will keep you busy for hours.

Up the south arm there is Captain's Cove Marina for haulouts, repairs and service as well as some overnight moorage, fuel, ice and a pub, The Rusty Anchor, which serves good meals seven days a week. Beyond Captain's Cove past the low bridge of Highway 99 is the Riverhouse marina with adjacent restaurant and pub.

Shelter Island docks on the Fraser River.

5. Shelter Island Marina & Boatyard

120–6911 Graybar (South Arm)
Richmond BC V6W 1H3
Ph: 604-270-6272 Fax: 604-273-6282
Toll Free: 1-877-270-6272
infodesk@shelterislandmarina.com
www.shelterislandmarina.com
Fresh water permanent and transient moorage. **Power. Showers, laundry, washrooms.** Public pay phones. Marine hardware, repairs, service. Two travel lifts to 150 tons–vessels to over 130', 30' beam. Workyard for up to 500 boats. Beer and wine store. Restaurant and pub adjacent.

6. River Rock Marina (Mid Arm)

Gary Cross
8831 River Rd, Richmond BC V6X 1Y8
Ph: 604-273-8560 Fax: 604-276-8000
Chart 3491
Fresh water moorage. Transient visitors welcome. **Power, showers, laundry, washrooms**. River Rock Casino Resort at this marina site. Fuel dock nearby. Moorage includes use of pool and fitness facilties.

7. Delta Marina **Chart 3491**

Manager: Rick Cockburn
3500 Cessna Dr (Fraser Middle Arm)
Richmond BC V7B 1C7
Ph: 604-273-4211 Fax: 604-273-7531
Delta Charters and Marina,
Toll Free: 1-800-661-7762
deltacharters@telus.net
www.deltacharters.com
Fresh water permanent and transient moorage–reservations. Customs clearance. **Power**, full service shop, 50 ton lift. Free shuttle to Vancouver International Airport. Hotel facilities and services. Elelphant & Castle restaurant. Near Richmond city facilities, restaurants and shopping centres.

The village of Ladner is tucked away down Ladner Reach which opens off the south arm of the Fraser River at the entrance to Captain's Cove. A large public dock at Ladner welcomes mariners when the fishing fleet is away. Phone 604-946-8430 for information. Another good facility with marine pub and restaurant is at Shelter Island a little farther up river. If you need a haulout or a workyard in which to block it up Captain's Cove or Shelter Island Marina can provide the necessary facilities. Marine service is available also at Bridgeview Marine.

You could cruise to New Westminster and return to the Strait of Georgia by going down the north arm of the Fraser. Part way down you will come to Richmond's marinas just after passing under Knight Street bridge and Oak Street bridge. Fuel is available at Vancouver Marina just beyond the swivel bridge on the Middle Arm or just under the Arthur Laing bridge. Haulouts and repairs are available at Shannon Buoys Ph: 604-231-0599.

Visit the facilities in False Creek or stop right downtown in Vancouver. There is a customs dock in the harbour on approaches to Coal Harbour Marina. While in the harbour cruise down to The Cannery and stay for a meal.

New Westminster

Delta Marina

Vancouver Marina

Above: The waterfront at New Westminster. While there are no facilities for mooring at this Fraser River waterfront city, it affords a spectacular view as you cruise by, perhaps en route to the Pitt River or Mission.
Left: Delta Marina docks opposite Vancouver Marina in the Middle Arm.
Left: Vancouver Marina includes the gas dock, prominently located at the west end of the docks and boathouses.
Opposite: Shelter Island in Richmond.

Marine Drive Golf Course 604 261-3212
Mayfair Lakes Golf Course 604-276-0505
Green Acres Golf Course 604-273-1121

8. Vancouver Marina (Mid Arm)

Michael Short
200-8211 River Road
Richmond BC V6X 1X8
Chart 3491 VHF 66A
Ph: 604-278-3300 Fax: 604-278-9788
mooring@vancouvermarina.com
www.vancouvermarina.com

Some transient moorage–up to 85' open, to 80' covered. Call to reserve. Check in at fuel dock. Water, power: : 15, 20, 30, 50 amps. **Fuel:** gas, diesel, oil, repairs, service. Within walking distance to Richmond city facilities, shops and restaurants. Close to airport. **Galleon Marine** chandlery at top of dock. **Adjacent bridge Max clearance 10 m (33').**

Vancouver waterfront

1. Harbour Cruises Marina

Fred Hercules **Charts 3311, 3493**
1 North Foot Denman St
Vancouver BC V6G 2W9
Ph: 604-605-6019 Fax: 604-605-6006
fred@harbourcruises.com
www.boatcruises.com

Moorage. **Power:** 15, 20, 30 amp. Fuel (nearby): Gas, diesel, stove oil, engine and outboard oils. Public pay phones. Chandlery, repairs, service, nearby. Located next to Stanley Park and charter vessel basin.

2. Bayshore West Marina

Managed by Thunderbird Marina
450 Denman, Vancouver BC V6G 3J1
Ph: 604-689-5331 Fax: 604-689-5332
bayshorewest@thunderbirdmarine.com
www.thunderbirdmarine.com

Marina Services: Limited transient moorage, security. **Power:** 30, 50,100 amp. Pumpout. **Fuel** nearby at fuel barges. **Washroom**. Garbage disposal. Ice. Wireless internet access. Yacht sales. Next to Westin Bayshore Resort. Near Stanley Park. Nearby laundry, restaurants, coffee shops and shopping.

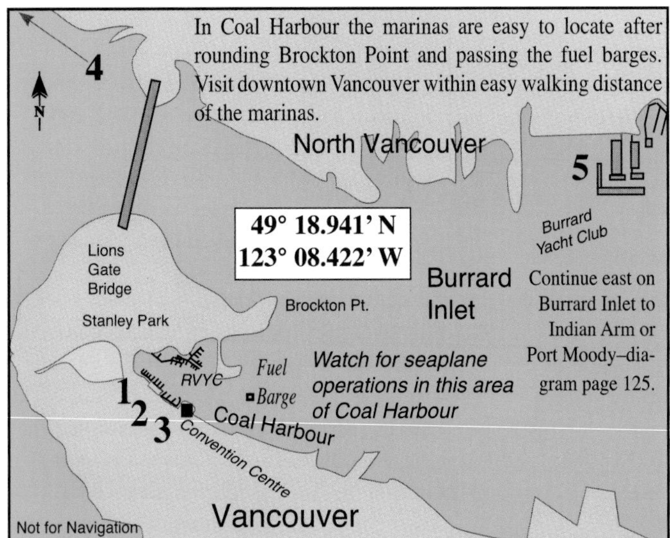

Opposite and right: Views of Coal Harbour. Below: Coal Harbour Marina is to the left and Harbour Cruises and Bayshore West marinas are in the lower right.

Photo: Justin Taylor.

3. Coal Harbour Marina VHF 66A

Danielle Brown

1525 Coal Harbour Quay

Vancouver BC V6G 3E7

Ph: 604-681-2628

Fax: 604-681-4666

info@coalharbourmarina.com

www.coalharbourmarina.com

Marina Services:

Moorage. Cable vision. **Washrooms. Power:** 30, 50, 100, 150 amp. Ice, garbage disposal. Fuel (nearby): Gas, diesel, stove oil, engine and outboard oils. Vacuum sewage pumpout system. Courtesy telephone and internet. Broadband Xpress Wireless Internet available. Coffee shop, convenience store. Wright Mariner Supply–chandlery nearby. Adjacent to city centre, restaurants, shops. Promenade. Easy walking to downtown Vancouver facilities and amenities.

Nearby medical services.

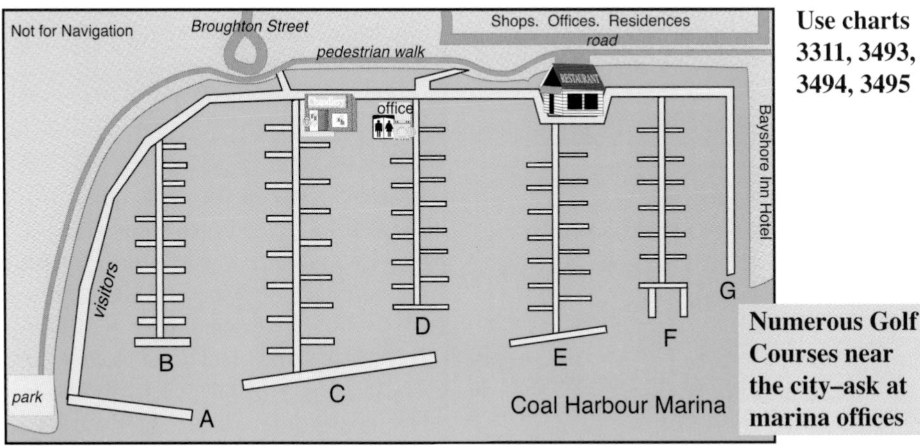

Use charts 3311, 3493, 3494, 3495

Numerous Golf Courses near the city–ask at marina offices

Diagram above: The basin at Coal Harbour Marina. To its right (not shown) are Thunderbird Marina and Harbour Cruises Marina. The Royal Vancouver Yacht Club is across the waterway.

Coal Harbour.

4. Thunderbird Marina

Manager: Fred McDonald
5776 Marine Dr West Vancouver BC V7W 2S2
Ph: 604-921-7434 Fax: 604-921-7486
Limited moorage. **Power**. **Fuel** dock (nearby): Gas, diesel, stove oil, engine and outboard oils. Marine store, tackle, bait, fishing licences, repairs, service. 25 ton travel lift for boats to 50 feet. Workyard, storage. *Also downtown Vancouver moorage at Bayshore West Marina.*

5 . Mosquito Creek Marina

Donny Mekilok
415 W Esplanade Ave
North Vancouver BC V7M 1A6
Ph: 604-987-4113 Fax: 604-987-6852
info@mosquitocreekmarina.com
www.mosquitocreekmarina.com
Guest moorage. Power: 15 amp. **Fuel:** Gas, diesel. Washrooms. Marine supplies, repairs, service. Crane. 55 ton travel lift. Cafe. Near North Vancouver restaurants, shops.

The Cannery

2205 Commissioner St
Vancouver BC V5L 1A4
Ph: 604-254-9606 F: 604-254-1820
info@cannery seafood.com www.cannery seafood.com
Private floating dock, moor and enjoy lunch, dinner or a picnic to go. 140' dock.

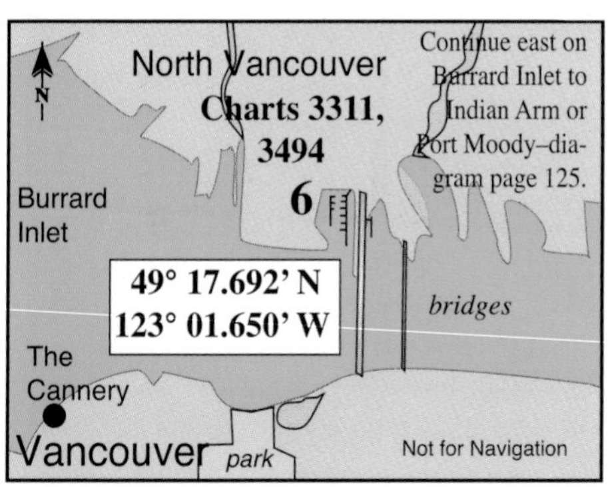

6. Lynnwood Marina

1681 Columbia
North Vancouver BC V7J 1A5
Ph: 604-985-1533 Fax: 604-985-8892
Service and yard. Visitor dock for restaurant only. 60 ton travel lift to boats 75' by 18.5' Mast Rigging. Wood and f/g repairs. Permanent moorage. **Power:** 15-100 amp. **Washrooms**. Chandlery, repairs, painting. Covered storage and work yard: service–six days a week. ***Hazard: strong currents at times.***

From east of Cambie Bridge looking Southwest.

Pelican Bay Marina

Mike Jensen
1708 W 6th Ave,Vancouver BC V6J 5E8
Ph: 604-729-1442 Fax: 604-683-3444
christianyensen@hotmail.com
www.globalairphotos.com/pelican_bay_marina
Visitor Moorage. In False Creek at Granville Island, adjacent to Granville Island Market, theatres, restaurants, shopping. **Power:** 30, 50 amp, washrooms. Cable and phone hookups.

Blue Pacific Yacht Charters

1519 Foreshore Walk, Granville Is, Vancouver BC V6H 3X3 Ph: 604-682-2161 Fax: 604-682-2722 Toll free 1-800-237-2392
info@bluepacificcharters.com
www.bluepacificcharters.ca

Call the Welcome Centre
VHF 66A. Ph: 604- 648-2628 or 1-866-677-2628
For transient moorage.

Cooper Boating

Ph: 604-687-4110 Fax: 604-687-3267
marla@cooperboating.com
www.cooperboating.com
Seasonal moorage, **power, showers.** Located on Granville Island–near the Granville Island Market and restaurants.

False Creek Yacht Club

1661 Granville St, Vancouver BC V6Z 1N3
Ph: 604-682-3292 Fax: 604-682-3614
fcyc@fcyc.com www.fcyc.com
Water, power, showers. Nearby recreational centre. Pumpout available.

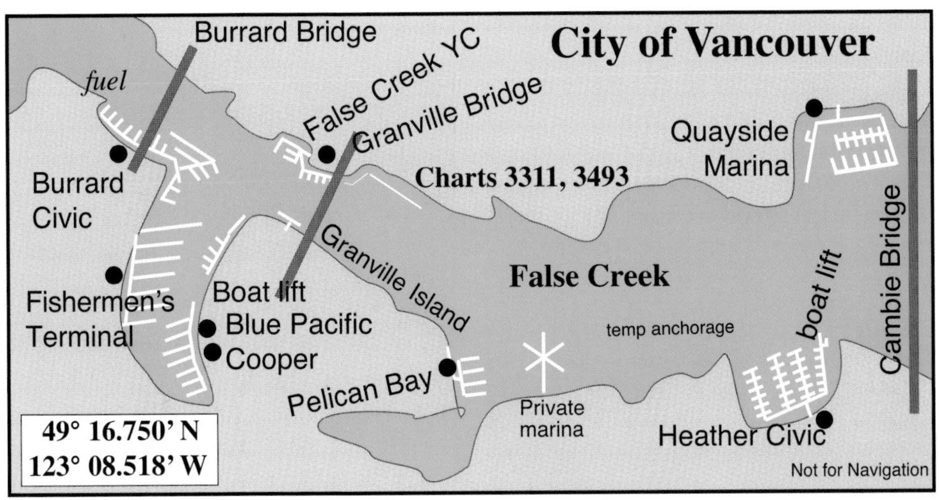

Fishermen's Wharf VHF 66A

False Creek, 1505 W 1st Ave
Vancouver BC V6J 1E8. Ph: 604-685-6924
manager@falsecreek.com www.falsecreek.com
Moorage, power: 20, 30 amp. Showers, laundry. Ice, garbage disposal.

Burrard Bridge Civic Marina

1655 Whyte Ave, Vancouver BC V6J 1A9
Ph: 604-733-5833 Fax: 604-733-9413
burrard.marina@vancouver.ca
www.vancouverparks.ca
Pumpout, power: 15 amp. Near Granville I.

Quayside Marina (pronounce 'Keyside')

Dockmaster: Dave Bird
1088 Marinaside Cres
Vancouver BC V6Z 3C4
Phone: 604-681-9115 Fax: 604-681-1932
qsmarina@ranchogroup.com
www.ranchovan.com/marina
Guest moorage. Space for large yachts. Located adjacent to downtown Vancouver.

Approaching Quayside Marina in False Creeek

Indian Arm

Deep Cove North Shore Marina & Rentals Ltd

2890 Panorama Dr
North Vancouver BC V7G 1V6
www.deepcovemarina.com
Ph: 604-929-1251 Fax: 604-929-7862
Moorage: call ahead, **water, power**: 15, 20, 30 amp. **Fuel**: Gas, diesel. **Washrooms.** Pumpout. Chandlery, mobile repairs, service. Ice, snacks, bait, fishing supplies. Boat rentals, certified marine technician on site and mobile. Walking distance to Deep Cove village, restaurants, stores.

Belcarra Park

Parks Board park and floats. Kiosk serves snacks, light meals. **Launch ramp at Cates Park. Ph: 604-257-8400.**

Charts 3495, 3311
Deep Cove Marina
49° 19.701' N
122° 56.128' W

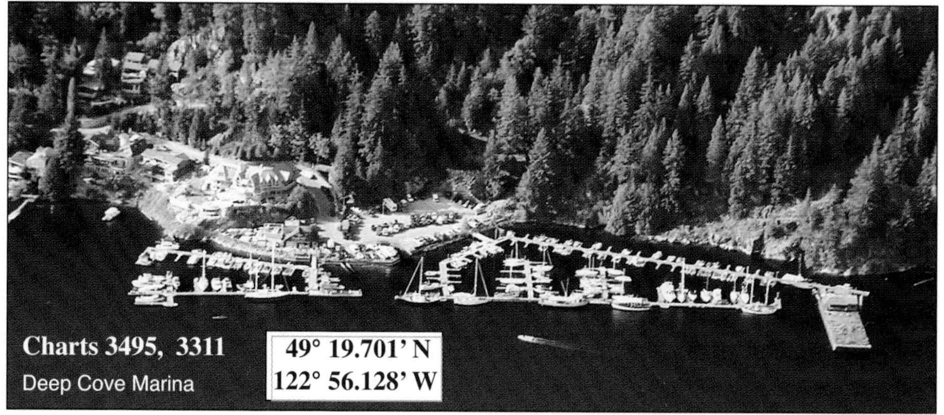

Above: The Deep Cove North Shore Rentals and Marina is located at the north side of Deep Cove. It has a fuel dock and convenience store. Nearby, in the cove, is the Deep Cove public dock (right) which allows convenient metered stops and excursions into the village.

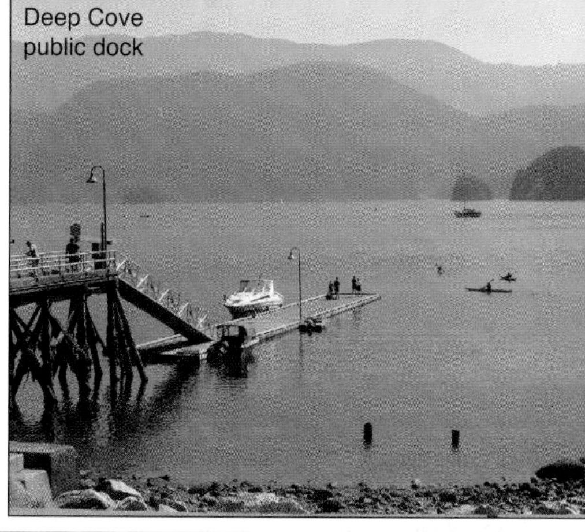

Deep Cove
public dock

Deep Cove Public dock
Diane and Roy Alton-Kaighin
Ph: 604-908-2151 Dock for day use only. Float length 44 m. Boats to 36'–pay at meter. Village–Restaurants, groceries, stores. Adjacent: Deep Cove Yacht Club.

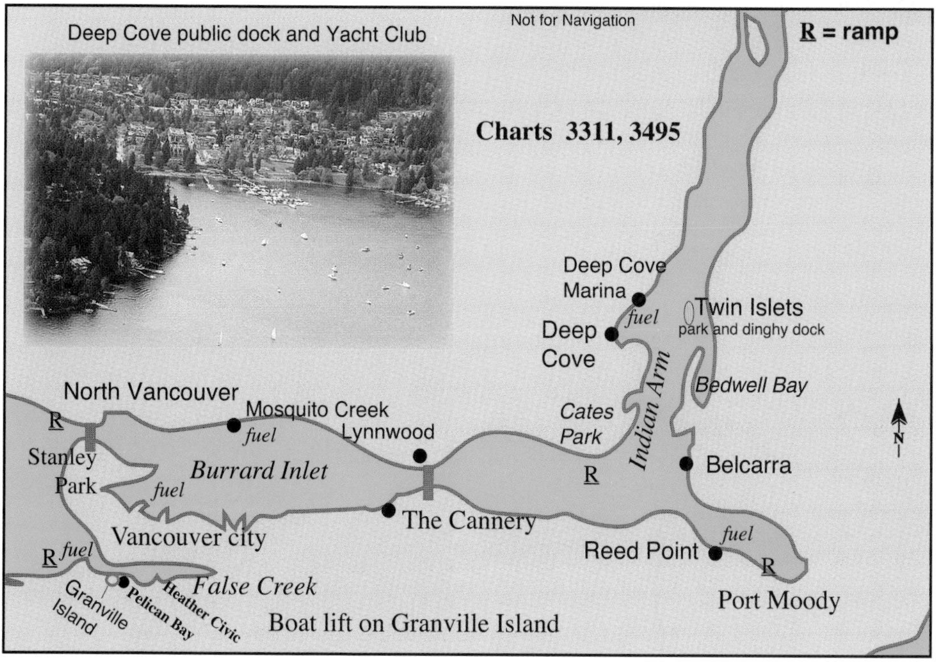
Deep Cove public dock and Yacht Club
Not for Navigation
R = ramp
Charts 3311, 3495
Deep Cove
Marina
fuel
Twin Islets
park and dinghy dock
Deep
Cove
Bedwell Bay
Indian Arm
Cates
Park
North Vancouver
R
Mosquito Creek
fuel
Lynnwood
Stanley
Park
Burrard Inlet
fuel
R
Belcarra
N
The Cannery
Vancouver city
Reed Point
fuel
R
R fuel
False Creek
Port Moody
Granville
Island
Pelican Bay
Heather Civic
Boat lift on Granville Island

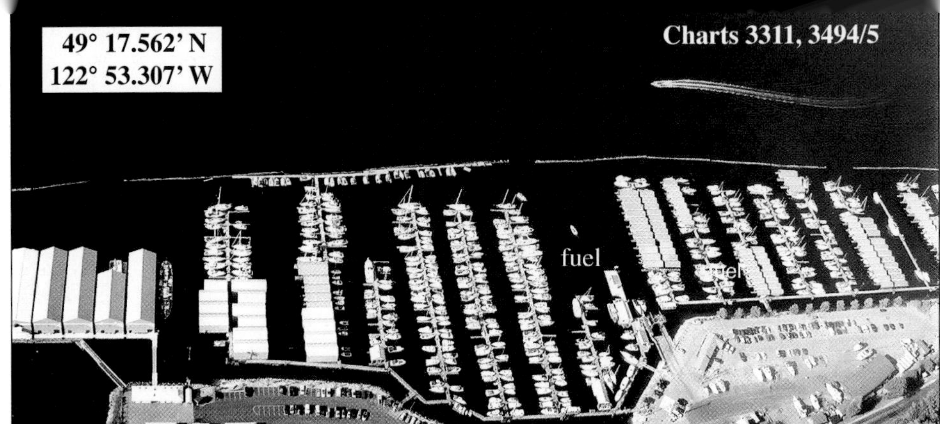

Reed Point

4. Reed Point Marina

Dave Harris
850 Barnet Hwy
Port Moody BC V3H 1V6
Ph: 604-937-1600 Fax: 604-937-1607
office@reedpoint.com
www.reedpoint.com

Marina services:
Fuel: Gas, diesel at fuel barge.
Moorage: Short and long term for boats of all sizes. **Washrooms. Power:** 20 amps. 38 ton travelift, dry storage and major work-yard. Full mechanical, fibreglass, woodwork and canvas work. Restaurant. Ample parking, full time security. Public pay phone. New and used boat sales. Chandlery, marine supplies, service, repairs. Major service centre.
For location of Reed Point Marina please refer to the diagram on the previous page.

Vessels launching at Port Moody (above) can fuel up at nearby Reed Point Marina.

Views of Reed Point Marina (top) and the fuel dock just inside the centrally located entrance (above). This is a major repair and service centre. Left: The launch ramp at nearby Port Moody. Below: View of Reed Point Marina looking west.

Sewell's Marina

Horseshoe Bay

Sewell's Ocean Adventure Centre

6409 Bay St
West Vancouver BC V7W 3H5
Ph: 604-921-3474 Fax: 604-921-7027
info@sewellsmarina.com
www.sewellsmarina.com

Marina Services
Moorage–limited space. Reserve.
Fuel: Gas, diesel, stove oil, engine and outboard oils.
Power: 15, 30 amp.
Washrooms nearby. Public phones, launch ramp. Propane. Marine repairs, service, fishing charters, licences, bait, tackle, rentals. Restaurants, Horseshoe Bay village, **The Boat Centre** marine store adjacent–boat sales & service available. Adjacent ferry terminal.

Howe Sound is one of the most active playgrounds for summer boating. It is the nearest relatively sheltered cruising area to Vancouver and a popular stop for vessels en route south to north. Several large marinas offer sheltered guest moorage and some smaller docks can accommodate boats for short durations while visiting local places of interest.

Horseshoe Bay — 49° 22.635' N, 123° 16.364' W
West Vancouver
Public dock adjacent to Sewell's Ocean Adventure Centre. • Manager • Lights • Power • Float length 64 m
Adjacent restaurants, shops, ferries to Vancouver Island and the Sunshine Coast via Langdale/Gibsons.

Charts 3534, 3311, 3526, 3512

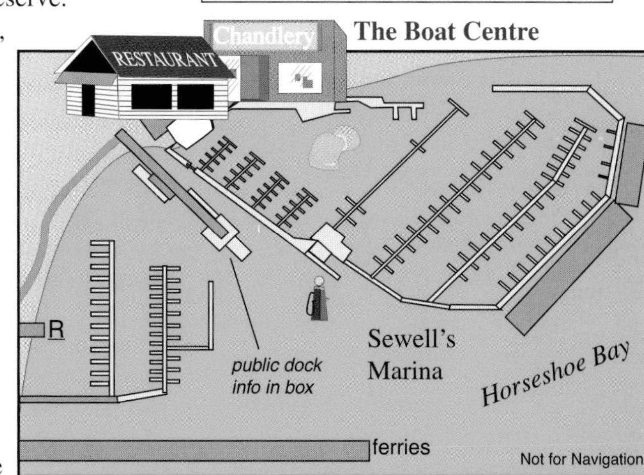

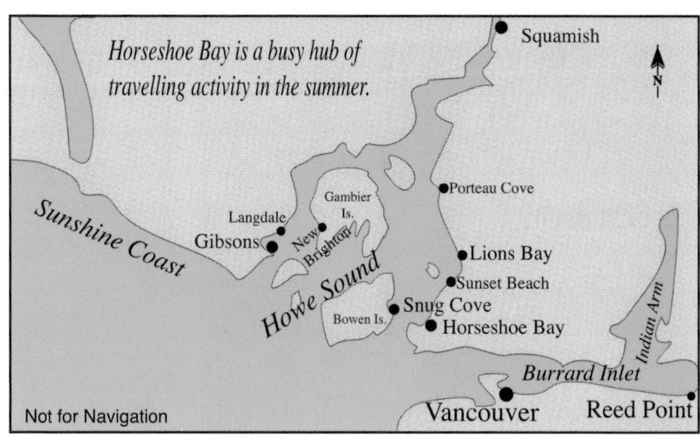

Not for Navigation
Howe Sound
Gambier I
Bowen I

Snug Cove

Union Steamship Co. Marina VHF 66A

Rondy and Dorothy Dike
PO Box 250 431 Trunk Rd
Bowen Island BC V0N 1G0
Ph: 604-947-0707 Fax: 604-947-0708
Charts 3534, 3311, 3526, 3512
ussc@shaw.ca
www.steamship-marina.bc.ca
Hazard: Shallows near beach beyond marina docks. Watch for ferry operations.

Marina services:
Moorage: Many slips. Maximum to 210 feet. Reservations suggested. **Power** at docks: 30, 50 amp. Laundry. **Showers, washrooms.** Pumpout.

49° 22.834' N
123° 19.501' W

Customer services:
Chandlery–boating supplies, gifts, novelties, charts, snacks. Garbage disposal. Nearby fresh produce, frozen foods, pharmacy, liquor, tackle, bait, hardware, ice and most supplies–at marina or in village. Also restaurants, pubs, art shops, bistro, bakery, health food, gift and specialty stores. Internet access.

Entertainment.
Annual summer events include live entertainment, (pub Saturday nights),
Bowen Island parade and festival (Saturday prior to Labour Day). Dog Days of Summer (Second Sunday in August). Walking roads and trails on island. Crippen Regional Park has many trails and walks. Including 600 acres surrounding Snug Cove and marina. Golf. Farmers market.

Adjacent facilities:
BC Ferries to Horseshoe Bay. Crippen Regional Park. Picnic ashore. Walking trails. Killarney Lake in Crippen Park area. Anchorage in Mannion Bay (temporary). ATM, Post office, medical services nearby.

Opposite: Snug Cove's Union Steamship Marina in the left of the photo. The public dock acts as a breakwater with the ferry landing and Bowen Island Marina in front. Mannion Bay is to the right. Opposite bottom: Inside the store at the marina.

Right: The Union Steamship Marina at Snug Cove is a busy place. Every summer, boats converge on this popular destination from all parts of the coast. The restaurants, bakery, farmers market, gift shops and specialty stores give this quaint village its particular charm.

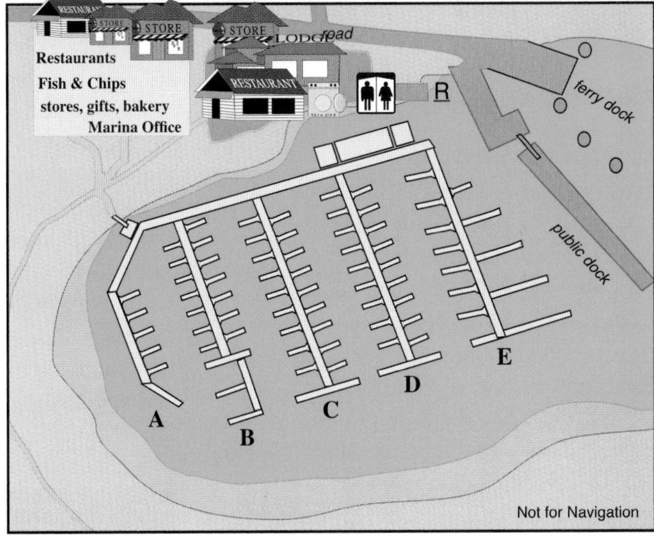

The village

One of the busiest boating centres on the coast, Snug Cove has been developed into a high profile marina and boating haven. It is a multi-slip dock facility with some 170 slips catering to boats up to 210 feet in length. The government dock that serves as a breakwater will dock about ten more boats depending on size. The ferry from Horseshoe Bay lands right alongside the government dock. Its wake and wash from the substantial propellers causes a stream that washes against boats moored to the dock so caution should be exercised when coming or going. When tying up-be sure to secure your boat adequately before leaving it for a walk up to the stores or the park and lake nearby.

The walk through the park is an easy one with well worn pathways as is the stroll up to Killarney Lake. Hiking around the lake is also not too taxing, unless you choose to do so in the middle of summer. Lots of shade helps reduce the discomfort in summertime and the cooler weather out of season does the same. Follow the trail up through the park, along the paved road a short distance to the right and then pick it up again for the stroll to the lake.

The village at the ferry landing is simply known as Snug Cove. There are several gift, handicraft and souvenir stores as well as refreshment establishments which include The Snug, a light meals and coffee shop, excellent cappuccino and latte. A bakery next door serves coffee to go along with any of the freshly baked bread and pastries available. The long-established restaurant at the lower end of the stores has been serving a variety of simple meals for many years and the restaurant at the main Union Steamship landing boardwalk offers a wide selection of fine dining and pub fare.

Union Steamship Marina occupies most of Snug Cove. Bowen Island Marina, bottom right in the photograph, has limited overnight moorage and facilities but the shore attractions include crafts and gift shop, bicycle rentals and a kayak shop.

49° 27.257' N 123° 14.476' W

Lions Bay Marina

Ken Wolder
60 Lions Bay ave Lions Bay
West Vancouver BC V0N 2E0
lionsbaymarina@telus.net
www.lionsbaymarina.com
Ph: 604-921-7510 Fax: 604-921-0782
Charts 3311, 3526, 3512

Guest moorage, water, power at fuel dock. **Fuel:** gas, engine and outboard oils. Washrooms. Garbage disposal. Public phones. Launch ramp, store–marine supplies, Haul out. Ice, snacks, fishing licences, bait.

Sunset Marina

49° 24.312' N 123° 14.821' W

Sue Rauter
34 Sunset Beach
West Vancouver BC V7W 2T7
Ph: 604-921-7476 Fax: 604-921-7477
sunset marina@shawlink.ca
Charts 3311, 3526, 3512

Visitors–call ahead. Open Feb 15 to Nov 15. Wet and dry moorage, power at gas dock. **Launch ramp, marine store. Fuel:** Gas, engine and outboard oils. Tackle, fishing licences. Washrooms. Repairs, service, power wash. Bait, ice. Snack bar. Parking.

Caulfeild Cove

West Vancouver Public dock Charts 3311, 3526, 3463 Float length 16 m
Lights • Garbage • Water •
see number 10 on map

Bowen Island Marina

Norma and Dennis Dallas
Bowen Island BC V0N 1G0
Ph/Fax: 604-947-9710 VHF 16 call 'Norma D'
norma@bowen-island.com
www.bowen-island.com

Marina located to starboard approaching Snug Cove ferry landing, public dock and Union Steamship Marina. Limited transient moorage. Tackle and bait shop. Ice, ice cream. Gift shop, kayak, bicycle rentals. Fresh fish and vegetables. Nearby hiking trails, shops, liquor outlet, grocery store, B&Bs, beach. Musicians. ***Hazard: Ferry dock alongside.***

Above: The public dock at Snug Cove forms a breakwater to Union Steamship Marina. Tie up on a first come basis. Rafting allowed.

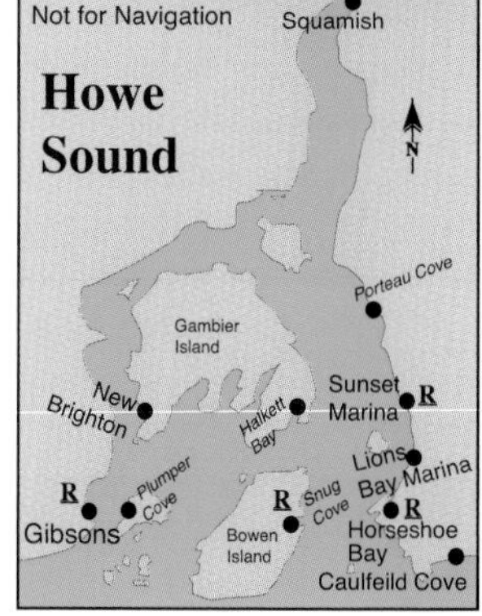

The marine park at Keats Island includes the Plumper Cove docks seen above lower right in the cove in the above photograph. The islands provide shelter from most conditions but occasional westerlies blow in, causing some discomfort when anchored or tied to mooring buoys.

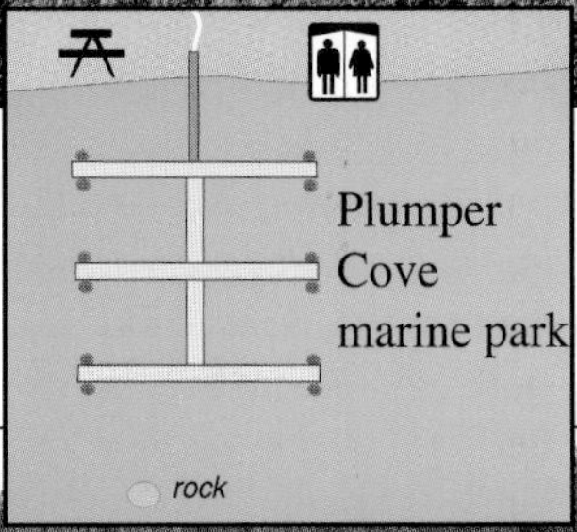

Right: A warm summer day at the marine park docks in Plumper Cove on Keats Island.

Parks in Howe Sound

For more information on marine parks see ***Anchorages and Marine Parks.***

Halkett Bay
Fair weather anchorage (some wind conditions).
Dinghy dock.
Camping sites, toilets, hiking.

Porteau Cove
Temporary moorage.
Buoys mark location of artificial reefs.
camping/picnic sites, water, toilets, beach, scuba diving (wrecks as artificial reefs).

Plumper Cove
This is a popular all weather anchorage (some unsettling wind conditions do occur).
Mooring buoys. **Boat docks,**
camping/picnic sites, water, toilets, beach.
Hiking. Fishing nearby at The Cut.

Howe Sound Public Docks

Howe Sound

1. Squamish Public dock

Ph: 604-892-3725 Bill McEnery
Charts 3311, 3534, 3526, 3512
Manager • Float length 118 m • Garbage • Water • Lights • Power 20 amp • Public phone ashore • Near city restaurants, shops, churches, service and facilities. Adjacent yacht club may allow some transient moorage. Launch ramp. Pumpout.

2. Hopkins Landing Public dock

Charts 3311, 3526, 3512
Manager • Float length 17 metres • Lights on the dock.

3. Keats Island Public dock

Charts 3311, 3526, 3512 Manager • Float length 15 m Water • Lights •

4. New Brighton

Gambier Island Public dock
Charts 3311, 3526, 3512
Float length 120 m • Lights • Public pay phone • Walking–island roads.
Nearby store. Ferry service to Langdale/ Gibsons.

Top: Looking north up Queen Charlotte Channel. Opposite, lower: A favourite stop at Gibsons is on the outside of the breakwater at the pub dock.

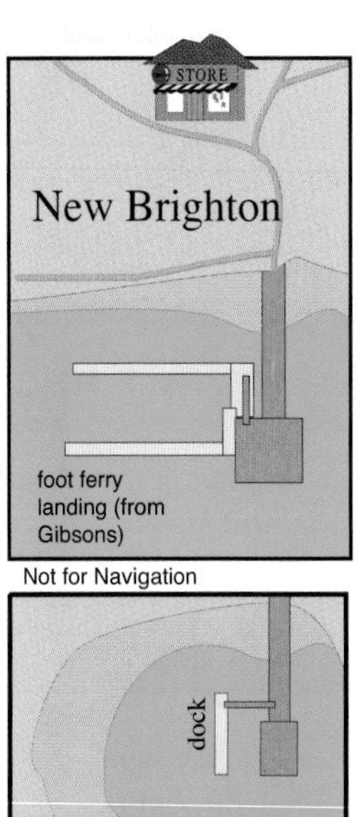

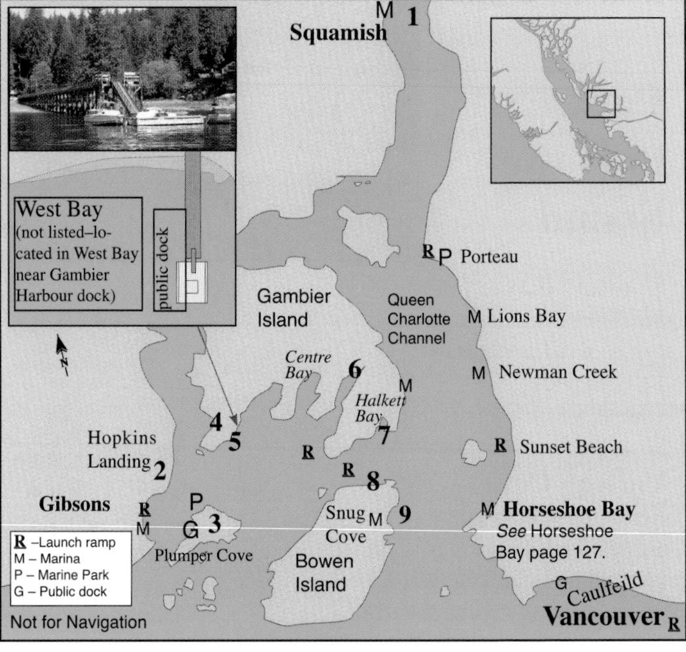

Above: Gibsons Landing Harbour Authority offices and facilities on the wharf.

Gibsons Landing Harbour Authority

PO Box 527, Gibsons BC V0N 1V0
Ph: 604-886-8017 Fax: 604-886-1347
glha@telus.net Bill Oakford
Charts 3534, 3311, 3526, 3512 VHF 66A
Transient moorage available. Rafting allowed.
Pumpout. Washrooms, Showers, laundry.
Launch ramp near • Garbage • Water • Lights • Power: 15, 30 amps • Nearby restaurants, shops.

Above: There are busy permanent and transient facilities in the protection of the breakwater at Gibsons.
Below: A waterfront pub at Gibsons.

5. Gambier Harbour

Gambier Island
Public dock
Charts 3311, 3526, 3512
Float length 30 m
Lights • Showers.

6. Port Graves

Gambier Island
Public dock
Charts 3310, 3512, 3526
Manager • Float length 10 m

7. Halkett Bay

Gambier Island
Public dock
Charts 3311, 3526, 3512
Float length 17 m
Adjacent marine park.

8. Mount Gardner Park

Bowen Island
Public dock
Charts 3311, 3526, 3512. Float length 17 m

9. Snug Cove

Bowen Island
Public dock
Charts 3534, 3311, 3481, 3512, 3526
Manager •
Float length 105 m
Garbage • Lights • Power • Public pay phone ashore • Washrooms ashore • Adjacent Union Steamship Marina. Near village arts and gifts, bakeries, restaurants, shops. All services. Ferry to Horseshoe Bay.

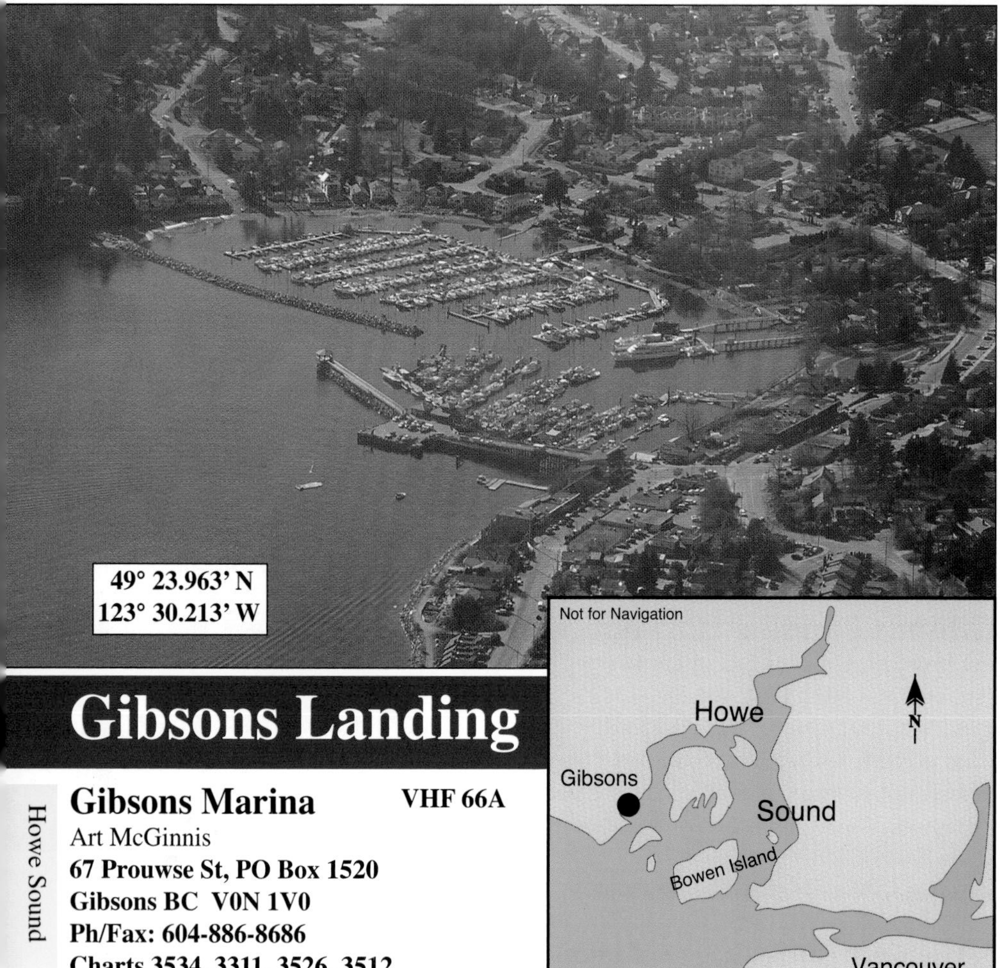

Gibsons Landing

Gibsons Marina VHF 66A

Art McGinnis
67 Prouwse St, PO Box 1520
Gibsons BC V0N 1V0
Ph/Fax: 604-886-8686
Charts 3534, 3311, 3526, 3512

Marina services:
400 permanent and transient berths. Reservations suggested for visiting boats. Dock A – main visitor dock. Portable pumpout. Garbage disposal. **Power** at docks: 15 amp at all slips. **Launch ramp.**

Customer services:
Laundry, showers, washrooms.
Marine supplies at chandlery/marina office. Fishing gear, licences, charts, bait, ice, repairs, accessories, books, binoculars. Nearby churches multi-denominational. Post Office. Walk to stores in village, also pharmacy and other necessities. Scuba diving at Sechelt up the Sunshine coast. Ask for information. Public pay phone ashore.

Walking: Road access walking or cycling. Waterfront walk, partial around bay. Walk, cab or bus up to main shopping centre. *Hourly bus service between Langdale ferry, Gibsons and Sechelt.*

Entertainment.
Fishing at The Cut a short run from the marina. Museum, local stores. Art galleries. Book store (Coast Books).

Adjacent facilities:
Fuel: Gas, diesel, oils. Outboard mix. Service, haul-outs.
Marine repairs available–mechanic on call. Marine and boat equipment sales. Bank machines, gifts, arts and crafts, snacks. Vehicle rentals. Public dock.

Top: At the city marina in Gibsons. Above: The store at Gibsons Marina. Above right and opposite: Views of Gibsons Marina docks.

Gibsons to Squamish

Gibsons today is a busy community of residents, transient ferry travellers, business people and boat operators docking their craft at Gibsons Marina. This large facility is one of the biggest and best of its kind in local coastal waters. It provides all services required by mariners from the chandlery store at the head of the dock to nearby repair facilities. The marina offers power and water, showers and laundry, fish cleaning, bait, tackle and accessories. In the waterfront village of Gibsons Landing there are stores, restaurants, a

Entrance to Squamish Harbour
49° 40.918' N
123° 10.031' W

Squamish

Moorage in Squamish

The Squamish Yacht Club Ph: 604-892-3942, has moorage alongside the public marina. There is often adequate room to tie up at the public docks and sometimes a yacht club member will invite you to stop for a while at their facilities, provided there is room. Many mariners tie up to log booms in the area but be careful not to hinder any work in progress if you do. Stop and enquire at the Yacht Club if the government docks are full.

Photos: From the wharf alongside the Squamish Yacht Club. Top: Looking north. Right: South side.

pub, post office, pharmacy, museum and convenience stores. A very handy delicatessen is located near the marina for excellent specialty items and a sit down cup of tea or coffee. Craft and art stores have become a major attraction.

From Gibsons to Squamish takes you either up the eastern shore of Howe Sound, where you can see numerous waterfront homes or small settlements, or up the western side with its islands and passages. One of the major landmarks on the steep-sloped eastern shore is Britannia Beach with its scarred hillside from former mining operations.

The passage up the western shore passes from Gibsons via New Brighton on Gambier, privately owned club facilities of Thunderbird Yacht Club and Burrard Yacht Club at Ekins Point and McNab Creek opposite.

Sunshine Coast

Howe Sound to Desolation Sound

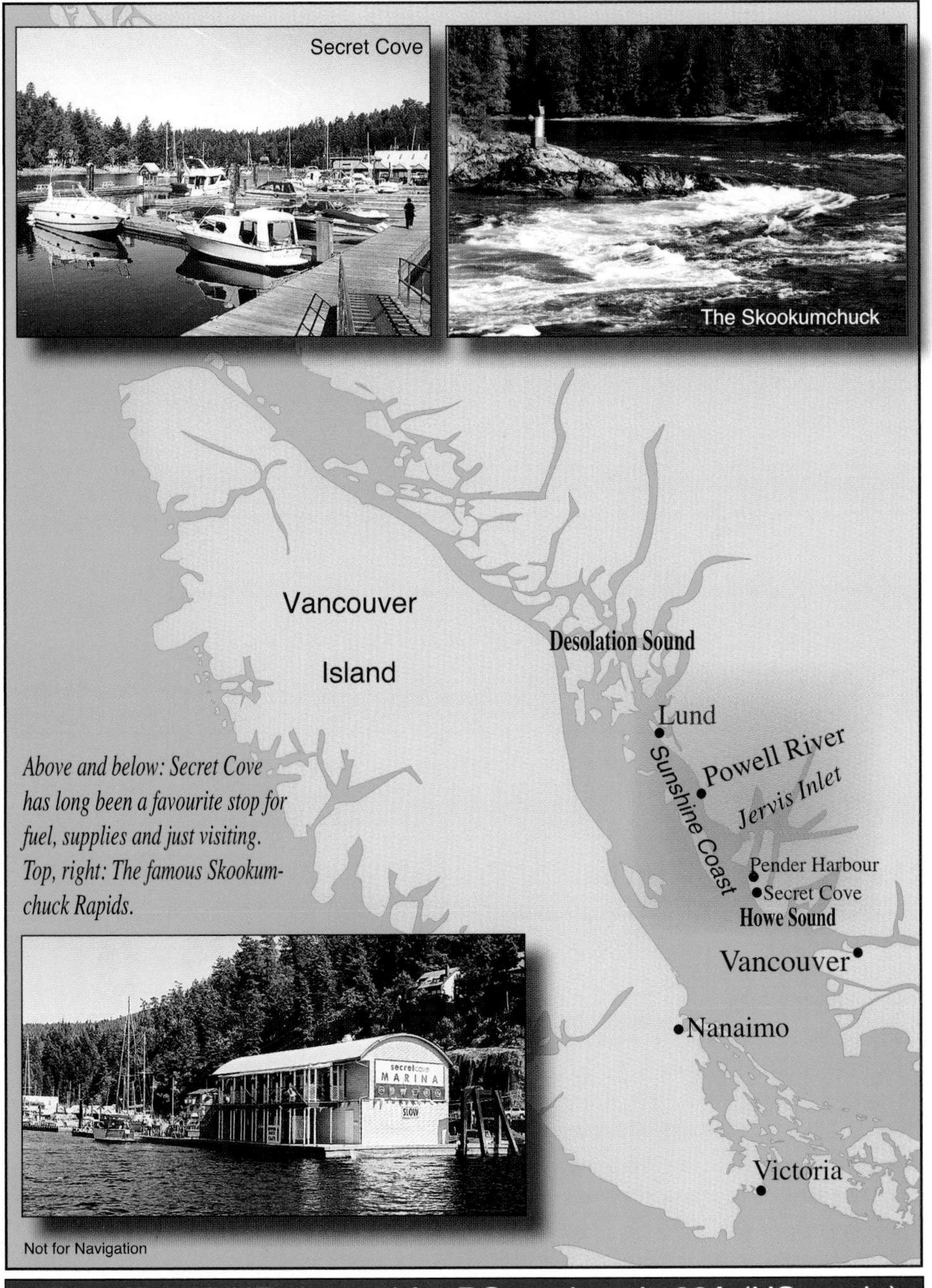

Above and below: Secret Cove has long been a favourite stop for fuel, supplies and just visiting. Top, right: The famous Skookumchuck Rapids.

The official VHF channel for BC marinas is 66A (US mode)

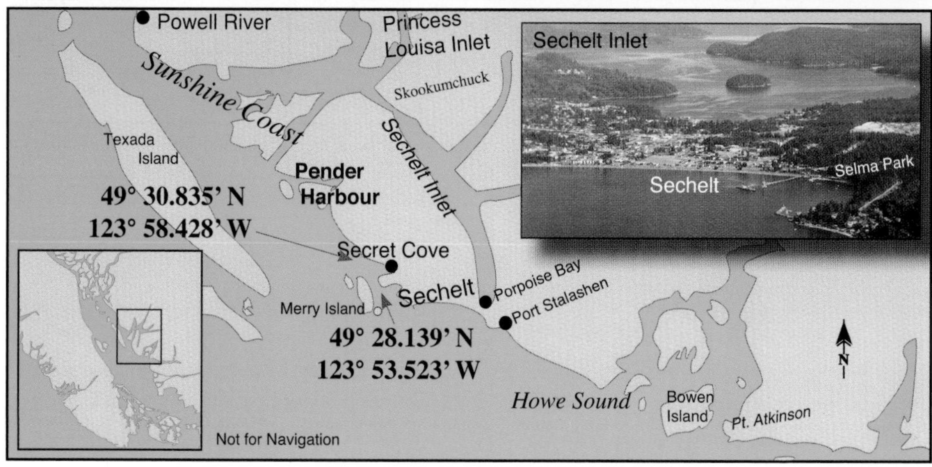

Above: Secret Cove Marina. Opposite page: The fuel dock at Secret Cove and boats at the marina. Inset, above: Selma Park, Sechelt Inlet and the isthmus at Sechelt (see also page 153).

Port Stalashen Marina

Art McGinnis *(see also Gibsons Marina)*
1585 Field Rd
Sechelt BC V0N 3A1
Ph: 604-885-7792
Charts 3311, 3512. VHF 66A
Marina services: Water.
Power: 30 amps. **No overnight moorage. While this is not a destination marina it may provide shelter in emergency on the exposed stretch of coast. Call to enquire.** *Use chart 3311 and enter with great care during rough conditions and at low tide. Depth at the entrance is 3' at zero tide.*

Port Stalashen is located off Sechelt. It is fully occupied with permanently moored boats and no berths are readily available for visitors.

Secret Cove

49° 31.620' N
123° 58.102' W

Charts 3535, 3311, 3512

Secret Cove Marina

Scott Rowland
5411 Secret Cove Rd, PO Box 1118
Sechelt BC V0N 3A0 VHF 66A
Ph: 604-885-3533 Fax: 604-885-6037
Toll free 1-866-885-3533
info@secretcovemarina.com
www.secretcovemarina.com

Marina services: (Seasonal)
Fuel: Gas, diesel, oil.
150 berth permanent and 25 transient slips. Seasonal–Easter to Thanksgiving.
Power at docks: 15, 30 amp.
Customer services:
Showers. Washrooms. Fish cleaning tables, picnic tables, garbage disposal for moorage customers only. Full grocery store, marine supplies. Fishing gear, licences, charts, bait, ice, electronics, repairs, accessories, books, gifts, wireless internet access. Fax service. Restaurant upstairs with patio, located on dock. General store. Liquor agency. Public pay phone ashore. Water Taxi available.
Walking: Road access walking or cycling. Cab or bus up to main shopping centres. Mountain bike rentals.
Entertainment:
Good fishing a short run from marina. Hotels, restaurants and facilities nearby.
Adjacent facilities:
Golf. Swimming.

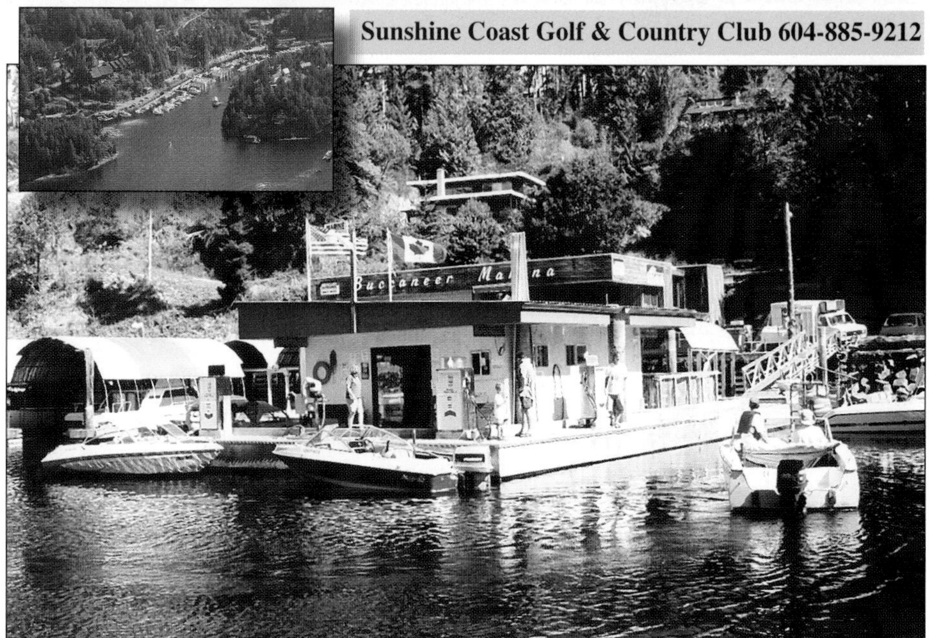

Buccaneer Marina

Bob, John, Jerry Mercer
5535 San Souci Rd
Halfmoon Bay BC V0N 1Y2
Ph: 604-885-7888 Fax: 604-885-7824
Toll free: 1-877-885-7888
buccaneermarina@telus.net
www.buccaneermarina.com
Charts 3311, 3512, 3535 VHF 66A
Marina services: Haulouts. **Fuel:** Gas, diesel, oil. Marine centre and store. Sales & service. Parts and repairs. Repair dock. Mercury Marine service. Guest moorage 6 slips. **Power** at dock. Garbage disposal. Boat rentals. Fishing gear, licences, charts, live and frozen bait, ice, propane, groceries, snacks. Marine ways 40'. Hull repairs, steam cleaning, bottom painting. Water taxi to Thormanby Island and Sechelt. Road access walking.

Halfmoon Bay

Sunshine Coast
Public dock
Manager: Linda
Ph: 604-885-2261
Charts 3311, 3512
Float length 26 metres • Lights.

Adjacent facilities:
Lord Jim's Lodge Ph: 604-885-7038 and Jolly Roger Inn Ph: 604-885-7184. Accommodations and some moorage.

Porpoise Bay
49° 29.045' N
123° 45.525' W

Inset: Hotels, their docks and the waterway to Buccaneer Marina (above) in Secret Cove.

Secret Cove

Public dock
Charts 3311, 3535, 3512 • Manager • Float length 44 m • Lights • Power • Public phone •
Adjacent marinas, lodges, provisions, fuel, repairs, service.

Porpoise Bay, Sechelt

Public dock. Mngr Bruce Haynes
District of Sechelt Ph: 604-885-1986
Fax: 604-885-7591 Charts 3311, 3512 • Float length 132 metres • Launch ramp • Grid • Aircraft float • Garbage • Water • Lights • Power • Pay phone ashore • Adjacent restaurant, hotels, nearby shops. Scuba diving in vicinity. Charters. Rentals. Photo page 153.

The dock at Princess Louisa. Pender Harbour is an ideal stop en route to Princess Louisa Inlet.

Entrance to Pender Harbour
49° 37.808' N 124° 03.986' W

Pender Harbour

The waterfront at Madeira Park has a park setting with adjacent facilities for transient mariners.

The location of Pender Harbour is central to many coastal areas, a favourite of which is nearby Princess Louisa Inlet (top of page). As a base to launch from or cruise from, Pender Harbour's 32 miles of shoreline has anchorages and facilities to meet most needs of cruising mariners. Entering Pender Harbour use your chart and pass between Martin Island to port and Charles and William Islands to starboard.

Yachts tying up at marinas in Hospital Bay will not be far from most available facilities. Visit Fisherman's Resort & Marina or try for space at the public float. The former hospital at Hospital Bay has functioned in more recent years as a lodge and restaurant. A short trip away is the famous Skookumchuck where the Sechelt Rapids tumble wildly over themselves during tidal changes. Pender Harbour or Egmont are staging areas for viewing the magnificent natural sight. There is good fishing nearby.

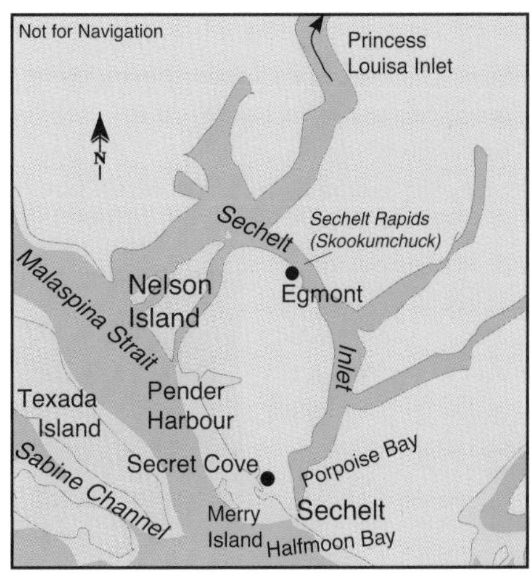

Pender Harbour

Entrance to Pender Harbour
49° 37.808' N 124° 03.986' W

Fisherman's Resort & Marina

David Pritchard, Jennifer Love
4890 Pool Lane PO Box 68 VHF 66A
Garden Bay BC V0N 1S0
Ph/Fax: 604-883-2336
fishermans@dccnet.com
www.fishermansresortmarina.com

Marina services:
Moorage. 2,200 feet. Reservations suggested. **Power** at docks: 20, 30 amp. Water.

Customer services:
Seasonal April–October. **Laundry, showers, washrooms,** ice, tackle. Waterfront cottages. Marine charts, books, clothing. Fishing gear, licences. Repairs. Secure parking.

Entertainment:
Fishing is good in the general area. Consult fishing guides.
Scuba diving arrangements and charters–ask marina for information. Road access walking or cycling. Four lakes nearby, swimming, golfing, mountain biking, animal and marine life. Internet access.

Charts 3535, 3311, 3512 VHF 66A

Fisherman's Resort

Adjacent and nearby facilities:
Groceries and **Fuel** at **John Henry's** general store–Ph: 604-883-2253. Post office, liquor, restaurants. Pharmacy and other necessities at store. Public marina. Anchorage in Garden Bay. Launch ramp. Float plane service.

Below: Fisherman's docks in Hospital Bay.

Fisherman's Resort. Inset: Owner David Pritchard talks to Carla about marina plans.

Fisherman's Resort

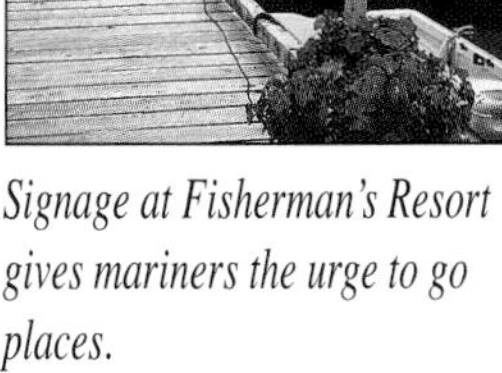

Signage at Fisherman's Resort gives mariners the urge to go places.

Centre: An aerial view of Fisherman's Resort (courtesy of the marina).

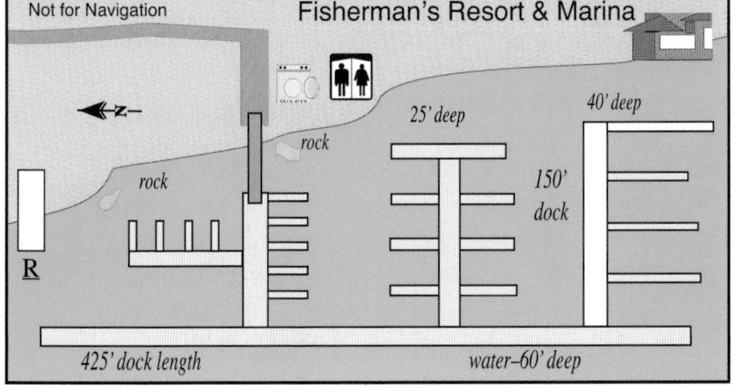

Opposite page, top to bottom: Overview of Pender Harbour, the dock at Fisherman's Resort, approaches to Hospital Bay.

Above: Hospital Bay and the fuel dock at John Henry's (to the right).

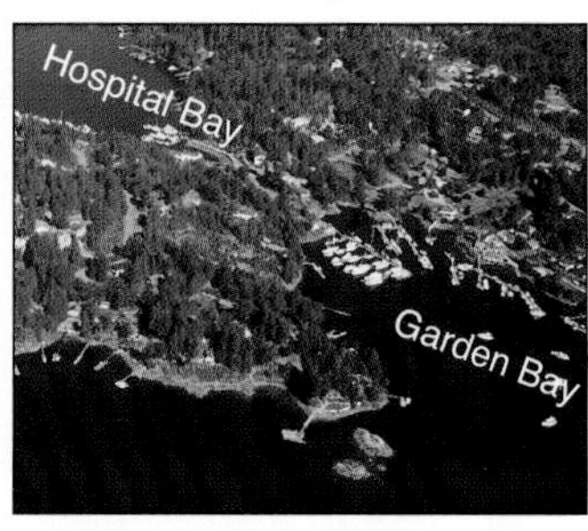

John Henry's Marina

Lucy & Wayne Archbold
4907 Pool Lane, PO Box 4907
Garden Bay BC V0N 1S0
Phone: 604-883-2253 Fax: 604-883-2147

Marina services: Launch ramp; gas, diesel, 50:1 mix, oil; propane; ice; full grocery/ liquor/marine/fishing supply store; bank machine.

Nearby facilities: Restaurants; playground; hiking trails; post office adventure charters. rant. Gift shop and art gallery,

Top: Garden Bay from Fisherman's Resort.
Centre: John Henry's docks and marina.
Above: The store at John Henry's Marina.

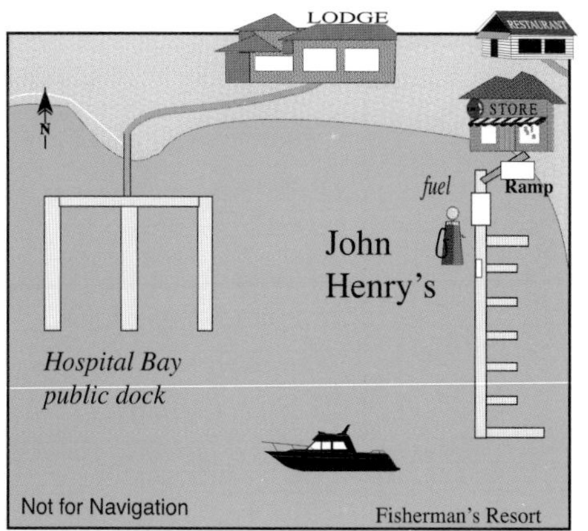

Hospital Bay

Public dock
Pender Harbour Authority
Manager Diana Pryde VHF 66A
Ph: 604-883-2234
Charts 3535, 3311, 3512
Float length 158 metres • Garbage • Water • Lights • 15, 20 amp power • Washrooms. Close to restaurants, groceries, liquor, boating needs. Anchorage. Fuel at John Henry's.

Garden Bay Hotel and Marina (left and below) has a popular pub and eating establishment. This marina is directly adjacent to the Royal Vancouver Yacht Club outstation at Pender Harbour.

Garden Bay Hotel & Marina

Ron Johnston
4985 Lyons Rd, PO Box 90 VHF 66A
Garden Bay BC V0N 1S0
Ph/Fax: 604-883-2674
gbhm@dccnet.com
www.gardenbaypub.com

Marina services:
Guest moorage: 1,200', reservations suggested, seasonal March-Oct. Water at dock.
Power: 15, 30 amp.

Customer services:
Fine dining at pub and waterfront restaurant. Gift shop and art gallery, kayak and canoe rentals, on dock. Fishing charters. Air charters. Nearby churches. Golf course.
Public pay phone ashore.

Washrooms, laundry, showers.

Entertainment. Live entertainment in pub. Jazz Festival in September. Good fishing and scuba a short run from the harbour.

Golfing, kayaking, hiking, easy walking or cycling.

Nearby facilities: Fuel: At **John Henry's Marina** in Hospital Bay. Gas, diesel, stove oil, outboard fuel, propane, tackle.
Post office, liquor agency, restaurants.

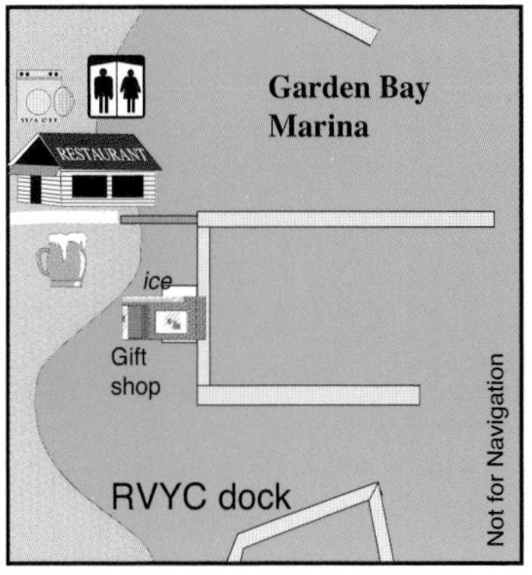

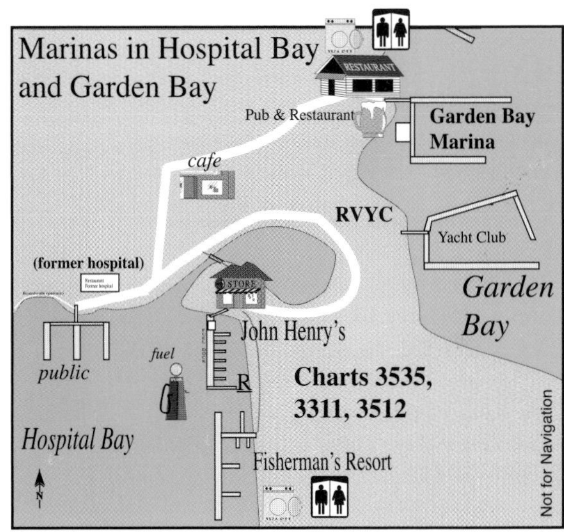

Pender Harbour Resort at Duncan Cove

Pender Harbour Resort

4686 Sinclair Bay Rd
Adam Boothy
S-15, C-13 Garden Bay BC V0N 1S0
Ph: 604-883-2424 Fax: 604-883-2414
info@penderharbourresort.com
www.penderharbourresort.com
Toll free 1-877-883-2424
Charts 3512, 3535, 3311
Marina services: Showers, laundry, washrooms. Ice, **water, power:** 20, 30 amp. Groceries, fishing tackle, licences, garbage disposal, rental boats. Access to pool. Walking. Launch ramp.

Coho Marina Resort

Dwayne and Brenda Balon
12907 Shark Lane, PO Box 160
Madeira Park BC V0N 2H0
Ph: 604-883-2248 Fax: 604-883-2237
coho@dccnet.com
Hazard: Rocks in bay–marked by beacons. Consult charts.
Marina services: Limited visitor moorage. Launch ramp. **Showers. Power:** 15 amp.

Pender Harbour Hotel & Marina

Manager: Bal Brar
12671 Sunshine Coast Hwy
Pender Harbour BC V0N 2H0
Phone: 604-883-9013 Fax: 604-883-9014
bal@penderharbourhotel.com
www.penderharbourhotel.com
Marina services: Guest moorage. **Power:** 20-amp, pub/restaurant, liquor, beer & wine store. **Chart: 3535**

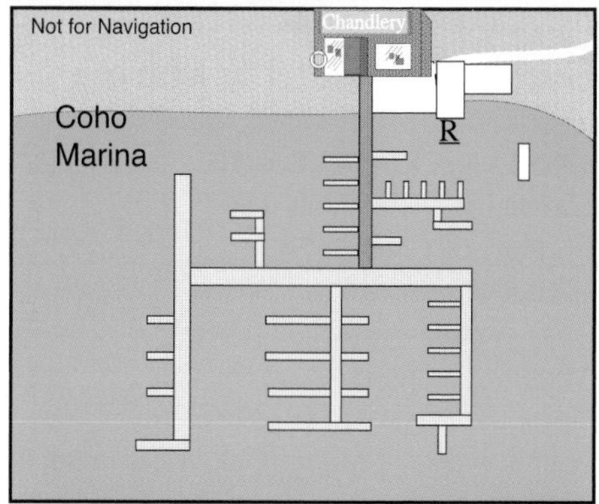

Entrance to Pender Harbour
49° 37.808' N 124° 03.986' W

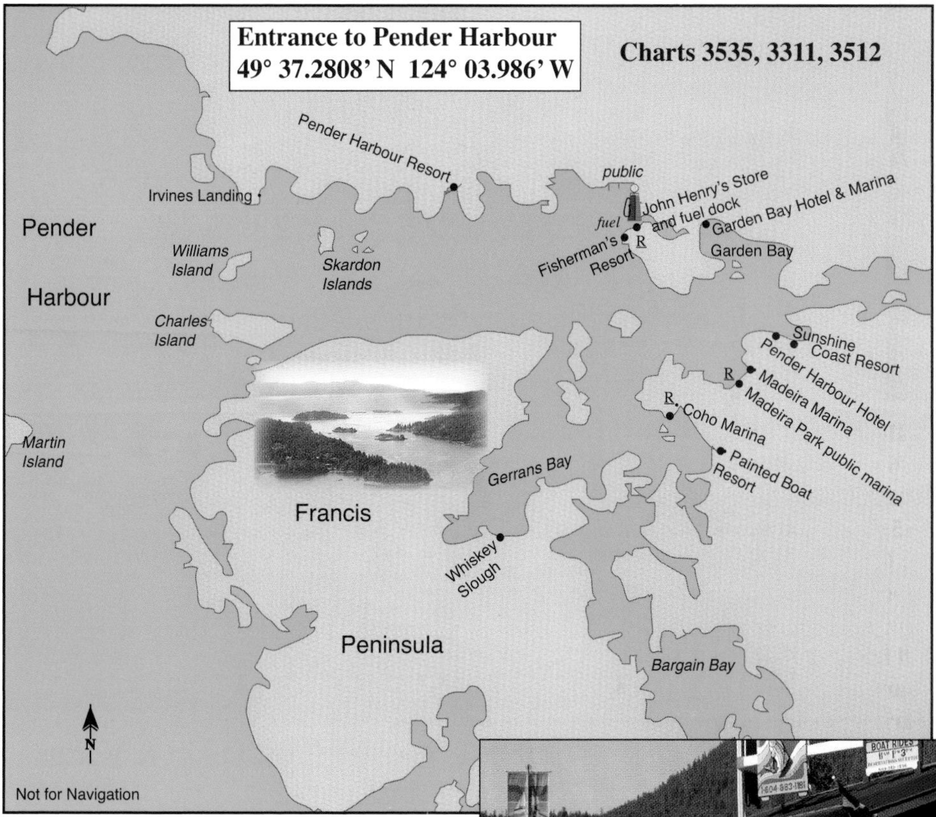
Entrance to Pender Harbour
49° 37.2808' N 124° 03.986' W
Charts 3535, 3311, 3512
Pender Harbour Resort
public
John Henry's Store and fuel dock
Garden Bay Hotel & Marina
fuel
Fisherman's Resort
R
Garden Bay
Irvines Landing
Pender
Harbour
Williams Island
Skardon Islands
Charles Island
Sunshine Coast Resort
Pender Harbour Hotel
Madeira Marina
Madeira Park public marina
R
Coho Marina
Painted Boat Resort
Martin Island
Gerrans Bay
Francis
Whiskey Slough
Peninsula
Bargain Bay
N
Not for Navigation

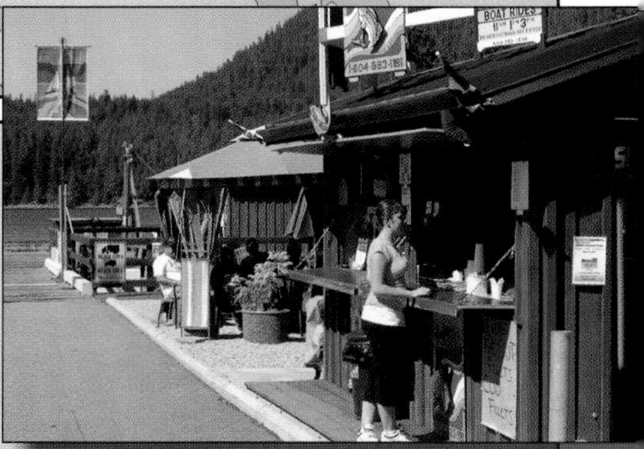
BOAT RIDES

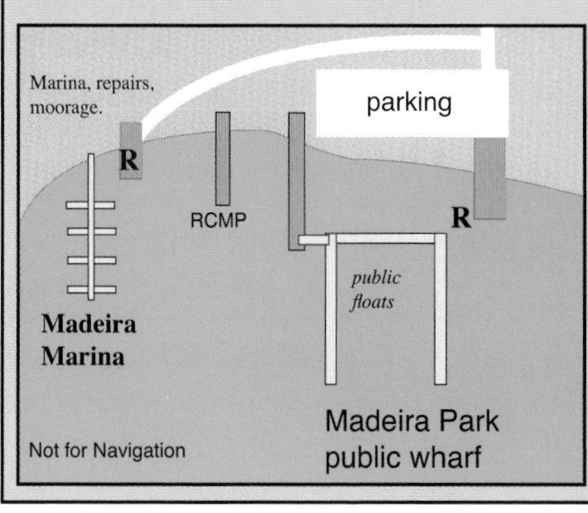

Concession at Madeira Park, Pender Harbour.

Whiskey Slough public dock

Harbour Authority of Pender Harbour
Diana Pryde
Ph: 604-883-2234 VHF 66A
Charts 3535, 3311, 3512
Moorage, 15, 20 amp power, water.
Two fingers–300' plus in summer.
See location of public docks on diagram above.

Marina, repairs, moorage.
parking
R
RCMP
R
public floats
Madeira Marina
Madeira Park public wharf
Not for Navigation

Madeira Park public wharf

PO Box 118, Madeira Park V0N 2H0
Harbour Authority of Pender Harbour.
Manager Diana Pryde.
Phone: 604-883-2234 VHF 66A.
• Float length 500' • Launch ramp • Barbecue • Aircraft float • Coffee, snack bar • Garbage • Laundry • Washrooms • showers • Water • Lights • Power: 15, 30, 50 amps • Pumpout • Nearby restaurants, supermarket, shops. Marine mechanic.

Sunshine Coast Resort & Marina

Photo courtesy Sunshine Coast Resort & Marina

Sunshine Coast

Sunshine Coast Resort, above and below, is located opposite Garden Bay, to the east of Madeira Park.

Photo courtesy Sunshine Coast Resort & Marina

Sunshine Coast Resort & Marina

Ralph Linnmann **VHF 66A**
PO Box 213 12695 Sunshine Coast Hwy
Madeira Park BC V0N 2H0
Ph: 604-883-9177 Fax: 604-883-9171
vacation@sunshinecoast-resort.com
www.sunshinecoastresort.com

Marina services: Guest moorage. Seasonal Easter to Thanksgiving. **Power:** 15, 30 amp. **Laundry**, **washrooms, showers. Garbage disposal.** Boat rentals, live bait, accommodations. Sundeck and hot tub. Nearby: shopping centre, restaurant, **launch ramp** at Madeira Park. Free transportation to and from golf course for marina guests. Playground nearby. Internet access.

Marina locations shown on previous page.

Irvines Landing (closed 2006/7)

This was the original Union Steamship stop at Pender Harbour. It is located at the entrance to Pender Harbour and was a favourite stop for sports fishermen with its close proximity to the entrance of the harbour. Its fuel dock is also closed.

Above: Aerial photo shows Lowe's Resort (Painted Boat Lodge) right and Coho Marina to the left.

Madeira Marina

Karen and Rick King
12930 Madeira Park Rd
PO Box 189, Madeira Park BC V0N 2H0
Ph: 604-883-2266 Fax: 604-883-9250
Charts 3311, 3535, 3512
Location: next to Madeira Park public docks and ramp. No transient moorage.
Marina services: (Photo page 148). **Moorage**. Haulout to 35'. Marine repairs. **Water** at dock. No power.
Customer services:
Marine store. Saltwater licences, charts.

The Painted Boat Resort Spa and Marina

Planned opening 2008
Formerly Lowe's Resort: PO Box 153
Madeira Park BC V0N 2H0
Ph: 604-883-2456 Fax: 604-883-2474
Toll free 1-800-527-7776
Charts 3535, 3512
(As Lowe's Resort)t information–Moorage. Limited–primarily for lodge customers. Boats to 28/30 feet. **Water, power, showers, washrooms**, laundromat, tackle shop, snacks. Accommodation. Shops nearby.

It is a scenic trip from Pender Harbour to Princess Louisa Inlet. This photo shows the dock at the head of the famous inlet.

entrance to Bathgate Marina docks and fuel

49° 44.989' N
123° 55.689' W

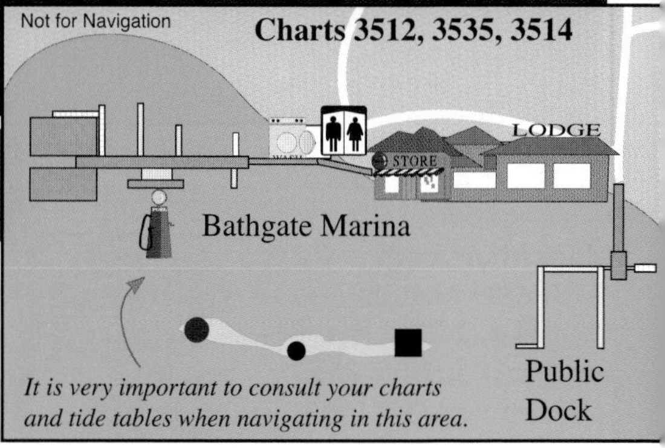

Not for Navigation

Charts 3512, 3535, 3514

LODGE

STORE

Bathgate Marina

Public Dock

It is very important to consult your charts and tide tables when navigating in this area.

Sechelt Inlet

Bathgate General Store Resort & Marina

Doug and Vicki Martin
6781 Bathgate Rd, Egmont BC V0N 1N0
Ph: 604-883-2222 Fax: 604-883-2750
bathgate@lincsat.com
www.bathgate.com

Marina services:
Fuel: Gas, diesel, propane, oils.
Moorage. Visitor moorage–reserve. Marine ways to 40 tons. Marine mechanic on duty. Water at dock. Ice. Internet access.
Power at docks: 15, 20, 30 amp.
Customer services:
New deluxe waterfront motel–wheelchair accessible. Liquor agency. Grocery store–fresh meat and vegetables. Fishing tackle, licences. Bank machine. RV tent sites.
Water taxi service. Washrooms for Bathgate Marina customers**, showers, laundry.**
Boat, cabin, video rentals.
Walking: Road access walking or cycling. Playground. Trail to the Sechelt Rapids viewpoint, bakery; Skookumchuck Rapids Provincial Park Egmont Heritage Centre; ferry to Princess Louisa Inlet & Malibu Club, Young Life *www.mailbuyachts.com.*
Entertainment.
Kayaking. Scuba diving and fishing in the immediate vicinity are rated very highly.
Adjacent facilities:
Public dock. Egmont–nearest base before trip to Princess Louisa Inlet. Automobile fuel. Fishing and scuba diving.
Hazard: Drying reef in middle of bay on approaches to fuel dock and another off the government dock. Check your chart.

Above: The museum at Egmont.
Left: Docks and fuel float at Bathgate Marina.
Left, lower: Egmont Marina at the Back Eddy Pub, Egmont.

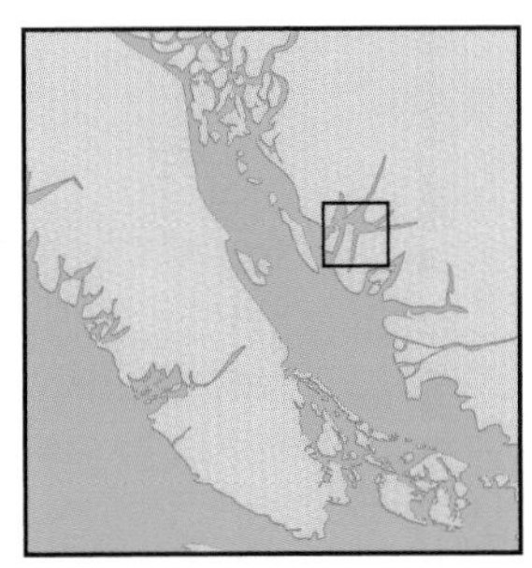

Egmont Marina

John and Margaret Mills
16660 Backeddy Rd
Egmont BC V0N 1N0
Ph/Fax: 604-883-2298
Toll free: 1-800-626-0599
Charts 3312, 3512
info@egmont-marina.com
www.egmont-marina.com

Marina services: **VHF 66A**

Fuel: Gas diesel, oils, two stroke oil, frozen bait at fuel dock. Garbage disposal. Guest moorage available 500'.

Power: 15, 30 amp. Potable water. Ice, tackle, fishing licences, book exchange, groceries.

Laundry, showers, washrooms. public phone ashore. Rental boats.

Entertainment: Backeddy Marine Pub, summer long-weekend live entertainment. Pool table. Nearby restaurant, trails to Skookumchuck rapids. Tours to Princess Louisa Inlet. Boat US participating marina.

Opposite Top: Bathgate Marina and public docks.
Bottom: The public dock at Egmont.

There is a public launch ramp nearby at Egmont. Another, gravel ramp, is located at Egmont Marina.

Egmont Public Dock

Egmont Harbour Authority.
Manager Betty Silvey
Ph: 604-883-9652 604-883-9463
Phone at store. Charts 3512, 3514.
Float length 145 m
Aircraft Float • Garbage • Lights.
West Coast WIlderness Lodge nearby has fine dining and occasional dock space.

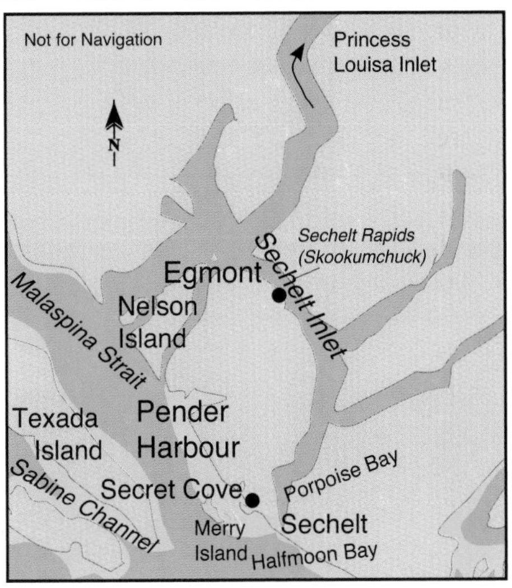

The Skookumchuck–to be avoided at tide changes in Sechelt Inlet.

Saltery Bay

Sunshine Coast public dock
Ph: 604-885-3714 Chart 3514
• Float length 133 metres • Garbage • Lights • Adjacent ferry dock to Egmont.

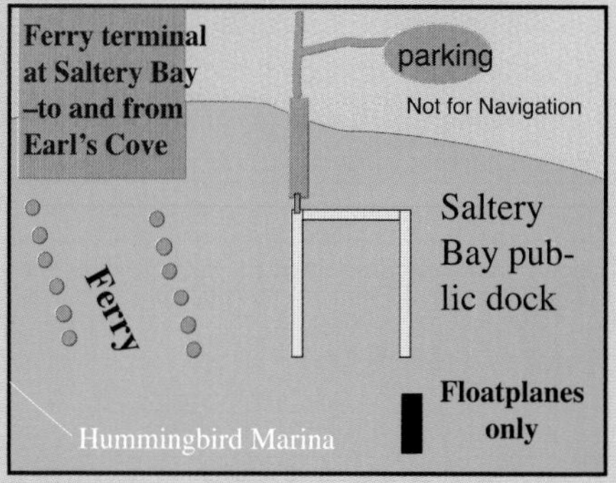

Justin Taylor photo.

Photo Justin Taylor

Hummingbird Marina

Hummingbird Cove Saltery Bay, BC
Ph: 604-487-1499 Fax: 604-487-1205

Located to west of ferry landing.
Located in Hummingbird Cove near Saltery Bay. The marina is small and space limited. Cottages.
BBQ available for oceanside dining.
Walking trails and the beach. Wildlife, birds, sea life.

Left: The dock at Saltery Bay.
Above: Hummingbird Marina in the foreground and the Saltery Bay ferry terminal.

Left: The public docks at Porpoise Bay in Sechelt Inlet are adjacent to the launch ramp and Lighthouse Marina. *See listing on page 138.*

Lighthouse Marina

Pub and Beer and Wine store

Manager: Dale Schweighardt
5764 Wharf Rd PO Box 137
Sechelt BC V0N 3A0
Ph: 604-885-9494 Fax: 604-885-3382
Charts 3312, 3512
info@lighthousepub.ca
www.lighthousepub.ca
Marina services: Fuel: gas, diesel. Guest moorage. Ice, laundry, showers, washrooms, pumpout, garbage disposal, restaurant/pub, internet access, ATM, launch ramp.
Nearby: Floatplane service, golf, hospital.

Poise Cove Moorage

Helen and Roy Wigard
5991 Sechelt Inlet Rd, Sechelt BC V0N 3A0
Ph: 604-885-2895
Charts 3311, 3512 (Inside Sechelt Inlet)
Some visitor moorage available, power at dock: 15 amp. Launch ramp.

Top: Sechelt Inlet and the isthmus on which Sechelt is located. Strait of Georgia to the left, marinas right. Below: Lighthouse Marina at Sechelt's Porpoise Bay. Poise Cove Marina's dock and launch ramp are shown at bottom right. Time your passage through the Skookumchuck rapids with care.

Porpoise Bay 49° 29.045' N 123° 45.525' W

Lighthouse Marina

Poise Cove

49° 47.974' N
124° 31.308' W

Powell River

Beach Gardens Hotel And Marina

Joan Barszczewski
7074 Westminster Ave
Powell River BC V8A 1C5
Ph: 604-485-6267 Fax: 604-485-2343
Toll free 1-800-663-7070
beachgardens@shaw.ca
www.beachgardens.com
Charts 3563, 3311, 3513 VHF 66A

Marina entrance is at the breakwater just south of Grief Point.

Marina services:

Fuel: Gas, diesel, oil. ice (in season). Mechanic and services available from local and nearby marine operators.

Moorage: Large permanent marina with overnight moorage slips. Reserve.

Power at docks: 15, 30 amp.

Laundry, showers, washrooms.

Customer services:

Hotel with waterfront accommodations. Liquor store nearby. Cold spirits, wine and beer. Public pay phones ashore. Walking trails or road access. Some beachfront walks.

Fishing charters. Sail charters (Cooper Boating). Sea kayaking. Wilderness canoe routes. Scuba diving arrangements and sightseeing charters–ask hotel for details.

New waterfront restaurant.

Adjacent and nearby facilities:

Grocery store, post office nearby.

Shuttle service to town in season, restaurants–pick up for dinner reservations.

Shopping, golf and hiking in the area.

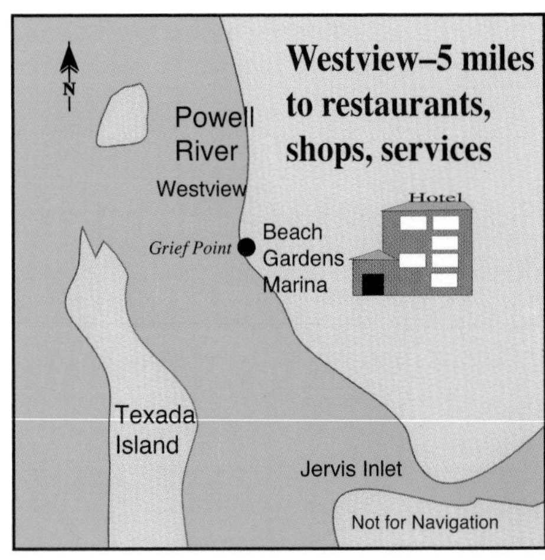

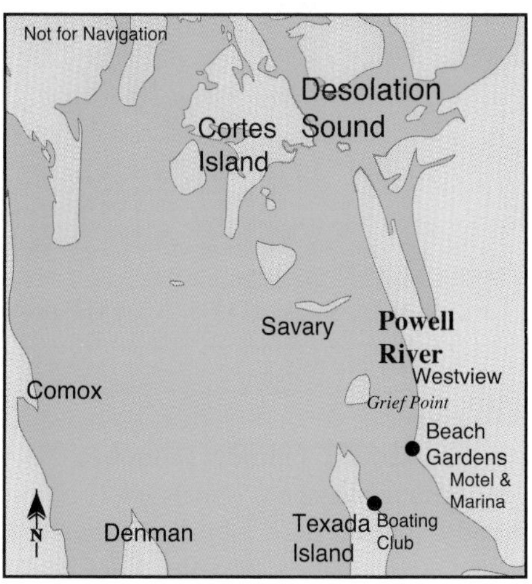

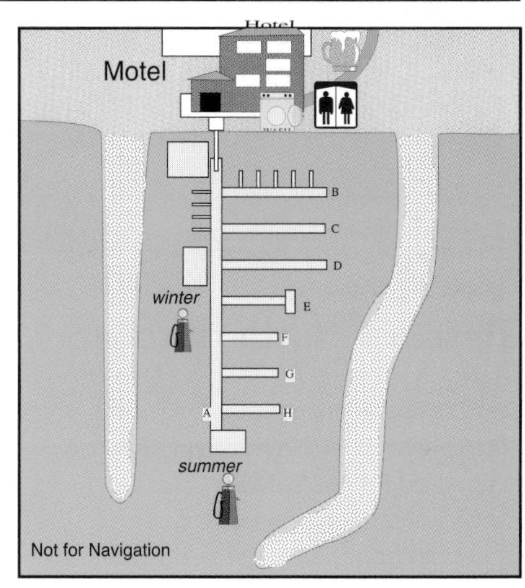

Texada Boating Club

Wharfinger: Barb Soepboer

PO Box 196

Van Anda BC V0N 3K0

Phone: 604-486-7574

Chart: 3513

Located on northeast side of Texada Island. Marina Services: Guest moorage, power: 15-amp, garbage disposal, launch ramp.

Nearby facilities: Hotel nearby offers showers, restaurant, bank machine, ice, liquor store, grocery store, laundry at the garage, walking club on Saturdays, old mine on opposite beach.

Rough in strong SE winds. Not suitable for larger boats in windy weather.

The Boating Club at Sturt Bay on Texada Island. Visitors are welcome to the guest dock at the far end of the marina. Boat size restricted by the type of anchored dock moorings. Good anchorage opposite in favourable winds.

Fuel dock inside south breakwater

South harbour

fuel

North harbour

MARINE FUELS 604-485-2867

49° 50.055' N
124° 31.766' W

Westview North Harbour

Charts 3311, 3563, 3513 **VHF 66A**

Transport Canada dock/Boat Harbour
Jim Parsons manager.
Ph: 604-485-5244 No transient moorage.
Charts 3311, 3536, 3513
Breakwater and permanent moorage.
Launch ramp located at north end.
Near ferry landing, city restaurants, shops.

Westview South Harbour

6910 Duncan St, Powell River V8A 1V4
Ph: 604-485-5244 Fax: 604-485-5286
www.powellriver.ca

• Float length 625 m • Garbage • Waste oil disposal • Water • Lights • Power: 15, 30 amp. Washrooms. Rafting permitted.

Moorage:
No reservations. **Laundry, showers**, Near city restaurants, shops, hotels. Golf course nearby. Marine store a block up the road. Enter south marina past the **Fuel dock:** located inside breakwater. Gas, diesel. Outboard mix. Propane, Ice. Small boat rentals. Internet access.
Nearby: fishing tackle, marine supplies. Free shopping shuttle bus to mall July, August. Also Blackberry festival, Seafair, Music Folk Fest (September).
Community events–Powell River Visitors Bureau Ph: 604-485-4701.

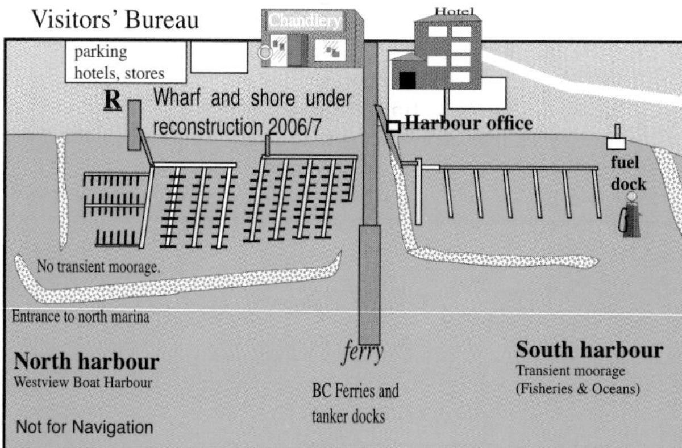

Flights daily Powell River–Vancouver on Pacific Coastal Airways 1-800-663-2872.
Ferries to Comox, Vancouver Island and to Texada Island.

Westview Fuel dock
Ph: 604-485-2867 Fax: 604-485-7238
Gas, diesel, outboard mix, naptha, water, ice (located in South Harbour).

Texada and Lasqueti Islands

The dock at False Bay has very limited space. It is used primarily for the local water taxi.

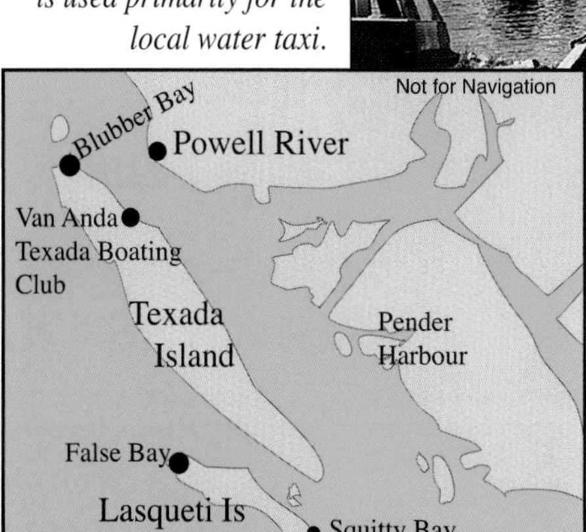

Blubber Bay

49° 47.924' N
124° 37.134' W

Texada Island dock

BC Ferries. Chart 3311. Ph: 250-978-1307 Limited facilities and moorage at 13 m float. Shore access by dinghy. Try the Boat Club docks at Van Anda to the south. Recommend docks also at Powell River and good moorage at Beach Gardens marina.

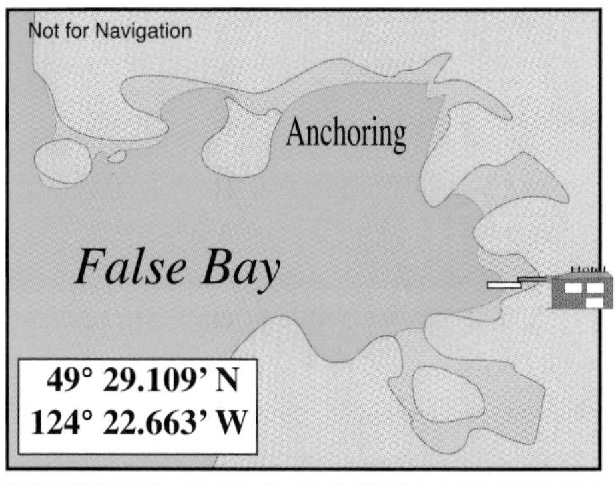

Lasqueti Island

Hotel and Resort

(see False Bay public dock)

Lasqueti Island BC V0R 2J0
Ph: 250-333-8846 Fax: 250-333-8897
Charts 3312, 3512, 3513

Local services: *Poor dock space at nearby public dock*–**Moorage** is limited. No facilities. No fuel. **Adjacent:** Hotel with facilities including convenience store, ice, showers. Washrooms. Restaurant–licensed, pub. Anchoring at opposite end of bay–see diagram top right–is sometimes windy.

False Bay public dock

Lasqueti Island (adjacent hotel)
Wharfinger–Bruce Bird
Charts 3536, 3512, 3513. Float length 36 m • Aircraft Float • No facilities at dock. Transport Canada.

Squitty Bay

49° 27.110' N
124° 09.762' W

Lasqueti Island
Public dock. Chart 3512 Float length 47 meters • Walking, trails, island roads.

49° 58.891' N
124° 45.827' W

Lund

Lund Small Craft Harbour

Rosie O'Neill
Ph: 604-483-4711 **VHF 73**
Marina services:
Moorage: Over 500 feet for transient use. **Water. Power**: 20, 30 amp. Public pay phone. **Washrooms. Showers.** Launch ramp. Adjacent Lund Hotel, restaurants, shops. ATM. Laundry. Rafting permitted at public docks. 30-ton travel lift at service dock.

The fuel dock at Lund.
Below: Rosie O'Neill, harbourmaster at Lund.

Lund Fuel dock and the historic Lund Hotel

Steve Tipton & Kathy Thomas
Ph: 604-414-0474 Fax: 604-414-0476
Fuel: Gas, diesel, propane. Some moorage. Paid garbage drop. Hotel accommodation, restaurant, pub–open 7 days a week. **Showers, laundry.** Ice. Art store in hotel building. Post office. General store: groceries, tackle, marine supplies. Some hardware. Liquor agency. Deli/bakery, fresh produce, butcher. Walking trails or road access. Some beach-front walks. Boardwalk. Fishing charters. Water taxi service.

Adjacent and nearby facilities: Stores, coffee house, arts, souvenirs and gifts. Restaurants. Ice cream. Pizza. Clothing store.

Photograph above shows a view of the Lund Hotel. It overlooks the wharf and fuel dock. The fuel dock can be seen in the foreground. The dock to the left serves the adjacent marine service facility.

Public docks

Okeover Inlet

Okeover dock
49° 59.511' N
124° 42.643' W

Public dock
Charts 3512, 3514, 3312, 3559
Manager • Float length 35 m
Breakwater • Lights • Power •
Public pay phone ashore •
This public dock provides access to the nearby Laughing Oyster restaurant.

Finn Bay, Lund

Public dock-No ramp to shore.
Charts 3311, 3513, 3538
Manager • Float length 49 m

49° 56.940' N
124° 46.433' W

Savary Island

Public dock Transport Canada
Charts 3311, 3538, 3513
Float length 11 metres.
No moorage–for loading only.

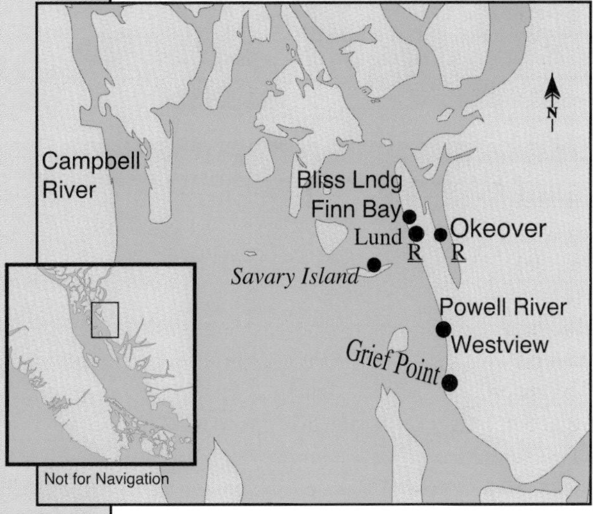

Lund is an interesting place, existing as the northernmost town on the Sunshine Coast road. It has an historic hotel, restaurants and numerous facilities including a well-stocked grocery store selling a fair selection of marine hardware, fishing gear, books and charts. There is a waterfront marine service centre and chandlery, catering year-round to the local community. Lund is a busy fuel stop before entering Desolation Sound.

Bliss Landing is located at the north end of Thulin Passage. They offer overnight **moorage** to visitors when resident boats are away. Check with them at 604-483-8098.

Bliss Landing, north of Lund, marks the entrance to Desolation Sound. Overnight moorage is available when space allows.

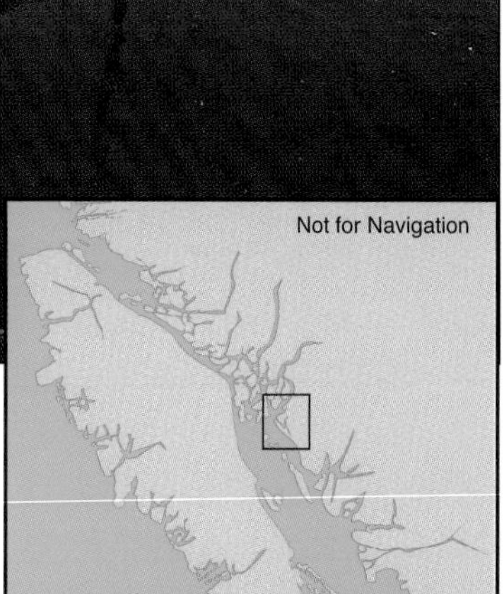

Not for Navigation

After Lund pay a visit to Okeover (top) where the cuisine at the restaurant is exceptional. Many mariners anchor in Grace Harbour and dinghy down to Okeover for dinner at the Laughing Oyster – Ph: 604-483-9775. The public docks (above) accommodate dinghies or a few small boats.

Above: The Copeland Islands provide a protected waterway from Lund to the entrance of Desolation Sound.

Finn Bay at Lund is an interesting spot, but there is no shore access and seldom space for tie-up at the public dock.

Vancouver Island

Central East Coast

Section 4

Union Bay is steeped in history. Its launch ramp and historic jailhouse.

49° 17.238' N
124°08.003' W

Schooner Cove Marina

Fairwinds Golf & Country Club 250-468-7666

Schooner Cove

Fairwinds Schooner Cove Resort & Marina

Wayne Newport
3521 Dolphin Dr
Nanoose Bay BC V9P 9J7
Marina Ph: 250-468-5364
Ph: 250-468-7691 Fax: 250-468-5744
Toll free 1-800-663-7060
marina@fairwinds.ca
www.*fairwinds.ca*

Hazard: Drying rock in entrance to marina. Keep red marker to starboard and keep close to floats inside the basin.

Marina services:
Fuel: Gas, diesel, oils, service available–can be arranged at dock. 360 permanent and up to 30 visitor docks. **Water** at all docks. **Power**: 15, 30, 50 amp. Some 125, 240 amp. Pumpout station–at end of G dock.

Customer services:
Hotel, accommodation, restaurant, lounge, pub. Coffee shop. Internet access. **Laundry, showers, washrooms.**

Charts 3512, 3459 VHF 66A

Outdoor pool, hot tub. Public pay phones. **Marine supplies**, fishing gear, licences, charts, bait, **ice,** books, gifts, snacks. Cold beer, wine and spirits store. ATM. Nearby churches**:** multi-denominational.

Post Office:
Courtesy shuttle to golf course.

Walking: Road access walking or cycling. Nearby parks.

Entertainment:
Fishing excellent near marina.
Tennis court, fitness centre. Dive shop, kayak and bicycle rentals. nature walks.

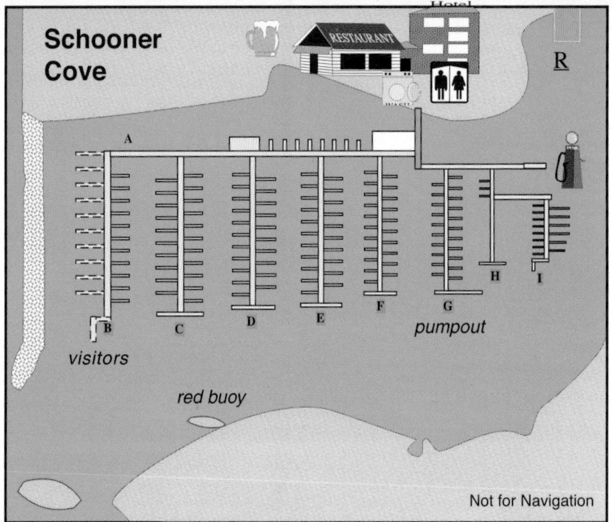

Above: A wide, segmented view of Schooner Cove Marina.

Schooner Cove is in one of the most beautiful settings on the coast. Nearby golf courses and developments have turned the area into a prized piece of real estate and the adjacent waters into prime fishing and scuba diving destinations. The hotel marina office is adjacent to restaurants and other facilities, including marine supplies.

Schooner Cove adjacent facilities: Courtesy shuttle to golf at Fairwinds 18 hole course. Group facilities. **Launch ramp**. Picnic area overlooking marina.

Beachcomber Marina

Manager: Leslie Barnes
7-1600 Brynmarl Rd,
Nanoose Bay BC V9P 9E1
Ph/Fax: 250-486-7222
ldbarnes@shaw.ca **Charts 3512, 3459**
Some visitor moorage, store with marine supplies and groceries. Launch ramp. Marine mechanic.

Refer to charts for reefs. Enter between the red and green buoys.

From Nanaimo to Campbell River take the time to stop at Schooner Cove. This is one of the largest and finest facilities anywhere with hotel and all amenities including golfing nearby, good fishing and scuba diving.

Farther north up Vancouver Island's east coast is Deep Bay, a pleasant place to visit and sheltered from windy conditions. If it is too long a stretch from Schooner Cove to Deep Bay drop in at French Creek, not always the easiest entrance, but shelter from rough seas and a place to break a long stretch along the coast. After Deep Bay, passing along Baynes Channel comes **Fanny Bay** and **Union Bay** then Comox with its vast set of docks, private and public. Fanny Bay offers possible moorage as well as semi-sheltered anchorage. Union Bay has a launch ramp for small boats. Comox Marina or those adjacent have lots of transient moorage. There are restaurants ashore and a park and stores nearby. Other facilities along with events such as Nautical Days each August will keep you entertained and enthused about the stop-over.

French Creek harbour

French Creek to Comox

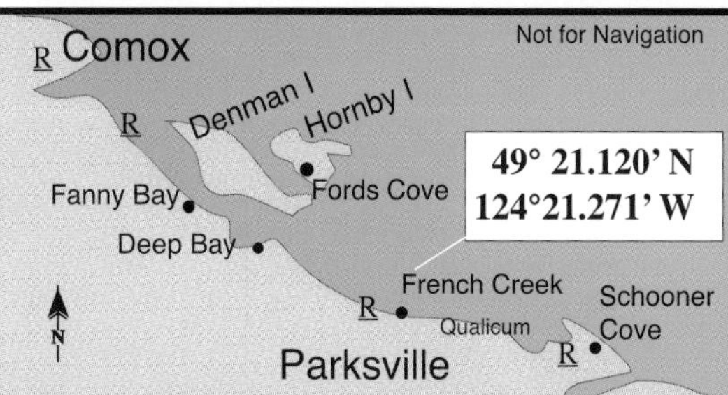

French Creek Charts 3512, 3513

Managed by FC Harbour Authority
1055 Lee Rd, Parksville BC V9P 2E1
Ph: 250-248-5051 Fax: 250-248-5123
hafc@frenchcreekharbour.com
www.frenchcreekharbour.com
Float length 804 metres. Breakwater. Garbage. Waste oil disposal. **Water**. Lights. **Moorage**. Rafting required. **Fuel:** Gas, diesel, pumpout. Laundry. Showers. **Power:** 20, 30 amp. Washrooms. Mobile service, repairs. Adjacent restaurants, shops, seafood store. Foot ferry to Lasqueti Island. Coast Guard station. **Launch ramp.**

Deep Bay Chart 3527

Deep Bay Harbour Authority
Ph: 250-757-9331 Fax 250-757-9319
deepbay-mgr@shawcable.com
www.dfo-mpo.gc.ca
Large, protected marina near Hornby and Denman Islands. Guest moorage–about 34 slips. **Launch ramp.** Tidal grid. Trailerable boats. Store and Restaurant. Water. Power: 15 amp. Pumpout, washrooms, showers.

Right: Deep Bay. Use caution in adjacent shallow waters. Launch ramp access with store and fuel for trailerable boats. Public dock is near the ramp. Larger boats anchor in bay.

Hornby Island

Ford Cove Hornby Island

Harbourmaster: Una Keziere
PO Box 2-6, Ford Cove BC V0R 1Z0
Ph: 250-335-2141 Fax: 250-335-2121
www.hornbyisland.com
Charts 3527, 3513

Float length 86 metres–about 650' rafting allowed • Breakwater • tidal grid • Garbage • Waste oil disposal • hydraulic crane • Lights • **Power:** 15, 30 amp • toilets • Grocery store, ice, fishing supplies. Art gallery • Sport kayaks and canoe rentals. Diving charters.

49° 29.811' N 124°40.704' W

It is safe to anchor to the north of the harbour in most conditions. However, avoid northwesterly winds. This anchorage is generally used in preference to the harbour because it is usually occupied by commercial vessels. Hornby Island is inhabited by a large community of very talented artists.

A small village and community centre on the island offers restaurants, arts and craft stores and a grocery store. It is adjacent to Tribune Bay where anchoring is popular in summer. It is a short walk from the beach to the centre.

Above: Ford Cove docks. There is an eclectic group of artists and musicians resident on the island. They can be seen at the local shopping centre.

Ford Cove on Hornby Island. Anchorage can be taken to the north of the docks and shallows.

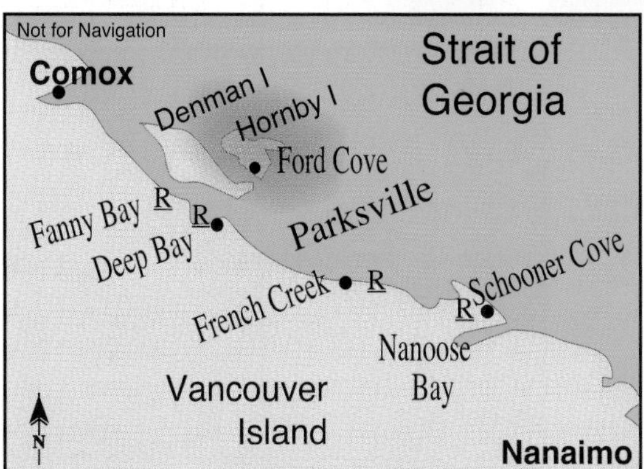

49° 30.430' N 124°49.341' W

Denman Island Public dock
Charts 3527, 3513
Float length 24 metres • Breakwater • Launch ramp on island. .

Fanny Bay Public dock
Ph: 250-335-9171
Charts 3513, 3527
Manager–Peter Golden • Float length 42 m • Breakwater • Grid • Power • Yacht sales.

Top: Ford Cove views showing also The Thatch pub dock at Hornby Island ferry landing and a boutique at the shopping centre. Diagrams show the sequence of harbours between Nanaimo and Comox. Above: A wide selection of local art is available at the gallery at Ford Cove.

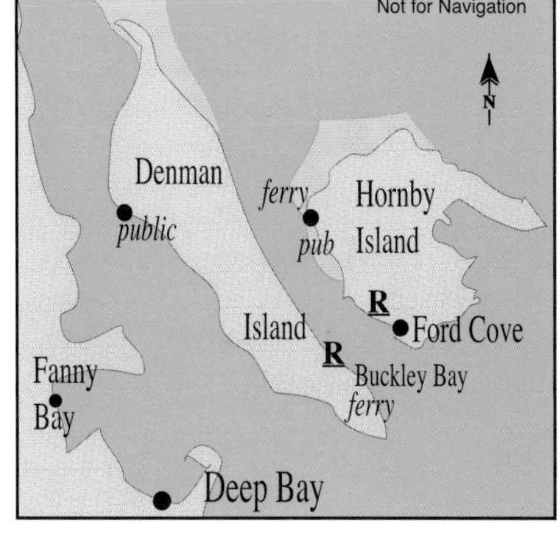

The outer dock has space available for visitors. Comox Municipal Marina lies in the centre of the complex, with Comox Bay Marina and Gas N Go docks to the left. Bottom: A view from shore of the public outer visitors' dock (far right this photo).

Entrance to harbour 49° 39.155' N 121° 54.973' W

Comox–Courtenay

Comox

Comox Harbour is home to over 500 pleasure boats and a commercial fishing fleet. It offers plenty of moorage for boaters visiting the Comox Valley. The marinas are protected by a rock breakwater which in turn is protected by Goose Spit making it one of the safest harbours on Vancouver Island.

For fishing enthusiasts there is a large launch ramp adjacent to Marina Park with lots of parking, washrooms and a play area for children. At the harbour, well-maintained guest floats are accessed around the east end of the breakwater on D and H floats.

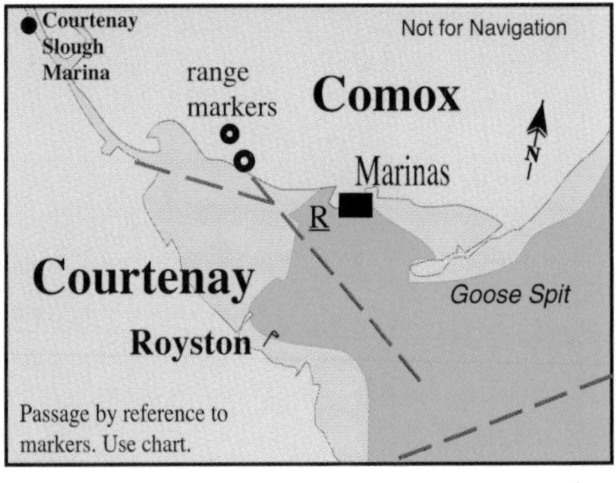

Visitor docks at east side of the harbour.

The harbour managers and staff are usually on hand to meet arriving vessels, but mariners can also check in at the office on the wharfhead. No reservations are required but a phone call ahead to 250-339-6041 will determine availability of space.

The Comox harbour puts on a warm welcome to visitors. There are nearby restaurants, shops and a golf course.

A variety of fresh seafood is available in season, direct from local fishermen at the popular fish sales dock.

Gas N Go Marina VHF 66A

Manager: Joan Benda
132 Port Augusta St, PO Box 1296
Comox BC V9M 7Z8
Phone: 250-339-4664

Two or three slips available at times for visitors. Gas, diesel, ice and convenience store.

Nearby facilities: Edgewater Pub located ashore. Launch ramp. Charters. Shopping centre, liquor store. Medical facilities.

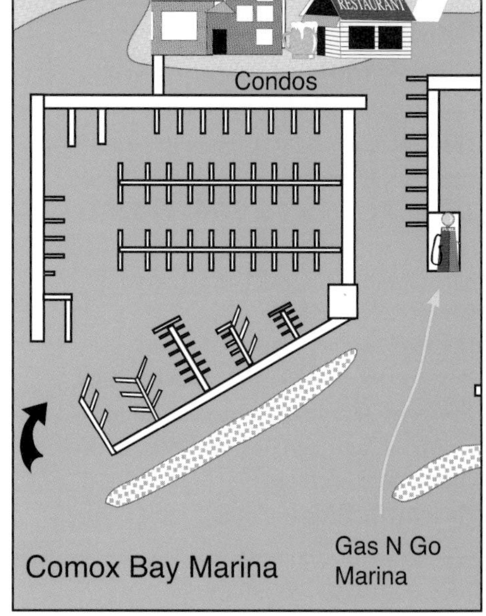

Comox Bay Marina VHF 66A

Manager: Brad Jenkins
1805 Beaufort Ave Comox BC V9M 1R9
Phone: 250-339-2930
manager@comoxbaymarina.com
www.comoxbaymarina.com

Moorage: Transient and permanent. Reservations suggested. Water, power-15, 30 amp. Showers, laundry, washrooms. Garbage disposal. Mechanic.

Entertainment:
Town pier–walk. Nautical Days celebrated every August. Picnic facilities at Marina Park. Rental vehicles available.

Adjacent facilities:
Restaurant, golf, shopping centre, yacht club. Float plane service. liquor store.

Comox Bay Marina

Comox visitors docks. Entrance from the east side.

Fisherman's Wharf

Comox Valley Harbour Authority

Liz McLeod & Mo Nordstrom
121 Port Augusta St, Comox BC V9N 7Z8
Ph: 250-339-6041 Fax: 250-339-6057
Town of Comox Ph: 250-339-2202
info@comoxfishermanswharf.com
www.comoxfishermanswharf.com

Charts 3527, 3513

Guest moorage, rafting allowed.
Power: 15, 20, 30-amp. **Washrooms, showers**, free internet access, laundry, pumpout, garbage disposal, ice, hydraulic crane, dogs welcome.
Nearby facilities: Comox: golf course, restaurants, grocery store, marine chandlery, marine mechanic, liquor store; pubs, playground, hiking trails, medical services, post office, banks, airport, float plane service, golf, adventure charters.
Canadian Armed Forces base.
HMCS Quadra camp at Goose Point.
Ferry to Powell River departs Comox.

Comox Bay Marina and launch ramp

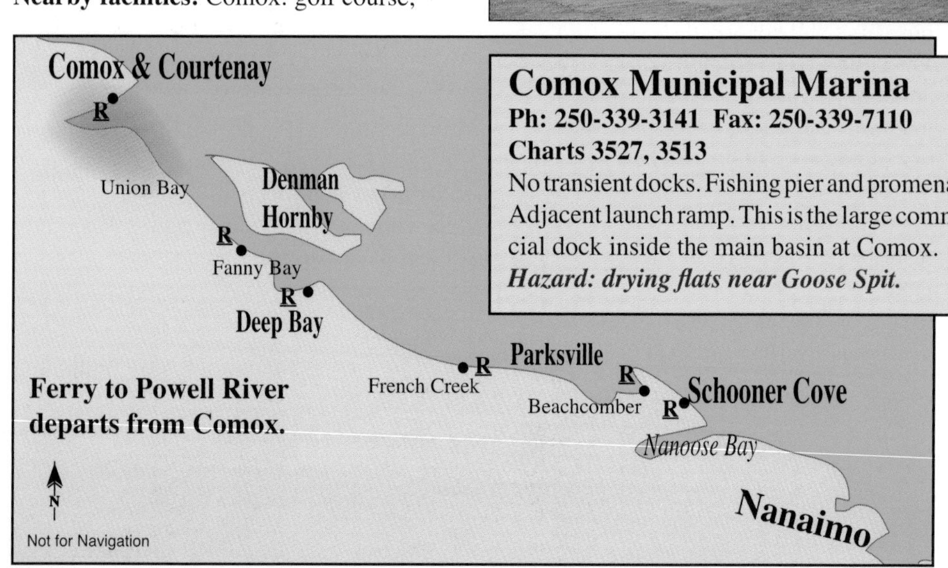

Comox Municipal Marina

Ph: 250-339-3141 Fax: 250-339-7110
Charts 3527, 3513
No transient docks. Fishing pier and promenad Adjacent launch ramp. This is the large comme cial dock inside the main basin at Comox.
Hazard: drying flats near Goose Spit.

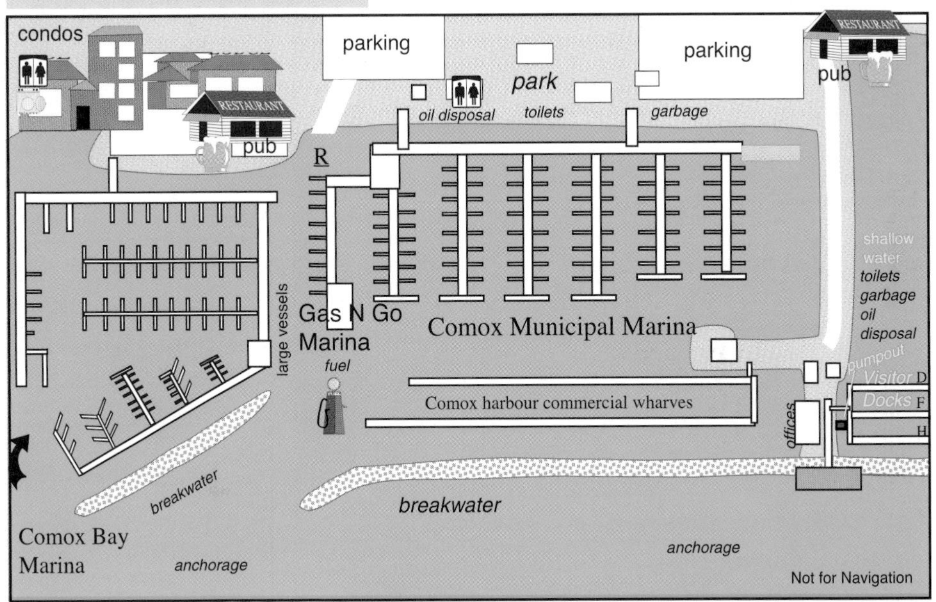

Courtenay Slough Marina

Ph: 250-339-6041

Comox Valley Harbour Authority. Launch ramp. Limited moorage for small boats. Walking distance to Courtenay. ***Hazard: Shallow river. Depths allow boat with shallow draft only– about 4 feet. Use chart*** *3527*. This marina is accessible only for small boats with shallow draft. The river delta dries at places at low tide. Range markers indicate the channel. Check with harbour authority before attempting to navigate the river. Note: Magnetic disturbance affects compass readings by two degrees in excess of normal in the vicinity of Comox. Adjacent airfield.

Right: Courtenay River drops to about four feet. There are range markers. Small craft only. Use chart, tide tables and caution. Slough Marina (pictured above).

49° 51.897' N
125°06.505' W

Saratoga Beach Golf Course 250-337-8212

Pacific Playgrounds Hazard–Channel may be entered at 4 foot (plus) tides. Follow pilings.

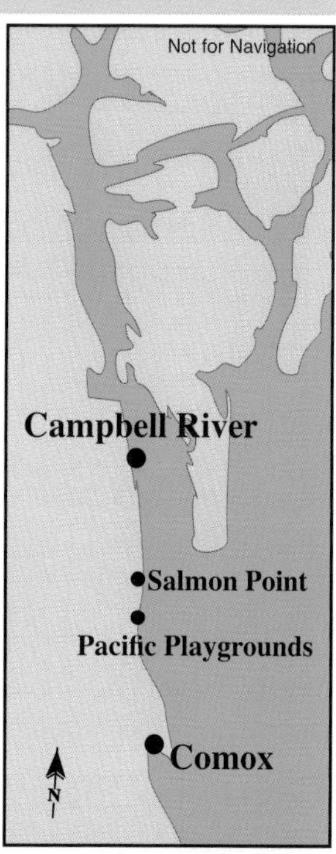

Comox to Campbell River

Pacific Playgrounds Resort & Marina

9082 Clarkson Dr
Black Creek BC V9J 1B3
Ph: 250-337-5600 Fax: 250-337-5979
info@pacificplaygrounds.com
www.pacificplaygrounds.com
(Alongside Oyster River Mouth.)
Call marina for guidance.

Marina: Moorage. Sheltered basin. Slips to 40 feet. **Fuel**: Gas. **Power:** 15 amp. **Marine store:** Supplies, tackle, charts, fishing licenses, groceries, public pay phone. Resort facilities including heated pool, grassy playground. **Showers, laundry, washrooms.** Garbage disposal.
Entertainment and nearby facilities: Golf, mini-golf, driving range, tennis, hiking roads and trails. Stores and restaurants. Scenery, sunsets and eagles. Nearby beach walks, bird watching. Fishing guides available.

Salmon Point Resort & Marina

Monica and Don Best
2176 Salmon Point Rd
Campbell River BC V9H 1E5
Ph: 250-923-6605 Fax: 250-923-7572
Toll free 1-866-246-6605
sales@salmonpoint.ca
www.salmonpoint.ca

Marina: Limited guest moorage for resort guests by land or water–no stayaboards. 150 slips (to 27ft). **Fuel:** Gas. Propane.
Water, power: 30, 50 amp.
Services: Many amenities–for resort moorage and RV guests. Restaurant. Grocery store. Hot tub, heated pool. Nature trails, tenting. **Laundry**. **Restrooms, showers**. Fishing guides and charters. Garbage disposal. Fish freezing. Internet access.
Entertainment and nearby:
Golf, mini-golf, driving range, tennis, hiking roads and trails. Stores. Scenery, sunsets and eagles. Nearby beach walks, bird watching. Fishing. Launch ramp at marina.

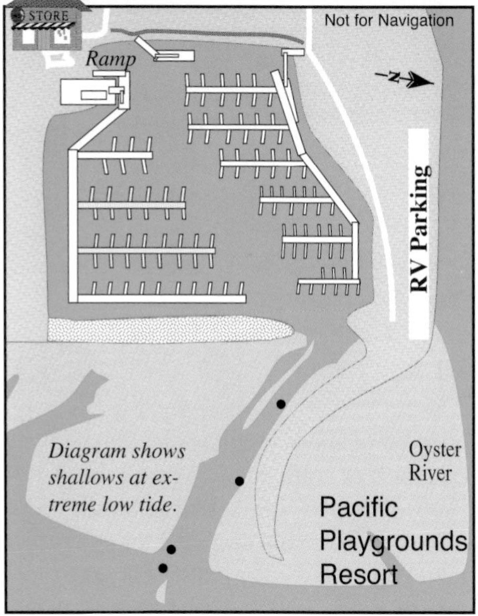

Above: Pacific Playgrounds launch ramp and the marina's entrance at high tide (opposite page). Top: Salmon Point Marina (diagram below).

Hazard: Narrow, shallow channel into Salmon Point Marina. Boats need a minimum of a 5' tide. Proceed between floats off breakwater. Call marina for guidance.
Phone: Toll free 1-866-246-6605

Opposite, top: Pacific Playgrounds with its open water entrance. Its approaches are shallow but clearly marked. NOTE: It dries at zero tide. Line up with the channel about 100 yards out. Check with marina.

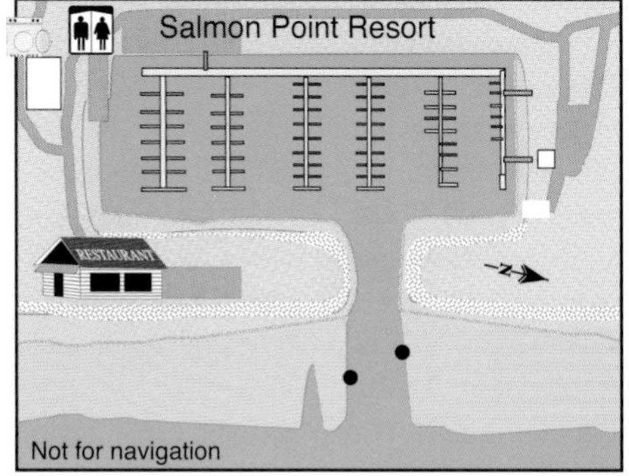

50° 01.917' N
125° 13.273' W

The Guest marina at April Point. Inset: Resort spa at the point.

Campbell River

April Point Resort & Spa

50° 03.927' N
125° 14.149' W

900 April Point Rd
Quadra Island BC V0P 1N0
Ph: 250-285-2222 Fax: 250-285-2411
april_point@obmg.com
www.aprilpoint.com
Charts 3312, 3540, 3539 VHF 66A

Many visiting boats in Campbell River head for the April Point Marina tucked into Quadra Island on the other side of Discovery Passage. The marina is located just beyond April Point.

Moorage. Large permanent marina with 4,000' overnight or extended seasonal moorage. Reservations recommended. Cable TV. Laundry, showers, washrooms. Ice. Garbage drop. Launch ramp.

Power at docks: 15, 30, 50 amp.

Customer services:
Lodge with full numerous amenities. Internet access. Fishing guides and charters. Restaurant. Breakfast, lunch, dinner. Open 7 days a week. Lounge, sushi bar. Coffee shop. Gift shop. Spa. Conference rooms. Walking trails or road access. Some beachfront walks. Scuba diving arrangements and charters–ask lodge for details.
Scooter rentals. Kayak rentals, eco-tours. Accommodations at lodge and bungalows. Transport to golf courses. Airport limo. Shuttle to and from Painters Lodge in Campbell River and access to their facilities including dining room, Sushi bar, gift shop, pub, swimming pool, exercise room.

Adjacent facilities:
Kenmore Air regular flights.
Liquor, grocery, arts and crafts and other stores including post office nearby.
Hiking trails at Rebecca Spit Provincial Park on Quadra Island. There is a large public marina at Quathiaski Cove.

Keep red channel marker close to starboard when approaching marina, red right return.

Above: Campbell River Fisherman's Wharf.

Fisherman's Wharf

Campbell River Harbour Authority
Linda Franz
Ph: 250-287-7931
Fax: 250-287-8495
fishermans@telus.net

50° 01.516' N
125° 14.274' W

VHF 66A

Open all year • Commercial and pleasure boats welcome–reservations suggested • Three tidal grids • Electric winches • Garbage disposal • Pumpout • Power: 20, 30, 50 amp • Pumpout • Washrooms • Showers • Ice, bait, tackle, seafood sales, charts. Wireless internet access. Marine service, mechanic, repairs, stores nearby. Near ferry to Quadra Island. Maritime museum.

April Point visitor docks.

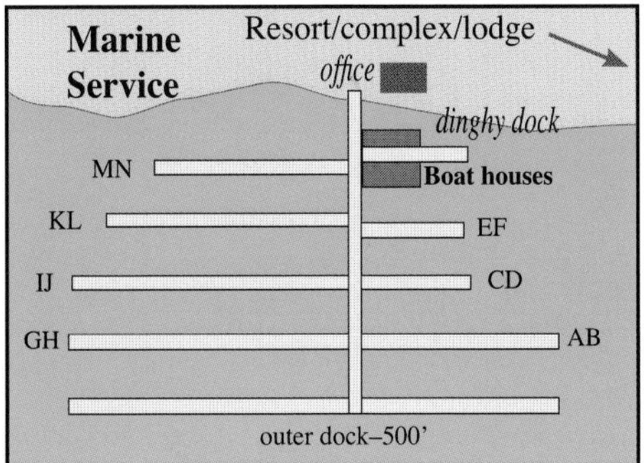

Above: The April Point Resort gift shop.

Cape Mudge
49° 58.55' N
125° 09.748' W

Cape Mudge

Quadra Island Harbour Authority
Ph: 250-285-3622 Charts 3540, 3539
The float is north of the tip of Cape Mudge, on First Nations land.
It was reported in poor condition in 2006.

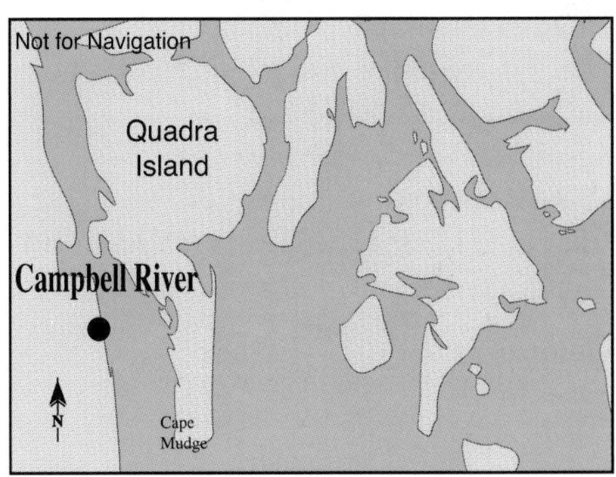

Above: Diagram shows location of Cape Mudge. A small community dock in Discovery Passage is exposed to wind and tidal currents.

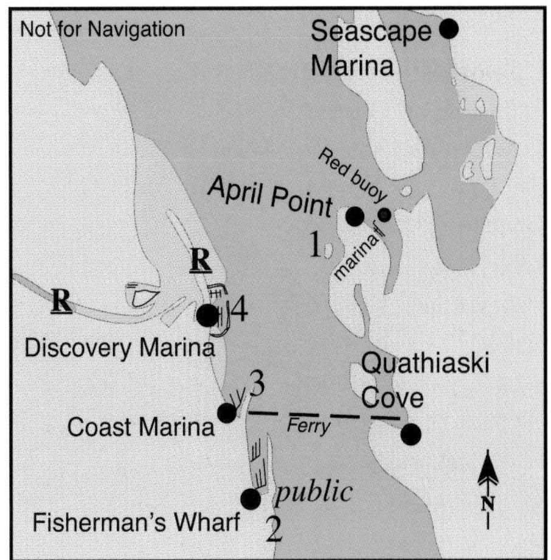

Above: Seascape Resort Marina dock. Seascape is located in Gowlland Harbour as seen in the diagram and the photograph below. Shallows at north end.

Seascape Marina

Mark & Jennifer Wanstall
PO Box 250
Quadra Island BC V0P 1N0
Ph: 250-285-3450 Fax: 250-285-2101
Toll Free 1-888-893-1626
info@seascapewaterfrontresort.com
www.seascapewaterfrontresort.com

Charts 3312, 3540, 3539 VHF 66A (10)

Marina services: Guest moorage, reservations preferred. **Power:** 15-amp. **Washrooms, showers,** laundry, ice, internet access, kayaking, power boat rentals, sauna/hot tub, video rentals.

Nearby facilities: Vineyard, restaurants, grocery store, post office, bank, marine mechanic, adventure charters, liquor store, float plane service.

Freshwater Marina

2705 Island Hwy
Campbell River BC V9W 4Z9
Ph: 250-286-0701 Fax: 250-286-1343

Above: Freshwater Marina on the Campbell River.

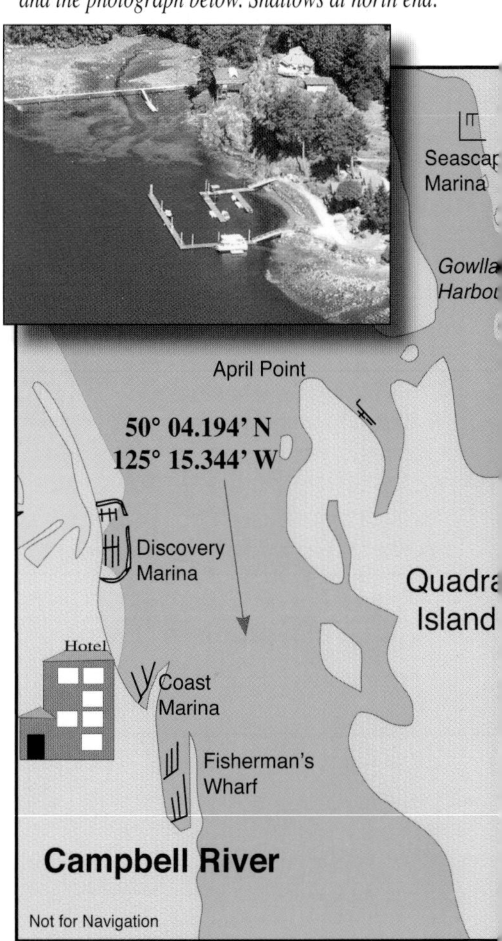

Coast Discovery C.R. Inn & Marina

975 Shoppers Row
Campbell River BC V9W 2C4
Ph: 250-287-7455 Fax: 250-287-2213
www.coasthotels.com
Charts 3540, 3539, 3312 VHF 66A

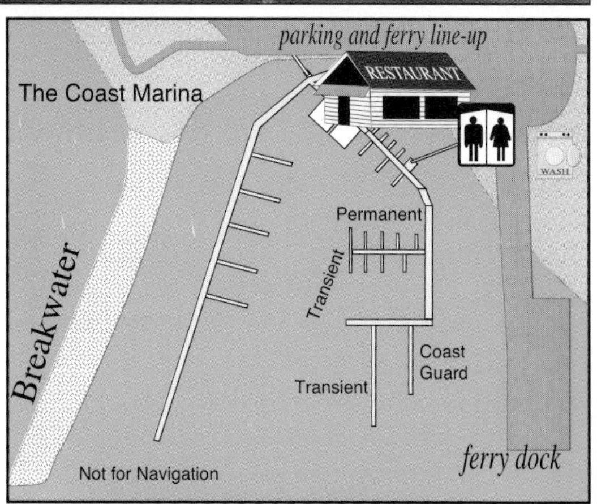

Marina Services:
Moorage. 1,900 feet docks. Boats to 150'. **Power:** 30, 50, 100 amp. Garbage disposal. Dockside services.
Customer services:
Showers, ice, bait. Cold beer, wine and spirits store. Laundry, washrooms, restaurant, pub, fitness centre, hot tub.
Entertainment:
Foreshore Park with walkway to scenic downtown Campbell River. Scuba diving arrangements and charters–ask marina for details. Fishing excellent in general area. Charters, boat rentals. Tours. Water taxi.
Adjacent facilities:
Opposite the marina is the Coast Discovery Inn and adjacent downtown shopping centre. Services, shops and retaurants are located in the city centre. Marine charts, books, fishing gear, licences and boat supplies are available at nearby marine stores. There is a large, modern shopping centre in Campbell River just north of this marina. Adjacent to the marina is the ferry landing for Quathiaski Cove on Quadra Island. Medical services nearby.

Above: A First Nations display near the Coast Marina.

Below: Coast Marina docks are near the ferry terminal.

Discovery Harbour Marina

Discovery Harbour Marina

Manager: Vicky Logos
392-1434 Island Hwy VHF 66A
Campbell River BC V9W 5T7
Ph: 250-287-2614 Fax: 250-287-8939
Charts 3540, 3539, 3312
dhml@oberon.ark.com
www.discoveryharbourmarina.com

Marina services:
Fuel: At Esso dock. Gas, diesel, oils.
Moorage: 150 berths for guest moorage. Boats to 100 feet and over.
Power at docks: 20, 30, 50, 100 amp.
Water. The launch ramp is a short distance north of the marina. Dockside marine service arranged. Expansion to docks is ongoing.
Customer services:
Laundry, showers, ice, bait. Garbage disposal. Road access walking or cycling. Vehicle rentals in town. All amenities.
Entertainment:
Sport fishing and scuba diving are excellent in the area. There are strong tidal currents and it is suggested that divers use local dive operators as guides. House of Treasure native art gallery next door.

Above: Quathiaski Cove public dock.

Quathiaski Cove

Quadra Island Harbour Authority
Public dock (DFO)
Paul Ryan manager
Ph: 250-285-3622
Charts 3540, 3539, 3312
Manager • Float length 195 metres • Launch ramp • Garbage accepted for a fee • Waste oil disposal • Lights • Power • Public pay phone • Shipyard. Shops nearby. Adjacent ferry to Campbell River. Fuel at Discovery Marina, Heriot Bay–Ph: 250-285-3212. : Diesel, gas, outboard mix, water, propane, oil.

Travelling North–use the guide: *North of Desolation Sound*
Going south– use *The Gulf Islands Cruising Guide*

50° 02.573' N
125° 13.045' W
Quathiaski Cove

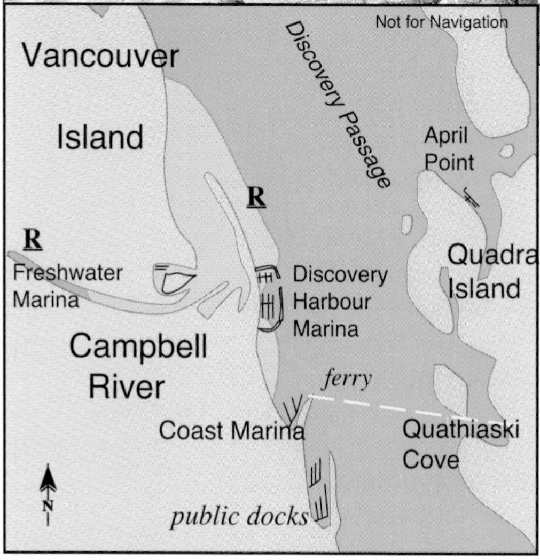

Not for Navigation
Vancouver
Island
Discovery Passage
April
Point
R
R
Freshwater
Marina
Discovery
Harbour
Marina
Quadra
Island
Campbell
River
ferry
Coast Marina
Quathiaski
Cove
N
public docks

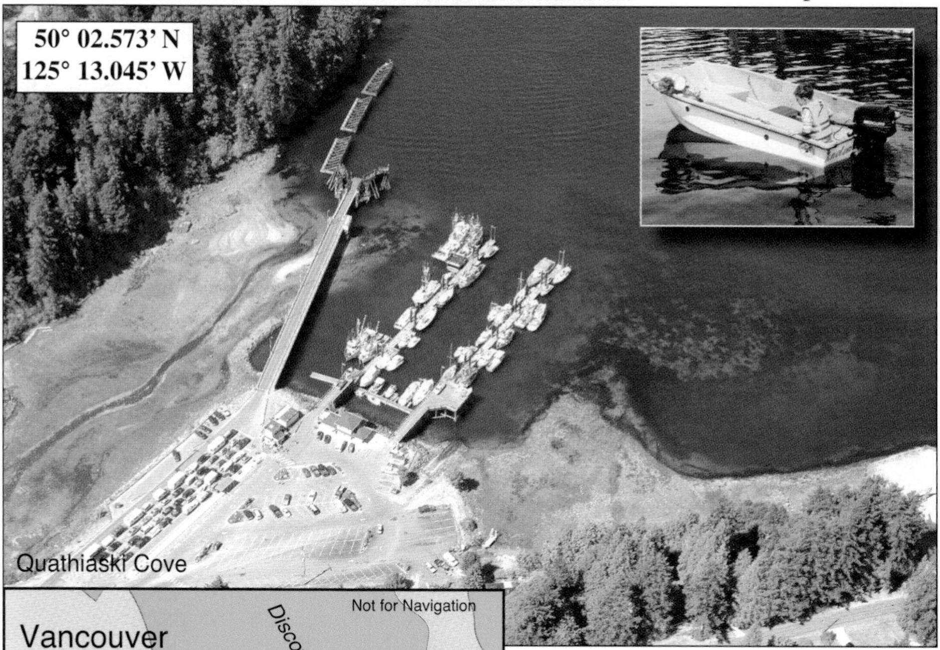

Above: Quathiaski Cove dock and ferry landing at Q Cove (Quathiaski Cove)
Opposite: Discovery Harbour Marina is a large facility with a vast breakwater.
It is on First Nations land and is operated by the local native band.
There is a large shopping complex adjacent to the marina.
Below: Dock A is for 18 foot boats, B is for 20, C & D for 24, E & F for 30, H is for 36, I and J are for 40 and K for 100 footers.

Not for Navigation
Discovery Harbour Marina
Fuel
A
B
C
D
E
F
G
H
I
J
K
office

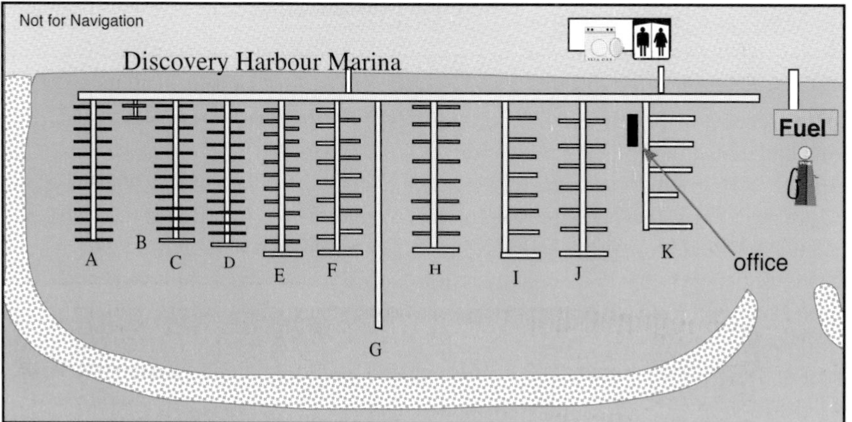

Brown's Bay Marina

Jon Dawson and Mike Sparks
15021 Brown's Bay Rd
Campbell River BC V9W 7H6
Ph: 250-286-3135
Fax: 250-286-0951
www.brownsbayresort.com
Charts 3539, 3513, 3312

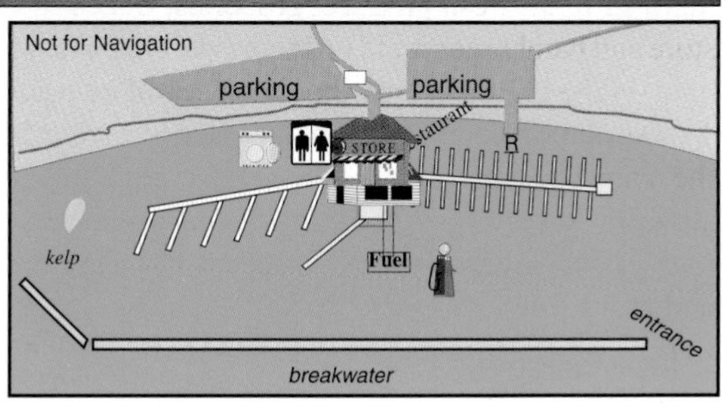

Marina services: Seasonal fishing resort. **Fuel:** Gas, diesel, oils. Moorage. Transient moorage available. Boats to 90 feet. **Power** at docks: 15, 30 amp. Water. Ice. Garbage disposal.

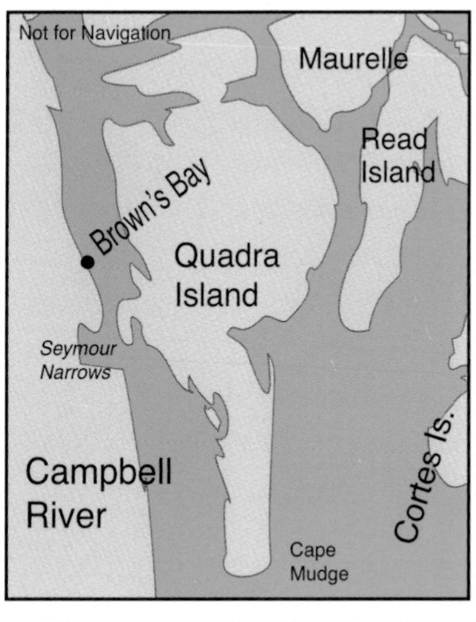

Customer services:
Bed and breakfast accommodation. RV sites. **Laundry, showers.** Bait, public pay phone ashore. Store. Foul weather gear, clothing, tide tables, tackle, fishing licences. Fish cleaning station. **Launch ramp.** Seasonal restaurant–licensed.
Entertainment: Boat rentals. Fishing. Wildlife viewing. Guides available. Charters.
Walking: Unpaved road in fair condition. Walking or cycling. Cyclists beware of road traffic. Fishing superior in general area near the harbour.
Adjacent facilities:
Ripple Rock RV Park–many facilities.

Campbell River is a busy place. There are resorts at this international sportfishing playground that cater to fishermen and eco-tourists, offering guided salmon fishing and tournaments and adventure tourism. Some lodges with marinas offer no transient moorage while others have an open door to overnight boating stops. The velocity of water surging through Seymour Narrows just north of the town is dangerous. Be mindful of tides and currents, especially when venturing through the narrows or around the bottom of Quadra Island and its infamous Cape Mudge during gusty winds and swift moving tidal waters.

Fuel up at Campbell River or just beyond Seymour Narrows at Brown's Bay, because you may not find fuel too conveniently for a while if you are heading north up Johnstone Strait. There is fuel at Blind Channel or Refuge Cove in Desolation Sound. It is available at Heriot Bay on the east side of Quadra Island as well as at Gorge Harbour on Cortes Island.

Desolation Sound
and the Discovery Islands

Section 5

Once in Desolation Sound you will not be stuck for fuel because there is a full service fuel stop at Refuge Cove. This facility is a centre for all boating needs to serve the cruising mariner. It has fresh produce, groceries, frozen foods, books, charts, liquor and more. The store and hamburger stand on the property above the marina makes an ideal place to wander or sit in the sun and enjoy the ambience of being out boating.

Desolation Sound is a popular place to anchor for days on end in the summertime. From the many coves and bays of Grace Harbour or Prideaux Haven to Pendrell Sound and Walsh Cove, or Roscoe Bay, Theodosia Inlet, Van Donop Inlet and Squirrel Cove to name a few, one can find the ideal place to set up home aboard for a few days or play musical moorages and move from one to the next as one spends a summer vacation in this warm water oasis in BC. Move early in the day to avoid difficulty in finding a place to drop anchor in some of the busier bays.

To the west is Heriot Bay for moorage and fuel and Drew Harbour with its anchorage behind Rebecca Spit. Kayaking is drawing increasing numbers to this area each year. Go to Surge Narrows from Heriot Bay, or cross over and spend the rest of your vacation at Gorge Harbour, one of the most sheltered large bays in the area, with a fine marina and restaurant to keep you in comfort for your stay. There is fuel at Gorge Harbour, a store, all facilities plus petroglyphs on the sheer rock face at the entrance. In the vicinity you may want to stop in for a stroll at nearby Whaletown. Dock space is limited. *See* **Anchorages and Marine Parks** *for more information on Desolation Sound.*

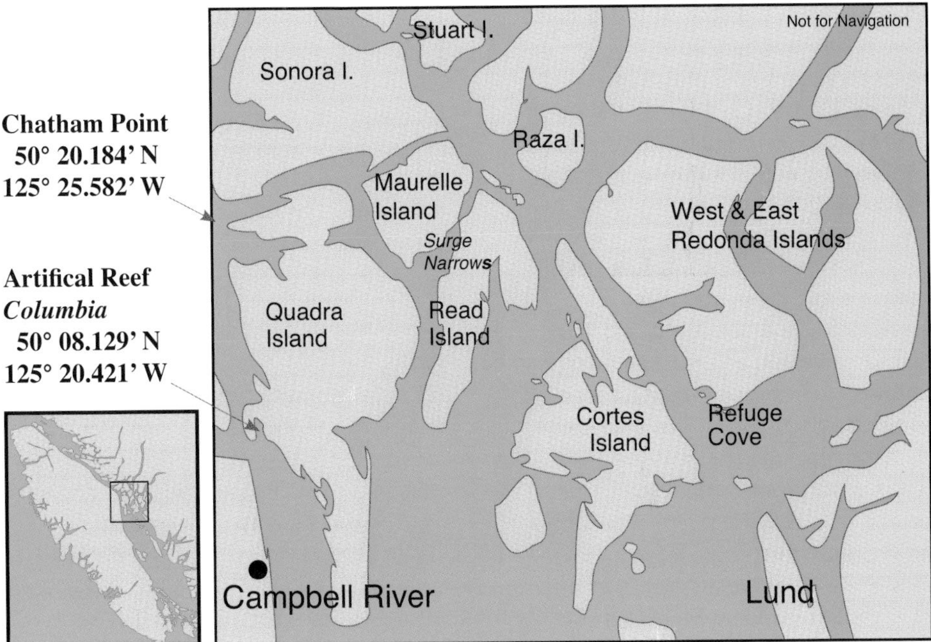

50° 05.419' N
125° 02.227' W

Gorge Harbour

1. Gorge Harbour Marina Resort

Barb Hansen & Grant Clarke
1374 Hunt Rd, PO Box 89
Whaletown, Cortes Island BC V0P 1Z0
Ph: 250-935-6433 Fax: 250-935-6402
info@gorgeharbour.com
www.gorgeharbour.com

Charts 3538, 3312, 3311 VHF 66A

Marina services: Fuel: Gas, diesel, oil. **Moorage:** 1,800' guest moorage. Water. **Power** at docks: 15, 30 amp.

Customer services:
Grocery store. Coffee counter, pastries, fishing licences, tackle. ice, books, gifts, charts, propane, postage stamps. Internet access. **Laundry, showers, washrooms.** Garbage drop. Boat rentals. Private rooms with showers. Charters arranged. Fish cleaning station on docks. Gazebo for groups or casual use.

Entertainment:
Adjoining campground with facilities. Trail to roadway. Walk to rustic Whaletown. Art Gallery nearby. Video and DVD rentals. Restaurant dining. Library, store, post office at Whaletown.

Adjacent facilities:
Licensed restaurant on property. Dinner only May 1–September 30 and weekends off season. Breakfast, dinner and lunch–July & August only. Art and museum on island. RVs, Campground. Vehicle rentals.

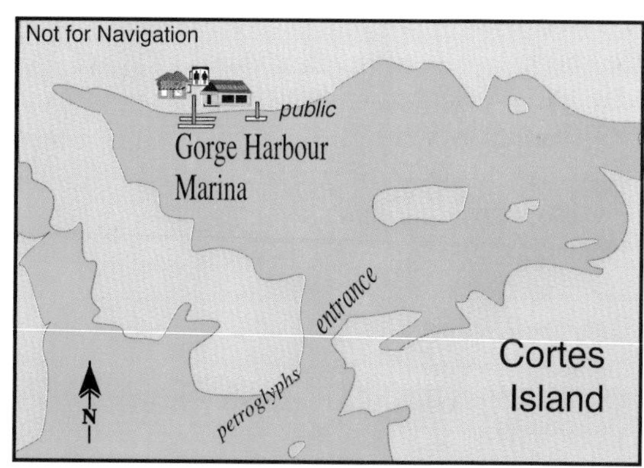

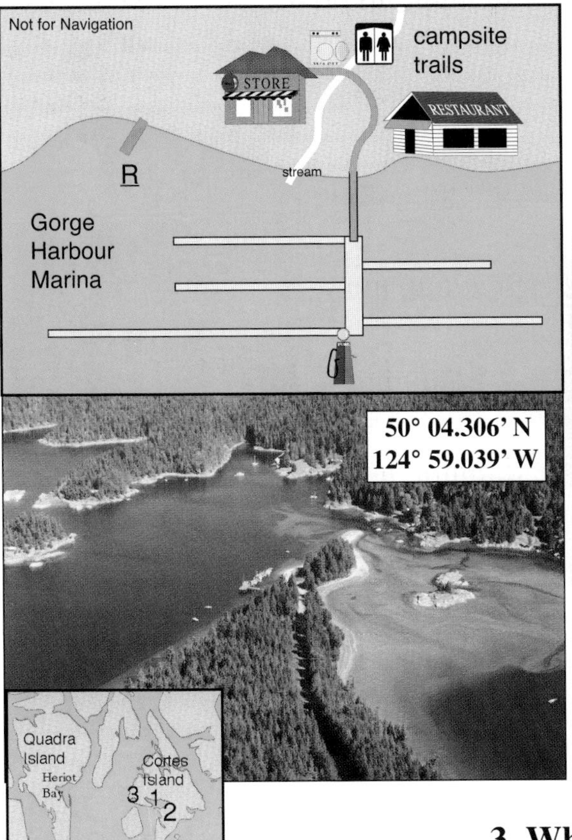

Below: The entrance to Gorge Harbour is narrow and subject to current. There are petroglyphs on the rock face to port. Bottom left and right: Manson's Landing and Whaletown. Opposite: Gorge Harbour Marina. Grant Clarke and Barb Hansen.

2. Manson's Landing

public dock and marine park

Merle Boley

Ph: 250-935-0053

Charts 3311, 3538 VHF 66A

Hazard: Exposed to westerly winds. Shallows on north approaches.

Moorage:

Limited moorage at small government dock. See the companion guide to this one– *Anchorages and Marine Parks*.

Alternative services:

Groceries nearby at Gorge Harbour. Road to store and cafe.

Entertainment:

Walking on island roads. Beaches. Lagoon.

Adjacent facilities:

Marine Park, toilets Public pay phone.

50° 06.479' N
125° 03.179' W

3. Whaletown

Whaletown General Store

George Frost

PO Box 26, Cortes Island BC V0P 1K0

Ph: 250-935-6562 Fax: 250-935-6624

Charts 3538, 3311

Hazard: Rock near government dock. See chart 3538.

Marina services: *No garbage.*

Transient, limited moorage at public dock.

Customer services:

Post office (Mon, Wed, Fri). Store: groceries, bakery goods, fresh produce, ice cream cones, milk, frozen foods, propane, ice, water, tackle, bait, charts, novelties, gifts. Video rentals. Liquor agency.

Entertainment:

Walking on island roads, swimming, scuba diving, fishing, kayaking, bird watching.

Adjacent facilities:

Ferry to Quadra. Public pay phone. Library nearby.

50° 06.159' N
125° 12.737' W

Heriot Bay

Heriot Bay Inn and Marina

Manager Steve Addison
PO Box 100, Heriot Bay
Quadra Island BC V0P 1H0
Ph: 250-285-3322 Fax: 250-285-2708
Toll free 1-888-605-4545
Charts 3538/9, 3312   VHF 66A
info@heriotbayinn.com
www.heriotbayinn.com

Marina services:
Fuel: Gas. Diesel. Oil. Propane.
Moorage 1800' of docks. Reservations recommended. **Power**: 15, 30 amps. Fish cleaning station. Water taxi service.

Customer services:
Restaurant–patio service (seasonal), pub–The Logger & The Fisherman. Kayak rentals. Fishing licences, bait, tackle. Store. Ice, books, gifts, charts. **Laundry, showers, washrooms.** Private rooms at Inn. Cottages. Water taxi.

Heriot Bay Public dock
Quadra Island Harbour Authority
Paul Ryan manager Ph: 250-285-3555
giha@island.net
Year round guest docks • Launch ramp
• Garbage • Lights • Power: 15, 30 amp
• Charts 3538, 3539, 3312

Entertainment:
Historic Heriot Bay Inn and its classic pub. Internet connection. Fishing, sight-seeing charters. Good scuba diving nearby. Bicycle rentals at marina. Walking–roadway and some beach access at nearby Rebecca Spit. Whale and bear watching. Kayaking, adventure packages. Guides fishing and kayak tours.

Adjacent and nearby facilities:
Repairs and marine service. Heriot Bay Store, liquor store and mini shopping centre–delivery to boats–Ph: 250-285-2436. Post office, grocery store at centre. RV Park. Hook-ups, tents. Popular anchorage in Drew Harbour at Rebecca Spit Marine Park. Public dock.

Taku Resort

PO Box 1, Heriot Bay
Quadra Island BC V0P 1H0
Ph: 250-285-3031 Fax: 250-285-3712
Toll free 1-877-285-8258
Charts 3538/9, 3312   VHF 66A
info@takuresort.com www.takuresort.com
Guest moorage 800'. **Power** at docks: 30, 50 amp. **Washrooms, laundry, showers.** Luxury resort. Accommodations by reservation. RV site. Easy walk to small shopping centre–groceries, coffee shop.

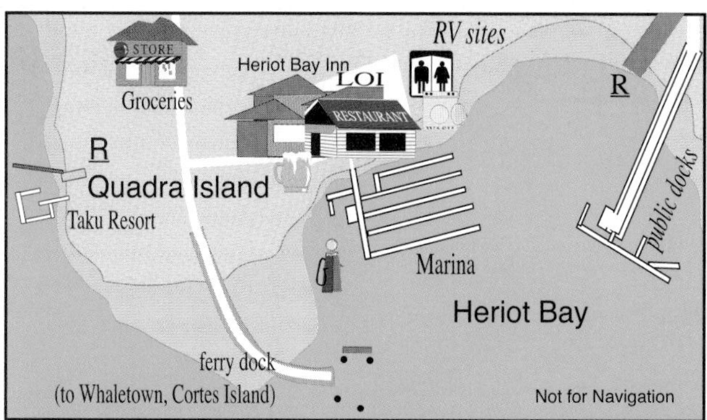

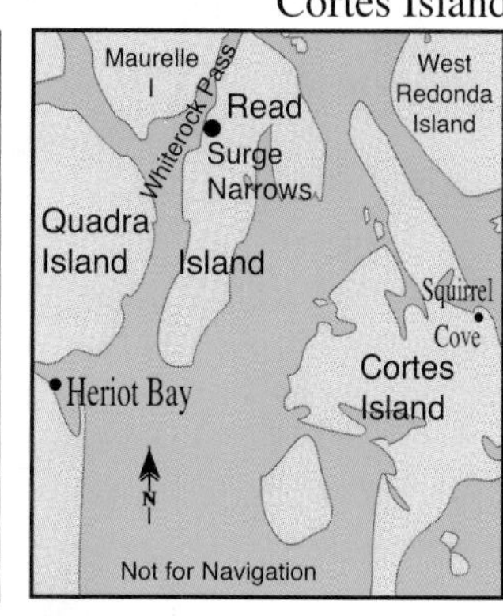

Whiterock Pass (north end)
50° 15.055' N
125° 06.061' W
(south end)
50° 14.561' N
125° 06.877' W

Surge Narrows
50° 13.629' N
125° 06.756' W

Surge Narrows

Doug and Teresa Beyerstein
PO Box 31, Surge Narrows
Read Island BC V0P 1W0 VHF 12
Ph: 250-287-6962

Charts 3312, 3537, 3539

Moorage: 200 foot public dock and aircraft float with post office–open Mon, Wed, Fri 1 to 4 pm. **General store:** Island fresh produce, baked goods and provisions. Coffee, snacks. Some hardware and marine supplies. Near south entrance to Whiterock Pass.

Below: The store and the post office on the wharf at Surge Narrows. This is a classic old fashioned store.

Passage through nearby Whiterock Pass to the Rendezvous Islands is a good alternative route to Big Bay. Check charts for depths.

Opposite page: The Heriot Bay Inn marina lies between the Cortes Island ferry dock and the public marina. It is used also by families checked into the adjacent RV park. Inset: Inside the gift shop at Heriot Bay Inn. Above: The historic Heriot Bay Inn. Below: Taku Resort in Drew Harbour. The marina is opposite Rebecca Spit.

Cortes Bay

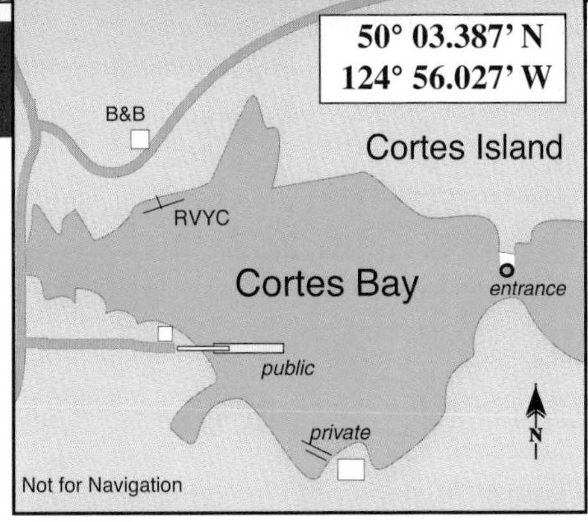

Cortes Bay public dock

Cortes Island
Harbourmaster: Siri Ellingsen
PO Box 243
Manson's Landing BC V0P 1K0
Phone: 250-935-6545, 250-935-0181
Charts 3555, 3538, 3312

Hazard: Entering bay–keep rock and day marker at entrance to starboard (passage south of marker).

Moorage at government dock. About 200 feet of dock, wide and solid. **Power** at dock: 20 amp. Seaplane dock. Pay phone ashore although cell phone reception is good. Launch ramp nearby.

Cortes Bay

The public dock is wide and sturdy although not anchored at the deep end. It is controlled by a wharfinger and shared with local residents owning pleasure and commercial craft. Space is limited. Many yachtsmen favour anchoring out in the bay.

Check with the wharfinger for island attractions such as the craft stores and the market. There are two yacht club out-stations in the bay, the Royal Vancouver and the Seattle yacht clubs. Neither of them permits non-member moorage.

Cortes Public Dock

Top: Cortes Bay with public dock to left, entrance to right. Note passage to south of the reef at the entrance.
Right top and bottom: Cortes Bay public dock.

Squirrel Cove General Store

O'Byrne Taylor
1611 Forest, Cortes Island BC V0P 1R0
Ph: 250-935-6327 Fax: 250-935-6327
Charts 3555, 3538, 3312 VHF 66A
squirrelcovetrading@yahoo.ca
www.cortesisland.com/squirrelcove

Public dock. Lights and power. Additional, free high tide dock (to left of main dock in photo–dries at low water). Garbage drop.

Squirrel Cove Store Customer services: Gas, diesel. Groceries. Organic foods. Fresh meat, prawns and salmon. Baked goods and fresh produce, milk, frozen foods, ice, water, tackle, bait, charts. Propane. Liquor. Gifts. Marine and hardware supplies. Marine batteries. Post office. Small launch ramp. Fuels. **Showers, laundry**. Dining at The Cove Restaurant on the beach with a large patio overlooking Desolation Sound. Home baking, full menu. Licensed. Ph: 250-935-6350. Hiking. Island roads. Beaches. Lagoon.

Above: The dock at Squirrel Cove is outside the actual cove. Below: Aerial view of Squirrel Cove. Entrance is the passage at lower right.

Adjacent/nearby facilities:
Squirrel Cove Marine Park. Anchorage. Crafts and garden store. Outdoor market on Wednesdays and Sundays.

50° 07.436' N
124° 50.411' W

Refuge Cove

Charts 3555, 3538, 3312 VHF 66A

Refuge Cove

Colin and Lucy Robertson, Bill Shillito
Refuge Cove BC V0P 1P0
Ph: 250-935-6659
refcov@twincomm.ca

Marina services:
Fuel: Gas. Diesel, oil, propane.
Water at dock. **Power**: 15 amp.
Moorage: Overnight moorage, 1,100 feet of docks. Rafting permitted. Internet access.
Customer services:
Laundry, showers, washrooms.
Grocery store, post office. Liquor, ice, books, gifts, charts, Public pay phone.
Adjacent facilities:
Hamburger stand.

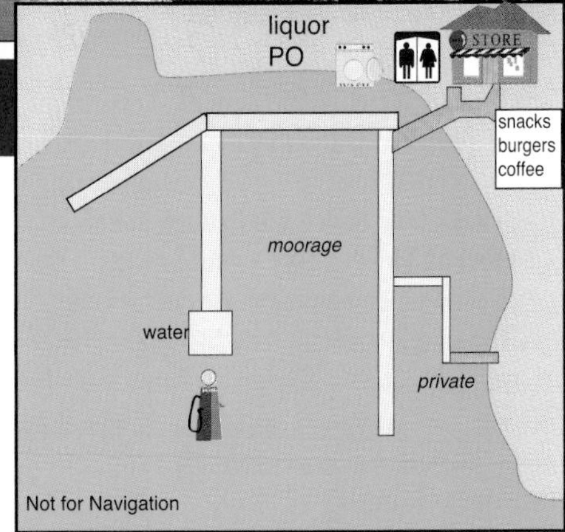

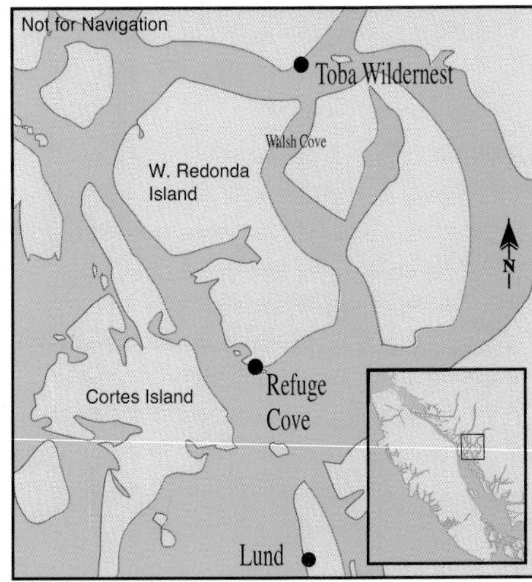

Above: Lucy Robertson (centre) and friends at the Refuge Cove General Store. Below: Tied up at the foot of the ramp to the store. Opposite page, top: A visiting boat slowly approaches the busy marina and fuel dock.

Desolation Sound

En route to all parts of Desolation Sound, Refuge Cove is a busy stop during the brief summer season. It affords replenishment of everything from fuels and fresh water to liquor, fresh produce, bread, meat and groceries. Charts, books and a limited selection of clothing are also sold at the store, as well as ice and fishing supplies. The store is positioned high and dry above the high-water mark. It and the fuel dock are run efficiently to accommodate the heavy traffic of the short summer season and survive the balance of the year.

50° 20.236' N
124° 46.116' W

Toba Wildernest

Toba Wildernest
Kyle and Andrea Hunter
Mouth of Toba Inlet at
Double Island VHF 66A
Desolation Sound Ph: 250-830-2269
Charts 3312, 3541
tobawildernest@lincsat.com
www.fishingwildernest.com

Moorage for overnight or longer-350 feet. Facilities: Shower and washroom. Small store with basic goods. Ice. Fishing supplies. Forest trails to nearby waterfall which provides power for resort. This is a nature resort offering rental cabins for boaters and fly-in guests. It is located at the mouth of Toba Inlet just north of Walsh Cove in Desolation Sound.

Top: Dock at Toba Wildernest. Above: Falls in Toba Inlet. Below: Kyle Hunter at the resort and marina office. This is a nature resort for mariners and fly-in guests.

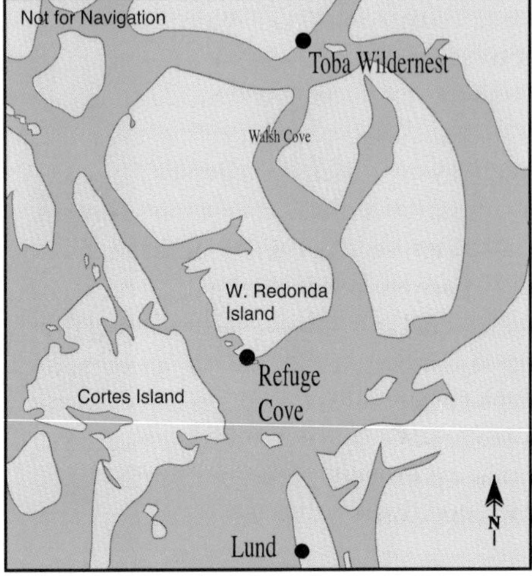

Big Bay to Port Hardy

North of Desolation Sound

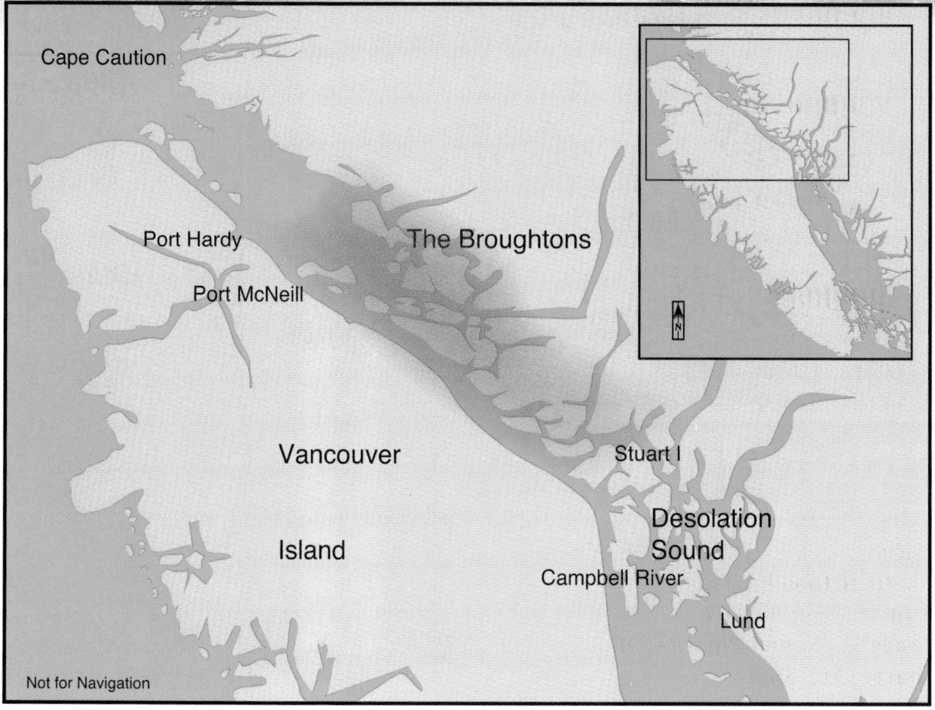

Travelling north of Desolation Sound the mariner must plan passage through the famous Yaculta Rapids, Dent Rapids, Green Point Rapids and Whirlpool Rapids. Or travel via Seymour Narrows and Kelsey Bay into Johnstone Strait. Slower boats would do well to plan stops through the waterways in which these rapids lie so as to take advantage of the best tidal currents. High water slack is usually best and it is particularly easier when the tidal changes are minimal. Stopping at places along the way rather than rushing through as many of the current-swept passages as possible in one leg allows for interesting meetings with local residents. Stop at the marinas along the Cordero Channel route to Port Neville in Johnstone Strait. Take advantage of the facilities provided at the various marinas and resorts and make that an integral part of your trip, if not your actual destination.

Churchhouse First Nations settlement just south of Stuart Island. It is slowly succumbing to nature.

Stuart Island

Stuart Island Community Dock

Stuart Island BC V0P 1V0 VHF 66A
Manager: Roger & Cathy Minor
Phone: 250-202-3625
Charts 3312, 3543
stuartislandca@aol.com
Docks expanded and reconfigured.
Guest moorage: water, washrooms, showers, laundry, coffee shop, grocery store, liquor store, post office, ice, fishing supplies.
Nearby facilities: Water taxi, float plane service, adventure charters.

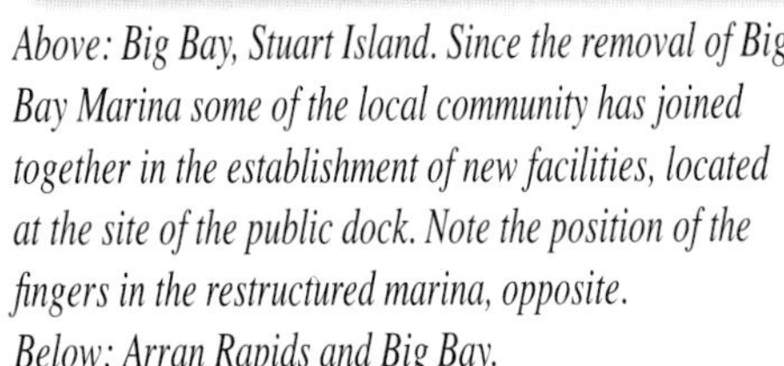

Above: Big Bay, Stuart Island. Since the removal of Big Bay Marina some of the local community has joined together in the establishment of new facilities, located at the site of the public dock. Note the position of the fingers in the restructured marina, opposite.
Below: Arran Rapids and Big Bay.

Big Bay marks the beginning of the run through the rapids north to Cordero Channel, Johnstone Strait, the Broughton Islands and beyond. It is the passage of choice over Seymour Narrows for most small craft.
Be mindful of the strong currents in the area. Use charts and tide and current tables to plan your passage.

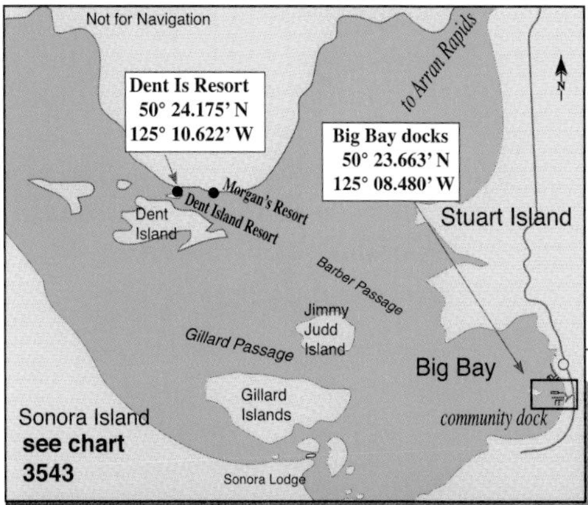

Not for Navigation

Dent Is Resort
50° 24.175' N
125° 10.622' W

to Arran Rapids

Big Bay docks
50° 23.663' N
125° 08.480' W

Morgan's Resort
Dent Island Resort
Dent Island
Stuart Island
Barber Passage
Jimmy Judd Island
Gillard Passage
Big Bay
Gillard Islands
community dock
Sonora Island
see chart 3543
Sonora Lodge

Below: The way north. From Big Bay, mariners travel through Gillard Passage and along Cordero Channel. Avoiding the worst of the currents takes careful planning. Use the tide and current tables.
Seen in the photo is the exclusive Sonora Lodge, a well-known fishing resort. Its docks may accommodate a few visitors overnight as space permits.

Morgan's Landing Resort

Bob and Jodé Morgan
PO Box 5-3 Stuart Island BC V0P 1V0
Ph: 250-287-0237 Fax: 250-287-1237
Charts 3543, 3312 VHF 66A
morgans@morganslanding.bc.ca
www.morganslanding.bc.ca

Marina services: Moorage, Open May to Sept 15. 200' dock space. **Fishing Resort. Water. Power** at docks: 30, 50 amp. Fish cleaning station.

Customer services:

Showers, Washrooms. Restaurant. Breakfast, lunch, dinner. Patio tables. Fishing licences, bait, tackle, ice. Cabin available.

Fishing charters. Guides. Good fishing.

Scuba diving nearby.

Entertainment:

Walk in coastal trails. Wildlife viewing/guided. Bear watching tours–Grizzlies August 15/September 15.

Nearby facilities:

Post office. Seaplane landing and mooring. Big Bay public dock. The public dock has been expanded and new facilities added. Note: Nearest fuel is at Refuge Cove or Blind Channel.

Morgan's Landing Resort offers overnight stops and facilities. Home baking and a cosy atmosphere attract many regular guests.

Hazards: Shoal in centre of Big Bay near the community dock. Strong currents in the area. Please slow to 5 kn on approach.

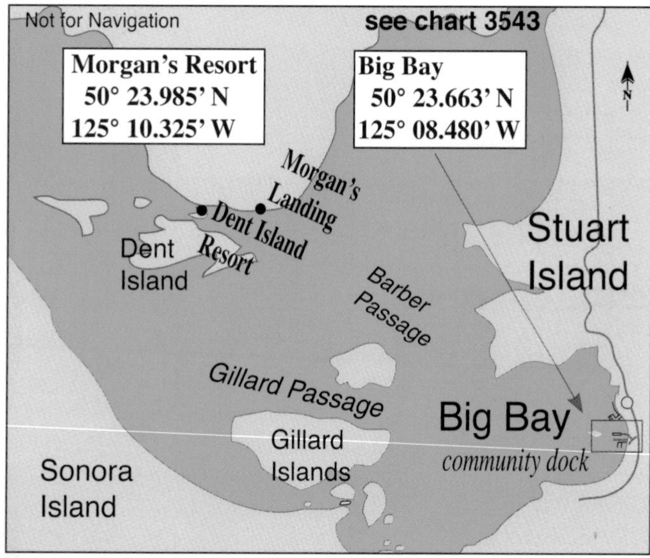

Arriving at Dent Island Lodge docks. This is a luxury resort providing marine moorage and lodge facilities to overnight guests (docks below left). Below: Morgan's Landing Resort dock.

Dent Island Resort

Henry Moll, Denise Mitchell-Hills
Stuart Island BC V0P 1V0
Ph: 250-203-2553 Fax: 250-203-1041
Charts 3312, 3543 VHF 66A
www.dentisland.com
marina@dentisland.com
Moorage. Visitors dock–700 feet.
Facilities: Lodge with overnight accommodation and full service. Restaurant. **Power:** 30, 50 amp. Showers. **Water. Washrooms. Showers.** Ice. Laundry. Hot tub and sauna. Fishing guides. Scheduled seaplane. Water taxi service.

In Big Bay mariners are advised to enter and leave with caution, noting the shallows near the shore facilities. Consult your chart and watch for kelp–a summertime marker for the reef.

At Shoal Bay a public dock with fairly generous moorage provides overnight accommodation. Owner Mark MacDonald offers fresh laid eggs and homegrown garden greens.

Shoal Bay Lodge is open May 1 to October 1. The facility offers outdoor adventure. It is a good overnight spot to tie up or anchor out in calm conditions. Usually it is only winter time when one has to be mindful of adverse winds coming down out of Phillips Arm.

Cordero Channel

50° 27.751' N
125° 21.995' W

Shoal Bay Lodge & Marina

Mark MacDonald **VHF 66A**
Ph: 250-287-6818
Charts 3543, 3312
mark.mac@shoalbaylodge.com
www.shoalbaylodge.com

Laundry, washrooms, showers. Cosy cabin restaurant. Liquor/pub. U-pick fresh vegetables. Eggs. Hiking trails. Logging roads. View points along a network of paths. Fishing can be arranged. View animals, marine life and eagles.

Nearby: Canoeing and kayaking. Day trips in the adjacent waterways. Includes Thurston Bay.

Public dock managed by Shoal Bay Lodge.
Shoal Bay, East Thurlow Island.
Float length: 300 feet.

Charts 3538, 3539, 3312

Owen Bay

Read Island public dock
Manager • Float length 9 metres

Evans Bay

Read Island Public dock
Float length 18 metres

Slow down when passing. The floating lodge pictured above, in Cordero Channel–is known internationally for fine dining and successful fishing charters. Inset: Doris Kuppers.

50° 26.717' N
125° 26.906' W

Cordero Lodge **VHF 66A**

Reinhardt and Doris Kuppers
G D Blind Channel BC V0P 1B0
Ph: 250-287-0917 Fax: 250-287-8840
info@corderolodge.com
www.corderolodge.com
Charts 3543, 3312
Marina services: 500' guest moorage. No power or water.
Customer services: Lodging–up to eight guests. Restaurant–fine dining. Fishing: Boats–guided or unguided. Mariners are requested to slow down when passing by.
Entertainment:
Sunsets and views. Animal and marine life. Bears and eagles.
Adjacent facilities:
Cordero Islands anchoring–***use caution as strong currents sweep through the area.***

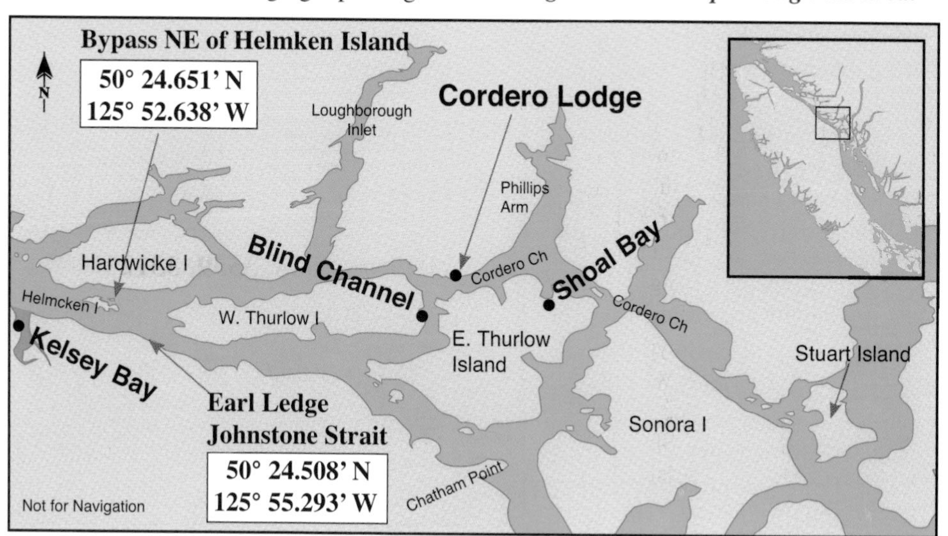

50° 24.797' N
125° 29.984' W

Blind Channel waterfront restaurant.

Blind Channel

Blind Channel Resort

Philip Richter
Blind Channel BC V0P 1B0
Ph: 250-949-1420
Toll free: 1-888-329-0475
Charts 3544, 3543 VHF 66A
info@blindchannel.com
www:blindchannel.com

Marina services:
Moorage: Transient moorage.
Fuel: Gas, diesel, propane.
Spring drinking water at dock. Ice.
Power at docks: 15, 20 amp–30 amp plug
Wireless Internet access.

Customer services:
Restaurant open June—Labour Day. Fine dining-excellent cuisine. Patio. Post office. Public pay phone. Groceries. Baked goods, bread, fresh produce, milk, frozen foods, ice, tackle, bait, charts.
Rental cottage available.
Laundry, showers, washrooms.
Liquor. Art, crafts, g ifts.
Excellent fishing and prawning nearby.
Scheduled flights.

Entertainment:
Hiking trails. Logging roads. Several view points along a network of paths. See the huge "Thurlow" Cedar tree. Incredible sunsets and views. Animal and marine life. Eagles. Docks are wide with tasteful embellishments.

Adjacent facilities:
Picnic area.

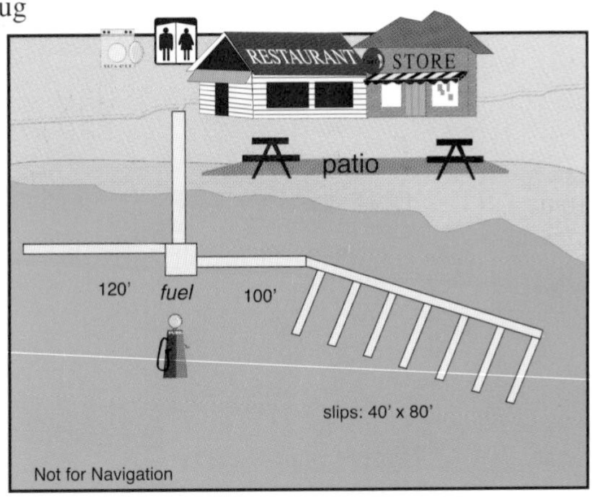

Blind Channel **Fine Dining and good facilities**

This long-established marina in one of the coast's busy waterways has evolved over the years to become a well maintained and contemporary facility for cruising yachtsmen. Three generations of Richters are busy around Blind Channel when guests are moored at their docks. Philip Richter's parents established the marina. Founder Edgar Richter still lives at the property and continues to be involved with planning and preparing further additions. Philip manages the store while his wife, Jennifer, can be found preparing bread and other baked delectables for the store and restaurant. She also attends a productive vegetable garden and landscape planting on the property. The marina offers moorage, fuel, water, propane and 20 amp shore power at the dock. The services include showers, laundry, ice, liquor agency, store and post office.

Nature lovers and hikers will be kept busy for days hiking trails that have been established by a large logging and sawmill company on West Thurlow Island. These trails, which begin about 300 meters from Blind Channel Marina, are designed to show the features of a second growth forest. There are three different trails, one to a spectacular viewpoint overlooking Mayne Passage and East Thurlow Island, a second to the "Big Cedar", a tree with a diameter of 16 feet, via a forest of 80-year old second growth and the third through a thinned western hemlock stand that was naturally established in 1964.

Years ago the Richters lobbied to have the first growth Thurlow cedar preserved when the logging company intended to log the hillside. The family persuaded them it would be advantageous to establish interpretive trails.

The final segment of the second trail descends through 100-year old second growth.

The stop at Blind Channel has been a favourite among mariners for many decades and the Richter family continues to cater to their needs with fresh produce, baked goods and gourmet cuisine in a fine waterfront restaurant. Note the bottle wall behind Philip in the store.

Johnstone Strait

Kelsey Bay to Port Hardy

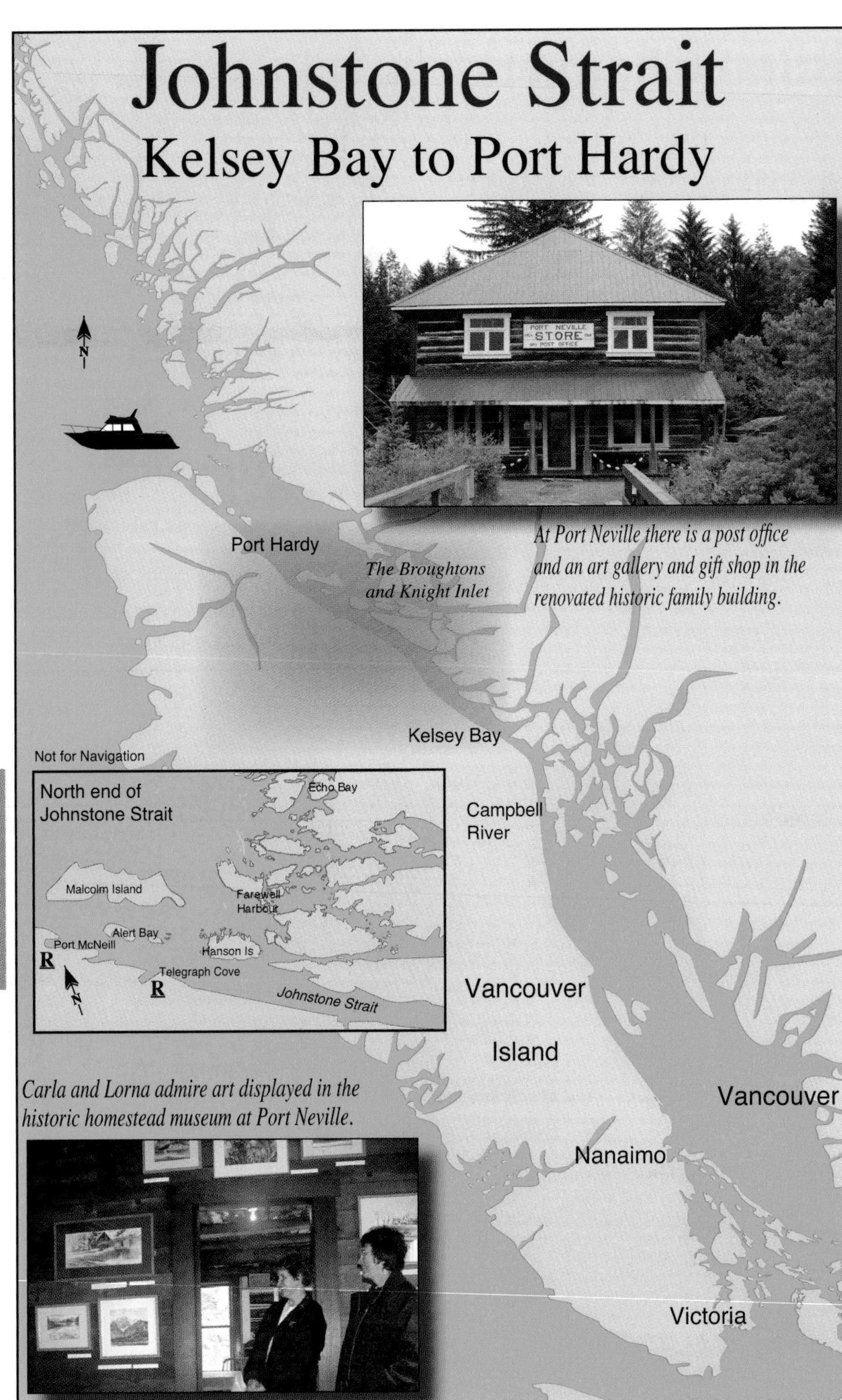

At Port Neville there is a post office and an art gallery and gift shop in the renovated historic family building.

Carla and Lorna admire art displayed in the historic homestead museum at Port Neville.

The dock at Port Neville.

The dock and old store at Port Neville.

Port Neville.

Kelsey Bay

Public dock, Vancouver Island
Sayward Harbour Authority
John Bakker Ph: 250-282-3851
Ph: 250-282-3463 Chart 3544
Float length 177 metres
New floating breakwater • Three fingers with additional length • Garbage • Water • Lights • Electric winch at loading bay (220 v) Power: 20, 30 amp • Restaurant in summer. Showers. Toilets. Groceries available–call from pay phone on the dock.

Deep Sea Port of Kelsey Bay
Sayward Futures Society dock
Wharfinger Ph: 250-282-0018
• Float length 31 metres
Breakwater • Water • Lights

Photo right: Erica Chesluk Hansen. Her family settled at Port Neville in 1891.

Port Neville

50° 28.646' N
125° 05.595' W

Historic settlement.
Johnstone Strait
Transport Canada dock
Port Neville BC V0P 1M0
Ph: 250-949-1535 Charts 3564, 3545
Call: *Ransom Point* VHF 6.
Lorna Chesluk Hansen (and Erica)–post office manager. Float length 34 m. Post Office open every day. Mail received and dispatched Wednesdays. Forwarded mail held for arriving boats. Antique display, art gallery and gift store in family building. Anchored out people welcomed–pot luck suppers and dessert nights. (Pets on leash.)

Above: The Minstrel Island post office is located in Chatham Channel. A small landing serves to access the property and a small store offers bread and baked goods. Right and below: Overlooking the public docks at Minstrel Island.

Drawing of a fallen totem at Mamaliliculla.

Minstrel Island

50° 36.868' N
126° 18.148' W

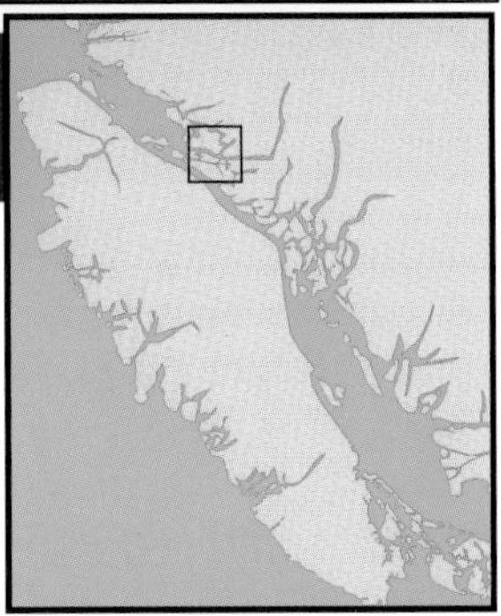

Minstrel Island

Public dock

Charts 3564, 3545, 3515

Manager • Float length 135 m • Aircraft float • Lights • Facility not in operation in 2006.

Use Chatham Channel via Havanah Channel and Port Harvey entrance to reach Minstrel Island from Johnstone Strait.

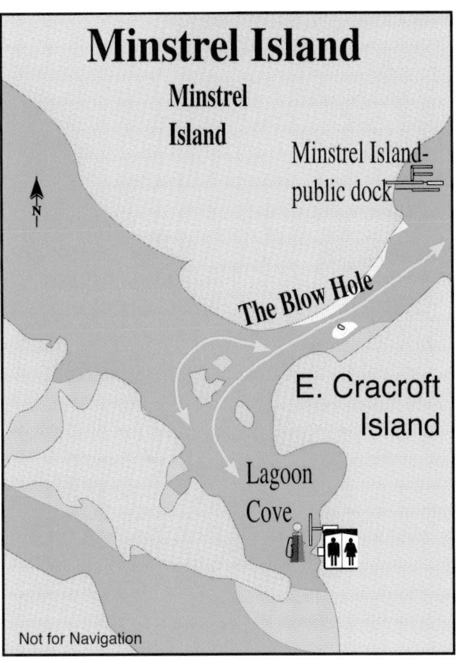

Charts 3564, 3545, 3515

GPS South end of channel:

50° 34.786' N

126° 12.646' W

GPS North end of channel:

50° 34.781' N

126° 14.244" W

Post Office located near the north end of Chatham Channel, close to Minstrel Island.

The docks at Minstrel Island are protected from most wind and weather. The public dock is adjacent to the private, historic property on Minstrel Island and is subject to government maintenance and regulations. New ownership of the property was reported in 2006.

Lagoon Cove

50° 36.061' N
126° 19.065' W

Lagoon Cove Marina

Bill and Jean Barber
Minstrel Island PO BC V0P 1L0
Charts 3564, 3545
VHF 66A
Post office is located in Chatham Channel

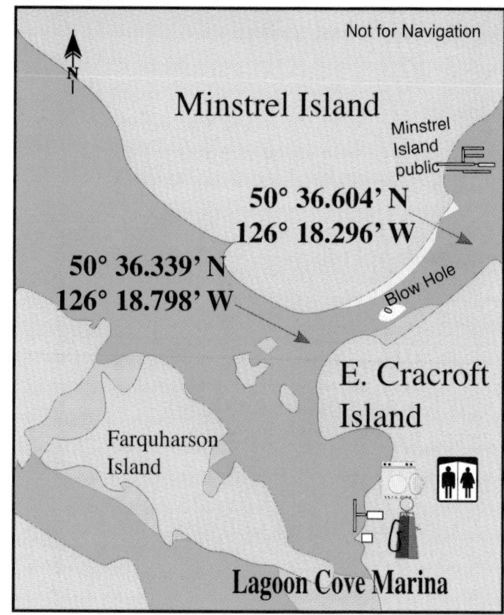

Marina services:
Moorage: Transient moorage. Open year roound. Rafting allowed.
Fuel: Gas, diesel, propane. Oils.
Some repairs subject to available help. Haulouts to 40'. Charts, books.
Water at dock. **Power:** 30 amps.
Customer services:
Coffee kiosk. Pot luck appetisers. Fishing licences, ice, tackle, bait, sodas, candies. Crab and prawn traps. Float plane service.
Showers, washrooms.
Excellent fishing and prawning nearby.
Entertainment:
Hiking trails. Sunsets and views. Animal and marine life. Bears and eagles.

Many people have chosen to anchor in Lagoon Cove over the past, but with secure docking and the associated peace of mind when the wind is up it is worth while stopping at the marina. There are showers, washrooms, additional accommodation and the friendly greeting of owners, Bill and Jean Barber.

Former owners accumulated an incredible collection of marine and other hardware, enough for a museum. Some items have been discarded but many remain in a work shed display area and patio coffee nook. Plan to attend the barbecues and other group get-togethers in summer.

Left: Bill Barber with freshly caught prawns for his famous afternoon "Appy hour."
Top: The marina at Lagoon Cove. Below: Lagoon Cove showing the marina at left and shallow non-navigable passage beyond, leading to Port Harvey.

50° 32.817' N
126° 50.159' W

Telegraph Cove

Telegraph Cove Marina

Elaine and Bob Sanford
1824 B Telegraph Cove Rd VHF 66A
Telegraph Cove BC V0N 3J0
Ph: 250-928-3163 Fax: 250-928-3162
telcove@island.net **Chart 3546**
www.telegraphcove.ca

Moorage: 130 slips (small). Also commercial dock for loading. **Pumpout, power, water.** Hotel accommodations.

Laundry, washrooms, showers. 50' wide launch ramp. Fuel: Available at entrance to cove. Gas, oil (no diesel), restaurant, pub, general store. Whale watching and scuba diving–contact Stubbs Island Charters on the boardwalk via the fuel dock ramp at the entrance to Telegraph Cove. RV park.

The store at Telegraph Cove Resort.

Small launch ramp at Telegraph Cove

Telegraph Cove Resort

Moorage reserved for resort clients. Slips to 25'. General store. Small launch ramp.

Seven Hills Golf & Country Club 250-902-2657

Right: Tied up at the whale watching boat dock. Opposite page top and bottom: Telegraph Cove Marina and entrance, showing the fuel dock and whale interpretive centre (museum). Below: Fog lies across the Strait opposite Telegraph Cove.

Telegraph Cove **Marina** offers overnight visitor moorage. Telegraph Cove **Resort** accommodates resort guests only. Stop briefly at the fuel dock and visit the craft shop on the wharf. The fuel dock is operated by Telegraph Cove Resort. There is fuel also at Alert Bay and Port McNeill.

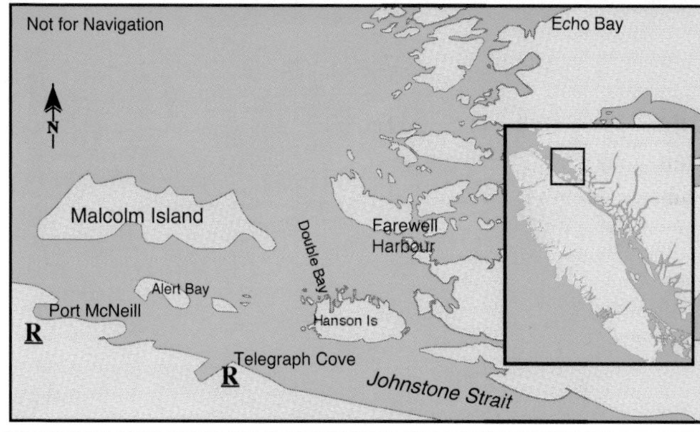

Stubbs Island Charters

Jim and Mary Borrowman
PO Box 7
Telegraph Cove BC V0N 3J0
Ph: 250-928-3185 Fax: 250-928-3102
stubbs@island.net
www.stubbs-island.com

Chart 3546 VHF 10

Customer Services:
Store. Gifts. Fine art. Books. Whale watching, day trips. Scuba diving charters. Accommodation. Cabins on boardwalk. Whale museum.

Opposite right: There is a public dock at the centre and another at the north end of Alert Bay and a small exposed one to the south. Left: Sointula has protected docks with lots of room. The settlement has many artists, a fine museum and lots of history. Sointula is a long established fishing village. It was settled by Fins early in the last century. Restaurant, grocery store, museum and liquor agency near the ferry dock.

Sointula

*** 50° 37.733' N**
127° 02.640' W

North of Desolation

Sointula Boat Harbour

Malcolm Island Lions Club Harbour Authority
Manager Lorraine Williams
710 First St, Sointula BC V0N 3E0
Ph: 250-973-6544 **Chart 3546**

milha@island,net *www.dfo-mpo.gc.ca*
Float 745 metres. Washrooms, laundry, showers. Power 20, 30 amp. Walk to hardware, snacks, restaurant, ferry to Port McNeill. **Mitchell Bay** has a small public dock.

Caution: Enter public docks past the floating breakwater (added since the photo at top of page).

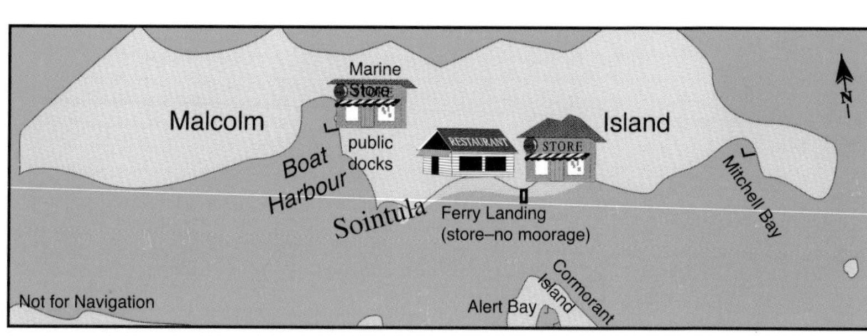

Queen Charlotte Strait

Alert Bay

Chart 3546
VHF 66A

50° 34.957' N
126° 56.151' W

Alert Bay Boat Harbour

Corporation of Village of Alert Bay
Bag Service 2800, Alert Bay BC V0N 1A0
Dan Kennedy
Ph: 250-974-5970 or 250-974-8255
boatharbour@alertbay.ca *www.alertbay.ca*

Marina services: Transient moorage. Float length 533 metres.

Power: 20, 30 amp**. Water.** Breakwater. Aircraft float. Waste oil disposal. Laundry, washrooms, garbage disposal.
Internet access.

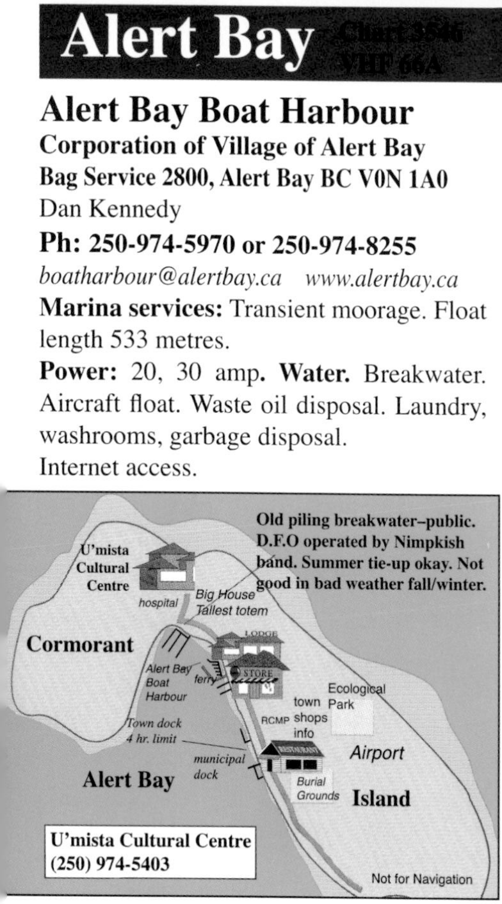

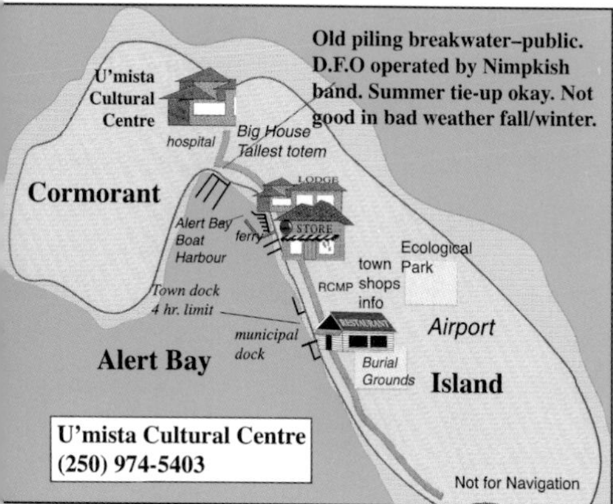

Customer services:
ATM. Restaurants. Dining. Groceries. Tackle, bait, charts. All services at village of Alert Bay. Accommodations, meals. Liquor, drug store. Library. Dental, medical services.

Entertainment:
Walking–hiking trails and roads. Visit the **Ecological Park** on the hill above the town. Animal and marine life. Prime whale watching and scuba diving nearby.

U'mista Cultural Centre.

Visit this outstanding display of native history. World's tallest totem and Big House at the north end of the bay.

Nearby facilities: Paved airstrip (2800').

Alert Bay travel information

Travel Info Centre Ph: 250-974-5213.
info@village.alertbay.bc.ca

Municipal dock

Chart 3546 • Manager Steven Souch
Ph: 250-974-5727 • Free launch ramp
• Float length 61 metres • Garbage •
Water (on wharf only) • Lights.

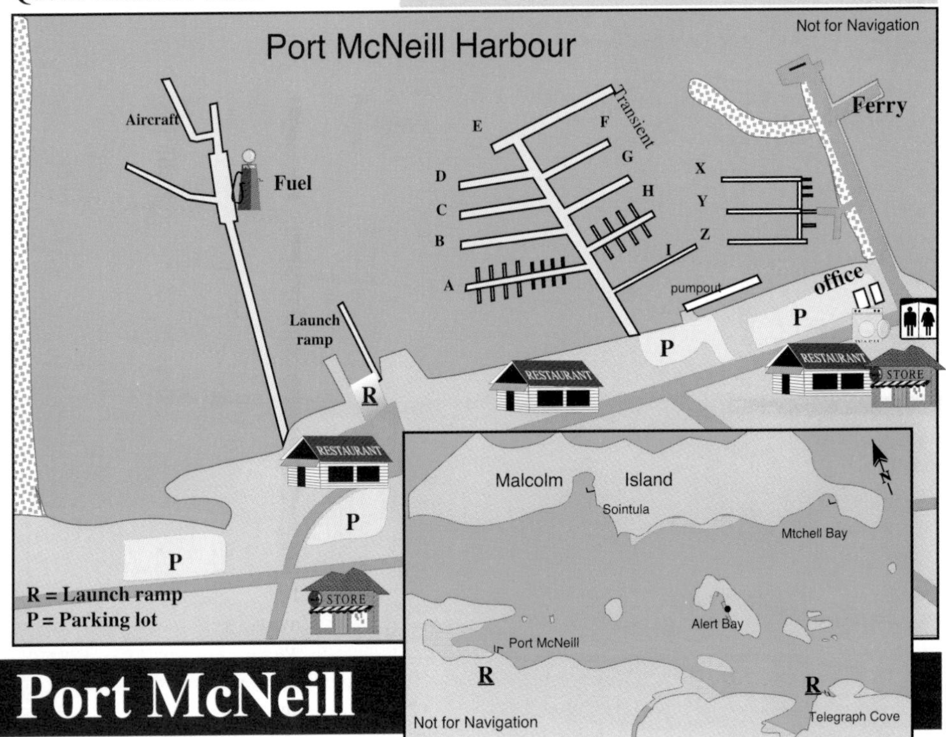

Port McNeill

Port McNeill Boat Harbour

Hiltje Binner
PO Box 1389
Port McNeill BC V0N 2R0
Ph: 250-956-3881 Fax: 250-956-2897
Charts 3546, 3548 VHF 66A
pmharbour@telus.net
www.town.portmcneill.ca

Moorage: Extensive sheltered docks to 5,000'. Outer floats D-G are reserved for transient moorage. No advance guest reservations. Oil disposal. Water. **Power**: 15, 20, 30, 50, 100 amps. **Fuel** (adjacent)**:** Gas, diesel. Propane. Oils. Aviation fuels. **Launch Ramp** adjacent.

Chamber of Commerce Ph: 250-956-3131

Services: Garbage disposal. Tidal grid. Fish cleaning station. Oil disposal, washrooms, showers, laundry. Pumpout, garbage disposal. Internet access.
Entertainment: Walk along shore and sea wall. Uptown facilities–hotels, restaurants, shops, Heritage buildings. Scenic flights.
Adjacent and nearby facilities:
Ferry to Sointula, Alert Bay. Marine repairs–fuel barge. Ice, laundry, showers, groceries. Marine store and service. Hospital nearby.
Overnight moorage also available at fuel dock: 250-956-3336.

Opposite, top: Port McNeill is a gateway to the Broughtons. The fuel dock is usually busy with commercial and pleasure boats as well as float planes. Bottom: Ecological Park on the hill near the radio tower.

Alert Bay

A ferry ride to Alert Bay and Sointula makes a good alternative way to visit those places from Port McNeill.

Alert Bay attracts mariners as a stop for replenishment and an opportunity to go ashore for some exercise as they travel en route to points north or home again. For many Alert Bay is a final destination on their northward travels. Among the reasons for stopping at Alert Bay, one is definitely for a visit to the Ecological Park. It is more like something you would expect to stumble across on a tour of

Florida. The park is a marshy, swampy glade complete with large still pools of water afloat with the massive leaves of various forms of vegetation and sprouting large sprays of skunk cabbage. Wooden boardwalks have been erected across the park to allow access for easy walking and viewing. The most prominent feature of the park is its incredible trees which appear to have been struck by lightning at one time. These massive trees are broad and tall and mostly scarred and craggy with eerie looking branches and cracks and splits appearing as though they were the inspiration for the tale of Sleepy Hollow. And the surprising thing is that the entire park is not where you would expect to find it, down near sea level, but rather up on top of the hill overlooking Alert Bay. From the government marinas of Alert Bay to the Ecological Park is a good uphill walk to the back of the residential area overlooking the bay. There are several routes, marked here and there by signs indicating the way. All routes end up alongside or near the transmitter station and entrances to the park, although not well marked, will eventually lead you to the wooden planked walk through the glades.

Alert Bay boasts the once tallest totem in the world. It is located a short walk up the hill next to the Big House behind the U' mista Native Cultural Centre which is on the shore adjacent to the government docks north of town.The museum at the cultural centre is well worth a visit. Among other interesting items it has on display segments of the exhibits that were shown at Expo 86 in Vancouver.

You may be lucky when visiting Alert Bay and experience some rare calm, sunny weather. If not you should watch the currents and sea conditions that sweep around the northern channel en route to Port Hardy or the open northern reaches of Johnstone Strait. In windy conditions it is usually possible to sneak around the bottom end of Malcolm Island and through the rocky channels and islets in the area. We once took shelter for two days in the Plumper Islets while the wind raged. It is not really a suitable anchorage for more than a temporary stop because the current rips through quite fast especially at high tides.

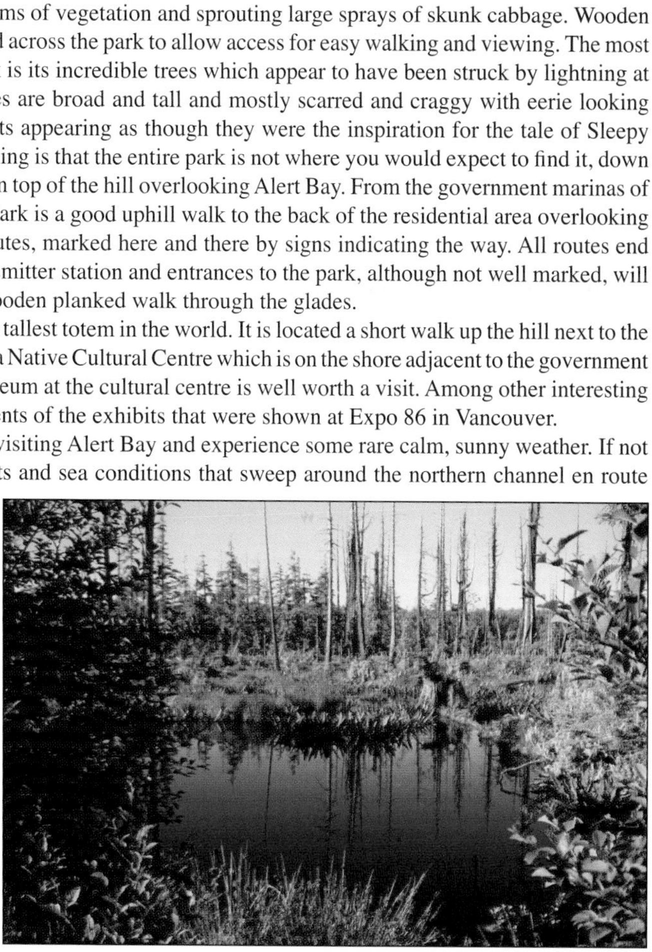

Echo Bay Resort on the right of the bay, Windsong Sea Village to the left.

Echo Bay

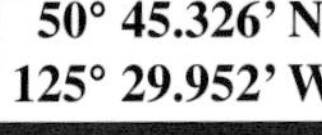
50° 45.326' N
125° 29.952' W

Echo Bay Resort

Chart 3515 VHF 66A

Bob and Nancy Richter
Simoom Sound PO BC V0P 1S0
Phone: 250-974-7139 Fax: 250-861-9891
echobay@island.net
www.echobayresort.com

Marina services:
Transient moorage 1,400'. Reserve in peak season–July, August. Open three days per week in winter. Internet access.
Fuel: Gas, diesel, kerosene, oils, propane.
Water at dock. Ice. **Power:** 15, 30 amps.
Laundry, showers, washrooms (for overnight guests.) Post office.
The main dock is a part of the former Lake Washington floating bridge.
Customer services:
Use Interac/Debit card.
Check your email at the marina office. High speed satellite connection available from your boat. Public pay phone.
Store–groceries.
Post office. Bakery goods and fresh produce, milk, frozen foods, ice, tackle, books, charts, film and gifts.
Eight lodging units. Hotel for groups of six or more. Boat and motor rentals.
Popular fishing and prawning nearby
Block and party ice. Covered picnic float.
Entertainment:
Park access and hiking trail to scenic view. Incredible sunsets and views. Animal and marine life. Potluck dinners:
July 8 to August 23–Wednesday nights. Resort supplies baby back ribs. Covered 40'x50' float with picnic tables and barbecue for use by overnight guests.
Adjacent facilities:
Regular scheduled flights. Local arts and crafts shops and artists. Billy Proctor's Museum. Nearby anchorage and public float at marine park. Playground.

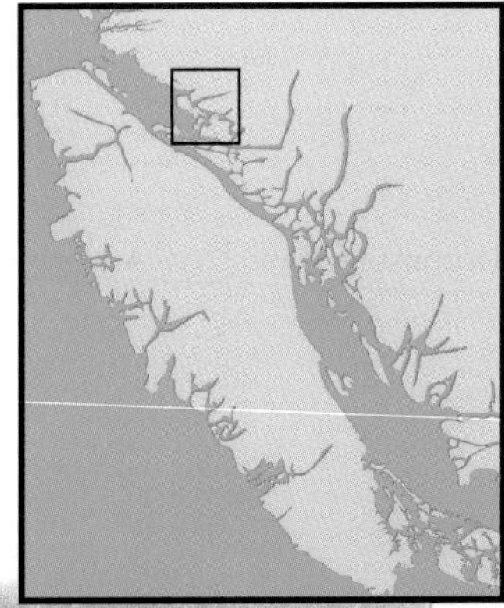

Above: Entering Echo Bay, Windsong Sea Village Marina lies on the north side. Note the small public dock and beach in the photo opposite. Billy Proctor's property is at upper right. Inset: We enjoyed visiting the owners of this yacht tied up at Echo Bay Marina.

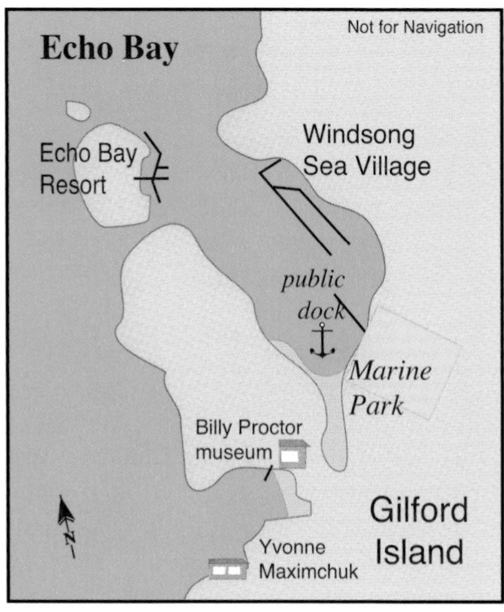

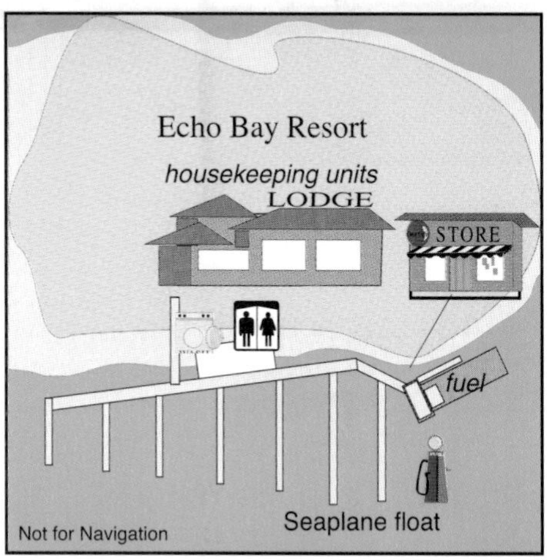

Echo Bay

History and commerce converge at Echo Bay. It is a hub of activity drawing summertime travelling boaters, whale watching tourists out of Telegraph Cove, sportfishing groups from near and far and a constant flow of local people from neighbouring logging camps and fish farms to pick up and drop off their schoolgoing children and their mail. Or to replenish some of their grocery needs. The lodge on the island at the entrance to the cove, for that's all that Echo Bay is–a tiny sheltered cove, caters to a steady flow of itinerant visitors in for a few days of fishing or stopping by in their boats for a spell in the area. Fuel and moorage with power and water are available from Echo Bay Marina which also serves as post office and store.

A marina on the opposite shore, Windsong Sea Village Resort, has large floats which will accommodate a good number of boats and offers moorage for seaplanes too. This marina offers no fuel or dockside electricity.

Artist Yvonne Maximchuk has a house

Pierre's Bay Lodge and early aerial view, inset.

50° 45.326' N 125° 29.952' W

Windsong Sea Village

Jerry and Carol (The Bead Lady)
Owner: Jim O'Donnell
c/o Pacific Eagle Air
Port McNeill BC V0N 2R0
windecho@Island.net

Marina services: Moorage: Transient moorage about 1,000'. Showers, washrooms. Arts and crafts store.

Customer services:
Floating cabin rentals. Floathouse moorage.

Entertainment: Hiking trail and marine park access. Incredible sunsets and views. Animal and marine life viewing. Billy Proctor's museum at Echo Bay.

Adjacent facilities:
Regular scheduled flights. Marine park and trail. Local artists live in the vicinity.
Bakery moored at marina during the season. Small boat tie-up, subject to availability, at nearby Marine Park public dock.

Chart 3515

50° 46.250' N 126° 28.850' W

Pierre's Bay Lodge & Marina

Pierre and Tove Landry **VHF 66A**
c/o PO Box 257
Gabriola Island BC V0R 1X0
Lodge 250-949-2503 Fax: 250-247-9551
Ph: 250-248-9704 in Winter
info@pierresbay.com
www.pierresbay.com

Marina services: Transient moorage 1,200'. Rafting. Showers, laundry, washrooms. Power at the docks: 15 amp. Limited water.

Customer services: Self-contained rental suites or sleeping rooms. Lady Di's Lighthouse Bakery. Dinners, barbecue. Saturday pig roasts. Internet access.

Entertainment: Christmas in July dinner. Movie nights–Wednesdays. Des Moines Yacht Club donated a huge barbecue for use at the resort. Gift shop, arts and crafts.

Hazard: Avoid Powell Rock and Evangeline Rock near the entrance to Scott Cove.

---

just outside the entrance to Shoal Harbour and provides an opportunity for artists or tyros to brush up on their skills. Here, in her gallery studio, she conducts instruction and classes in art, water colour, acrylics and oils, available to people on visiting boats.

She also has a fine selection of works for sale and can be reached by calling her at *Sea Rose* on channel 16.

Meet Billy Proctor, a long-time resident of Echo Bay. With Yvonne Maximchuk and another local artist, he has co-authored several books about the area. His museum is worth a visit, especially if you get to talk to him.

Right: Pierre's Bay Lodge in Scott Cove with its bakery store lighthouse.
Inset: Pierre Landry.
Bottom: Billy Proctor, whose nearby museum should not be missed.

Kingcome
Transport Canada
Chart 3515
Float length 55 m
Windy and exposed.

Gilford Island
Gilford Village
Chart 3515
Float length 60 m
Aircraft float.

Echo Bay
(Marine Park)
All weather anchorage. Boat dock-70', camping sites, water, toilets. Waddington Bay–part of Broughton Archipelago (Park). See *Anchorages and Marine Parks.*

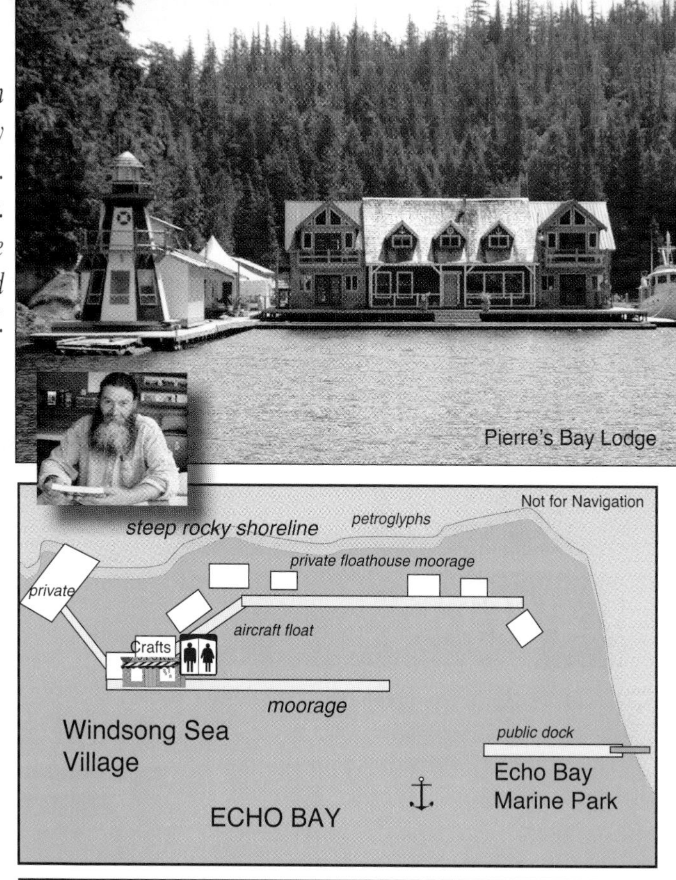

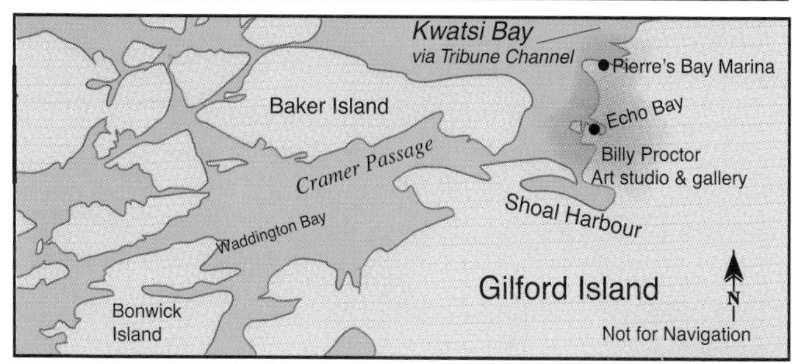

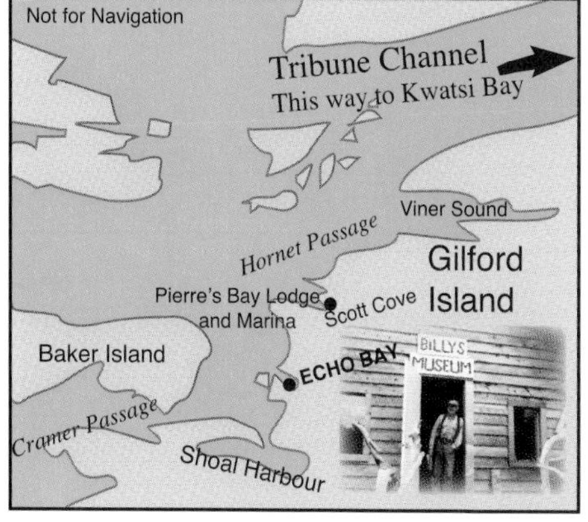

50° 51.020' N
126° 35.099' W

Shawl Bay

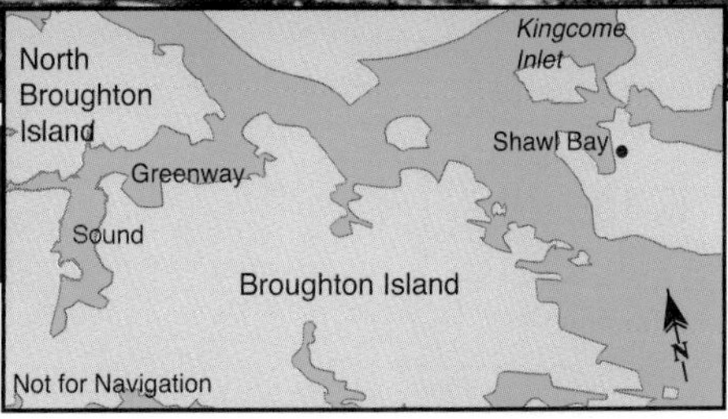

North Broughton Island
Greenway Sound
Broughton Island
Kingcome Inlet
Shawl Bay
Not for Navigation

Shawl Bay Marina

Lorne and Shawn Brown
c/o Simoom Sound PO BC V0P 1S0
Ph: 250-483-4169
Chart 3515 VHF 66A
shawlbaymarina@hughes.net
www.shawlbaymarina.com

Marina services:
Moorage: Transient (1,000') and floathouse moorage. **Power. Water. Showers.** Store. Groceries. Home baked bread, cinnamon rolls and pies. Ice. Rental cabins. Internet access. Public satellite TV at picnic float.
Entertainment: Pancake breakfast included with moorage. Coffee hour 8-9 pm. Animal and marine life.
Adjacent facilities:
Water in good supply but use sparingly during summer. Daily scheduled flights to Port McNeill and Campbell River. Near Kingcome Inlet entrance and Broughton Islands
Look for the turquoise docks to locate the marina in the bay.

Above: A shelter over the entertainment deck protects from sun and rain.

Shawl Bay is a busy place during the summer season. Many regular boating friends and customers of the family that owns and operates the cosy marina at the far corner of the bay, return each year to tie up at the spacious docks. These docks and the structures on them comprise Shawl Bay Marina, operated until the mid 1900s by the late Edna Brown and her sister Johanne along with Edna's son Gary.

Brother Alf Didriksen ran a logging camp in the bay for many years and the family's hospitality is legendary among fishermen, loggers and pleasure boaters alike. It is now being run by Lorne and Shawn Brown, their son Robert and Aunty Jo.

Aerial photo shows the location of Shawl Bay Marina at the far corner of the bay. Buildings on the dock include the store and residences. Adjacent to the docks is a covered entertainment deck.

Next stop Kwatsi Bay and Greenway Sound

Continuing from Echo Bay towards Sullivan Bay stop at Greenway Sound. It was opened in 1985 by Tom and Ann Taylor. The bay is large and the docks extensive totalling one half mile in length. The Taylors laid out the marina docks in a wide square 'u' with a finger pointing into the square near the far corner where the facilities are located. These facilities set the floating resort apart from others in the area. The Greenway Sound store is part of a restaurant with an airy, clean kitchen that serves up mouth-watering dinners and ice cream in waffle cones. Moorage is typically busy with large visiting yachts, some of which remain during summer. The resort literally gives arriving boats the red carpet treatment, from the smiling attendance of young dock helpers to the full length coverage of the floats with red indoor/outdoor carpet.

Kwatsi Bay Marina lies beneath towering coastal mountains off Tribune Channel.

50° 50.622' N
126° 16.932' W

Kwatsi Bay

Kwatsi Bay

Anca Fraser and Max Knierim
c/o Simoom Sound BC V0P 1S0
Cell Ph: 250-949-1384
Chart 3515 VHF 66A
kwatsibay@hughes.net
www.kwatsibay.com

This is a small marina at remote Kwatsi Bay off Tribune Channel. Cruise from Echo Bay or from Minstrel Island via beautiful scenery in Tribune Channel area.

Guest moorage. open year round. Water (good and plentiful), showers. Nearest fuel at Lagoon Cove, Echo Bay or Sullivan Bay. Gift store, 2 rental cabins, evening pot luck appetizers. Wilderness facilities. Peaceful and quiet. Anchorage at head of bay in 30 ft.

The Kwatsi Bay owners Anca Fraser (also above) and Max Knierim with their children Russell and Marieke.

Walk the length of the floats at Greenway twice and you have walked a mile. Another favoured walk is to the lake a short distance up the mountainside. A dinghy float and ramp provide access to the path that leads to the lake. The resort offers fly in service from points south including Seattle, Campbell River, Port McNeill and Vancouver. The store carries

fresh and frozen foods, books, charts, clothing, fishing tackle and ice. In separate buildings attached to the adjacent docks are laundry and shower facilities as well as a book exchange library. The docks are serviced with water and 120/208 volt shore power. The resort stands by on VHF radio channel 66A and is equipped with regular telephone service. See *www.greenwaysound.com* for more information. Cellular service is available to amplified phones with good antennas. This marina, like many now has good Wi-fi internet service.

Kwatsi Bay is a small inlet off Tribune Channel. From Echo Bay. Turn east after Viner Sound and travel along this picturesque waterway to find one of the loveliest spots on the coast. It is so remote that the less said about it here the more it will be enjoyed when you reach it. It lies about midway between Minstrel Island and Echo Bay. When you are in the Knight Inlet area use Tribune Channel from Minstrel Island.

Top: The marina in Kwatsi Bay continues to grow and attract more visitors. Centre: Regular visitor and friend Linda Lewis arrives at Kwatsi Bay. Above: Anca Fraser shares a light moment with the crew on a BC Forest Service boat.

Tom and Ann Taylor

Greenway Sound

North of Desolation

Greenway Sound Marine Resort

Tom and Ann Taylor
PO Box 759, Port McNeill BC V0N 2R0
Ph: 250-974-7044 (Alert Bay number)
Toll free: 1-800-800-2080
Ph: 360-466-4751 (winter)
Charts 3547, 3515 VHF 66A
tomnann@ncia.com
www.greenwaysound.com

Marina services:
Moorage: Large destination marina with plenty of transient moorage with up to 2,200 feet of red carpeted docks. Good for power walking. Reserve dock space in peak season. **Garbage** accepted. **Water** at dock is good and abundant. **Shore Power**: 15 and 30 amp/120 volt and 50 amp/208 volt. Free W-Fi to all locations on dock. Uses 802.11.
Restaurant. (Reservations essential for dinner). Dinner 6:30-8 pm. Licenced. Menu on website. Steak, prawns, chicken, pastas, awesome desserts. Groceries. Milk, produce, frozen foods, bread, deli, sticky buns, ice, bait, tackle, books, charts, film, and gifts, great clothing, hardware, sundries.

Laundry, showers, washrooms.
Postal service, telephone, fax.
Conscientious boat sitting.
Excellent fishing and prawning nearby.
Ice cream and espresso.
Free video and pocketbook exchange.
Flown-in fresh dairy and produce.

Entertainment:
Adjacent park for hiking, walking, swimming, exploring. Incredible sunsets and views. Animal and marine life.

Customer services:
Regular scheduled flights to Port Hardy, Port McNeill, Campbell River, Vancouver, Kenmore and Renton (Seattle). See website. Assistance with travel arrangements or customs as needed. Local cruising and exploring advice. Reasonably current newspapers to borrow. VISA, Mastercard, Discover. (No Amex.)

Broughton Island

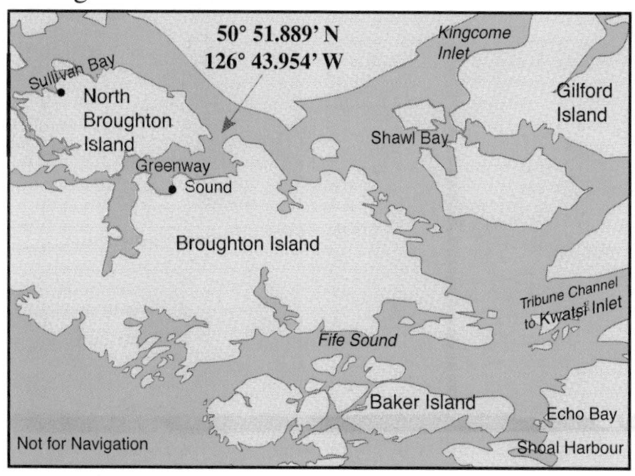

Greenway Sound

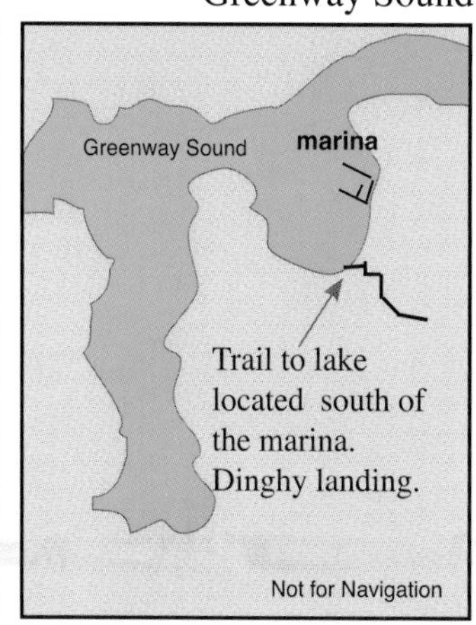

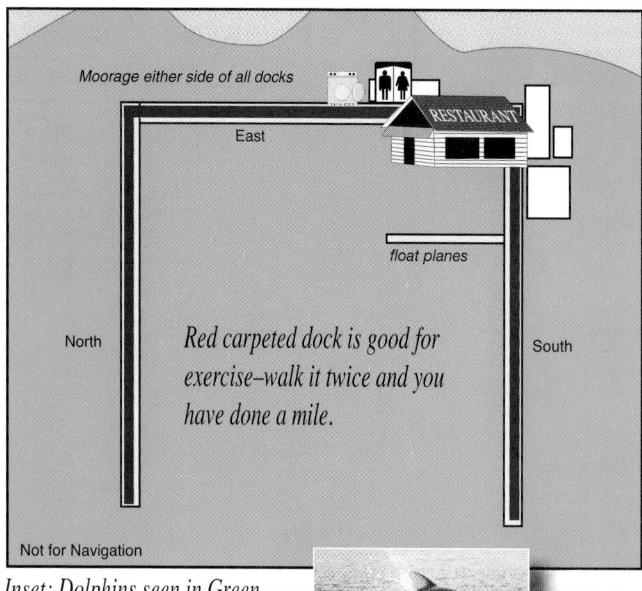

The restaurant is on a float alongside the dock. It also houses a small store as well as the marina office. The aircraft float is reserved for floatplanes arriving regularly in summer.

Inset: Dolphins seen in Greenway Sound. Tom Taylor photo. Opposite: An aerial view of Greenway Sound Marine Resort. Nearby, there is a hiking trail from a dinghy dock leading to Broughton Lake Park. Right and inset opposite: Restaurant and marina. Access off Sutlej Channel to the marina at Greenway Sound is very easy.

Sullivan Bay

Sullivan Bay Marine Resort

Chart 3547 VHF 66A

Pat Finnerty and Lynn Whitehead
GD, Sullivan Bay BC V0N 3H0
Phone: 250-483-6881
palyn@telus.net
www.sullivanbay.com

Marina services: Fuel: Gas, diesel, oil, ice, bait. Mechanic and services at Vancouver Island towns and ports. Some repairs possible. Internet access.

Moorage: Large permanent marina with plenty of guest moorage at up to 2,500 feet of dock. Reserve in peak season.

Water at dock. Plentiful. **Power** at docks: 15, 30, 50, 120 amp (240V).

Laundry, showers, washrooms.

Customer services: Restaurant. Liquor store. Groceries. Post office. Fresh produce, dairy products, frozen foods, ice, tackle, and souvenirs. Video movie rentals.

Smokehouse. Boat sitting.

Fishing and prawning in vicinity.

Entertainment:

Library. Novel building structures, street names on docks.

Adjacent facilities:

Regular scheduled flights. Private floating homes village.

Flying activity. This facility was a seaplane refuelling stop but no longer. It has an interesting aviation history.

Left: Lyn Whitehead at the store and post office in Sullivan Bay.

Above: Sullivan Bay Marine Resort with its floating sidewalks. Left: Lyn Whitehead with Carla, inside the Sullivan Bay store.

Jennis Bay in Drury Inlet.

Jennis Bay Extreme Expeditions, Ltd.

Managers/Hosts: Tom and Allyson Allo

PO Box 456 **Chart: 3547**

Port McNeill BC V0N 2R0

Phone: 403-987-9410

jennisbay@hughes.net

www.jennisbay.com

Location: Jennis Bay, Drury Inlet.

VHF 66Av

Marina services: Guest moorage, gift shop, eco-tourism, Geo-cache "treasure" hunting, hiking/biking trails, bike & sit-atop kayak rentals, guided trail & lake excursions, Cajun cookouts Tuesday nights, washroom, shower, campfire get-togethers, pets and children are welcome.

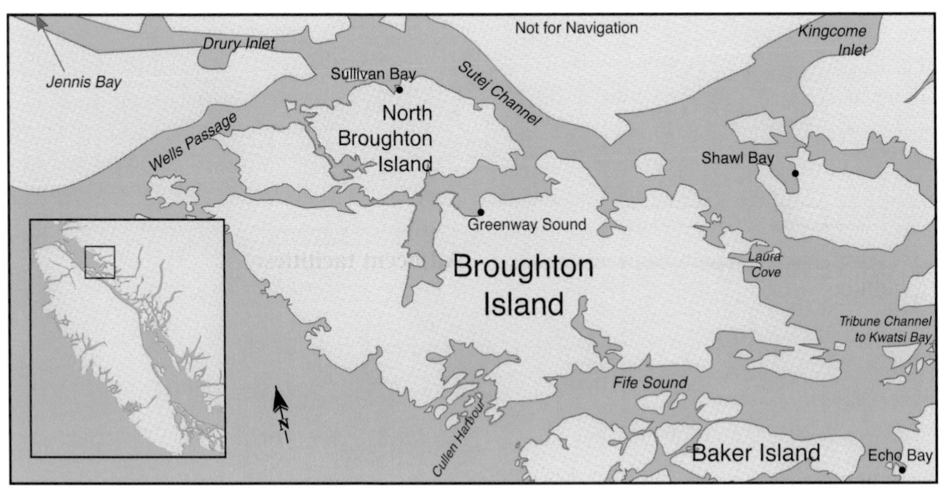

Port Hardy outer dock

North of Desolation

Quarterdeck Inn & Marina Resort

Owner/manager: I.V. Villani
6555 Hardy Bay Rd
PO Box 910
Port Hardy BC V0N 2P0
Ph: 250-949-6551 Fax: 250-949-7777
info@quarterdeckresort.net
www.quarterdeckresort.net
Charts 3548, 3605 VHF 16, 66A

Marina: Fuel: Gas, diesel, propane. **Showers, laundry**. **Moorage** Guests 100 slips to 32'. Reservations suggested. **Power** 15, 30, 50 amp. **Water.** 60 ton travel lift. Repairs. Pressure wash. Marine store. Charts, ice, dry ice, propane, natural gas, fishing tackle. Internet access. 40 room Motor Inn. Courtesy Car.
Available services: Flights, bus service, ferry nearby. Pub restaurant, wine and beer store, hotels nearby. Taxi and limo service to airport, BC Ferries and shopping. Adventure charters. **Launch ramp**.

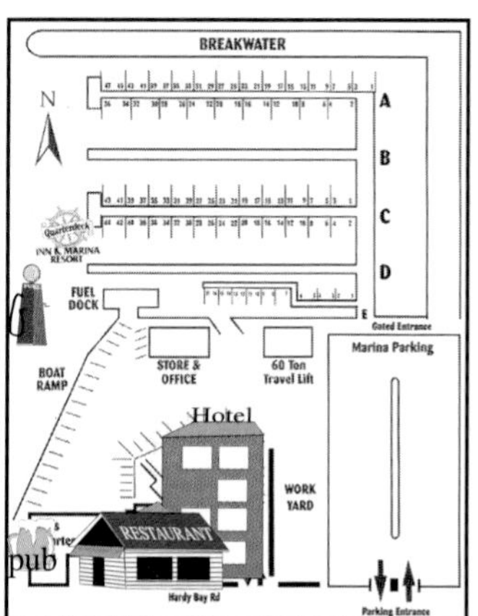

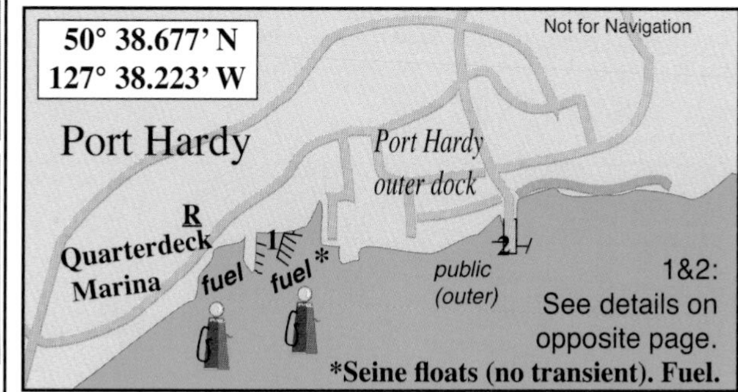

Bull Harbour

Hope Island
Government dock
Charts 3921, 3549
Float length 35 m
Anchor in bay. Use dinghy.

Port Hardy outer dock

1. Port Hardy Inner dock

(Inside breakwater-Fisherman's Wharf)
For pocket cruisers and commercial boats.
Port Hardy Harbour Authority
PO Box 68, Port Hardy BC V0N 2P0
Pat McPhee and Mary-Ann Smith
Also manages Seagate.
Ph: 250-949-6332 Fax: 250-949-6332
phfloats@cablerocket.com
www.district.porthardy.bc.ca
Charts 3548, 3605

• Float length 574 m • **Launch ramp** • Breakwater • Grid • Garbage • Waste oil disposal • **Water** • Lights • **Power**: 15, 30 amp • Public pay phone • **Washrooms** • Customs • **Fuel** nearby • Pumpout.

Near city restaurants, services, shops. All services and facilities in Port Hardy and local adjacent marina.
Ferries nearby for northern route.

2. Port Hardy Outer dock

Seagate Marina.
Ph: 250-949-6332 Fax: 250-949-6332

• Float length 250 m • **Garbage** • Waste oil disposal • **Water** • **Power** • **Moorage**: Commercial but some transient when space available. Floats in place May to September only. Excellent scuba diving nearby. Enquire at dive facilities in town. Coast Guard station adjacent. Downtown Port Hardy location with access to shops and services.

Hurst Island

50° 50.394' N
127° 35.694' W

God's Pocket

Bill Weeks & Annie Ceschi
PO Box 130, Port Hardy BC V0N 2P0
Ph: 250-949-1755 Toll free 888-534-8322
Charts 3921, 3549, 3605 VHF 66A
info@godspocket.com
www.godspocket.com

Moorage and facilities: Limited, sheltered docks. Washrooms. Water taxi. Some accommodation available. Cabins. Some provisions, gifts.
Restaurant-July only as available.

Entertainment:
Walking trails on island. Hiking. Scuba diving. Kayaking charters.

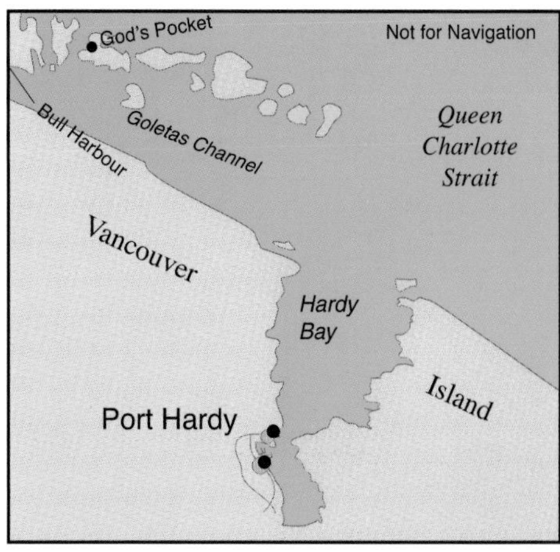

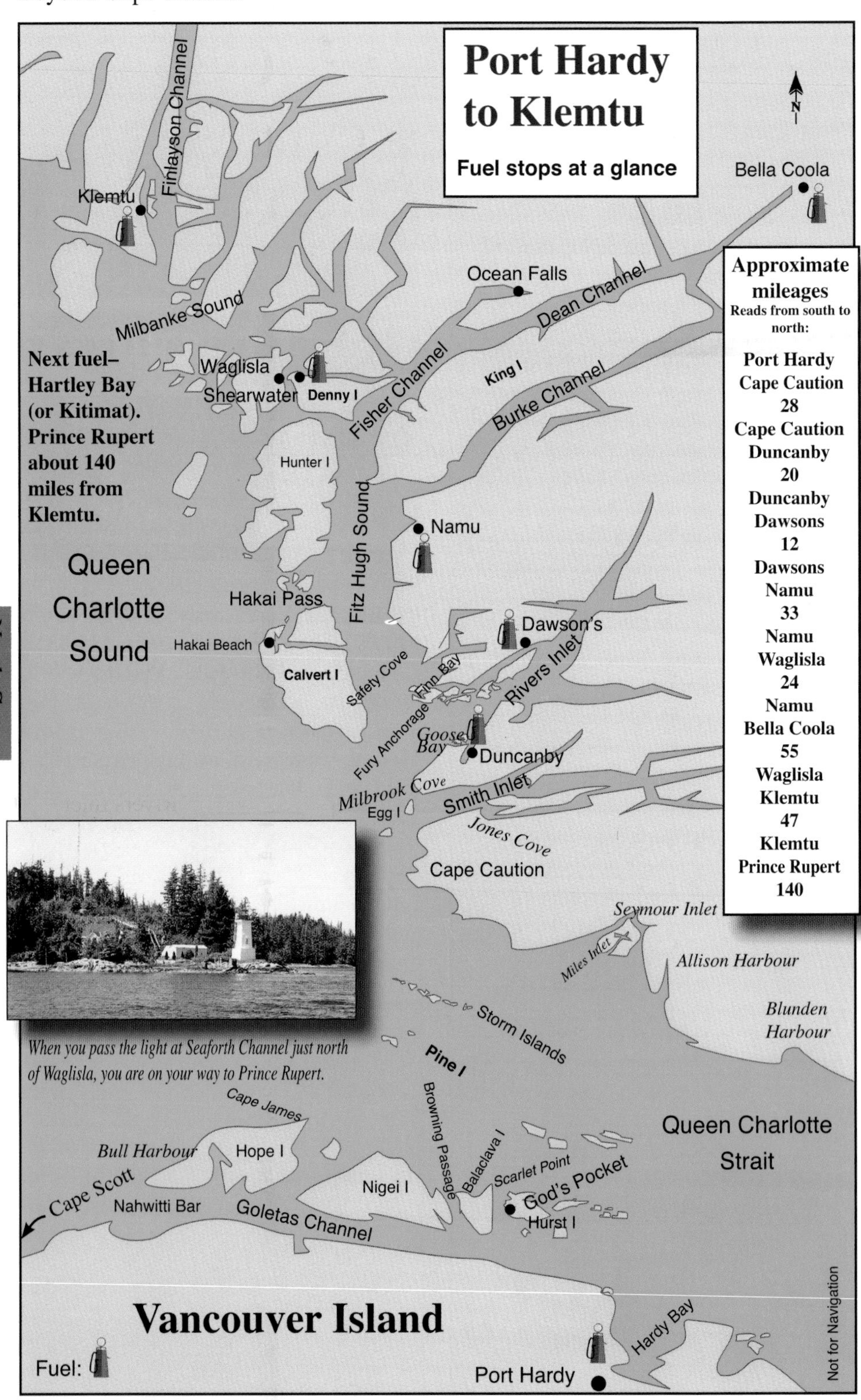

When you pass the light at Seaforth Channel just north of Waglisla, you are on your way to Prince Rupert.

The North Coast

Beyond Cape Caution

Section 6

Photo: Norman Elliot

Rivers Inlet

Chart 3934

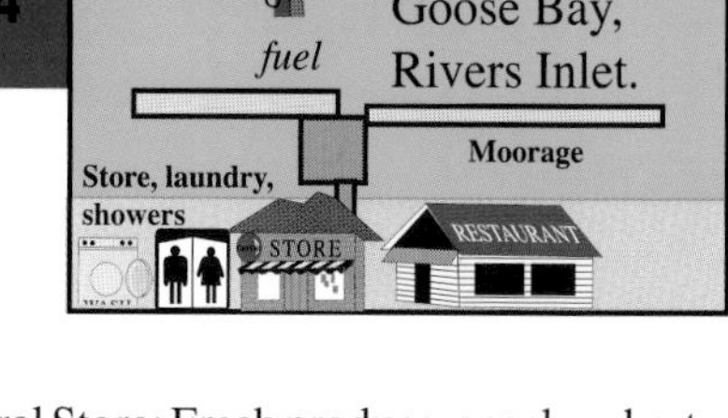

Duncanby Landing Lodge & Marina

Dean McLaren
Rivers Inlet PO BC V0N 1M0
Ph: 1-604-628-9822 VHF 06
reservations@duncanby.com
www.duncanbylodgemarina.com
Moorage. Water, power: 30 amp.
Fuel: Gas diesel, propane, lubricants.
Showers, laundry, washrooms.

General Store: Fresh produce, snacks, charts, books, tackle, bait, fishing licences, equipment, charters, boat rentals. Groceries. Liquor store. Accommodations. Restaurant–breakfast, lunch, dinner. Located at Goose Bay at the entrance to Riverse Inlet.

Photos: Norman Elliot

Duncanby Landing

North Coast

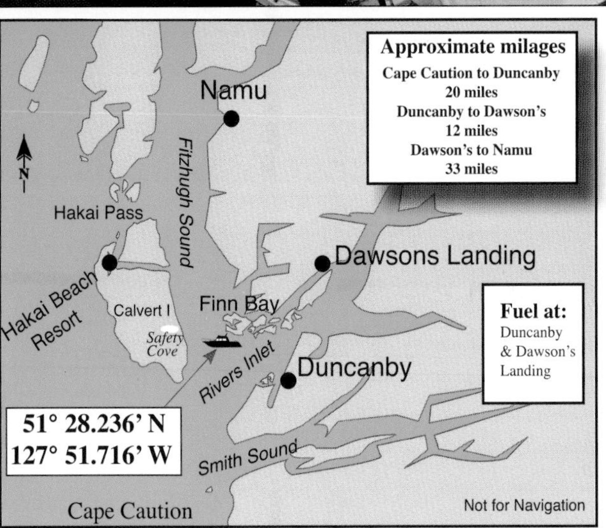

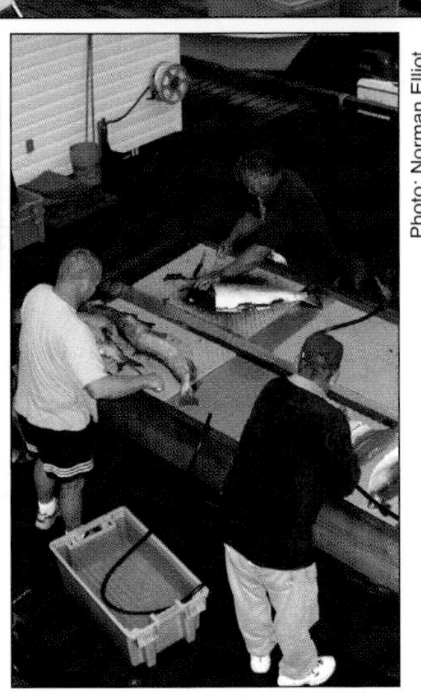

Photo: Norman Elliot

To reach Rivers Inlet from Port Hardy it is necessary to round Cape Caution and pass the entrance to Smith Inlet. There are no facilities between God's Pocket just out of Port Hardy, and Rivers Inlet. If weather is a deterrent temporary anchorage is possible off Hurst Island or moorage at God's Pocket dock if space is available. Bull Harbour, slightly out of the way for a passage around Cape Caution is a good anchorage. It is shallow off Cape Caution and many yachtsmen round the Cape about five miles off. Local mariners cut close to the Cape and take passage behind the islands, rocks and islets off Smith Inlet to slide around into Rivers Inlet off Goose Bay. Choose to round Cape Caution in gentle wind and sea conditions and be wary of fog. On the passage around Cape Caution one can find temporary and some good protected overnight anchorages at places such as Blunden Harbour, Allison Harbour, Miles Inlet, Seymour Inlet, Jones Cove and Milbrook Cove. Please refer to **Anchorages and Marine Parks**.

The first fuel stop is at Duncanby Landing in Goose Bay, or farther up Rivers Inlet at Dawson's Landing. Some mariners travel past Rivers Inlet, stopping, if necessary for overnight anchorage, at Safety Cove on Calvert Island, or at Fury Anchorage at the entrance to Rivers Inlet.

Photo: Norman Elliot

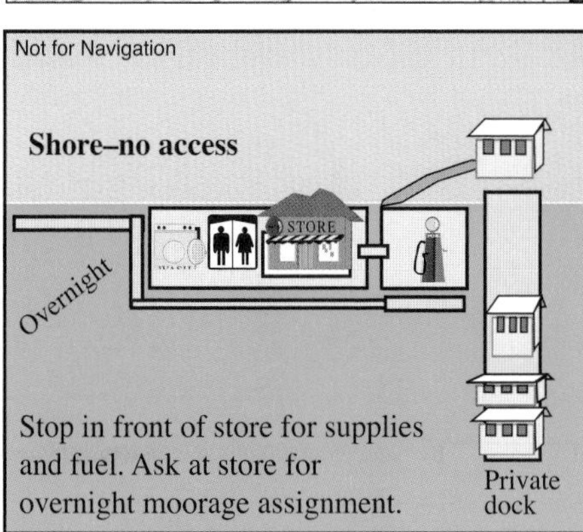

Photo: Norman Elliot

Tied up to the fuel and store dock at Dawsons Landing. Inset shows an aerial view with current dock layout and improved condition (photo courtesy of Dawsons Landing). Inside the store there is always a warm welcome. Opposite page: The dock at Duncanby on the south side of Rivers Inlet.

Dawsons Landing General Store

Robert and Nola Bachen
Dawsons Landing BC V0N 1M0
Ph: 403-987-9058 Fax: 250-949-2111
dawsonslanding@hotmail.com
Charts 3934, 3932 VHF 66A
Marina services: Moorage. Water. Washrooms. Fuel: Gas, diesel, stove oil.
Customer Services: Showers, laundry.
General store: tackle, fishing licences, bait, groceries, block and cube ice, fish freezing, liquor agency. Scheduled air service to Port Hardy.

Photo: Courtesy Dawson's Landing

Post office, gifts, toys, souvenirs, books, charts, supplies for marine maintenance and repairs.
Anchorage among nearby islands.

Photo: Sharon Allman

Fitzhugh Sound

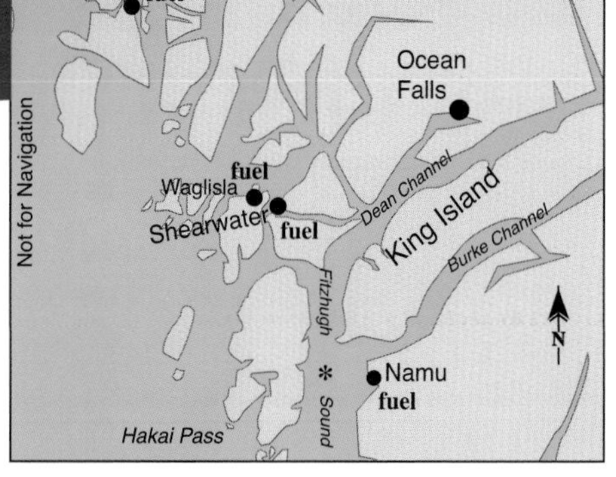

Hakai Beach Resort

Dock manager
Pruth Harbour, Calvert Island
PO Box 3819, Smithers BC V0J 2N0
Ph: 250-847-9300 Charts 3935, 3727
fishon@hakai.com
www.hakai.com

Anchor in bay. This is not a public dock or marina. Shore access–tie up small dinghies under ramp inside marina. Resort offers restaurant and accommodations when available. Store–gifts, film, snacks, cappuccino. Walk to white, sandy beach on open Pacific.

Anchorage–Pruth Bay.

Boats at anchor receive welcome flyer.

Guided fishing excursions available.

Hakai Beach Resort
51° 39.296' N
128° 07.438' W

***Mid channel (Namu)**
Fitzhugh Sound
51° 52.044' N
127° 57.841' W

Namu to Bella Coola 55 miles
Waglisla to Ocean Falls 30 miles
Waglisla to Klemtu 47 miles

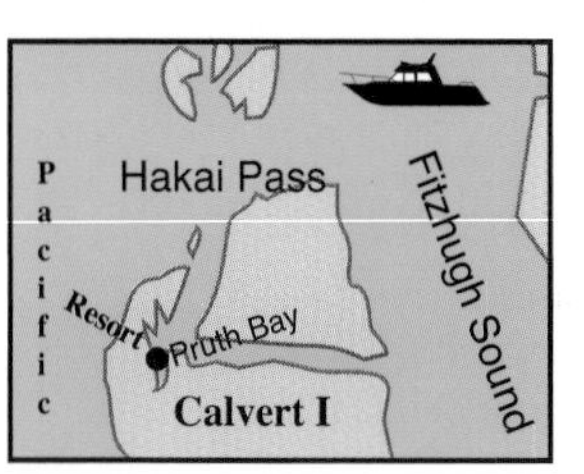

Above and right: The resort at Hakai Pass. Anchor off, row ashore and stay for dinner in season.

Photo: Sharon Allman

51° 51.597' N
127° 52.116' W

Namu

Namu BC V0T 1Z0
Pete and Rene Darwin
General Delivery Waglisla BC
Ph: 250-949-4090 Fax: 250-624-8984
VHF 10 monitored at times.
Charts 3936, 3727
rene_d_7@hotmail.com

Moorage. Water at main dock. **Showers, laundry, washroom**. Restaurant.
Fuel dock nearby: Gasoline, diesel.
Customer services: Constant changes are in place. Buildings and docks are in a mixed state of repair but the operators are redeveloping some facilities for visitors.
This stop is an interesting historic and archaeological site. This is a popular area for kayaking, with many kayakers making nearby Hakai Pass a destination of choice.

Caution: Beware of unmarked rocks in the bay. See chart 3785 for Loo Rock.

Photos: Sharon Allman

Top and bottom: The docks and buildings at Namu.
Above: The fuel dock at Namu sells gas and diesel. There is a small gift shop at the landing.

Waglisla (Bella Bella)

226 Waglisla
Waglisla BC
V0T 1Z0
Campbell Island
Ph: 250-957-2440
Charts 3938, 3939

52° 09.706' N
128° 08.457' W

Marina: Fuel: Gas, diesel, stove oil.
Customer services: Moorage. Water. Store. Public pay phones, **showers,** pub, coffee shop. BC ferry stops weekly. RCMP station. Hospital. ATM. Liquor store. Repairs, haul out facility. Taxis. Airport. Short distance to Shearwater Marine Group. Waglisla is a First Nations village.

Top and below: The docks at Waglisla have been replaced. Right: Going into the village. The old store has since been repainted.

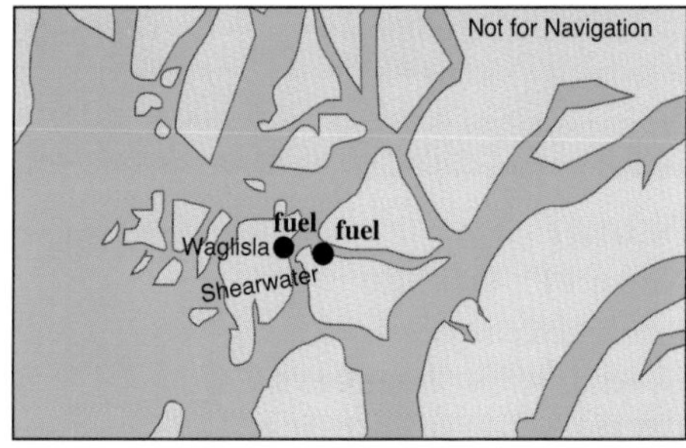

Photo: Sharon Allman

Shearwater

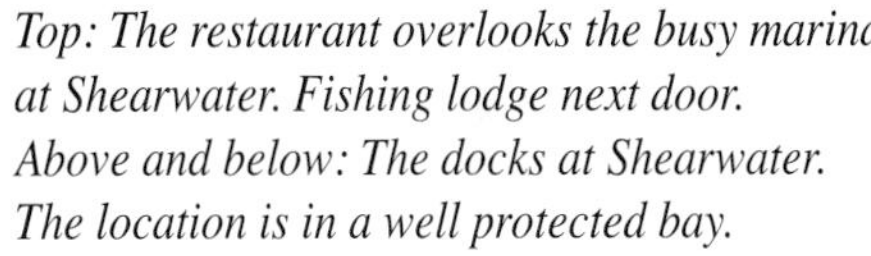

Sharon Allman

Top: The restaurant overlooks the busy marina at Shearwater. Fishing lodge next door. Above and below: The docks at Shearwater. The location is in a well protected bay.

Shearwater Marine

PO Box 68,
Denny Island BC V0T 1B0 VHF 66A
Ph: 250-957-2666 Fax: 250-957-2422
Toll free Vancouver: 1-800-663-2370
Charts 3938, 3939
www.shearwater.ca

Marina services: Fuel: Gas, diesel. Propane. Marine service. Lubricants. **Moorage.** 1,600 feet of docks (1,500 of concrete dock) **Water, Power** 15, 30, 50 amps. **Laundry, showers, washrooms.** Public pay phones. Pub. Liquor. Boat and engine repairs. 70 tonne travel lift. Boat launch. Grocery/hardware stores. post office. Internet access.

Customer services: Electronics shop. Store: tackle, fishing licences, bait, gifts. Charts, marine supplies. ATM. Pub. Off-sales. **Restaurant Ph: 250-957-2366.**

40 room hotel. 3,000 foot airstrip. Yacht charters. Fishing charters, boat rentals. Scuba air station. Daily plane service nearby. B.C. Ferry terminal. Transport Canada dock. Floating breakwater. Launch ramp. Seabus to Waglisla.

Photo: Sharon Allman

Ocean Falls

Namu to Bella Coola 55 miles

Namu to Waglisla 24 miles

Waglisla to Ocean Falls 30 miles

Waglisla to Klemtu 47 miles

Ocean Falls to Bella Coola 50 miles

Namu to Kitimat 181 miles

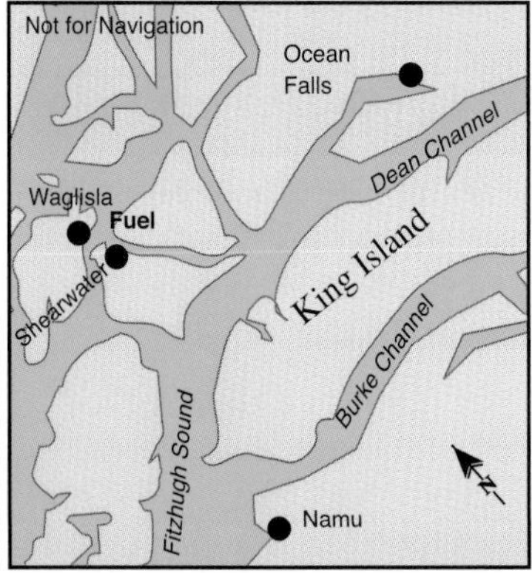

Ocean Falls

Butedale

Photo: Sharon Allman

Photo: Iz Goto

Ocean Falls

Ocean Falls Harbour Authority

Herb Carpenter–manager
Sally Isaksen–wharfinger
GD, Ocean Falls BC V0T 1C0
Ph: 250-289-3859/3211
Fax: 250-289-3859 **VHF 09**
Charts 3939, 3729

Marina: Moorage. Power: 20, 30 amps. **Water.** Fish cleaning station. The docks are in good shape, unlike the decaying town of Ocean Falls. Between the remnants of Ocean Falls and the nearby community at Martin Valley there are accommodations and amenities. These include medical services, a saloon, gift shop, groceries at Jim Owen's Rain Country store, fresh produce, a post office, liquor store, laundry, showers, and a marine ways. There is a cafe in the old church building. Walk the roadway to Link Lake and the dam. There is a hatchery and rearing pen for fish farming. The old powerhouse and mill are barricaded for safety. Tours are available during ferry stopovers.

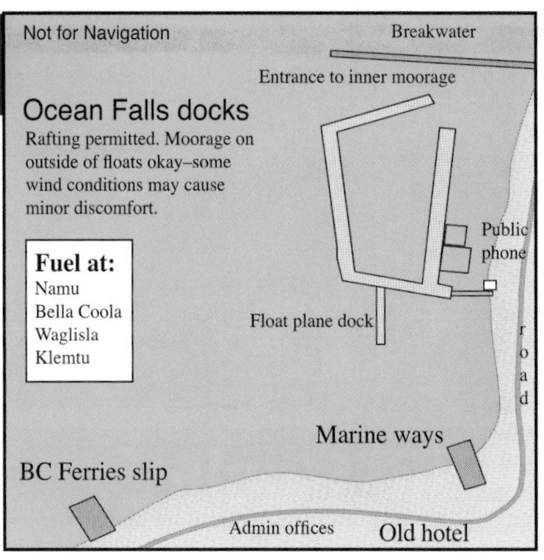

Above and below: Ocean Falls docks. Opposite page top: An old house at Ocean Falls. Centre: Ocean Falls floats include a small shack that serves as the dock manager's office. Bottom: Butedale, farther up the coast, has some dock space for visitors.

Photo: Iz Goto

Bella Coola main street.

Bella Coola

Charts 3730, 3729

52° 19.319' N
126° 45.840' W

Bella Coola Harbour Authority

Manager: Shirley Willson
PO Box 20, Bella Coola BC V0T 1C0
Ph: 250-799-5633
Fax: 250-799-5632 **VHF 10**
bcha@belco.bc.ca

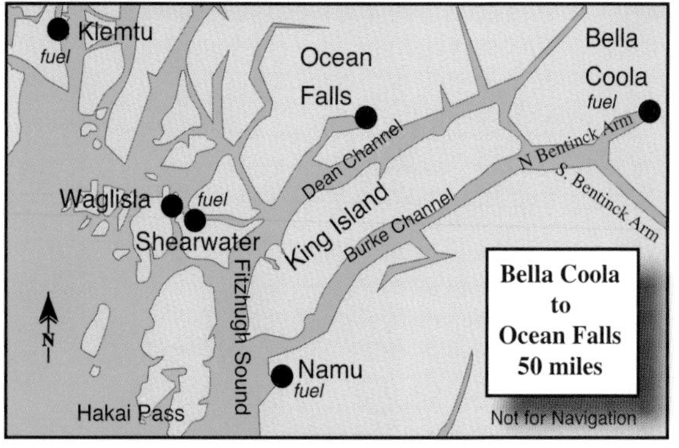

Marina: Rafting necessary at pleasure boat moorage near shore on east side of marina. Larger vessels easy access guest moorage. **Power:** 20 amps. **Water.** Pumpout. Garbage disposal. **Showers, laundry**, **washrooms**. **Fuel dock** 250-799-5580: Gas, diesel. One and a half miles to uptown stores, restaurants, museum, motel, car rentals. Post office, credit union, hospital. Store: Tackle, fishing licences, bait, groceries, liquor, gifts. Charts, marine supplies. No food services at marina. Poor VHF radio reception. Broadband internet service is available. Wharfinger office open 8.30 - 4.30 pm (weekdays). BC Ferries.

If you ask the townsfolk at Bella Coola where their favourite hot springs is located, they may tell you. Just down North Bentinck Arm to South Bentinck Arm and turn south. Several miles down the arm just beyond Bensins Island and on the opposite shore is Talheo hot springs at the mouth of Hotsprings Creek. Anchor off and row ashore for a hot soak in the sulphur waters of this delightful pool. It has been improved by the local people of Bella Coola so please respect it and leave it clean.

Bella Coola may be reached overland from Williams Lake but it is far easier by water. And the town is worth a visit. The walk into town from the harbour is pleasant, about three kilometres, with magnificent views over the delta and the high adjacent mountains. History was made in this area with the arrival of Alexander Mackenzie in July, 1793 when he completed the first recorded crossing of North America. This was ahead of Lewis and Clark by some 13 years. He was not far behind Captain Vancouver who had passed through the area only seven weeks previously.

In Bella Coola visit the museum where the president of the Museum Society may have some surprise information in store for you. Ask about tours of nearby petroglyphs. Read the book *Bella Coola* by Cliff Kopas, early settler and author who founded Kopas General Store. In summer months the town is busy with festivities ranging from a rodeo, a music festival and a fall fair and parade.

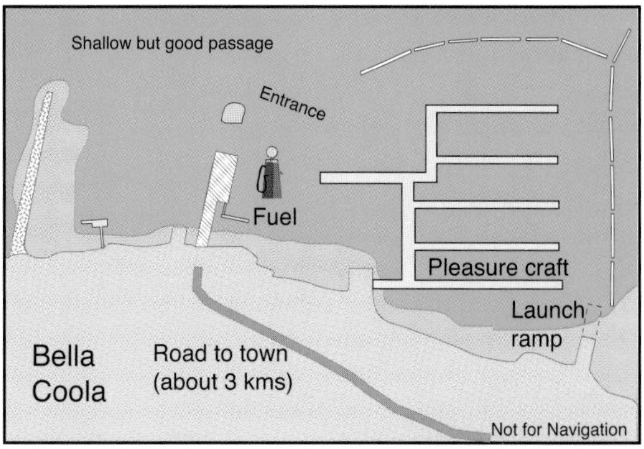

Above, centre and top: Views of Bella Coola harbour and dock plan.

Photo: Sharon Allman

Klemtu–Hartley Bay

Charts 3711, 3742

North Coast

Klemtu Tourism Dock

Wharfinger. **Ph: 250-839-3246** **VHF 06**
GD, Klemtu BC V0T 1L0
Ph: 250-839-1233 Charts 3711, 3734, 3902
info@klemtutourism.com
Website: www.klemtutourism.com
Moorage: Mooring float for guests at nearby band operated dock. Two stores. **Fuel:** Gas, diesel, stove oil, propane, water. Store at fuel dock. Groceries; ice; marine/ fishing supplies, ATM, hiking trail to water tower lookout, medical services, post office, guided tours; kayak rentals, Floathouse Inn, Klemtu Lodge, cabin rentals. Up town Robinson-Mason general store (near the church): groceries. Visit the Big House. Ask at fuel dock for directions.

Hartley Bay (Txal giu)

Fuel dock attendant: Mary Dundas
GD, Hartley Bay BC V0V 1A0
hbvc@gitgaat.net
Ph: 250-841-2500 Fax: 250-841-2679
Marina: Moorage at public docks behind breakwater. **Fuel:** Gas, diesel. Credit cards accepted. **Power:** 20 amps. **Water**. Groceries. Post office. General store. Garbage drop. Emergency helipad. Nearby mooring buoys in Stewart Channel. This is a government dock run by the local band–office at 445 Hayimiisaxaa Way in the village.

Klemtu Band membership, reception at Kitasoo-Xai'xais Government House: Warren Edgar Ph: 250-839-1255
Klemtu and Hartley Bay are the last significant stops before Prince Rupert or Kitimat.
Fuel at Hartley Bay.
Distance Klemtu to Prince Rupert 150 miles.

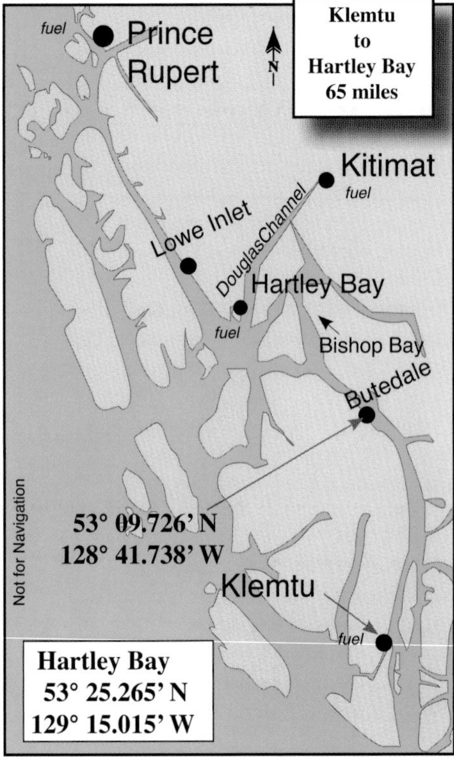

Opposite: The village dock and the Lodge at Klemtu. Above: The docks and fuel dock at Hartley Bay. Right: M.K. Bay Marina in Kitimat. It is located on the east side of Douglas Channel adjacent to the Haisla First Nations Kitimaat village. Bottom: M.K. Bay Marina. Below, right: Moon Bay Marina on the northwest side of Douglas Channel (southwest of the town of Kitimat), just beyond the Alcan smelter wharf.

Kitimat

53° 59.200' N
128° 40.572 ' W

M.K. Bay Marina **VHF 68**

Manager: Richard Smeal
Kitamaat Village Rd, PO Box 220
Kitimat BC V8C 2G7
Phone: 250-632-6401 Fax: 250-632-6889
www. mkbaymarina.com
Chart 3743, 3736 Launch ramp.
Marina: Fuel: Gas, diesel, oils. **Water.** **Moorage:** 150 slips. **Power** 15, 20, 30, 50 amp. **Laundry, showers, washrooms.** Haulouts to 20 tons. ATM. Charts, fishing licences, tackle, bait. Campground adjacent. Playground. Taxi to stores–7 miles (11 km) to town on Minette Bay Rd. Liquor store, post office, hospital. Marine stores.

Moon Bay Marina

Don Pearson
PO Box 196, Kitimat BC V8C 2G7
Ph: 250-632-1541.
Monitors Channel 16–Call: *Moon Bay.*
Fuel: Gas, diesel.
Water, toilets, showers.
Power can be made available.
Marine repairs and service. Rental fishing boats. Camping, boat launching ramp. Located northwest side of Douglas Channel past Alcan smelter wharf.
Visit Bishop Bay hot springs off Douglas Channel and Verney Passage.

Photo: Sharon Allman

Prince Rupert Harbour.

Ketchikan–first stop in Alaska.

Prince Rupert

54° 19.219' N
130° 19.169' W

North Coast

Prince Rupert, BC, is a fishing town. Its docks in season are brimming with commercial vessels rafted as many as six deep at the town's two major public docks. Moorage overnight for pleasure craft is best at the Prince Rupert Yacht Club or nearby at Port Edward. Yacht Club spaces are tight and subject to being available only if members are away temporarily. It is necessary to call ahead to reserve space, although frequently boats arriving early in the day will be allocated a slip immediately or later in the day.

Directly above the marina there are friendly services for the transient mariner, from laundry and showers to nearby restaurants, pubs, shopping and marine repairs. Arts of local people can be found in stores up town. A good hotel with restaurant and pub sits atop the cliff overlooking the harbour.

Fuel is available at a number of fuel docks along the waterfront. Prince Rupert is the final major stop before continuing to Alaska. Mariners learn while talking to other yachtsmen during stops along the British Columbia coast that entering Alaska may not always be straight forward. Wind can prevent vessels, especially slow cruising yachts, from making the Rupert to Ketchikan run all in one stretch. And the reason most skippers plan it in one step is the belief that one has to do so as a customs clearing requirement. What one learns is that it is possible to stop en route, either on the Canadian side at Dundas Island or on the Alaskan side several miles up channel from Cape Fox at Foggy Bay. If there is any doubt whatever that you can make the run in one leg, it is best to call Alaska customs and ask for permission to stop at a specific place en route. Remember also that Alaska, unlike BC, remains on Standard Time all year.

Once in Ketchikan there is much to do and see, from a visit to the Totem Heritage Center to walking the old town with its infamous Creek Street, once the place of bawdy houses and frontier life at its most colourful.

It's a tourist town with several large cruise ships at a time lining the docks right alongside the downtown main streets. And it's a town which will prompt you to stay a while, test the delights of fine cuisine and then go on deeper into the Alaskan Southeast or Panhandle, whichever you prefer to call it. There are numerous books and guides on cruising Alaska. Once in the state you will find easy access to lots of cruising options with easy availability of fuel and services along the way.

The Prince Rupert Yacht Club. It is located on the east shore of the harbour, seen also in the photo on the opposite page, top. Call on channel 73 for moorage reservations.

Photo: Sharon Allman

Prince Rupert Yacht & Rowing Club

Jo-Lynda Hill
121 George Hills Way
Prince Rupert BC V8J 1A3
Ph/Fax: 250-624-4317
Charts 3964, 3957, 3958, 3955 VHF 73
info@prryc.com
www.prryc.com
Marina services: Customs station. **Moorage:** Boats to 250'. **Power:** 30 amps. **Water. Shower,** ice, bait, power wash available. No reciprocal club moorage.
Adjacent facilities:
Fuel: Esso 250-624-5000, Petro Canada 250-624-4106.
Up town Prince Rupert is five minutes walk. Also restaurants (Smiles, Breakers Pub, Crest Hotel).
Anchorages at Pilsbury Cove and Tuck Inlet.
Public docks nearby–busy during fishing season: Rafting. Fishing openings usually begin 6pm Sundays. BC Ferries, Alaska Ferries.

Note: Five knots speed limit strictly enforced in Prince Rupert Harbour. Vessel speeds are monitored by radar. Make no wash or wake.

Prince Rupert Chart 3958

Rushbrooke Harbour

Lydio Burias
288 George Hills Way
Port Edward, BC V0V 1G0
Ph: 250-624-9400 Fax: 250-624-9460
Marina services:
Large marina with about 400 slips. Power: 15 amps. **Water, washrooms, showers,** public pay phone, public launch ramp adjacent. Garbage disposal. 20 minutes walk into town.

Cow Bay Floats Lydio Burias

Next to Prince Rupert Yacht Club
Ph: 250-624-9400 Chart 3958, 3957
Commercial fishing float.

Fairview Harbour

South end of Prince Rupert harbour
Rick Hill
PO Box 1820
Port Edward BC V0V 1G0
Chart 3958, 3957
Ph: 250-624-3127 Fax: 250-624-9430
Marina Services: Power: 25, 30 amp, water, garbage disposal. Fishing harbour. 300 vessel capacity. Pleasure boats welcome.
Fuel alongside.

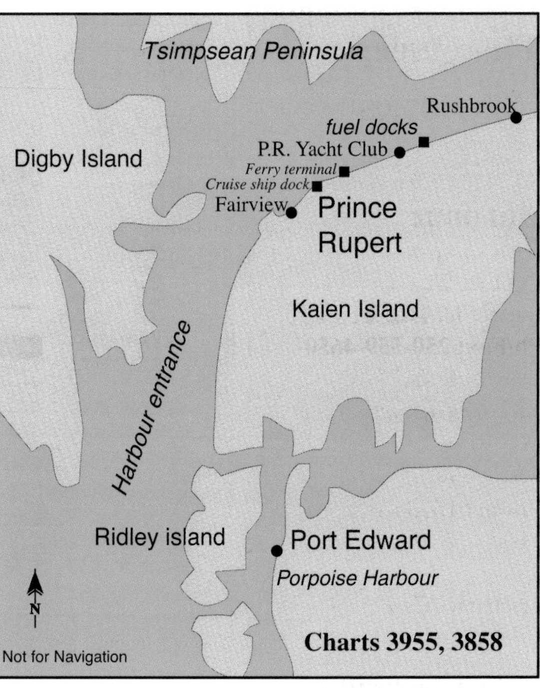

Left, top: Creek Street, Ketchikan recalls its past with souvenir and gift stores that are former bawdy houses, lining the boardwalk. Information on preceding pages. Left: Signpost at Prince Rupert.

Port Edward

Prince Rupert alternative moorage

Porpoise Harbour Marina Complex

Port Edward Harbour Authority
Rick Hill
200 Bayview Dr, PO Box 1820
Port Edward BC V0V 1G0
Ph: 250-628-9220 Fax: 250-628-9233
peharbor@citytel.Net
www.peharbour.ca
Charts 3955, 3957, 3958
Marina services: Fishing harbour–public moorage. **Power:** 20, 30 amp. **Water, laundry, washrooms,** public pay phone. Travel lift.
Adjacent facilities: Cab service to Prince Rupert–Skeena Taxi Ph: 250-624-2185. Convenience store. North Pacific Cannery Museum. Bus service.

The Queen Charlottes

Charts 3890, 3894

For those crossing to the Queen Charlottes there are a few marinas available for transient moorage. There is a large marina at Sandspit and several public marinas in other parts of the islands as listed below and on the following page.

Sandspit Harbour Marina

Kathy Goalder
PO Box 477, Sandspit BC V0T 1T0
Ph: 250-637-5700 Fax: 250-637-2460
Charts 3890, 3894 VHF 66A
sandspit@Island.net
Transport Canada dock
Marina services: Fuel: Gas, diesel. **Moorage** up to 100'. Power: 15, 30, 50, 100 amp. Pumpout. Garbage disposal. Water, **showers, washrooms**. Launch ramp. **Adjacent facilities:** Car rentals, shops and city services and amenities.

The Queen Charlottes

QC Small Craft Harbour

Steve Collinson
PO Box 68 **VHF 06**
Queen Charlotte BC V0T 1S0
Ph/Fax: 250-559-4650
Charts 3890,3894
harbour@qcislands.net
Marina services: Public dock. Water, garbage.
Power: 15, 30 amp.
Nearby fuel: gas, diesel, propane. Marine store, mechanic. City has all amenities.

Port Clements Small Craft Harbour

Chris Marrs
PO Box 126
Port Clements BC V0T 1R0
Ph: 250-557-4295
Fax: 250-557-4568
marrs@islands.net
Power: 20 amp. Launch ramp. **Chart 3893**
Caution: shallow at low tide.

Delkatla Slough

Harbour Authority
Dale Otto
PO Box 35
Masset BC V0T 1M0
Ph: 250-626-5487
Fax: 250-626-5193
Charts 3892, 3895
VHF 66A
Marina services: Fuel.
Power: 20, 30 amp.
Water. Tidal grid.
Shower, laundry. Shops.

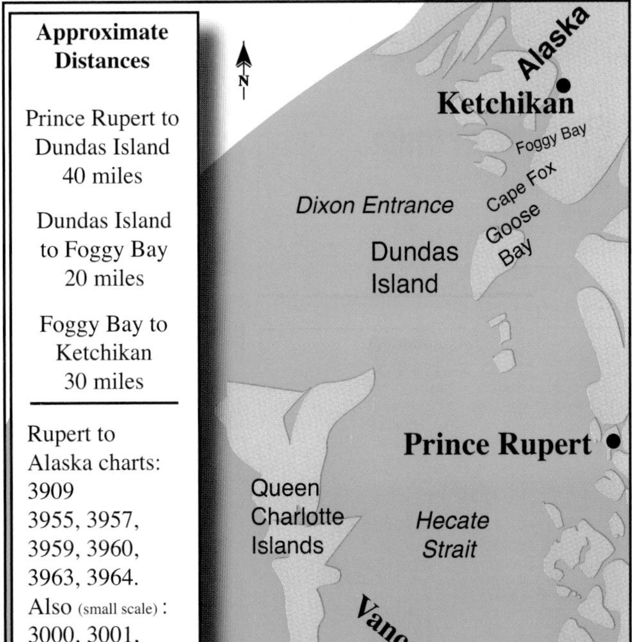

Next stop—Alaska

If you are proceeding to Alaska, your fist stop will be Ketchikan, probably via a short stop at Foggy Bay. This protected bay is a short distance beyond Cape Fox which you pass as you venture across Dixon Entrance into Alaskan waters. If you are planning to stop in American territory before reaching Ketchikan, an official customs port of entry, you must obtain permission from customs in Ketchikan first. This can be done by calling 907-225-2254 and advising customs that you will need to stop at Foggy Bay. Ask for permission to do so rather than telling the customs officer that you are going to stop there. And if the weather permits a straight, uninterrupted run into Ketchikan simply dock at a convenient slip and call customs. They may ask you to walk up town to their offices to clear. Note: It is important to read the customs document you are issued, as it instructs you to notify customs at certain other Alaskan points as you proceed farther along the coast. This is the case, even though you have cleared at Ketchikan (or elsewhere in Alaska). Customs hours are office hours, week-days only. Special arrangements are required for clearing at weekends.

A safe harbour to spend time waiting for suitable wind and sea conditions to cross Dixon Entrance is at Goose Bay on the north end of Dundas Island. If you set out from Prince Rupert in calm seas but the wind picks up and dictates a rough passage beyond Dundas stop a while and do some fishing, reading and relaxing. Then travel when conditions improve. At Dundas you are about 20 miles from Foggy Bay or about 70 from Ketchikan. Rupert to Ketchikan is 90 miles.

West Coast Vancouver Island

Section 7

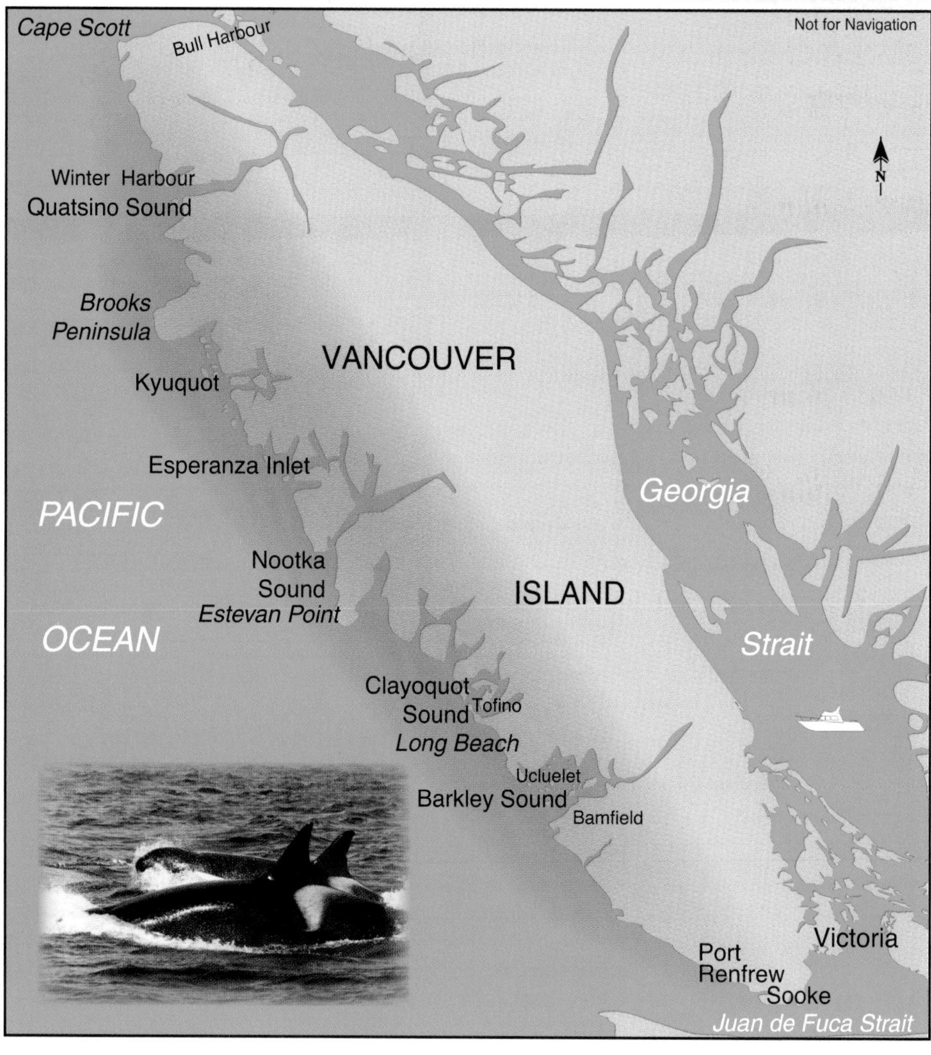

The west coast of Vancouver Island enjoys a short summer season of recreational boating. All year around, however, there is maritime activity catered to by a small number of marine facilities. These are scattered among the inlets and coves that indent the rugged coast and serve as a home away from home to those out working the coast. They serve also as havens of safety and replenishment for those seeking to extend their pleasure boating experiences in British Columbia. It is possible to travel along the Pacific west coast of Vancouver Island yet remain in sheltered waters a good deal of the time.

The open coast is broken up by numerous islands, large and small, forming inlets and protected waterways. One can travel along these waterways, poking out into the open Pacific during calm conditions and moving along to the next inlet which in some cases is no more than about 25 miles distant. The longest stretches of open water are between Juan de Fuca Strait and Barkley Sound to the south and between Quatsino Sound and Bull Harbour to the north.

Above: The dock at Whiskey Cove in Ucluelet with its overnighting fishing boats, makes a striking picture on a mild, grey day in summer. The main dock farther up the inlet accommodates visiting pleasure craft. Right: Adjacent to the public docks in Ucluelet is the Canadian Princess fishing resort.

Right: The Amphitrite Point lighthouse at Ucluelet. Since the advent of electronic navigation aids lighthouses on the Canada coast have been automated. Few are still manned.

50° 30.784' N
128° 01.729' W

Photos courtesy The Outpost

Winter Harbour

West Coast Vanc I

The Outpost (Former BC Packers dock)

Greg and Andrea Vance
GD, Winter Harbour BC V0N 3L0
Ph: 250-969-4333 Fax: 250-969-4334
winterharbour@telus.net
www.winterharbour.ca

Moorage. Over 900'. The marina does not have power. Water is G-gas, diesel, filters.

There is a coin operated **laundry** and **showers**. A general store (fresh produce, groceries, ice, fishing tackle) and liquor agency are on site. The marina serves 35 RV campsites which are fully serviced. Guided fishing charters available.

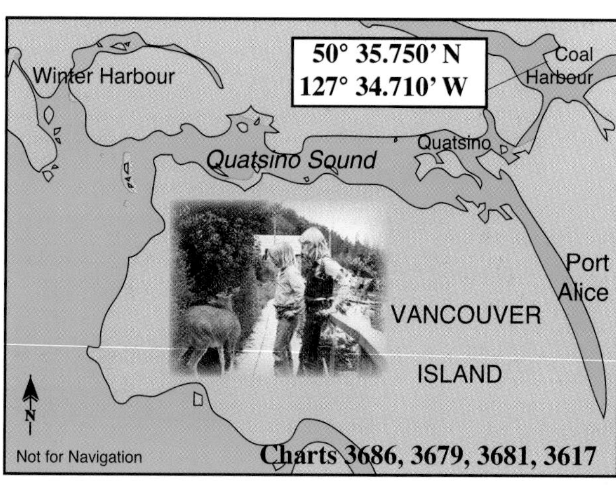

Coal Harbour

Transport Canada dock
Charts 3681, 3617
Large dock for public use • Garbage-waste oil disposal • Derrick • Lights • Power • The Coal Harbour public port facility is located on Holberg Inlet on Vancouver Island and includes a wharf, an approach and two floats.

Winter Harbour

Winter Harbour Authority
GD, Winter Harbour BC V0N 3L0. • Float length 171 metres • Garbage disposal • Derrick • Water • General store nearby. Washrooms, library, public pay phones at community building.

Quatsino

Transport Canada dock.
Charts 3681, 3679.
Loading dock.

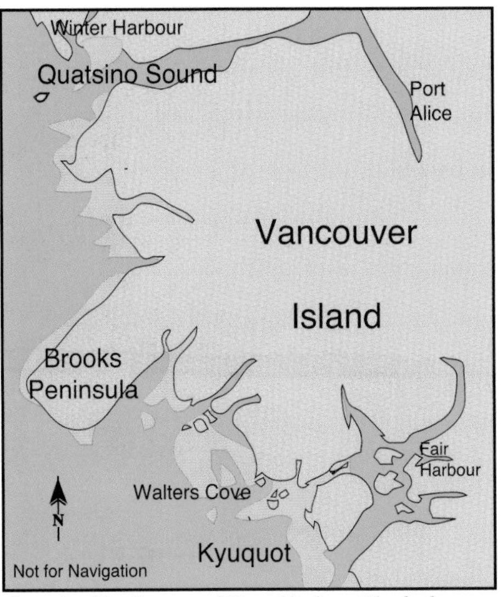

Opposite: The Outpost at Winter Harbour. The docks are at top in the inset photo. The photograph on the map opposite bottom was taken some years ago. Wildlife presence and the "main road" walkway have not changed.
Right: The visitor dock at Walters Cove, Kyuqout. The post office and store is at the head of the dock.

Photo: Robin Battley

Port Alice Yacht Club

50° 23.008' N
127° 27.312' W

Errol Stewart
Ph: 250-284-6100 Charts 3681, 3679
Power, water. Fuel on land.
Some moorage available. Launch ramp adjacent to club. Water, power.
It's a pleasant cruise down the inlet but if it is windy there is not much protection. The marina, which is a ten minute walk from the nearby settlement, provides shelter from windy conditions.

Kyuquot (Houpsitas)

Fisheries & Oceans dock
Float length 82 m
Charts 3651, 3682, 3683, 3623

Kyuquot Transport Canada dock

Float length 103 metres
30 m wharf • Derrick • Sheds
Charts 3651, 3682, 3683.

Kyuquot

50° 23.008' N
127° 27.312' W

Walters Cove

Susan Bostrom
PO Kyuquot BC Ph: 250-332-5209
Charts 3651, 3682, 3683, 3623
Marina services:
Moorage–public dock. Post office and store at head of dock (see photo above). Cafe adjacent to post office.

Swan Song

Located at Fair Harbour, Kyuquot.
Owner: Richard Leo
217-1434 Island Hwy
Campbell River BC V9W 8C9
Store phone: 250-830-2230
E-mail: swansong@crcn.net
Chart: 3682
Marina services: Guest moorage: approx. 8 slips. Reservations suggested.
Services. Water, outhouse, internet access, launch ramp, gas, diesel, propane, marine/fishing supplies, ice, groceries, water taxi service arranged, fishing charters, 10 campsites, reservations required, credit cards accepted.

Tahsis

49° 54.683' N
126° 39.676' W

Westview Marina

Cathy Daynes
PO Box 481, Tahsis BC V0P 1X0
Ph: 250-934-7672 Fax: 250-934-6445
Toll free 1-800-992-3262 Chart 3676
info@westviewmarina.com
www.westviewmarina.com

Moorage–year round. Summer transient available. Reservations recommended. **Fuel:** Gas, diesel, ice**. Power:** 15, 30 amp. **Water.** Store–groceries. Garbage disposal. Marina Cantina licenced restaurant/patio. **Laundry, showers, washrooms.** Internet access. Quarter mile to Tahsis. Pool, restaurants, supermarket, RCMP, Info Centre and Museum. **Launch ramp**.
Beware of logs in the harbour on approaches to Tahsis and the marina.

Tahsis

Public (Deep Water) dock
Charts 3676, 3604
Manager • Float length 30 metres • 42 m wharf • Garbage disposal • Derrick • Lights • Sheds • Public phone ashore • General store • Liquor agency • Post office • Shops and accommodations nearby.

Esperanza (two docks)

PO Box 398, Tahsis BC V0P 1X0
Charts 3676, 3604 **VHF 66A**
Transport Canada (Hospital Floats)
Manager • Float length 42 metres • Water • Lights • Moorage–summer transient space available.
Esperanza public dock/fuel dock.
Float length 15 m • Wharf 29 m • Derrick • Lights. Fuel: Gas, diesel, stove oil, naptha, kerosene • Water. Mini store • Showers. Laundry. Phone ashore (emergency use only). Food available at Nootka Mission camp.

Gold River Golf Course 250-283-7221

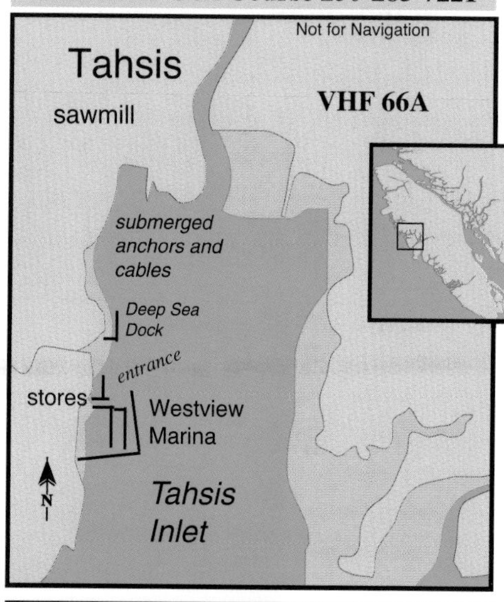

Zeballos

49° 58.685' N
126° 50.771' W

Weston Enterprises

Tom and Alice Weston
PO Box 100, Zeballos BC V0P 2A0
Ph: 250-761-4201 Fax: 250-761-4618
Charts 3676, 3664 VHF 66A
Fuel: Gas, diesel, propane, ice. Store, marine supplies. Seaplane landing and fuel dock**. Moorage** at nearby public docks. **Water, garbage** drop, public pay phone. **Nearby:** General store, liquor agency, museum, information centre, clinic, laundromat, Zeballos Hotel, restaurants, post office. Washrooms, showers.

Zeballos

Small Craft Harbour
Arlene Coburn
PO Box 99, Zeballos BC V0P 2A0
Ph/Fax: 250-761-4333
Charts 3676, 3604 **VHF 66A**
Guest moorage. Float length 191 metres. Garbage/oil disposal. Water. Power: 15 amp. Showers.Washrooms.
Fuel at Weston Ent. Launch ramp.

Zeballos Village Dock

Ph: 250-761-4229
For commercial vessels.

Gold River

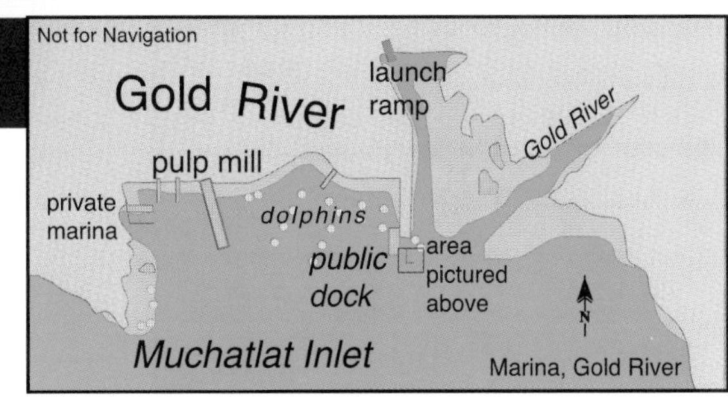

Critter Cove Marina

Cameron Forbes
PO Box 1118
Gold River BC V0P 1G0
Ph: 250-283-7364 or 604-886-7667
Fax: 250-285-7364
Charts 3675, 3603 **VHF 07**
info@crittercove.com
www.crittercove.com

Moorage: 1000 feet of dock space as available in summer May 16 to September 15. Call for reservations. Anchoring nearby. Rental cabins and suites available. Licensed restaurant, snack bar. **Fuel:** Gas. Store, licences, bait. Coffee House. Known for their chowder and home-made pies. **Showers, washrooms, water.** Launch ramp at Gold River.

Gold River

Public dock. Charts 3675, 3603
Manager • Float length 47 metres • Wharf • Aircraft float • Garbage disposal • Water • Lights • Power • Telephone • Sheds • Launch ramp

Tuta Marina

Larry and Shirley Andrews
490 Eagle Cresc, PO Box 765, Gold River BC V0P 1G0 Ph/Fx: 250-283-7550
tutamarina@cablerocket.com

Chart 3675 Located in Hanna Channel, Nootka Sound. 50 slips. Open summer only–July-Sept. **Fuel:** Gas, oil. Boat launch ramp. **Store,** licences, bait. **Showers,** Campground. Pit toilets.

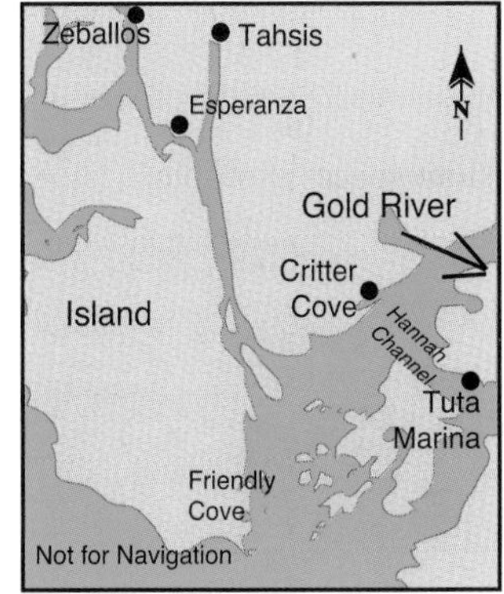

Long Beach Golf Course 250-725-3302

Hot Springs Cove

Parks Canada
300' visitors dock
Ph: 250-670-1149
Charts 3674, 3603 VHF 66A
Marine Park. Hot Springs.

49° 21.726' N
126° 15.927' W

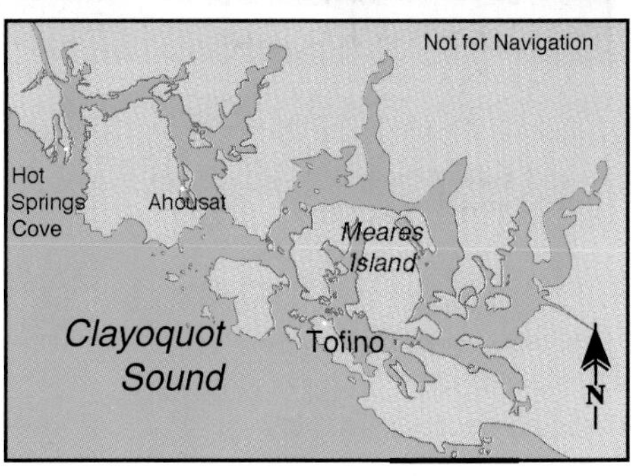

49° 16.939' N 126° 04.277' W

Ahousat, Matilda Inlet

Hugh Clarke **Ph: 250-670-9575**
Charts 3673, 3674, 3603
Moorage: 400' guest dock • Derrick • Lights • Sheds • Public phone.
Fuel: Gas, diesel, stove oil.
Attractions and amenities:
General store. Cafe. Post office. Fuel. Marine Ways. Water. Nearby is the Gibson Marine Park and Hot Springs.

Top and inset: Fourth Street public dock at Tofino. Fuel is available at Method Marine (opposite), whose service station is part of the marina complex and a major fuel stop on the west coast.
The lower photo shows Weigh West Marina and the waters of Tofino beyond.

Weigh West Marine Resort

385 Campbell St
PO Box 69
Tofino BC V0R 2Z0
Ph: 250-725-3277
Guest moorage, marina, restaurant and pub. This is a resort with accommodation and a marine adventure centre for fishing enthusiasts. Reservations recommended in summer.

Armitage Point dock at Tofino (Crab Dock)

Method Marine

Tofino

Tofino Harbour Authority
Fourth Street Harbour
VHF 78A
Vince Payette
PO Box 826, Tofino BC V0R 2Z0
Ph: 250-725-4441 Fax: 250-725-4461
tofhar@island.net
Charts 3685, 3673, 3603, 3674

• Float length 444 metres • 15 m wharf • Breakwater • Grid • Garbage/oil disposal • Derrick • Water • Lights • Power: 20 amp • Sheds • Launch ramp • Public phone ashore. General stores, liquor agency, Post office, shops, laundry and accommodations nearby. Note: Method Marine is a private marina and does not cater to transient boats. It is recommended mariners check in at the public docks.

Armitage Point (Crab Dock)
Vince Payette

• Float length 121 metres • Garbage disposal • Derrick • Lights. Public pay phone ashore. General stores, liquor agency, Post office, shops, laundry and accommodations in town nearby.

Top: Armitage Point public docks. Note buoys. Inset: Method Marine docks in Tofino. Fog is common in the summer months.

Method Marine Supply

Steve Bernard
380 Main St **VHF 6**
PO Box 219, Tofino BC V0R 2Z0
Ph: 250-725-3251 Fax: 250-725-2111
Charts 3685, 3673, 3603, 3674

Moorage for boats to 22 feet–regular guests. Overnight moorage usually not available. **Power:** 20 amp. **Fuel**: Gas, diesel, stove oil. **Water**, ice, propane, **laundry, toilets.**

Chandlery, marine service station–parts and accessories. Tackle shop–scoffee, snacks, Scuba air fills. Charts, bait.

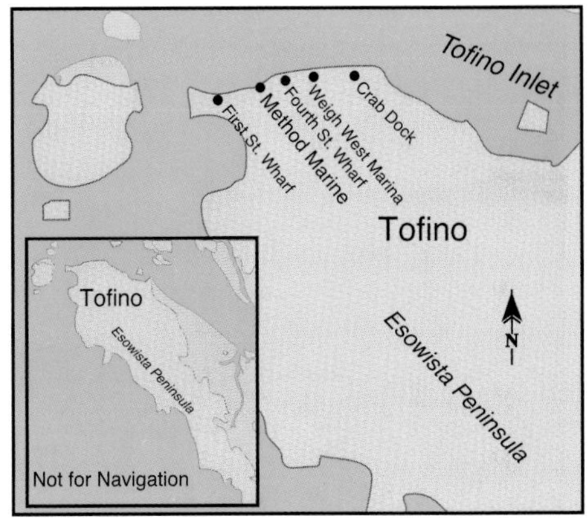

Ucluelet Boat Harbour docks–the entrance is off to the right. The Canadian Princess has a dock for its charter fishing vessels.
Opposite page: The docks at Islands West Fishing Resort early in the year await arrival of many small boats. Right: Pub at the marina.
Diagrams show: Ucluelet and Ucluth Peninsula–note approximate location of primary marinas; Barkley Sound (opposite) with Ucluelet and Bamfield locations.
Use a large scale chart for safe navigation;

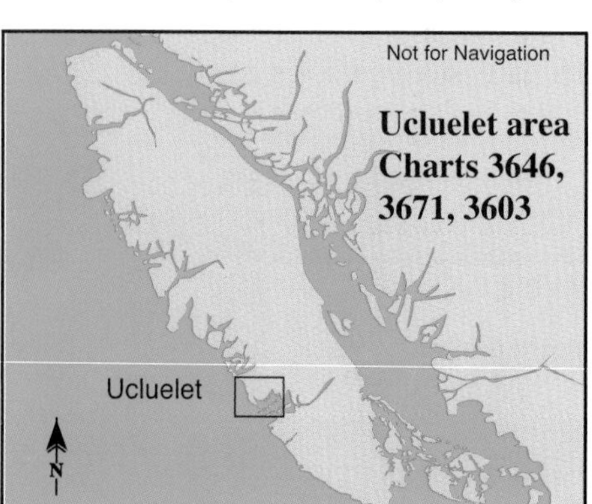

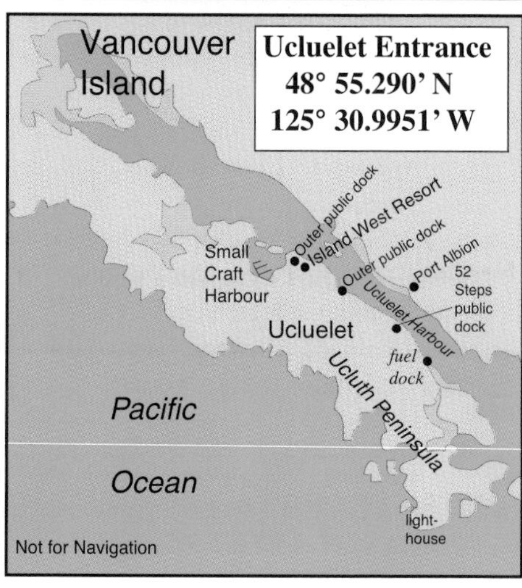

Uclulet

Ucluelet public docks
Boat Harbour– (inner harbour)
Hemlock Street
PO Box 910, Ucluelet BC V0R 3A0
Ph/fax: 250-726-4241 or 250-726-2473
Charts 3646, 3671, 3603
Manager Steve Bird. • Float length 820 metres • Garbage/oil disposal • Water • Lights • Power: 20 amp • Phone • Toilets • Near general stores, restaurants, Post office, shops, pool, laundry, accommodations, showers.

Other public docks (outer harbour):
Otter Street–(52 Steps)
Clear customs here.
No customs available at Bamfield.
CANPASS: Ph: 1-888-CANPASS
District of Ucluelet dock
Manager Steve Bird. • Float length 150 m • Garbage disposal • Lights • Public pay phone • Water •

Main Street–Ucluelet public dock
Manager • Float length 36 m • Wharf • Garbage disposal • Derrick • Lights

Port Albion facility dock
Float length 49 metres.

"52 Steps" Otter Street dock–
48° 56.474' N 125° 32.482' W

Island West Fishing Resort

PO Box 32 Ucluelet BC V0R 3A0
Ph: 250-726-7515 Fax: 250-726-4414
Charts 3646, 3671, 3603 VHF 66A
fish@islandwestresort.com
www.islandwestresort.com
Marina services:
Moorage–Summer transient available at times. **Power**: 15 amp. **Launch ramp.** Water, ice, tackle shop, **laundry, showers, washrooms**. Pub/Reswtaurant. Marine supplies, deli, accommodations. Fishing gear and charters. Fish freezing.
Nearby: Fuel: Gas, diesel, stove oil–at Eagle Marine Ltd Ph: 250-726-4262.
RV park, stores, restaurants, bakery.

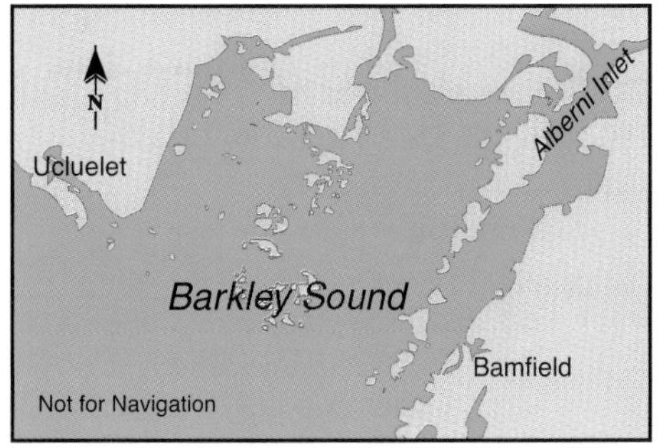

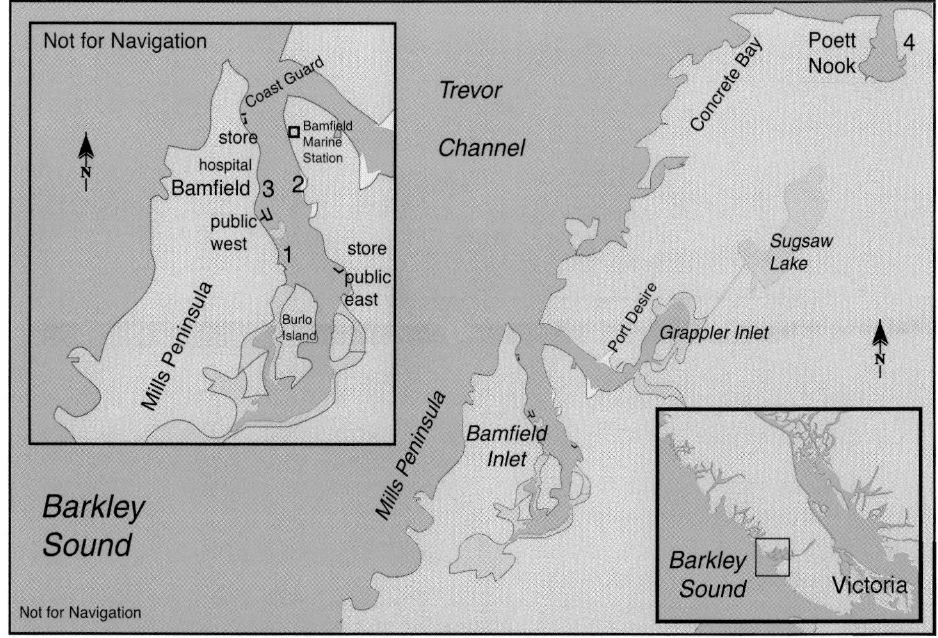

Bamfield

1. McKay Bay Lodge

Brian and Cheryl McKay
PO Box 116, Bamfield BC V0R 1B0
Ph: 250-728-3323 Fax: 250-728-3255
Charts 3646, 3671, 3602
mckaybay@island.net
www.bamfield-travel.com
Moorage–limited transient 300’.
Fuel: gas. Ice, washrooms. Fishing gear and charters. Accommodations (resort), restaurant (by reservation only).
Nearby: Post office, grocery, bakery, liquor store, marine store and medical services.

2. Kingfisher Marina

Scott Needham & Lori Parker
PO Box 38, Bamfield BC V0R 1B0
Ph: 250-728-3228 Fax: 250-728-3268
Charts 3646, 3671, 3602
kingfishermarina@telus.net
www.hawkeyemarinegroup.com
Fuel: Gas, diesel. **Water.** Ice. Tackle shop. Fishing licences. Accommodations. Charters. Limited visitor moorage.

Bamfield Public Docks

• **East**–Transport Canada dock
Charts 3646, 3671, 3602
Manager • Float length 128 metres • Wharf 18 m • Breakwater • Garbage disposal • Derrick • Lights • Phone • Sheds. Near general store.
• **Port Désiré**–Fisheries & Oceans dock
Manager • Float length 22 m • Launch ramp.
• **West**–Fisheries and Oceans dock
Manager • Float length 154 m • Garbage
• **West**–Transport Canada dock
Manager • Float length 24 m • Wharf 18 metres • Derrick • No water or power

Note: The hospital is located on the east side of Bamfield Inlet.

Barkley Sound is known for its fishing and scuba diving. The town of Bamfield is a good base for reaching some of the beautiful waters and beaches strewn throughout the Sound, especially in the islands of the Broken Group.

3. Bamfield Lodge and Cottages

Barry and Judy Otterson VHF 66A
PO Box 23
Bamfield BC V0R 1B0
Ph: 250-728-3419
Fax: 250-728-3417
barry@bamfieldlodge.com
www.bamfieldlodge.com
Charts: 3646, 3671, 3602
Moorage–limited transient when available. **Power**. **Water.** Ice. Fish freezers. Cappuccino bar. Accommodations (resort), cottages, charters, tours, marine field trips, kayaking, whale watching.

4. Poett Nook Marina

Dave Hooper
6170 Werners Way, Nanaimo BC V9V 1R7
Ph: 250-758-4440 or 250-720-9572 
poetnookmarina@hotmail.com
www.*poettnookmarina.com*
Charts 3671, 3688, 3602
Moorage: Boats to 26 feet. Campground. **Fuel**: Gas. **Washrooms, showers.**

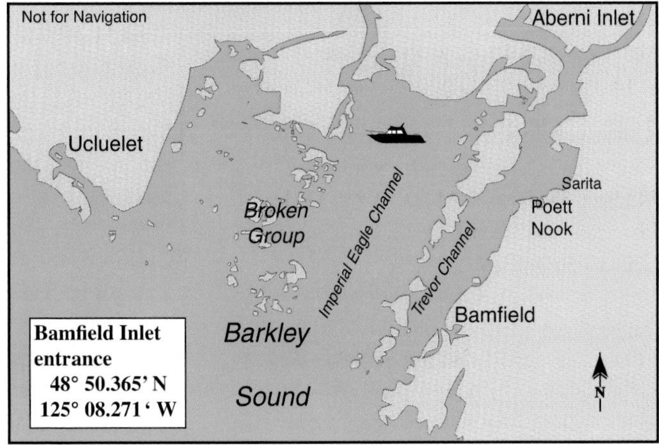

Top: Approaching the dock in Bamfield. Coast Guard at right. Above: The post office at Bamfield.

Port Alberni Golf Course 250-723-5422

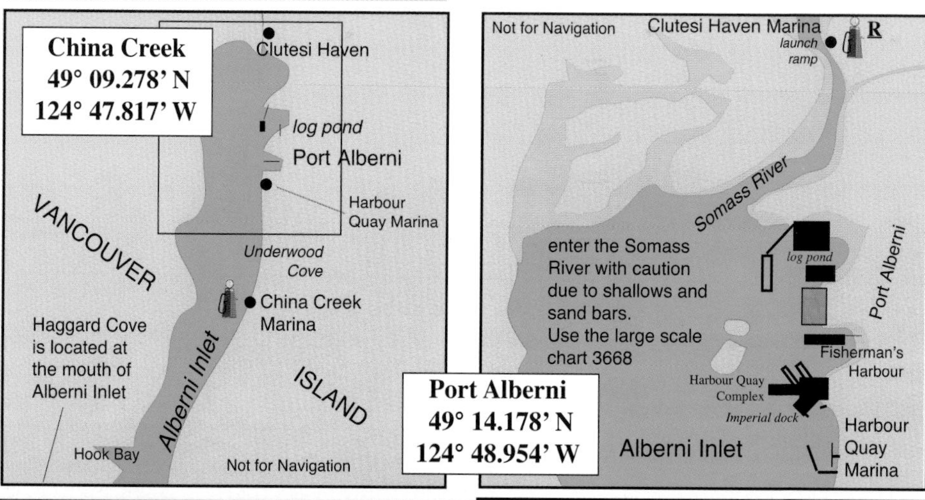

Port Alberni

Clutesi Haven Marina

Tom McMillan
5104 River Rd
Port Alberni BC V9Y 6Z1 VHF 66A
Ph: 250-724-6837 Fax: 250-723-1114
Chart 3668 (up Somass River)
Moorage–summer transient available at times. **Water. Power** 30 amp.
Fuel: Gas. Public pay phone. Launch ramp. Ice, **showers, washrooms**. Pumpout. Chandlery. Fishing gear and charters.
Nearby: Port Alberni: Grocery, hardware, propane, marine supplies, restaurants, bakery, laundry, liquor store and other facilities.

Haggard Cove Resort

Ron and Deborah Clark
PO Box 396, Port Alberni BC V9Y 7M9
Located near entrance to Alberni Canal.
Ph: 250-723-8457
haggardcove@shaw.ca
www.haggardcove.com
Charts 3668 VHF 27 (MV *Our Way*)
Moorage–Occasional summer transient available June to October. **Reservations.** Fishing Lodge. Fishing gear and charters. **Water.** Accommodations, meals.

Fisherman's Harbour

Port Alberni Port Authority
Mark Braithwaite
3140 Harbour Rd, Port Alberni
Phone. 250-723-2533
email: p.a.f.h.mark@shaw.ca
Chart 3668. • Float length 825 metres • Breakwater 70 m wharf • Garbage disposal • Sani-pumpout • Derrick • Water • Lights • Power.

China Creek Marina

Port Alberni Port Authority **Chart 3668**
Bruce Kramer
2750 Harbour Rd
Port Alberni BC V9Y 7X2 VHF 16
Ph: 250-723-9812 Fax: 250-723-9842
Moorage–summer transient moorage if space available. Reservations suggested.
Fuel: Gas, diesel, propane**. Water.**
Power: 30 amps. Garbage disposal, ice.
Customer Services:
Laundry. Showers. Washrooms.
Laundry. Launch ramp adjacent. Mini-store–fishing gear and supplies, cafe. Campsite, sani-dump.
Playground. 9 miles to Port Alberni.

Harbour Quay Marina

Richard Hartigan–Harbour Master
2750 Harbour Rd
Port Alberni BC V9Y 7X2
Ph: 250-723-1413
Fax: 250-723-1114
Cellular: 250-720-6256
Chart 3668

Moorage: Harbour–breakwater and retaining shoreline with primary docks. 116 resident slips.
Power: 20, 30 amps, **water** and nearby shore facilities. **Washrooms, laundry. Visitor moorage** is also available at the nearby Fishermen's Harbour. Visit the quay at Fisherman's Harbour for restaurants, gift and craft shops and the nearby The Boathouse chandler.
The local Marine Historical Society and the Port Alberni Museum have mounted the former Chrome Island lighthouse on top of the Discovery Centre on the pier.

Port Alberni Harbour Authority

Top: The launch ramp on the Somass River at Clutesi Haven (also above, top left) in Port Alberni extends in the river. Below: Fuel is available at Clutesi Haven and at China Creek (above, bottom left). Above right: Harbour Quay.

Clutesi Haven

Port Alberni Yacht Club

PO Box 37, Port Alberni BC V9Y 7M6. Located at Fleming Island in Barkley Sound, it has guest moorage of approx. 240' plus power, water, washrooms and showers.

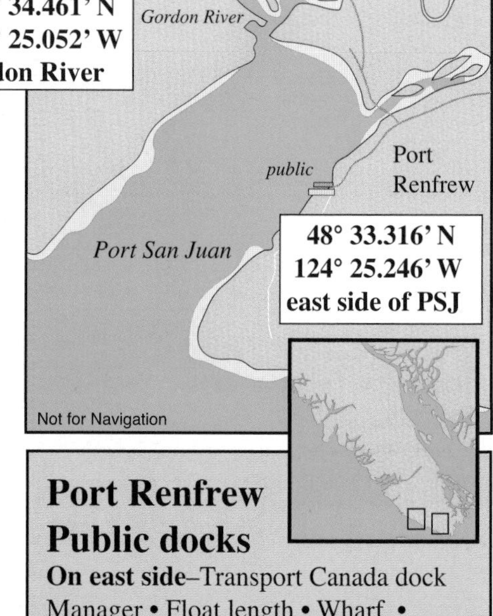

Port Renfrew

Port Renfrew Marina

Rex Colburn
Gordon River Rd, Port Renfrew BC
Ph: 250-478-3674 Marina 250-647-0002
Fax: 250-478-3696
cactusdevelopments@shaw.ca
www.portrenfrewmarina.com
Charts 3647, 3606 **VHF 66A**
Marina: Bait, tackle and fishing licences.
Fuel: Gas, oil. RV park. Campground.
Launch ramp.
Open May through September.

Enter up river on instructions from marina. Larger boats require high tide.

Photo above: The launch ramp at Port Renfrew is located on the Gordon River.
Opposite, top: The public docks at Sooke are located on the west shore of the harbour just after passing Whiffen Spit. Exercise great caution entering Sooke, using the channel markers to avoid hazards at the entrance.
Right: Sooke Harbour Marina–mostly small boats.

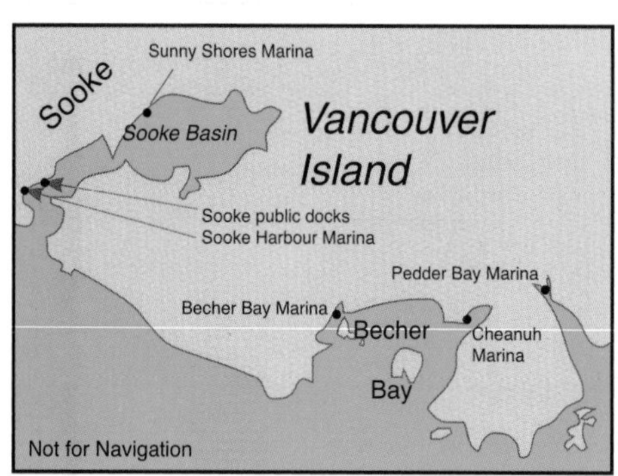

Port Renfrew Public docks

On east side–Transport Canada dock Manager • Float length • Wharf • (Breakwater) • Derrick • Lights • Phone ashore • Pub. Restaurant nearby.

Sooke

Sooke Harbour Resort & Marina

Matthew Mackenzie
6971 West Coast Rd, Sooke BC V0S 1N0
Ph: 250-642-3236
Chart 3410 **VHF 66A**
info@sookeharbourmarinia.ca
www.sookeharbourmarina.ca
Moorage–limited summer transient. **Power:** 15 amp. Water. Showers. Washrooms. Snacks. Garbage disposal. Nearby town–restaurants, shops. Launch ramp.

Sooke public dock

John Phillips Memorial Course 250-642-6344

Sooke Public Docks

Harbour Authority of Sooke
Ph: 250-642-4431
Chart 3461 • Manager • Float length 243 metres • Wharf 34 m • Garbage disposal • Derrick • Water • Lights • Power • Easy walk up into town for all shops and services.

Sunny Shores Marina

Andrew Planeta
5621 Sooke Rd, Sooke BC V0S 1N0
Ph: 250-642-5731 Fax: 250-642-5737
info@sunnyshoresresort.com
www.sunnyshoresresort.com
Charts 3410, 3411, 3461, 3606
(Enter from Eliza Point favouring the eastern shore)
Fuel: Gas, diesel, oil**. Power. Water. Launch Ramp.** Fishing licences. **Moorage**–some summer transient slips. **Showers. Washrooms. Laundry.** Mechanical service. Ministore–groceries. Pool. Nearby restaurants and bus service to Sooke and Victoria. This is mostly an RV and fishing facility.

Pedder Bay

Becher Bay Marina

Dolphin Loustalot
24 Becher Bay Rd, Sooke BC V0S 1N0
Ph: 250-642-3816 VHF 66A
Charts 3410, 3411, 3461, 3606
Marina: Power. **Water** Fishing, whale watching, boat rentals. Meals at the Smokin Tuna Restaurant on the waterfront.

Becher Bay Marina

Becher Bay Marina

48° 20.108' N
123° 36.147' W
Caffery Point

Cheanuh Marina

Mike Chipps
4901 East Sooke Rd, Sooke BC V0S 1N0
Ph: 250-478-4880 Fax: 250-478-5800
Charts 3410, 3461. VHF 16 switch to 68
Fuel: Gas only. **Moorage**–some summer transient–call for reservations. **Power:** 15 amp. Ice. Washrooms. Pumpout. Garbage disposal. Launch ramp. The marina is located behind Fraser Island in Becher Bay.

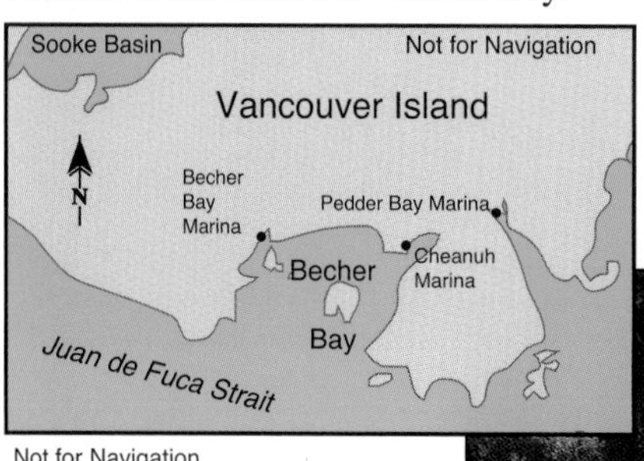

Not for Navigation

Pedder Bay Marina

Sean Moore
925 Pedder Bay Dr, PO Box 12
Metchosin BC V9C 4H1
Ph: 250-478-1771 Fax: 250-478-0285
pbm@obmg.com
www.pedderbaymarina.com
Charts 3410, 3461, 3606 VHF 66A
Fuel: gas, diesel. **Moorage**–some summer transient. Fishing licences. **Power:** 15 amp, **washrooms, showers, laundry**. Rental boats and fishing guides available. Camping, mini chandlery. **Launch Ramp.** *Beware of the reef at entrance to marina.*

Top: Cheanuh Marina, tucked away in Becher Bay.
Right: Pedder Bay Marina

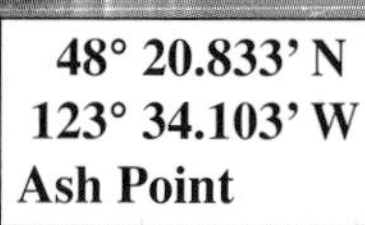

Southbound to Olympia

Section 8

Most vessels returning from a cruise in British Columbia or the San Juans to their home ports in Puget Sound are probably familiar with much of the following information.

Hopefully there are some docks in this section that you have not yet discovered and will experience pleasure in visiting them. The information relating to the marinas is intended to provide input for the mariner to check into the most suitable overnight facilities.

For those mariners who have spent all or most of their boating years in British Columbia waters, a pleasant surprise is in store for you when you travel south. There are destination marinas that are well equipped to cater to visiting boats. And there are surroundings that will make you want to stay longer than intended and return again soon.

Many Canadians are inclined to think of Puget Sound as a busy, commercial and built-up residential-lined waterway. But there are passages, bays and coves that compare with some of the most remote wilderness areas of northern British Columbia. In the following pages I have included those marinas which offer overnight moorage. Most have special visitor moorage, some have visitor docks and additional space available for guests while others offer space as available. This latter type of marina has been included only where I consider there to be adequate visitor moorage. There are other marinas I have not included. This is because they either do not offer visitor moorage, or do so on a very limited basis.

Whether returning home from northern destinations or just going south for a change, plan a visit to Admiralty Inlet, Puget Sound or Hood Canal and check out some of the outstanding facilities for yourself.

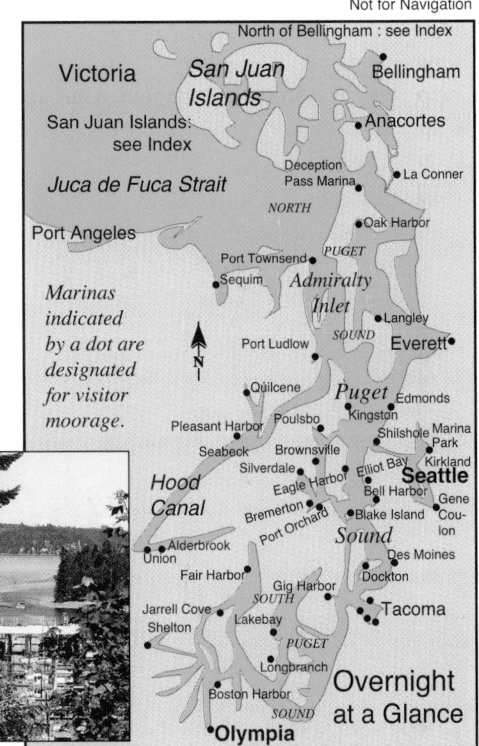

Right: Pleasant Harbour Marina and diagram with primary overnight moorage locations.
Top: Skyline Marina at Anacortes, where resident boats occupy hundreds of slips and special docks are set aside for visitors–see page 275.

Sekiu

48° 29.387' N
124° 43.676' W
Juan de Fuca
Strait (Racon)

Juan de Fuca Strait

NEAH BAY Charts 18485, 18484

Makah Marina

Port director: Bob Buckingham
Port of Neah Bay
PO Box 137, Neah Bay WA 98357
Ph: 360-645-3015 Fax: 360-645-3016
portofneahbayt@centurytel.net
VHF 16 switch to 66A

Moorage. Commercial boats to 100 ft. Pleasure boats check in with Big Salmon Resort. **Water. Power:** 30, 50 amps. **Fuel:** Gas, diesel. **Showers, washrooms.** Pumpout. Portadump. **Nearby:** Accommodations, shops, museum, culture center. **Launch ramp.**

Big Salmon Resort

PO Box 140, Neah Bay WA 98357
Ph: 360-645-2374 Fax: 360-625-0772
Toll free 1-866-787-1900 VHF 68
bigsalmon@centurytel.net
www.bigsalmonresort.com

Moorage at Makah Marina**.** Seasonal April to September–boats to 100 feet. **Water. Power:** 30 amps. **Fuel:** Gas, diesel. **Washrooms.** Pumpout. Ice. **Adjacent:** Launch ramp. Laundry, store–some supplies. Bait, tackle and gear. Boat rentals, charters. Delicatessen. Groceries and services nearby.

Launch ramp (off to left) at Makah Marina and Big Salmon moorage.

Neah Bay's Makah Marina

Snow Creek Resort

PO Box 248, Neah Bay WA 98357
Ph: 360-645-2284 Fax: 360-645-2997
Toll free 1-800-833-1464
snowcreek@centurytel.net
www.snowcreekwa.com

48° 21.442' N
124° 33.225' W

Charts 18460, 18484 **VHF 16, 17**

Moorage to 24' mooring buoys to 30'. **Water. Showers. Washrooms.** Portadump.
Nearby: Launch ramp, scuba air fills, camping, RV park, haulout, rail launch to 30 feet. Cabins. Charters.

SEKIU Chart 18460

Olson's Resort (Sekiu)

Donalynn Olson **CB 21**
444 Front St, PO Box 216, Sekiu WA 98381
Ph: 360-963-2311 Fax: 360-963-2928
info@olsonsresort.com
www.olsonsresort.com

Fuel: Gas, diesel, oil. **Moorage. Water. Washrooms, laundry, showers.** Camping. Convenience store. Motel accommodations. Fishing charters.
Nearby: Launch ramp. Air strip.

Top: Snow Creek's small dock for launched boats. Inset above: Olson's well-stocked store. Left: Olson's Resort marina Dock. Opposite, top: Olson's Resort and adjacent Van Riper's marina docks at Sekiu.

Coho Marina

SEKIU Chart 18460

Coho Resort & Marina

Chet Kimple
15572 Hwy 112, Sekiu WA 98381
Ph: 360-683-2333
Moorage: Boats to 25 feet. Launch ramp. **Washrooms, laundry, showers.** Pumpout. Campground, RV park, restaurant adjacent.

View along the beach from Coho Marina to Sekiu.

Van Riper's Resort

Valerie Mohr
280 Front St
PO Box 246
Sekiu WA 98381
48° 15.486' N
124° 17.515' W
CB 14
Ph: 360-963-2334 Toll free 1-888-462-0803
www.vanripersresort.com
Moorage nearby: 3000' dock. **Water. Showers, Washrooms.** Portadump. Rental boats. Groceries, charts, books, ice. Motel. Campground. Launch ramp.
Nearby: Restaurant. Marine store–5 miles.

Curley's Resort and Dive Center

48° 15.466' N
124° 17.518' W

Jim and Virginia Bartz
291 Front, Box 265, Sekiu WA 98381
Ph: 360-963-2281 Fax: 360-963-2291
Toll free: 1-800-542-9680
www.curleysresort.com
Moorage: May–Sept 30. Boats to 30 feet. Motel. Rooms and cabins to rent. Air fills.

Sequim Bay State Marine Park, Sequim Bay 424 feet of guest dock space at two floats. Washrooms, showers, Portadump. Park, picnic sites, scuba diving, launch ramp. Mooring buoys. Shallow at low tide.

Sequim Bay Marine Park dock

John Wayne Marina. Top photo shows its entrance. Left: The fuel and guest dock. Bottom left: The ramp at John Wayne marina. Bottom, right: A bronze of the famous actor in the office lobby.

SEQUIM Chart 18471

John Wayne Marina

Ron Amundson
2577 W Sequim Bay Rd, Sequim WA 98382
Ph: 360-417-3440 Fax: 360-417-3442
www.portofpa.com
Fuel: Gas, diesel. **Moorage**: Visitor dock at marina inside breakwater. **Power:** 30 amp. **Washrooms, laundry, showers.** Pumpout. Portadump.
Adjacent: Store–Bosun's Locker, books, marine supplies.Launch ramp. Nearby beach, picnic area, grocery store.
Follow channel to the marina.

Port Angeles Boat Haven

48° 07.271' N
123° 25.353 ' W

Launch ramp on Marine Drive alongside the Coast Guard station.

48° 08.362' N
123° 27.271 ' W

Launch ramp at the Boat Haven

Harbour: 48° 07.733' N 123° 24.030' W

PORT ANGELES Chart 18468

Port Angeles City Pier

312 E Fifth St, Port Angeles WA 98362
Ph: 360-457-4550 (Port Angeles Parks)
Moorage: Visitor dock, seasonal.
Washrooms. Public aquatic centre (showers), nearby stores, restaurants. Customs. Visit the Marine Science Center.

Port Angeles Boat Haven

Chuck Farris
832 Boat Haven Dr, Port Angeles WA 98363
Ph: 360-457-4505 Fax: 360-457-4921
pamarina@olypen.com www.portofpa.com
Fuel: Gas, diesel. **Moorage**: Visitor dock, boats to 150 feet. **Power:** 20, 30, 50 amp.
Washrooms, showers. Customs. Pumpout. Portadump. **Adjacent: Launch ramp.** Haulouts to 70 tons, 200 ton railway, repairs, service, marine supplies, charts, stove oil, kerosene. Cafe. Laundry nearby. Customs port 360-457-4311.

Going south from Juan de Fuca Strait or the San Juan Islands your choices are Hood Canal, Admiralty Inlet or Puget Sound. If you are in the vicinity of Crescent Beach or Point Roberts and intend to travel south down Puget Sound you may find a visit to Blaine worthwhile. The town has been embellished with paving and landscaping. The marina has many facilities and a warm welcome for visitors. The same can be said for Semiahmoo Marina on the opposite side

Left: Boat Haven visitors dock at Port Angeles. This page, centre and bottom: Views of the docks at Port Angeles City Pier and a beach alongside.

Opposite page: Boat Haven. Centre: The launch ramps across the harbour and at Boat Haven. Bottom: A mural on the Marine Science Center alongside the city pier.

of Drayton Harbor. This modern marina loves to have visitors. Call ahead to reserve moorage and look forward to a pleasant stay with options of golf or time in the spa. If you stay there and want to visit Blaine you can use the ferry in summer.

In the Puget Sound area most mariners are familiar with destinations such as Port Townsend known for its historic buildings and holiday atmosphere, or Anacortes for its bustling activity as a port for larger vessels, ferry traffic and business community. Check out these two places for their large, accommodating marinas. And visit other ports such as Poulsbo for its colorful Scandinavian village, Silverdale, Port Ludlow or Jarrell's Cove for remoteness from anywhere. These and other marinas and towns in the Sound and Hood Canal can provide lots of entertainment, new experiences and friendships, and a joyful boating experience. Moreover, getting to some of these places can be a lot of fun.

State marine parks which provide adequate or substantial visitor moorage and other facilities have been included in the following pages.

Semiahmoo Marina

Blaine

North Puget Sound

Semiahmoo Marina

Rick Greenhow
9540 Semiahmoo Pkwy
Blaine WA 98230
Ph: 360-371-0440 Fax: 360-371-0200
VHF 68 Chart 18421
semimarina@bbxmail.net
www.semiahmoomarina.com

Moorage: 500 feet, plus slips.
Fuel: Gas, diesel, propane. **Power:** 30, 50 amp. **Washrooms, showers, laundry,** portadump, **pumpout.**
Adjacent: Resort accommodations, golf course, health spa, chandlery, marina service, repairs, restaurants,snacks. Access to Blaine by ferry through summer–weekends.

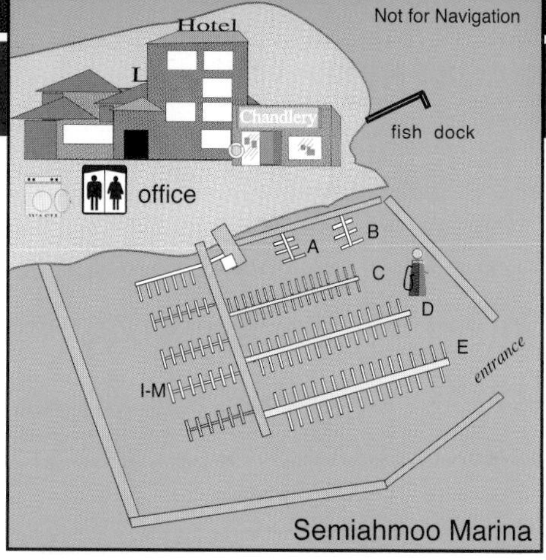

Semiahmoo Marina

Semiahmoo Marina

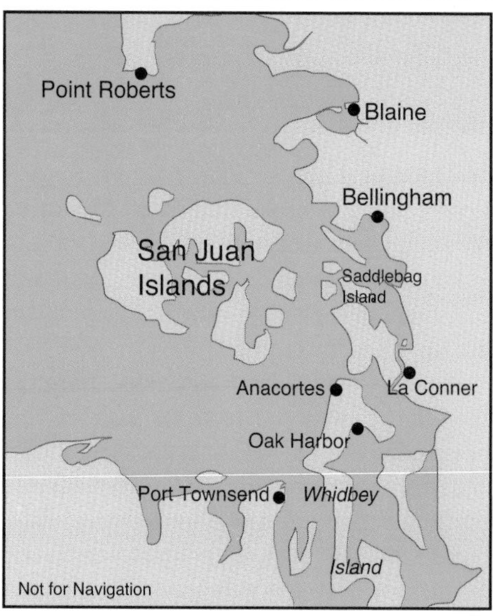

Blaine Harbor Marina

Operated by Port of Bellingham
Pam Taft
235 Marine Dr, Blaine WA 98231
Ph: 360-647-6176 Fax: 360-332-1043
VHF 16 switch to 66A Chart 18421
blaineharbor@portofbellingham.com
www.portofblaine.com

Moorage: 850 feet guest moorage plus slips. **Fuel:** Gas, diesel, propane, at Blaine Marina (Fuel dock 332-8425). **Power:** 30, 50 amp. **Washrooms, showers,** portadump, pumpout, **laundry. Customs phone in.**

Adjacent: Haulouts, repairs, supplies, restaurants. Launch ramp. Landscaped parkland. Short walk to uptown Blaine. **Blaine Marina (Fuel dock– 360-332-8425).** Internet access.

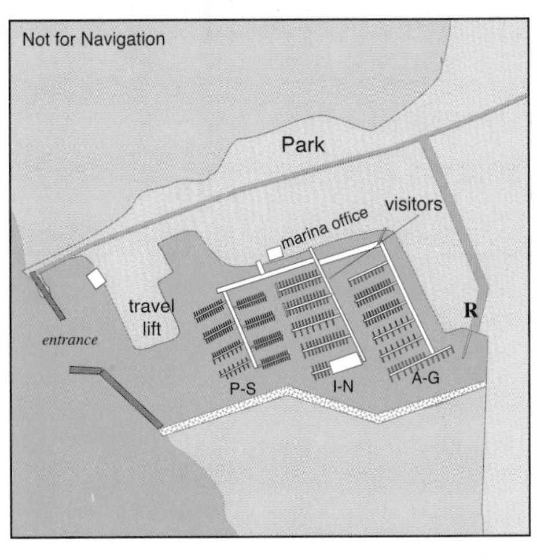

Photos above and opposite show the two marinas at Blaine. Note their juxtaposition (right). Just across the border, is the seaside British Columbia town of White Rock (top).

Squalicum Harbor

Shulsan Golf Course 360-293-3444

48° 15.101' N
122° 30.563' W

Bellingham

North Puget Sound

Squalicum Harbor Port of Bellingham

Harbourmaster: Pam Taft
722 Coho Way WA 98225
Ph: 360-676-2542 Fax: 360-671-6149
blaineharbor@portofbellingham.com
www.portofbellingham.com **VHF 16**
Chart 18424

Moorage: Visitor's dock–1,000 feet. **Fuel:** Gas, diesel, propane. **Power:** 30 amp**. Water. Showers, laundry, washrooms.** Garbage disposal. Porta-dump. **Pumpout.** Customs.
Adjacent: Marine supplies, service, 150 ton travel lift. Restaurant, groceries, stores, **4-lane launch ramp.** Free shuttle to town.

Squalicum Harbour

Top: Bellingham Bay from Fairhaven. Above: Inside the Squalicum Harbour marina near the launch ramp area and harbor offices. Inset above: Poster of docks displayed at Squalicum Harbor.

Fisherman's Cove

Lummi Nation
2557 Lummi View Dr
Bellingham WA 98226
Ph: 360-758-7050 Fax: 360-758-2806 Chart 18421

Located at near ferry dock at Gooseberry point, Hale Passage.**Fuel dock:** Gas. Monorail hoist. Deli. Store.

48° 43.831' N 122° 39.946' W

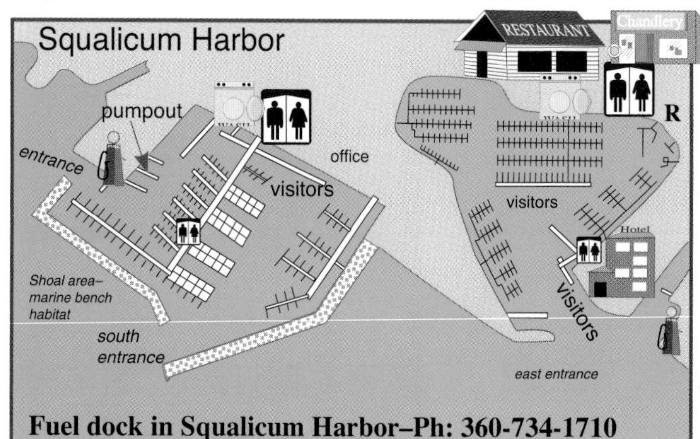

Fuel dock in Squalicum Harbor–Ph: 360-734-1710

Not for Navigation

Squalicum Harbour

Squalicum Harbour

Fairhaven launch ramp

Top and above left: East entrance and waterway in Squalicum Harbor's recreational yacht basin. Visitor docks parallel to the shore. Above right: Sand castle competition at Bellingham–first annual Sand-in-the-City event October 2006. Left: Fairhaven launch ramp. Bottom: Fairhaven's linear moorage for visitors. Inset shows Coast Guard dock at cruise ship terminal.

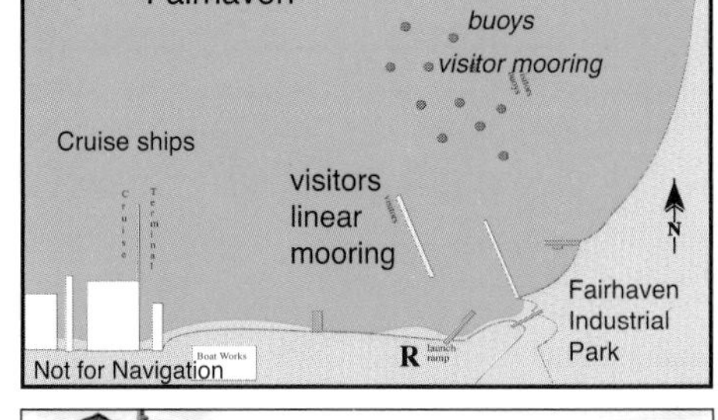

Fairhaven. Numerous mooring buoys and a linear floating dock for visitors (dinghy to shore) during boating season. Park, scenic and historic area adjacent. **Garbage** disposal. **Water. Launch ramp.**

Saddlebag Island Marine State Park

East of Guemes Island, Padilla Bay.
Chart 18429 Mooring, camping. Watch depths on all sides.

48° 43.415' N
122° 30.761' W

Fairhaven

La Conner

48° 23.930' N 122° 29.837' W Chart 18427

North Puget Sound

La Conner Marina

VHF 66A

Harbormaster: Paul Spannert
613 N Second St
PO Box 1120, La Conner WA 98257
Ph: 360-466-3118 Fax: 360-466-3119
paul@portofskagit.com
www.laconnermarina.com

Fuel adjacent: Gas, diesel, propane, ice. **Moorage:** 2,400 foot guest dock plus slips. Closed Sundays and holidays. Marine service. **Power:** 30 amp**. Water. Showers, washrooms, laundry.** Pumpout. Swinomish Yacht Club adjacent south. **Nearby:** Stores. marine supplies, service, light boat launcher to 7500 lbs (roller equipped trailers), 100 ton travel lift. Boat storage. Historic town of La Conner–stores, gifts, artisans, restaurants. Moorage available at several La Conner business and public docks.

1. La Conner Landing Marine Services. Fuel dock, PO Box 1020, La Conner WA, 98257 Ph: 360-466-4478 Washrooms, pumpout. Store: Groceries, beer and wine, fishing equipment, bait, ice.

2. Twin Bridges Marina under Hwy 20 on Swinomish Channel–boat storage, marine store. No visitor docks.
Launch ramp. Ph: 360-491-0850.

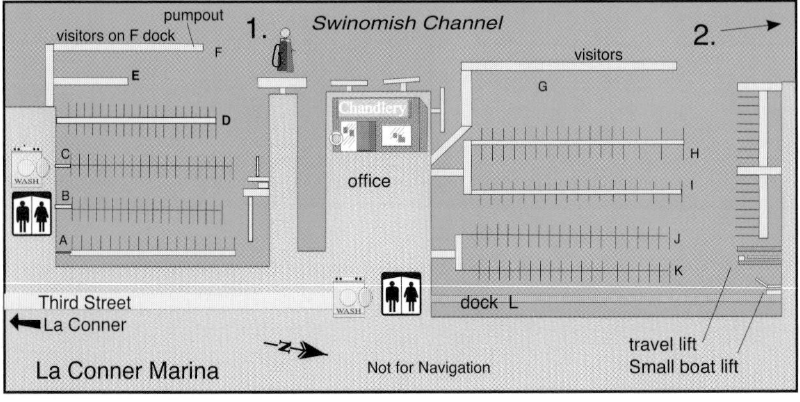

Top: Some docks in Swinomish Channel offer day or overnight moorage. La Conner Marina has transient moorage.

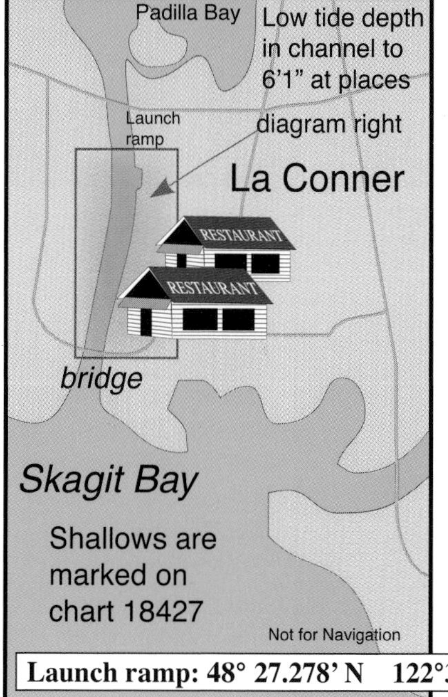

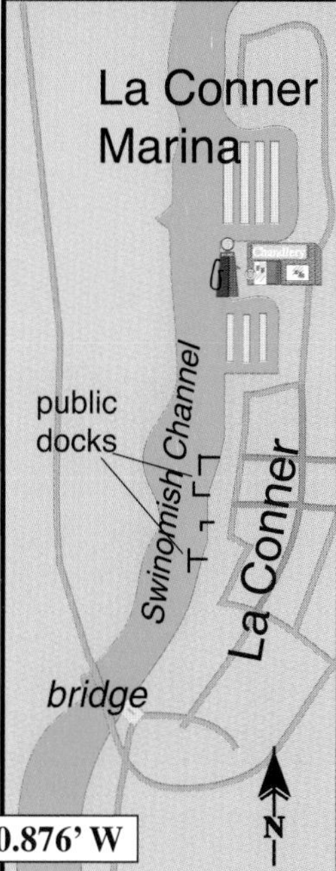

Top: La Conner and the channel looking north from the bridge. Center: The Swinomish Channel looking north from Champagne Cove. Insets and above: The Cove store inside and out. Tourism thrives at La Conner with art galleries and stores sharing space with restaurants on the waterfront.

Anacortes

North Puget Sound

Cap Sante Boat Haven

Harbourmaster/manager: Dale Fowler
PO Box 297 VHF 66A
1019 Q Ave, Anacortes WA 98221
Ph: 360-293-0694 Fax: 360-299-0998
marina@portofanacortes.com
www.portofanacortes.com
Charts 18421, 18427
Moorage: Guest docks. 150-200 slips. **Call. Fuel at Cap Sante Marine:** Gas, diesel, propane. **Power:** 20, 30, 50 amp. **Showers, laundry, washrooms.** Pumpout. Portadump. Internet access. **Nearby:** Food and other stores, marine supplies, service, historic town of Anacortes–stores, gifts, arts and crafts, restaurants.

Top and above: Cap Sante Boat Haven has guest moorage and facilities for visitors and is adjacent to restaurants and stores in the historic town of Anacortes.
Below: Farmers Market held at Anacortes on Saturdays.

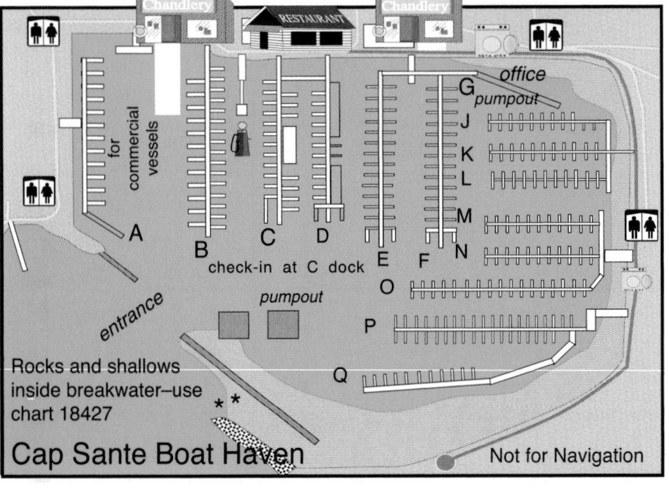

Adjacent: Cap Sante Marine Ph: 360-293-3145. Launching and service center located at Cap Sante Boat Haven. **Marine Service Center Ph: 360-293-820,** south of Cap Sante, has free pumpout, some moorage. **Power:** 30 amp, showers, washrooms fuel dock with gasoline, diesel and propane. Haulout facility and repair yards.

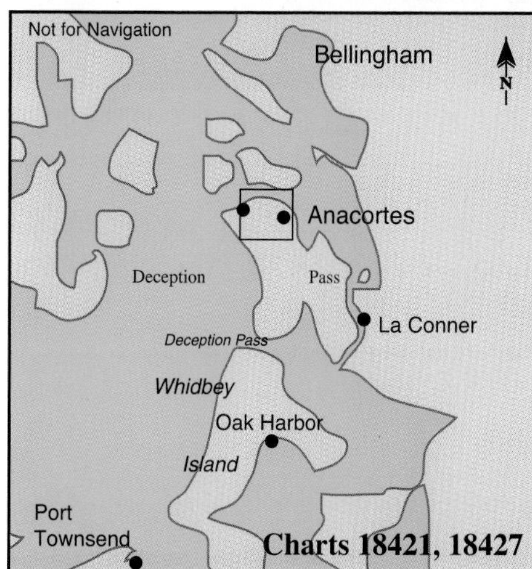

Skyline Marina

Manager: Kelly Larkin
2011 Skyline Way (Flounder Bay)
Anacortes WA 98221
Ph: 360-293-5134 Fax: 360-293-7557
skylinemarinecenter@verizon.net
www.skylinemarinecenter.com

Moorage: 40 slips. Internet access. **Fuel docks:** Gas, diesel. **Power:** 15, 20, 30, 50 amp. Garbage disposal. **Showers, laundry, washrooms.** Pumpout. Propane. Mechanic. **Adjacent:** Stores, marine supplies, fishing tackle, bait, charts, books, service, repairs. Sling launch.. Travel lift to 55 tons. Restaurants and groceries. Four miles to town.

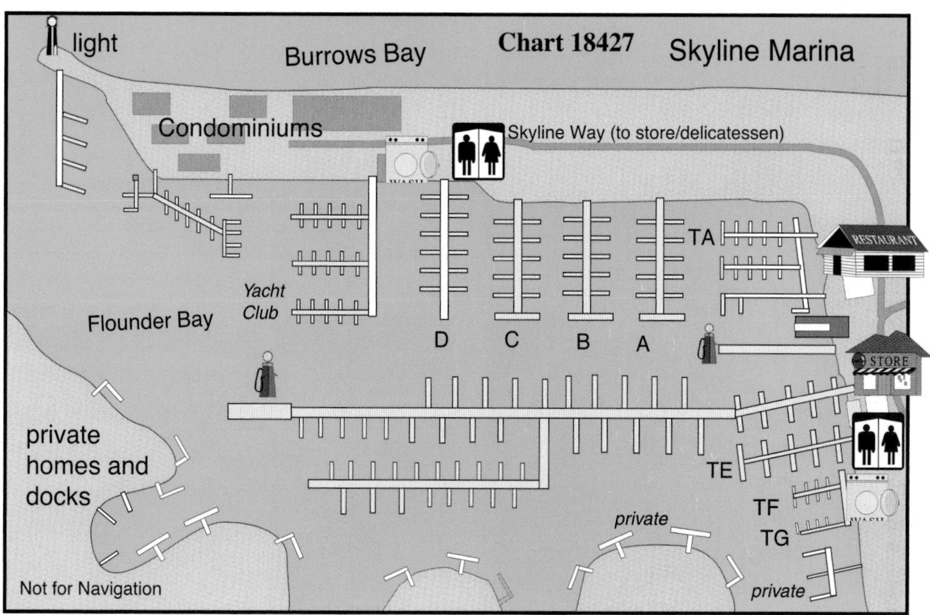

Deception Pass can be a tricky passage in strong currents.

North Puget Sound

Deception Pass Marina

Dundee Woods
200 W Cornet Bay Rd
Oak Harbor WA 98277
Ph: 360-675-5411
VHF 16, 68 Chart 18427

Moorage: Guest dock plus slips. **Fuel dock:** Gas, diesel, kerosene, stove oil, propane. **Power:** 30 amp. **Water. Garbage disposal. Laundry, washrooms.** Pumpout.

Adjacent: Store, fishing tackle, bait, charts, books, ice, fishing supplies, groceries, beer and wine store. Haulouts. Park.

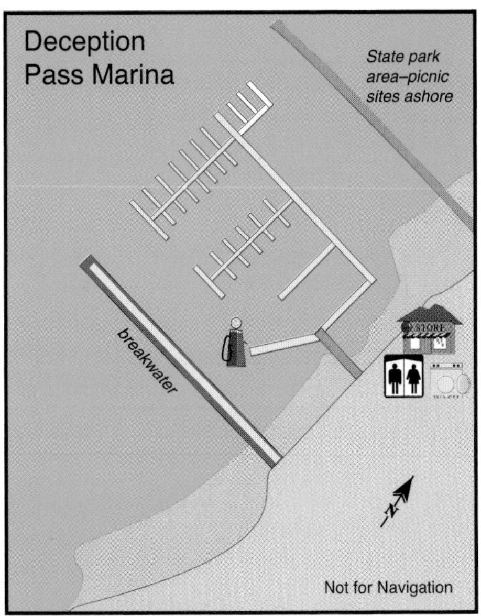

Deception Pass Marine State Park (Sharpes Cove, Bowman Bay) 128 foot guest dock. Picnic sites, campsites, washrooms, showers, portadump. Mooring buoys located at Skagit Island and Hope Island.

Oak Harbor Marina on Whidbey Island.

Whidbey Island

48° 17.051' N 122° 38.411' W

Oak Harbor Marina

Harbourmaster: Dave Williams

865 SE Barrington Dr, Oak Harbor WA 98277

Ph: 360-679-2628 Fax: 360-240-0603

Charts 18428, 18441

ohmarina@whidbey.net

www.whidbey.com/ohmarina **VHF 16**

Visitor moorage 52 40' slips. Internet access. **Fuel:** Gas, diesel, propane. **Power:** 30 amp**. Water. Showers, laundry, washrooms.** Pumpout. Nearby stores, Adventure Marine Supply, service, haulouts. **Launch ramp,** 6,500lb sling hoist.

Easy access to Oak Harbour. There are shops, stores and restaurants within walking distance of the marina. Playground.

Note: Rocks between R2 channel marker and Maylor/Forbes Point; deepest water is on red buoy side of channel; shoals on green buoy side.

Whidbey Golf and Country Club, Oak Harbor Ph: 360-675-4546
Useless Bay Country Club, Langley Ph: 360-321-5960
Lams Links, Oak Harbor 360-675-3412
Holmes Harbor Golf Club 360-331-2363

Above: The main guest dock adjacent the manager's office. Oak Harbor Marina is a large facility, as seen in the photo at the top of the page.

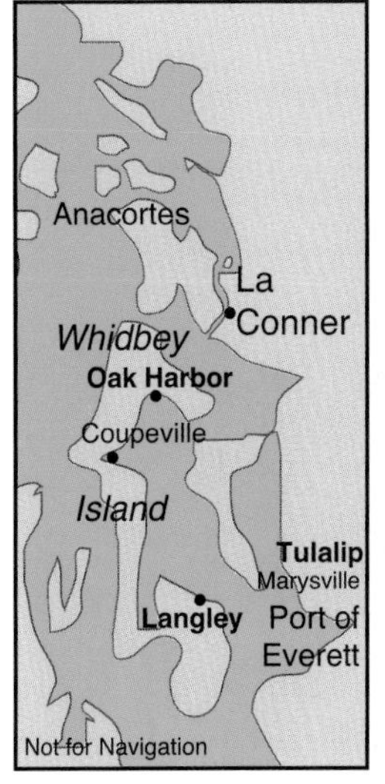

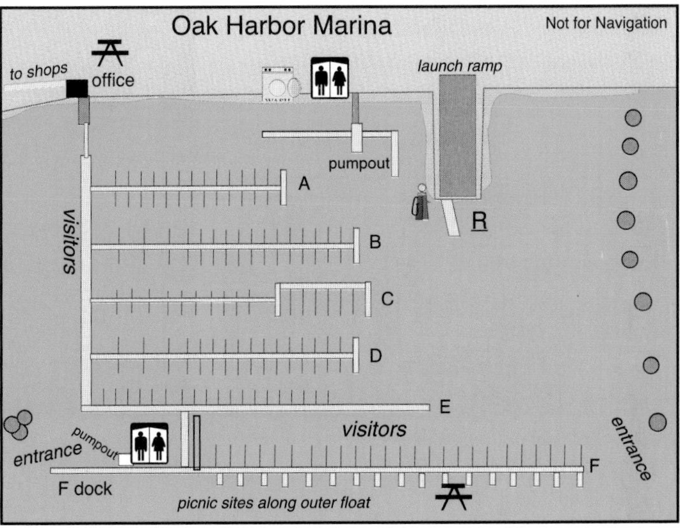

48° 13.381' N 122° 41.061' W

Coupeville dock

Port of Coupeville

Harbormaster: Long Bechard
Port of Coupeville, PO Box 577
Coupeville WA 98239-0577
Ph: 360-678-5020 Fax: 360-678-7424
execjim@verizon.net **Chart 18441**

Moorage. Seven feet at low tide. Two floats providing a total of 400 feet of moorage. **Fuel:** Gas, diesel, garbage disposal. **Water. Showers, washrooms. Adjacent:** Gifts. Store, ice, charts, books, art gallery. Gray whale exhibit. Whale watching, kayak tours. **Nearby:** Portadump. **Launch ramp**–parks, beach access, restaurants, stores, post office, public transit. Dine and lunch at County Deli on Main and other nearby restaurants.

Shops at Coupeville

Top: Coupeville dock. Above and right: Uptown Coupeville is along the waterfront. Visit other parts of Whidbey Island by free bus service.

Langley Boat Harbor

Harbourmaster: Ben Reams
PO Box 366, Langley WA 98260
Phone: 360-221-2611 Cell: 360-914-1739
Fax: 360-221-4265
harbor@langleywa.org
Website: www.langleywa.org
Moorage. **Power:** 20, 30 amp**,** water, **washrooms, showers, pumpout**. Launch ramp. Internet access.
Nearby: A short walk uptown–Post office, restaurants, liquor store, groceries. Art galleries, gift shops, bookstores, pharmacy. Accommodations. Marine mechanic. Bank machine. Medical services.

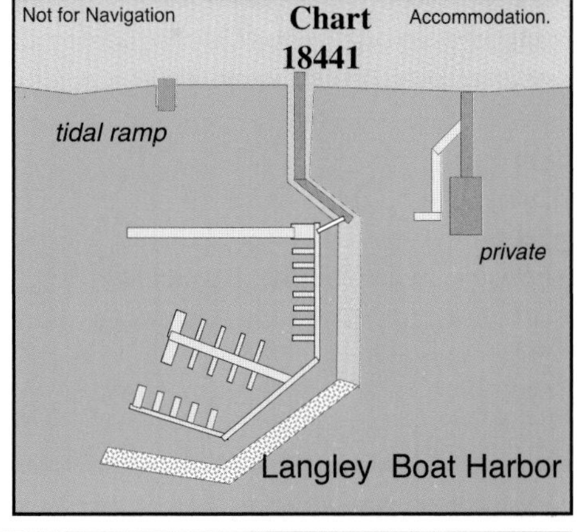

Top: Langley harbor. Right: Uptown Langley has many bakeries, coffee shops, restaurants and alleys with art, crafts and souvenir shops.

Top: Anchorage off the Langley Small Boat Harbour. Above: The launch ramp at Keystone, alongside the ferry landing. Right: Free bus service on Whidbey Island is available Monday through Saturday. Right: B&B at Langley waterfront located just above the launching ramp. Below: Marina entrance.

Photo courtesy of Port of Everett

Port of Everett

47° 59.790' N 122° 13.516' W

Port of Everett Marina

Kim Buike
1720 W Marine View Dr, Everett WA 98206
Ph: 425-259-6001 Fax: 425-259-0860
marina@portofeverett.com
www.portofeverett.com

VHF 16 –to 69 Charts 18444, 18443

Moorage: 1,800' guest dock plus slips. **Fuel docks:** Gas, diesel. **Power:** 20, 30, 50 amp. Snack bar. Garbage disposal. 25 ton travel lift. Recycling. **Showers, laundry, washrooms.** Pumpout. Propane.

Adjacent: Internet access. Village restaurants and shops. Marine stores, fishing tackle, bait, charts, books. Wheelchair access float. Haulouts, storage, repairs, service. Launch ramp. Be aware of the 500'Naval Station boundary.

Nearby: Restaurants, grocery stores, chandlery, liquor store, playground, hiking trails, medical services, post office, banks.

The marina at Everett is one of the biggest in Puget Sound. It has continuous expansion projects underway. The launch ramp is extensive with multiple lanes and spacious parking facilities.

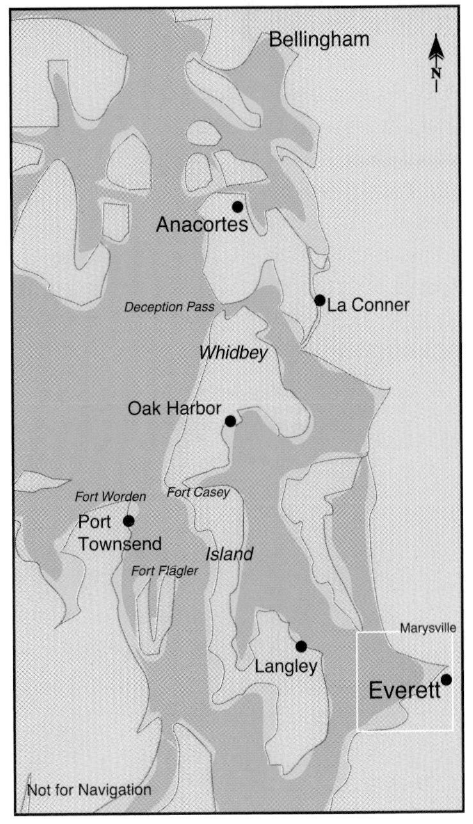

Port Townsend

Charts 18464, 18441

Point Hudson Marina & RV Park

Chris Wenger
103 Hudson St, PO Box 1180
Port Townsend WA 98368 VHF 09
Ph: 360-385-2828 Fax: 360-385-7331
info@portofpt.com
www.portofpt.com

Moorage: Slips to 40' lineal slips to 65'. Check in at the marina office on the north-east side of the marina. **Water. Power:** 30 amps. Internet access. Propane, **Fuel:** One mile south at Port of Port Townsend public docks. **Laundry, showers, washrooms.** Pump-out. Garbage disposal. **Launch ramp**. Several town docks near marina. **Nearby:** Restaurants, stores, groceries, medical services, **Fleet Marine chandlery** adjacent to harbor–travel lift, mechanical service and repairs. Bank, post office.

Port Townsend is a quaint, historic town with many antique stores, arts and craft shops, classic restaurants and specialty stores.

Note diagram layout of docks–changed since some photographs on these pages.

Above: Approaching Point Hudson Marina. Right, top to bottom: docks and Wooden Boat Foundation at Point Hudson.

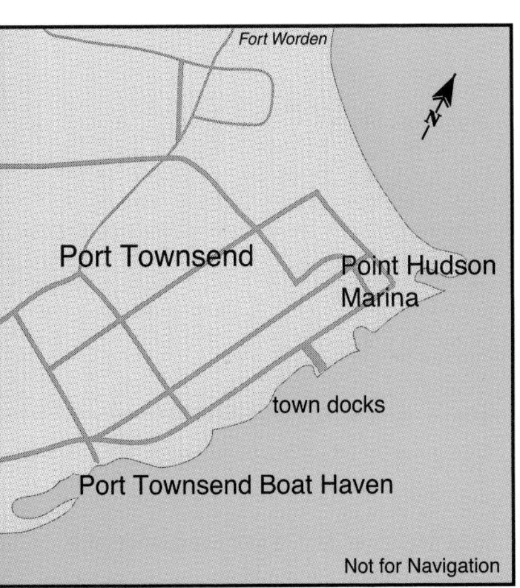

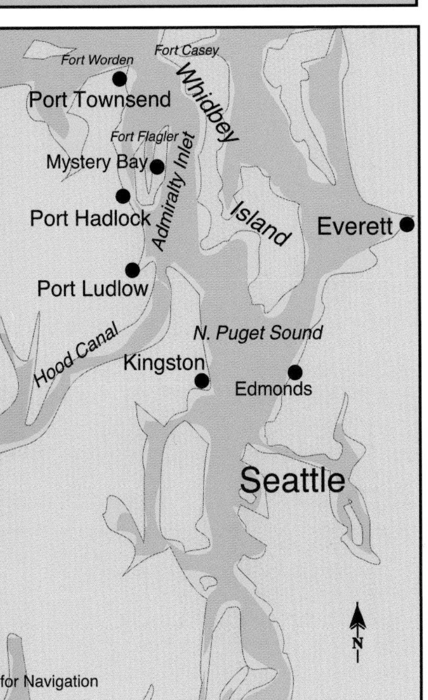

Point Hudson Marina entrance.

Wooden Boat Foundation at Point Hudson

Point Hudson Marina

Port Townsend Boat Haven

48° 06.411' N 122° 46.223' W

Port Townsend Boat Haven

Ken Radon
2601 Washington St, PO Box 1180
Port Townsend WA 98368
Ph: 360-385-2355 Fax: 360-379-8205
info@portofpt.com
www: www.portofpt.com

Charts 18464, 18441 VHF 66A
Moorage: Transient slips available.
Power: 30, 50 amps. Internet access.
Fuel: Gas, diesel, propane. **Laundry, showers, washrooms.** Pump-out. Garbage disposal. **Launch ramp**. Haul outs to 300 tons.
Nearby: This marina lies immediately south of the town. Restaurants. Stores, groceries, marine store, service and repairs adjacent. Customs: 360-385-3777.

Port Townsend. One of several town docks. First come basis. Open to wash and weather.

Top: The large public dock at Port Townsend has overnight moorage for visitors. Several exposed docks along the waterfront take recreational vessels on a first come basis.
Below: Anchorage is possible off the Port Townsend waterfront in calm conditions.

Port Townsend waterfront.

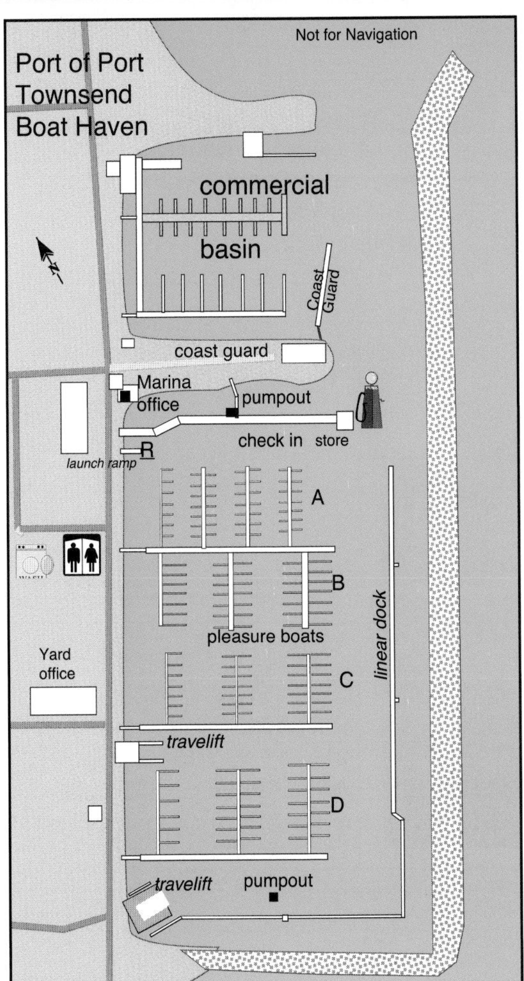

Historic Port Townsend and a section of its commercial docks adjacent to Boat Haven.

Fort Worden Marine State Park Port Townsend

Ph: 360-902-8844 360-385-4730
Charts 18441, 18464
Moorage. Washrooms, showers, laundry. Launch ramp. Mooring buoys. Scuba Diving. Marine Science Center. Campsites.

Port Hadlock

48° 01.877' N 122° 44.725' W

Anchorage near Port Hadlock marina

Admiralty Inlet

Port Hadlock Marina

Jerry Spencer **Charts 18464, 18441**
310 Hadlock Bay Rd
PO Box 1369, Port Hadlock WA 98339
Ph: 360-385-6368 Fax: 360-385-3067
Toll Free: 1-800-785-7030 VHF 16 –to 68
phmarina@mail.com www.innatporthadlock.com

Moorage: Some transient moorage. **Power**: 30, 50 amps. **Showers, washrooms.** Pumpout. Laundry. Internet access. **Nearby:** Inn at Port Hadlock with restaurant and hotel facilities. Kayak rentals. Float plane dock.

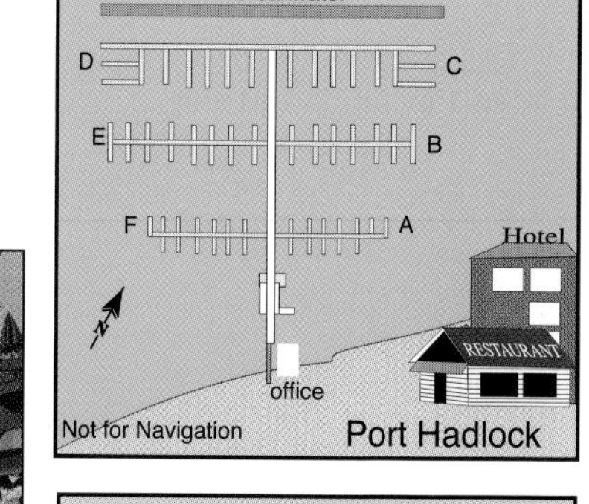

Mystery Bay Marine State Park (map page 283)

Kilisut Harbor, Marrowstone Island. Chart 18464. Visitor dock. Pumpout, portadump. Mooring buoys. **Launch ramp.**

Fort Flagler Marine State Park

Marrowstone Island. Chart 18464
Visitor dock. Washrooms, showers, portadump. Launch ramp. Mooring buoys. Scuba Diving. Mini store. Campsites. Boat rentals. Fishing supplies.

47° 55.170' N 122° 40.893' W

Port Ludlow Marina

Kori Ward
1 Gull Dr, Port Ludlow WA 98365
Ph: 360-437-0513 Fax: 360-437-2428
Toll free: 1-800-308-7991
Charts 18477, 18473, 18441 VHF 16 to 68
kward@portludlowresort.com
www. portludlowresort.com
Moorage: Visitor docks, available slips.
Water. Power: 30, 50 amps.
Fuel: Gas, diesel, stove oil, propane.

Above and bottom: Port Ludlow Marina visitor docks. Below left: A quiet garden at the marina. Opposite page: Port Hadlock Marina and the Inn overlooking the docks. The inset photo shows the view north from Port Hadlock.

Pumpout. **Laundry, showers, washrooms.** Garbage disposal. Ice.
Nearby/adjacent: Restaurants. Lounge. Golf course shuttle. Marina store, groceries, books, fishing tackle, bait, ice, fishing supplies. Marine mechanic. Repairs.

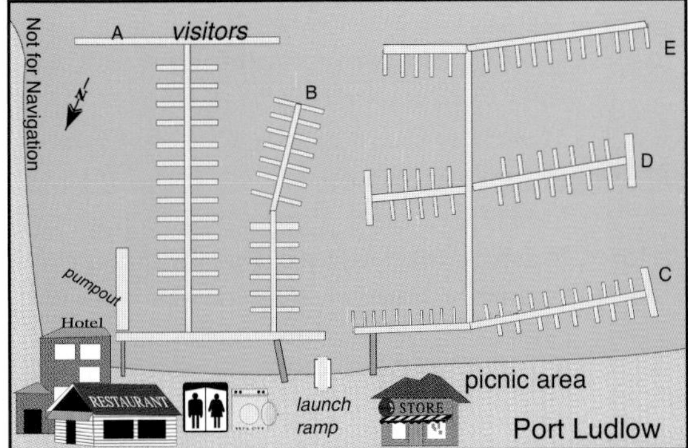

Alderbrook Golf Course 360-898-2560

Not for Navigation
Quilcene
Port Gamble
N
Dabob Bay
Bangor
Pleasant Harbor
Triton Cove State Park
Seabeck
Hood Canal floating bridge 360-779-3233
HOOD CANAL
Charts 18476, 18458
Belfair State Park
Belfair
Hoodsport
Potlatch State Park
Twanoh State Park
Tahuya (Summertide)
Union
Alderbrook Inn

Hood Canal

VHF 9, 16.
Chart 18476

Herb Beck Marina

Ken Radon
1731 Linger Longer Rd. PO Box 98,
Quilcene WA 98376
Ph: 360-765-3131
www.portofpt.com
Chart 18476

Guest moorage available. **Fuel:** Gas, diesel. **Power:** 20, 30 amp. **Washrooms, showers,** pumpout**. Launch Ramp.**

Above: Herb Beck Marina, at the head of Dabob Bay, was formerly known as Quilcene Boat Haven.

Adjacent: Ice, supplies. repairs, service. Camping. Barbeque. Town less than 1 mile. Shrimping popular in April and May. (Formerly Quilcene Boathaven).

Bangor is a restricted military area.
Use charts 18473, 18476 and 18477.

Pleasant Harbor Marina

Ryan Kaufman
308913 Highway 101, Brinnon WA 98320
Ph: 360-796-4611 Fax: 360-796-4898
Toll free: 1-800-547-3479
nfo@pleasantharbormarina.com
www.pleasantharbormarina.com

Moorage: Guest moorage 50 slips. Reservations suggested.
Fuel: Gas, diesel. **Power:** 30, 50 amp. **Washrooms, showers**–free for moorage cusomers, **laundry,** pumpout. Internet access**.** Garbage disposal. Launch ramp.
Adjacent: Hot tub. Boaters Lounge, swimming pool. Delicatessen.Groceries. Ice. Marine store, fishing and marine supplies. Repairs, service. Gifts. Beer and wine. Order-in or take-out Pizza. Check at the office.

Left: Pleasant Harbor is well named for its delightful surroundings. The nearby State Park is also popular.

Pleasant Harbor Marine State Park.
Ph: 360-796-4415. www.parks.wa.gov
Chart 18448 Guest dock 218 feet.
Portadump. Pumpout.

Pleasant Harbor Marina has space for visitors. This and Alderbrook Inn Resort are the marinas of choice in Hood Canal for larger boats.

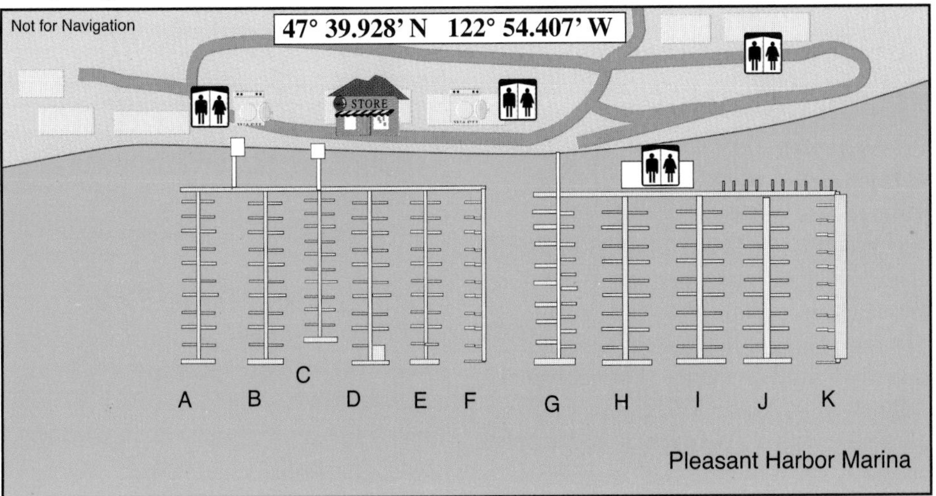

47° 24.512' N 123° 08.165' W

Hoodsport Marina & Cafe

24080 Highway 101
Hoodsport WA 98548
Ph: 360-877-9657
Adjacent: Restaurant–free use of public dock (check its condition). **Washrooms.**
Nearby: Grocery store. Sunrise Motel and Resort. Ph: 360-877-5301.
Gasoline available nearby.

Twanoh State Marine Park

Near Belfair Ph: 360-275-2222
Mooring buoys, pumpout, porta-dump. 200 foot dock for overnight use. Launch ramp, playground, picnic areas, campsites, toilets, tennis courts, hiking trails.

47° 20.983' N 123° 04.087' W

Alderbrook Resort and Spa

Harbormaster–Scott Glenn
10 E Alderbrook Drive, Union WA 98592
Ph: 360-898-2200 Fax: 360-898-4610
dock@alderbrookresort.com
www,alderbrookresort.com
Guest moorage 1500'. Power 30, 50 amp, water, pumpout, showers. Seaplane dock. Hotel rooms, cottages, indoor pool, 18 hole golf course, restaurant, banquet facilities, watercraft rentals. Boat launch nearby.

47° 22.099' N 123° 03.432' W

Summertide Resort & Marina

15781 Northshore Rd NE
Tuhuya WA 98588
Ph: 360-275-9313 Fax: 253-925-9277
summertide_resort@msn.com
Website: www.summertideresort.com
Moorage: Seasonal by reservation.
Boats to 45 feet. **Washrooms, showers, laundry.**
Adjacent: Launch ramp. RV sites. Cottage rentals. Store–ice, propane, groceries, fishing supplies and licences.

47° 21.215' N 123° 04.783' W

Hood Canal Marina

E 5010 Hwy 106
PO Box 86, Union WA 98376
Ph: 360-898-2252 Fax: 360-898-8888
Moorage: Guest moorage–check in ahead.
Nearby: Groceries, supplies. Repairs, marine service. **Kayaking.**

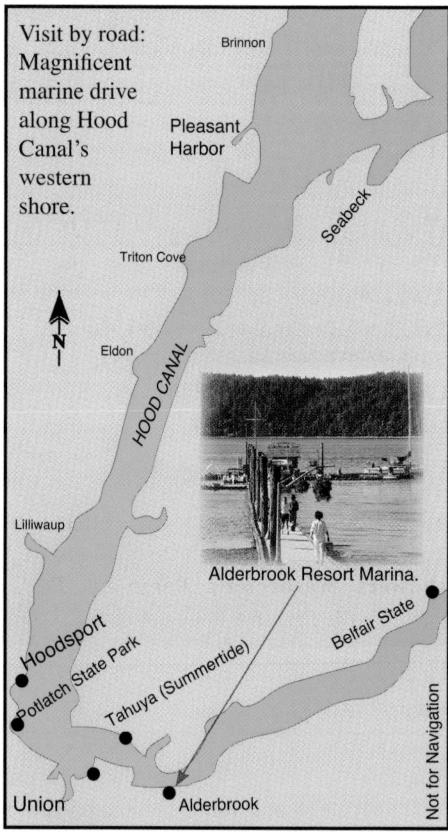

Triton Cove State Marine Park

Chart 18476 In Hood Canal
Seasonal dock. 100' for launching use.

Potlatch State Marine Park

Ph: 360-877-5361
Chart 18476 Near Hoodsport
Adjacent: Mooring buoys. Park, picnic sites, hiking trails, scuba diving, launch ramp. Washrooms, showers.

Fuel dock and visitor moorage at Kingston

Central Puget Sound

Port of Kingston 47° 47.635' N 122° 29.958' W

Harbormaster–Tom Berry
25864 Washington Blvd
PO Box 559 Kingston WA 98346
Ph: 360-297-3545 Fax: 360-297-2945
Charts 18446, 18473, 18441, 18445
VHF 65 Internet access.
ptkingston@aol.com
www.portofkingston.org

Moorage: Slips for 49 guests. **Fuel:** Gas, diesel, propane. **Power:** 30 amps. **Laundry, showers, washrooms.** Pump-out. Porta-dump. **Launch ramp.** Guest moorage located just inside breakwater. Limited reservation with advance notice.

Nearby medical services. Playground.

The ferry from Edmonds lands next to the marina at Kingston. Watch for the heavy motor traffic on shore as you wander into Kingston to visit the stores and restaurants.

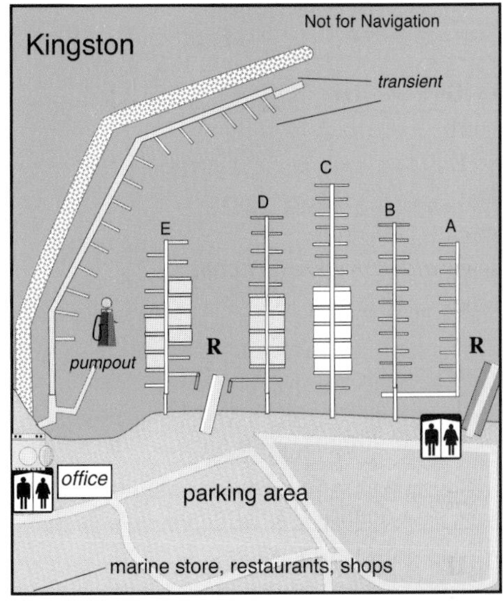

Launch ramp at Kingston

47° 48.5565' N 122° 23.485' W

Port of Edmonds Marina

Marla Kempt & Chris Keuss
336 Admiral Way, Edmonds WA 98020
Ph: 425-775-4588 Fax: 425-670-0583
info@portofedmonds.org
www.portofedmonds.org **VHF 69**

Charts 18441, 18446, 18473

Moorage: 1000' visitor docks plus slips.
Fuel docks: Gas, diesel. Pumpout. Ice. Garbage disposal.
Power: 20, 30 amp. Water. Haulouts, sling launch, boatyard, repairs, service.
50 ton travel lift. NOAA weather reports.
Showers, restrooms, laundry.
Adjacent: Marine stores, fishing tackle, bait, charts, books. Some groceries. Restaurants. Fishing pier.
Nearby: Restaurants and shops. Courtesy van available. Public beaches. Good scuba diving at nearby artificial reef.

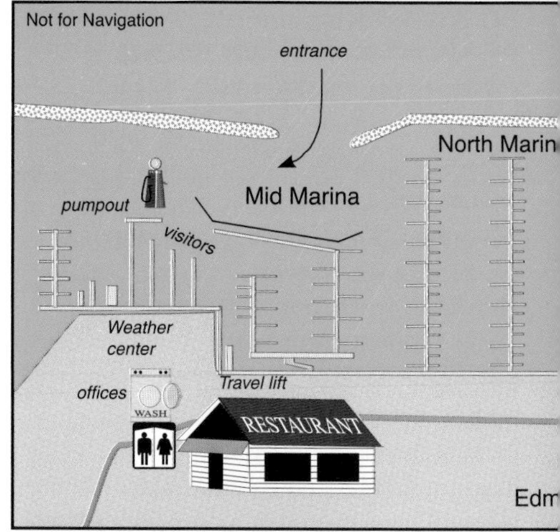

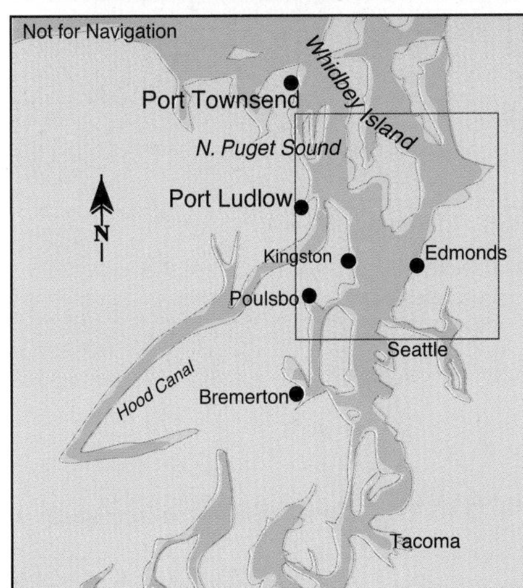

Above and opposite: Visitor and fuel dock at Edmonds. Traveling south to Seattle, convenient stops may be made at Kingston or at Edmonds. Either place is a pleasant stopover with spacious moorage, facilities and adjacent restaurants and nearby stores.
Below: The fuel dock is conveniently located alongside the visitor docks near the entrance to the marina at the Port of Edmonds.

Opposite bottom left: A large restaurant overlooks the marina at Edmonds. Opposite, bottom right, a substantial NOAA mariners' weather center provides helpful, instant weather reporting and navigation information for Puget Sound, including distances to other ports.

Poulsbo

47° 43.965' N 122° 38.963' W

Bainbridge Island vicinity

Port of Poulsbo **Chart 18446**

Kirk Stickles
18809 Front St
Poulsbo WA 98370
Ph: 360-779-3505 Fax: 360-779-8090
portofpoulsbo@yahoo.com
www.portofpoulsbo.net/portofpoulsbo

Moorage: Slips for 123 guests. Call for reservations. Internet access. **Water. Power:** 30 amp. **Fuel:** gas, diesel. **Laundry, showers, washrooms.** Free pump-out. Launch ramp. **Nearby:** Bistros, bakery, shops and all facilities for visitors. Playground.

Poulsbo

Poulsbo is a character town. The village is built in traditional Viking style and has a beautiful setting with ethnic restaurants, bakeries, gift and book stores.

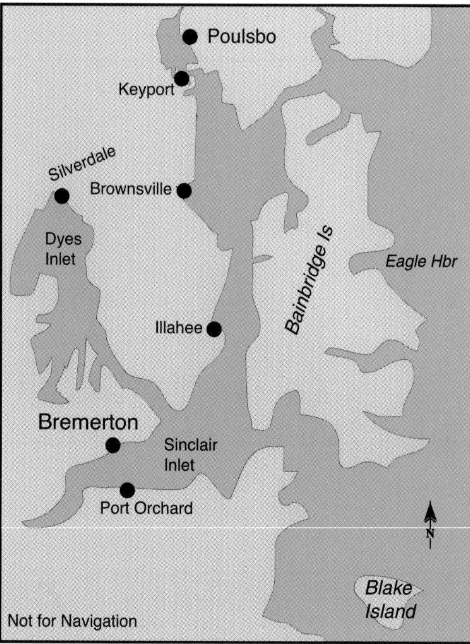

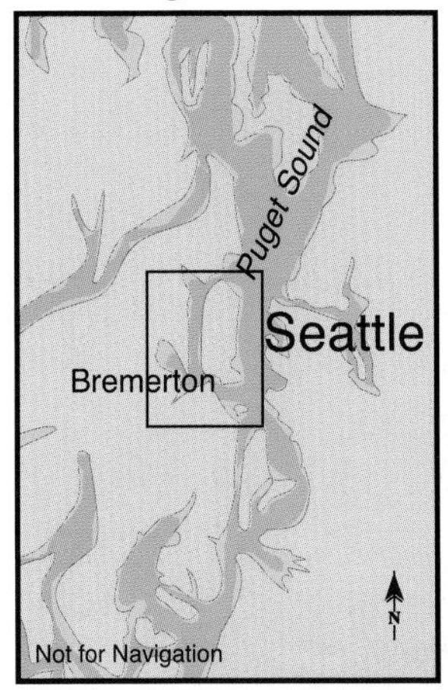

Poulsbo

Poulsbo

Opposite, top: The marina at Poulsbo. Left: A downtown street scene. Left, lower: Visitor docks at Poulsbo. Opposite, bottom: The fuel dock at the marina. This Norwegian village has a strong appeal to tourists.

Port of Silverdale Marina

PO Box 310 Silverdale, WA 98383
Phone: 360-698-4918 Chart 18449
Visitor moorage 1,300'. **Washrooms. Nearby**: Restaurants, shopping. **Launch ramp** adjacent in Waterfront Park. Picnic and play areas. Reservations available.

Below: The dock at Silverdale serves a park and a launch ramp. It can accommodate some larger boats.

Silverdale

47° 38.564' N 122° 41.526' W

Brownsville–visitors dock

Port of Brownsville

Jerry Rowland
9790 Ogle Rd NE
Bremerton WA 98311
Ph: 360-692-5498
Fax: 360-698-8023
pob@portofbrownsville.org
www.portofbrownsville.org
Charts 18446, 18449 VHF 16, 66A
Moorage: 1,000' breakwater plus visitor dock. **Water. Power:** 30 amp. **Fuel:** Gas, diesel, propane, snacks. **Laundry, showers, washrooms.** Launch ramp. Free pump-out. **Nearby:** Bank machine, park, deli, convenience store, meat market.

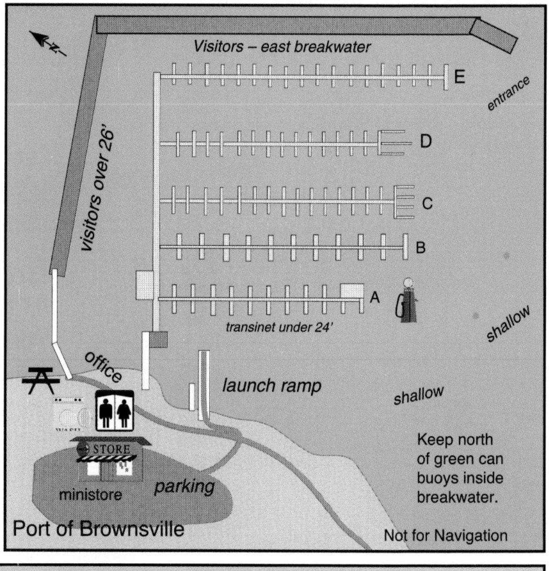

Illahee Chart 18449

Illahee State Park

Port Orchard Bay.
Ph: 360-478-6460 360-902-8844
Visitor dock. Up to 350 feet of dock space. Mooring buoys are located beyond floating breakwater adjacent to the dock area. **Washrooms.** Portadump.

47° 35.979' N 122° 35.584' W

Bainbridge Waterfront Park

370 Brien Dr, Bainbridge Island WA 98110 Manager–Tami Allen
Ph: 206-780-3733 Fax: 206-780-0955
tallen@ci.bainbridge-isl.wa.us
www.ci.bainbridge-isl.wa.us
Chart 18449. Moorage 100 ft. **Washrooms. Pumpout**. Playground, picnic tables.
Nearby: Launch ramp. 400' linear mooring buoys. Downtown location and near Seattle ferry. Speed limit 5 knots. Summer concerts on Wednesdays in season. speed limit 5 knots.

Winslow Wharf Marina

Harbour Marina

Fred Adams **Chart 18449**
231 Parfitt Way SW, Eagle Harbor Bainbridge Island WA 98110
Ph: 206-550-5340 Fax (pub)**: 206-842-5047**
Visitor moorage in available slips. **Shower, laundry, washrooms. Power:** 30 amp.
Facilities: Pumpout. Marina is adjacent to an English-style pub. Close to town.

Winslow Wharf Marina

Dave Lafave **Chart 18449 VHF 9**
141 Parfitt Way SW, Bainbridge Island WA 98110
Ph: 206-842-4202 Fax: 206-842-7785
Limited visitor moorage. **Power:** 30 amp.
Showers, laundry, washrooms.
Nearby: Launch ramp. Pumpout. Chandlery. This marina is very close to town and adjacent to the park and Seattle ferry.

There are public boat launching ramps at Fort Ward State Park, at Fay Bainbridge State Park and at Eagle Harbor Waterfront Park. Overnight moorage is available on the pier at Eagle Harbor Waterfront Park and anchorage buoys at Fay Bainbridge State Park.

Eagle Harbor Marina

Tod Hornick
5834 Ward Ave NE, Bainbridge Island WA 98110 Ph: 206-842-4003
harbormaster@eagleharbormarina.com
www.eagleharbormarina.com
Chart 18449
Guest moorage, 30' to 66'.
Power: 30, 50-amp, club house, mobile pumpout, cable; phone, wi-fi; high speed internet, shower, laundry, exercise room, sauna.

Left: Eagle Harbor Marina is across the bay from town. It is mostly permanent moorage.

Bremerton - Port Orchard

Port Washington Marina

Bob & Stephanie Stanberry
1805 Thompson Dr Bremerton WA 98337
Ph: 360-479-3037 Chart 18449
www.portwashingtonmarina.com

Moorage: Transient–call for slip assignment. **Water. Power**: 30, 50 amps. 80 slips. Cable and phonelines to all docks. Pumpout. **Laundry, showers, washrooms.**

(see location on diagram, opposite page)

Photo at top shows a view of the docks at Port Orchard. Right: The USS Turner Joy tied up at Bremerton.

Bremerton Marina

Steve Slaton (also Port Orchard Marina)
120 Washington Beach
Port Orchard WA 98367
Ph: 360-373-1035 Fax: 360-479-2928
Charts 18448, 18449 VHF 66A
guest@portofbremerton.org
www.portofbremerton.org

Moorage: Call for reservations. **Water. Power**: 30 amps. **Pumpout. Laundry, showers, washrooms.** Public pay phones, bus, ferry, restaurant. Adjacent City of Bremerton. Fuel and moorage at Port Orchard Marina. Restaurants, stores.

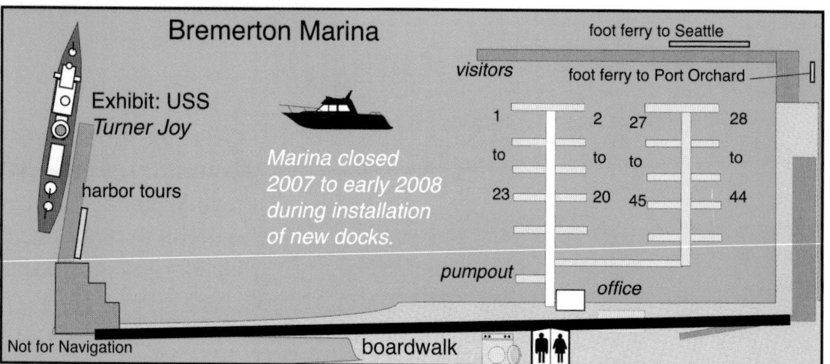

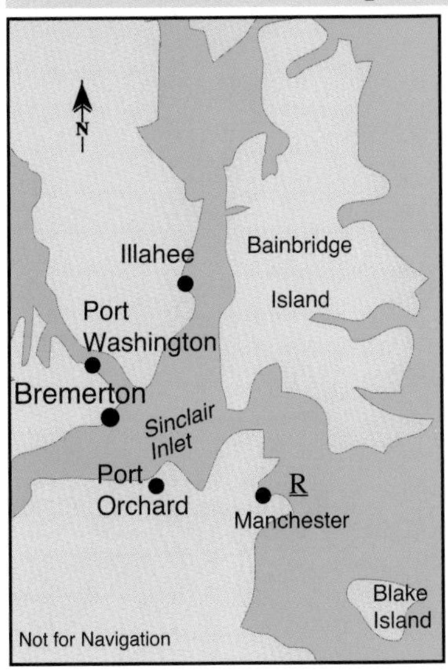

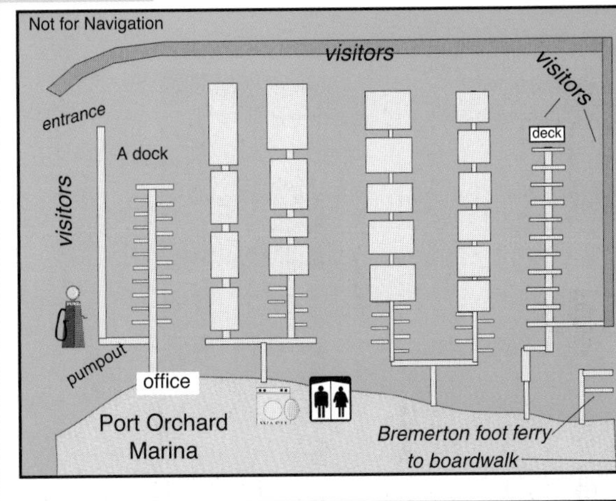

Port Orchard Marina

Steve Slaton (also Bremerton)
707 Sidney Pkwy
Port Orchard WA 98367
www.portofbremerton.org
Ph: 360-876-5535 Fax: 360-895-0291
Charts 18448, 18449 VHF 66A

Moorage: Permanent and transient–call for reservations. **Water. Power:** 20, 50 amps. **Fuel:** Gas, diesel, ice. **Laundry, showers, washrooms.** Garbage disposal. Internet access.

Nearby: Boardwalk and waterfront park. Playground. Ferry to Bremerton and Seattle. Bus, bank, restaurants, shops. Marine hardware and marine services off property.

Blake Island State Marine Park

Blake Island, Yukon Harbor, Puget Sound.
Ph: 360-731-833
Charts 18474, 18448, 18449, 18441
Moorage, water, 1700' dock space plus mooring buoys. Camping, trails, scuba diving nearby. Indian Loghouse replica and restaurant.

47° 33.328' N 122° 32.521' W

Port of Manchester

PO Box 3404 Manchester WA 98353
Ph: 206-722-3887 Chart 18448
Day moorage only. Launch ramp.
Nearby: Washrooms, Restaurants, stores. Potable water.
This is a state park. Visitor dock–200 feet. May dry at extreme low tides.

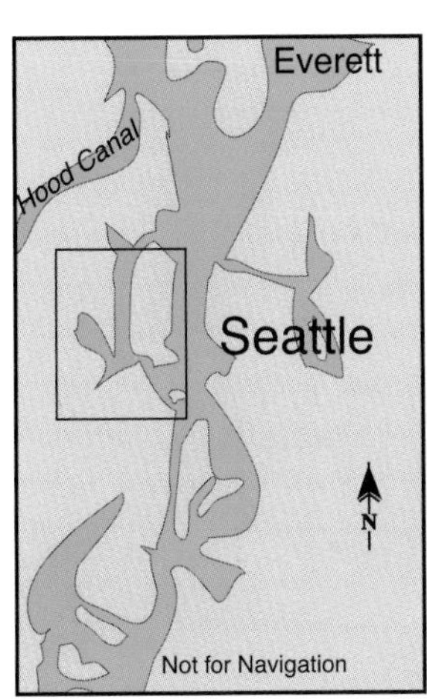

Closing marina June 2007 until early 2008 to expand docks by 300 slips. Guest moorage is available at Port Orchard Marina (Phone: 360-876-5335).

47° 33.281' N 122° 38.198' W for Port of Bremerton Marina

Seattle

Charts: 18447, 18474, 18448/9, 18441

Shilshole Marina
Hiram M Chittenden Locks
Ballard Mill Marina
Fishermen's Terminal (Salmon Bay)
Morrison's Fuel dock
HC Henry Marina
Chandler's
Elliot Bay Marina
Seattle
No Overnight Anchoring in Seattle
Elliot Bay
Bell Harbor Marina
Alki Point
Not for Navigation

Shilshole Bay Marina

Note: 2007: Many changes in new construction plans.

Sharon Briggs
7001 Seaview Ave NW, Seattle WA 98117
Ph: 206-728-3006 Fax: 206-728-3391
Toll free 1-800-426-7817 ext 3006
sbm@portseattle.org
www.portseattle.org/seaport/marinas/shilshole **VHF 17**

Fuel. Gas, diesel. **Power:** 20, 30, 50, 100 amp. Marine supplies. Mechanic. **Laundry, showers, washrooms.** Guest slips for over 100 boats. Internet access. Dry moorage for 92 boats to 40 feet. Garbage/recycling. Boat yard. Haul-outs. Pump-out. Hazardous waste disposal. Restaurants, conference facilities, pub. Groceries. Fishing supplies. **Nearby:** Shops. **Launch ramp.**
The marina's location makes it an ideal stop for those heading into or out of Lake Washington.

Artist's rendering of new docks at Shilshole Bay Marina

Shilshole Marina

Ballard Mill Marina

Willy Jenkins
4733 Shilshole Ave NW VHF 66A
Seattle WA 98107 Ph: 206-789-4777
bmm@surfbest.net
(located in ship canal, Salmon Bay). Limited moorage. **Power:** 20, 30 amp. **Washrooms. Showers. Pumpout.**
Nearby: Launch ramp.

Fishermen's Terminal–For location of listings on this page please see diagram on page 302.

Fuel at Morrison's **North Star Marine. Ph: 206-284-6600.**

Opposite and top: Shilshole Marina in concept and its dock structure. Above: Docks at Fishermen's Terminal.

Marina Park

25 Lakeshore Plaza Dr
123 Fifth Ave, Kirkland WA 98032
Ph: 425-587-3340 Fax: 425-587-3902
www.ci.kirkland.wa.us
Visitor moorage. Washrooms.
Nearby: **Launch ramp**. Kirkland city access. Medical services. Ice. Liquor store, post office. Restaurants in the area.

Fishermen's Terminal

3919 Commodore Way, Seattle WA 98199 Salmon Bay (at Salmon Bay)
Ph: 206-728-3395 Fax: 206-728-3280
ft@portseattle.org www.portseattle.org
Moorage.–7 slips. Boats to 250 ft. **Showers, laundry, washrooms. Power:** 15, 20, 30, 50, 100 amp. Boat repairs. Ways. Boat lift.

Salmon Bay Marina

Leslie Campbell
2100 18th Ave W, Seattle WA 98199
Ph: 206-282-5555 Fax: 206-282-8482
sales@salmonbaymarina.com
www.salmonbaymarina.com
Moorage: Visitors, **Power:** 30, 50-amp. Garbage/recycling, pumpout. Nearby restaurants, liquor store, groceries. Bank machine, shops, supplies.

Chandler's Cove

901 Fairview Ave N Seattle WA 98109
Ph: 206-262-8800
No overnight–2 hour stops only. Pumpout. Nearby restaurants.

Carillon Point Marina

Shelley Taylor
7000 Carillon Point, Kirkland WA 98033
Ph: 425-822-1700 Fax: 425-828-3094
shelley@carillonprop.com
www.carillon-point.com
Visitor moorage. Power: 30, 50 amp. **Showers, washrooms.** Pump-out station. Portadump. Adjacent hotel and shops.

Lake Washington moorage is available on a very limited basis. Stop at Parkshore Marina, the Kirkland dock or possibly at Gene Coulon Park. If you are a member of a yacht club with reciprocal privileges you will be able to stay on a first come basis at club facilities on the lake.

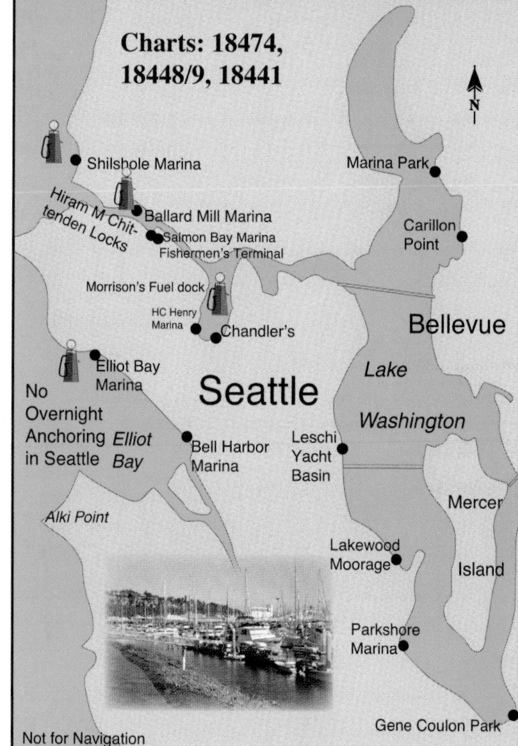

Top: Elliot Bay Marina can accommodate very large pleasure craft. Visitors should call ahead to arrange moorage.

Lakewood Moorage

Ell & Kathie Schober
4500 Lake Washington Blvd S
Seattle WA 98118 Ph: 206-722-3887
www.seattle.gov/parks
Limited visitor moorage.
Washrooms. Laundry, gift store, marine supplies, snacks. Picnic area.

Parkshore Marina

9050 Seward Park Ave
Seattle WA 98118
Ph: 206-725-3330 Fax: 206-418-6734
info@parkshoremarina.net
www.parkshoremarina.net
Visitor moorage in vacant tenant slips.
Washrooms, showers, laundry.
Pumpout station. Launch ramp.
Adjacent to Rainier Yacht Club.

Gene Coulon Memorial Beach Park

1201 Lake Washington Blvd
Renton WA 98055
Ph: 425-430-6700 Fax: 425-430-6701

Moorage for day use only. Park with facilities. Showers, washrooms. Tennis, playground.Nearby: 8-lane launch ramp. Restaurant. *www.ci.renton.wa.us*

Elliott Bay Marina **VHF 78A**

Dan Park
2601 W Marina Pl, Seattle WA 98199
Ph: 206-285-4817 Fax: 206-286-3129
info@elliottbaymarina.net
www.elliottbaymarina.net

Moorage. 20'-200' **Fuel:** Gas, diesel, **Water. Power:** 30, 50, 100, 150 amp. Garbage disposal, marine mechanic and repairs. Internet access. Restaurants, convenience store. **Showers, laundry,** washrooms, slipside **pumpout.**

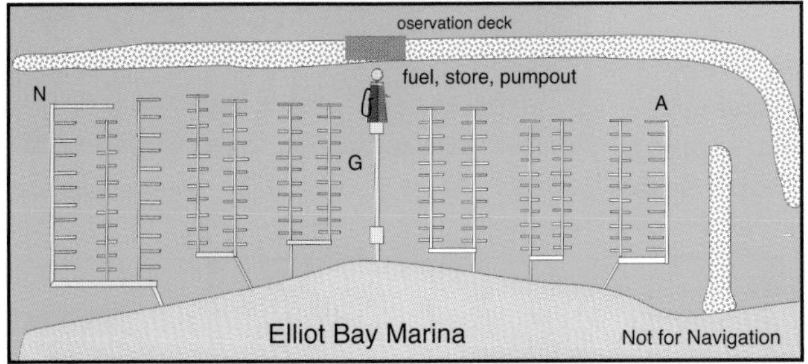

Below left: One of two restaurants at Elliot Bay Marina. It overlooks the marina and a view across Elliot Bay towards Seattle (photo above left). Below right: View from Elliot Bay Marina towards Seattle.

Restaurant at Elliot Bay Marina

47° 36.617' N 122° 21.061' W

Bell Harbor

Bell Harbor Marina VHF 66A

Ramel Winslow, Pati Lockeman
Pier 66, 2203 Alaskan Way, Seattle WA 98121
Ph: 206-615-3952 Fax: 206-615-3965
Toll free 1-800-426-7817 ext 3952
bhm@portseattle.org
www.portseattle.org

Moorage: Marina on Seattle waterfront. 36 visitor slips. Reserve online.
Power: 30, 50, 100 amp. **Washrooms, showers.** Garbage/recycling. **Pumpout.**
Nearby: Restaurants, stores. Near Aquarium maritime museum, science center, Space Needle and Pike Place Market. Waterfront trolley. Vessels over 120' should inspect entrance angle before entering.

Restaurant overlooking the dock

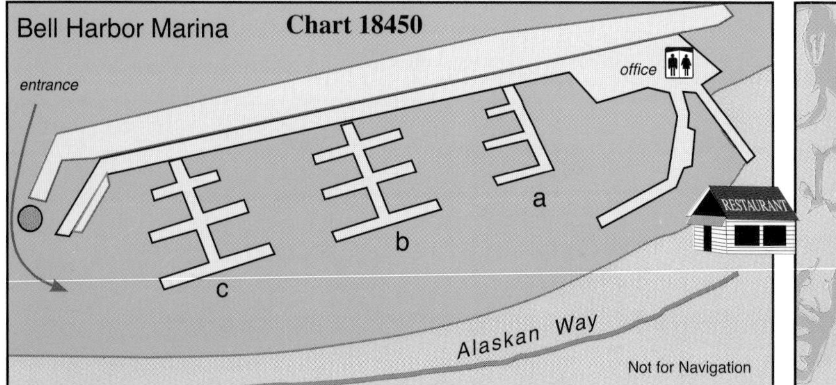

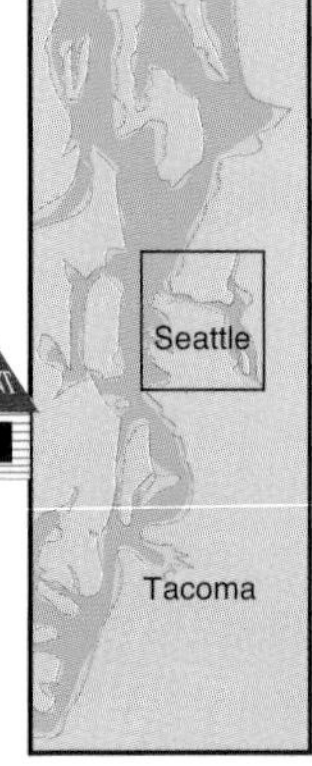

City of Des Moines Marina

Joe Dusenbury
22307 Dock Ave S
Des Moines WA 98198
Ph: 206-824-5700 Fax: 206-878-5940
Charts 18474, 18448 VHF 16
www.desmoineswa.gov

Moorage. Large permanent marina with section for visitors–about 65 slips. **Power:** 30, 50 amps. **Fuel:** Gas, diesel, propane, ice, engine and outboard oils. Marine repairs. Free pumpout. **Washrooms. Showers.**
Adjacent: Boatyard, Haul outs–30 ton sling hoist for haulouts and launching, marine store, snacks, restaurants. Playground. **Laundry** nearby.

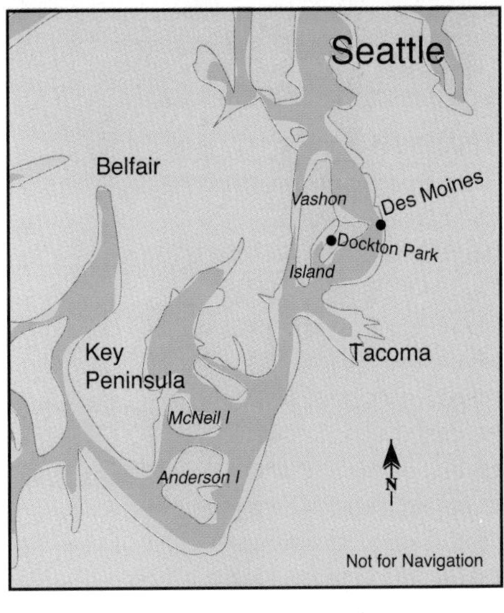

Above: The guest dock and sling hoist at Des Moines.

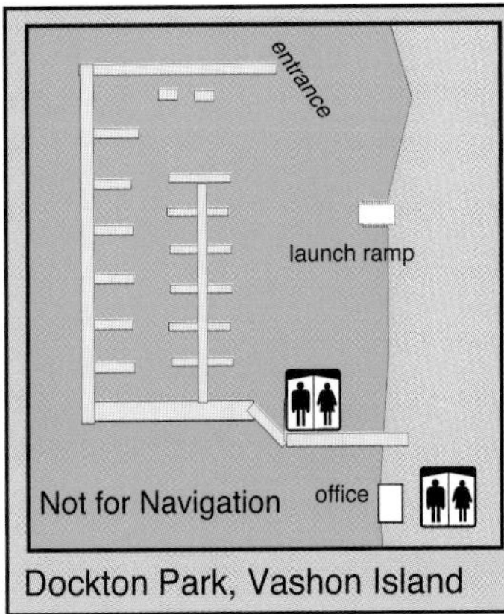

Dockton Park, Vashon Island

Vashon Island Dockton Park

9500 SW Dock St, Vashon WA 98070
Ph: 206-463-2947 Chart 18474
www.metrokc.gov/parks

Moorage. Visitor docks. Mar–October. **Water. Pumpout. Porta dump. Washrooms. Showers.** No garbage. Park adjacent to moorage. **Launch ramp.** Picnic shelter.

47° 22.451' N 122° 27.552' W

47° 19.601' N 122° 34.527' W

Jerisich Park dock

Gig Harbor

Jerisich Park

Gig harbor public marina
3510 Grandview St,
Gig Harbor WA 98335
Ph/Fax: 253-851-6170
www.cityofgigharbor.net

Moorage: Up to 420 feet of space for visitors' boats. Note the dinghy dock in the foreground of the photo above. Pumpout station at outer end of dock is open in summer only.

Adjacent: Picnic tables, walkways, gardens. Stores, groceries, restaurants and services nearby. The marina is located in the centre of downtown Gig Harbor. **Use chart 18474.**

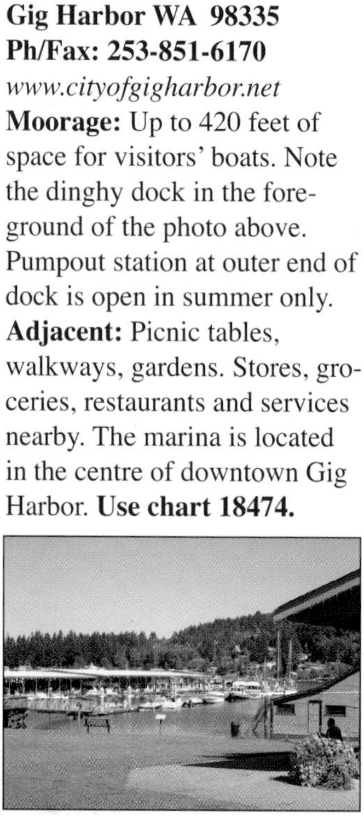

The public dock at Gig Harbor is close to all facilities. A sculpture commemorates fishermen. Gig Harbor is a top-rated destination.

Arabella's Landing

John Moist
3323 Harborview Dr
Gig Harbor WA 98332
Ph/Fax: 253-851-1793
arabellas@harbornet.com
www.arabellaslanding.com

Moorage: Up to 40 visitor boats at Bayview Marina dock. This is part of the same marina complex.
Water. Power: 20, 30, 50 amps. Garbage disposal. **Pumpout.** Lounge. **Laundry. Washrooms. Showers**. Clubhouse, walkways, gardens, wheelchair access. This is a high quality marina with all amenities. Stores and services nearby.

Above: Arabella's Landing at Gig Harbor.
Above: Another view of Arabella's Landing Marina.
Left: Arabella's docks.

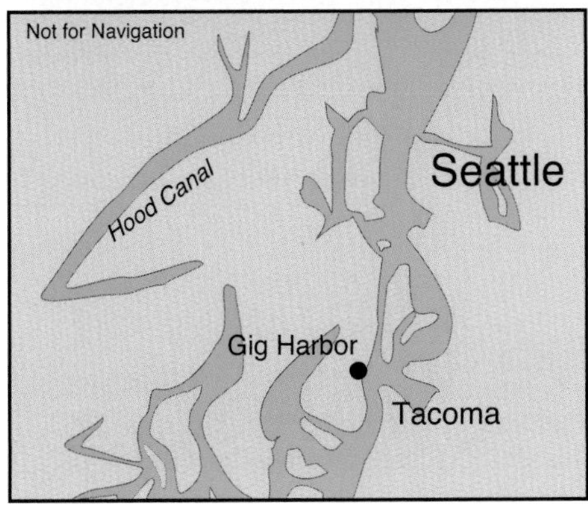

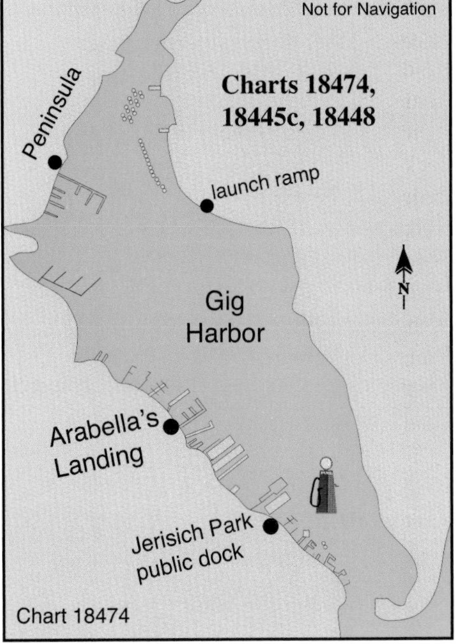

47° 15.725' N 122° 26.335' W

Charts: 18453, 18474, 18448

Pick up a copy of Cleats & Eats Tacoma *for restaurant guide information.*

Foss Waterway Marina

Delin Docks Marina.

Tacoma

Not for Navigation

Chinook Landing

Tacoma Harbor

Foss Waterway Marina

Totem Marina

Delin Docks

Dock Street Marina

Foss Landing Marina

Puyallup River

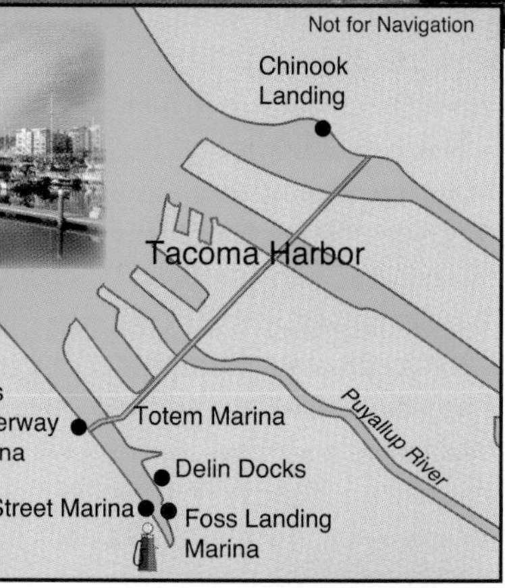

Dock Street Marina

Doug Hicks

Thea Foss Waterway VHF 78A

817 Dock St, Tacoma WA 98402

Ph: 253-272-4352 Fax 253-572-2768

info@dockstreetmarina.com

www.dockstreetmarina.com

Moorage. Visitor docks. **Water. Power**: 30, 50 amp. Garbage/recycling. Cable TV. Marine store. Propane. Slipside pumpout. **Free showers. Laundry, washrooms. Nearby: Fuel,** stores–groceries, restaurants, fishing supplies, post office. Tacoma city.

Foss Waterway Marina

Tracy McKendry

821 Dock St, Tacoma WA 98402

Ph: 253-272-4404 Fax 253-272-0367

tracy@fosswaterwaymarina.com

www.fosswaterwaymarina.com

Moorage. Transient moorage–reserve. Two hours free. **Water. Power**: 30, 50 amps. Hoist. Marine store. Propane. Pumpout. **Launch ramp. Showers. Laundry. Washrooms. Fuel,** stores–groceries, fishing supplies, post office. Dock Street Landing Bar and Grill, Tacoma city. Shoreline walkway. Toy Boat Museum alongside.

Above: Foss Waterway Marina store.

Thea Foss Waterway with Dock Street Marina in the foreground.

Foss Landing Marina

Tim Curry
Thea Foss Waterway
1940 East D St
Tacoma WA 98421
Ph: 253-627-4344 Fax: 253-627-4878
info@fosslanding.com
www.fosslanding.com
Moorage. Permanent moorage. Guest moorage by reservations.
Power: 50 amp. Fuel nearby.
Pumpout. Showers, washrooms

Foss Landing Marina .
47° 14.391' N 122° 33.671' W

Delin Docks

Doug Hicks
Thea Foss Waterway
1616 D St, Tacoma WA 98421
Ph: 253-572-256
Permanent moorage only.
The guest docks are at Dock Street Marina, which is managed by Delin Docks. **Power, showers, laundry.** Propane. Pumpout. Restaurant**. Washrooms.**

Totem Marina fuel dock on the Thea Foss Waterway and downtown Tacoma.

Dock Street: Fuel, moorage. See listing page 308.
NOTE: *A free tram service carries passengers along Tacoma's city streets.*

Chinook Landing Marina
47° 16.811' N 122° 24.218' W
Chinook Landing

Chinook Landing Marina

Dennis LaPointe
3702 Marine View Dr **VHF 79**
Tacoma WA 98422 **Chart 18453**
Ph: 253-627-7676 Fax: 253-779-0576
Moorage. Many slips.
Pumpout. Water. Power: 30, 50 amps.
Showers, Laundry. Washrooms.
Marina store. Espresso. Ice. Garbage disposal.

Point Defiance Boathouse

Boathouse Marina

Breakwater Marina

Michael Marchetti
5603 N Waterfront Dr
Tacoma WA 98407
Phone: 253-752-6663 Fax: 253-752-8291
info@breakwatermarina.com
www.breakwatermarina.com

Moorage. Many slips for visitors. Check in at Fuel dock. **Power:** 15, 30 amp. **Fuel:** Gas, diesel, propane, snacks. Internet access. **Pumpout. Laundry. Washrooms. Showers.** Garbage disposal. **Adjacent:** Vashon Island ferry. Launch ramp. Restaurant nearby. Visitors: Nearby liquor store, zoo, aquarium, Fort Nisqually historic site. Point Defiance Park adjacent.

Port of Allyn Dock

Lynch Cove. Near Belfair. Ph: 360-275-2430
Small dock–brief stops. **Launch Ramp.**

Lakebay Marina

Dewey Hostepler
15 Lorenz Rd Key Peninsula N
Lakebay WA 98349 Ph: 253-884-3350

Moorage. Water. Power: 15 amps.
Fuel: Gas, propane. **Washrooms.**
Store–fishing tackle, ice, groceries.

Boathouse Marina (Point Defiance)

Tim Hartman
5912 N Waterfront Dr
Tacoma WA 98407
Ph: 253-591-5325
boathouse@tacomaparks.com
www.metroparkstacoma.org

47° 18.125' N
122° 30.574' W

Boat rentals, small visitor dock and boat launching. **Water. Fuel:** Gas. **Pumpout. Washrooms. Adjacent:** Public fishing pier, restaurant. Gift and tackle shop.

Top: The launch ramp is at the entrance to Breakwater Marina and the Tacoma Yacht Club. Above: Two views of Boathouse Marina.

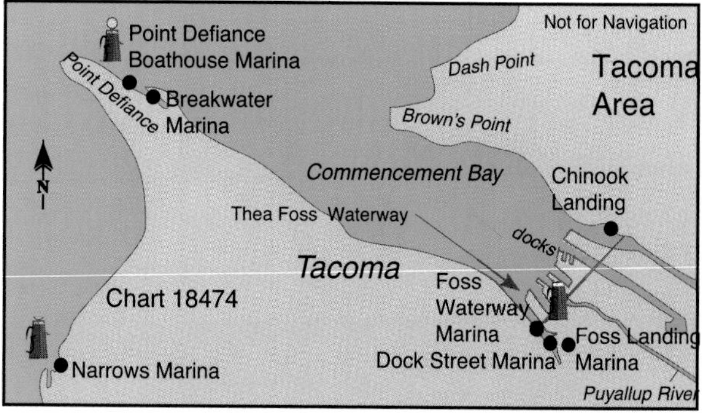

Fair Harbor **Charts 18457, 18448**

47° 20.021' N 122° 49.801' W

Fair Harbor

Fair Harbor Marina

Susan and Vern Nelson
5050 Grapeview Loop Rd
PO Box 160, Grapeview WA 98546
Ph: 360-426-4028 Fax: 360-275-8139
info@fairharbor.us www.fairharbormarina.us
Moorage. Visitors docks 350 feet.
Power: 20, 30 amps. **Fuel:** Gas, **Washrooms, showers.** Marine store–groceries, hardware, fishing tackle and bait, alcohol, kerosene, propane. Charts. Gift shop. Some repairs and service. Moorage guests–complimentary transportation to golf course. Picnic area.

Port of Shelton **VHF 16**

www.sheltonyachtclub.com
Ph: 360-426-9476 Reciprocal moorage.

Penrose State Marine Park
Chart 18448. Guest moorage 300 ft.
Mooring buoys. Pumpout, showers.

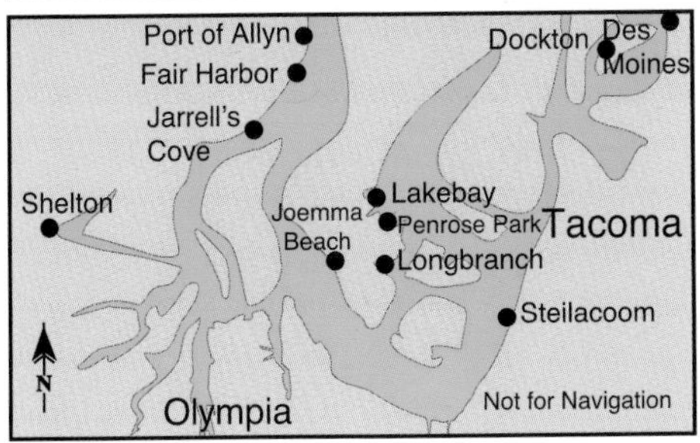

Longbranch

47° 12.588' N 122° 45.131' W

Longbranch Marina

Mark Jones **VHF16/68**
PO Box 111, Longbranch WA 98349
Ph: 253-884-5137
Moorage. Visitors, clubs welcome.
Portapottie toilets. Water. Power: 30 amps. Garbage disposal. Mechanic, divers available. Laundry. Dinghy dock.
Adjacent: anchorage nearby. Store across the road–*photograph below.*

Joemma Beach State Marine Park
Chart 18448. Guest moorage 500 ft.
Mooring buoys. Pumpout, campsite.

photo courtesy of Jarrell's Cove Marina

Jarrell's Cove

Jarrell's Cove Marina

Lorna and Gary Hink
220 East Wilson Rd Harstine Island
Shelton WA 98584
Ph: 360-426-8823 Fax: 360-432-8494
Toll Free: 1-800-362-8823 Charts 18457, 18448

Moorage: 200 feet visitor docks. **Check in at fuel dock. Pumpout. Water. Power:** 30 amps. **Fuel:** Gas, diesel, propane. **Laundry, showers, washrooms.** Marine store–Hardware, fishing tackle, licences, groceries, ice. Books, beer.

Adjacent: 4 RV sites, games area, picnic area, beach, public pay phone, point of interest–historic log cabin.

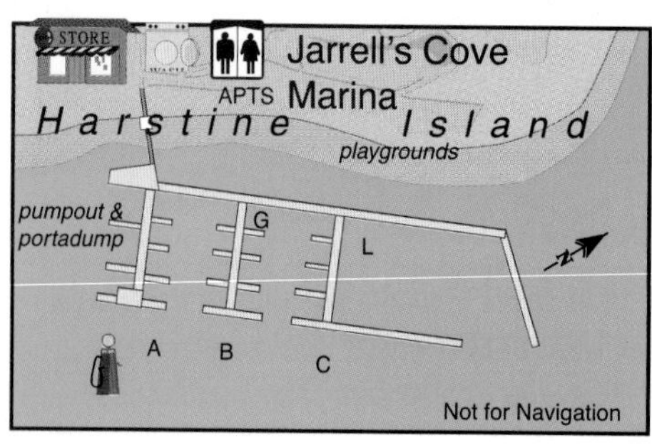

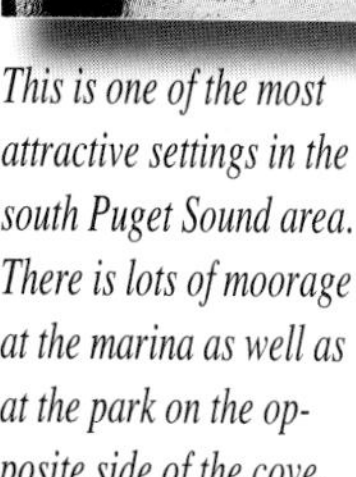
This is one of the most attractive settings in the south Puget Sound area. There is lots of moorage at the marina as well as at the park on the opposite side of the cove.

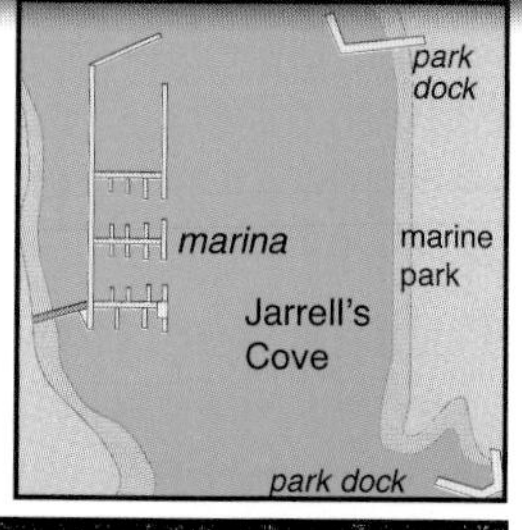

Jarrell's Cove Marine State Park, Harstine Island. Located opposite the marina. 682 foot guest dock. 14 mooring buoys, washrooms, showers, pumpout, portadump. Picnic areas. See *www.parks.wa.gov* for more.

Boston Harbor

Boston Harbor Marina

Don McHugh and Pam McHugh
312 73rd Ave NE **Chart 18448**
Olympia WA 98506 **VHF 16/68**
Ph: 360-357-5670 Fax: 360-352-2816
bhm@bostonharbormarina.com
www.bostonharbormarina.com

Moorage. Transient. Large vessels okay.
Water. Power: 20 amps.
Fuel: Gas, diesel, CNG.
Toilets. Marine store–gifts, marine supplies, fresh seafood, groceries, ice.
Adjacent: Launch ramp, picnic area, beach, park. Kayak and boat rentals.

Boston Harbor Marina is a good place to sit and watch the sunsets and the store has a friendly staff to welcome you to the harbor.

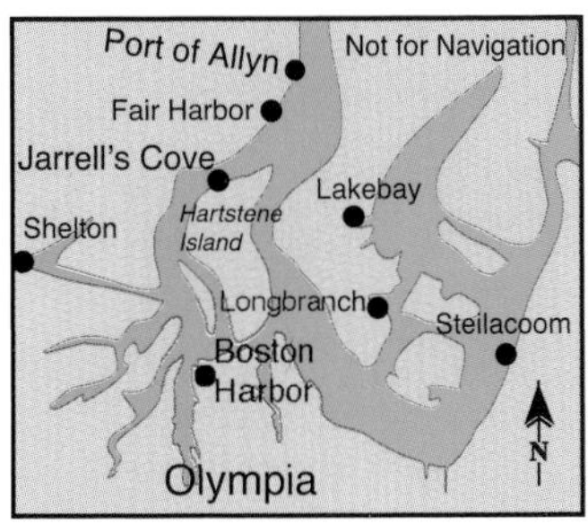

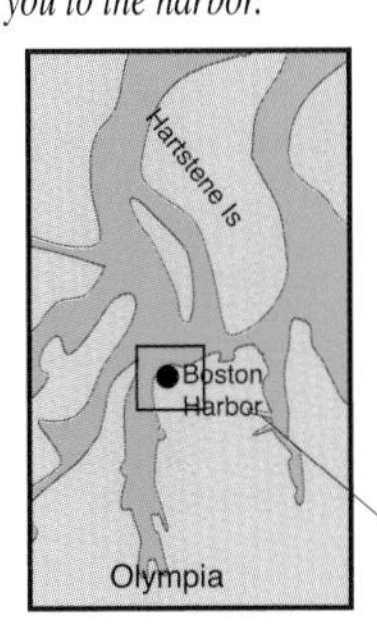

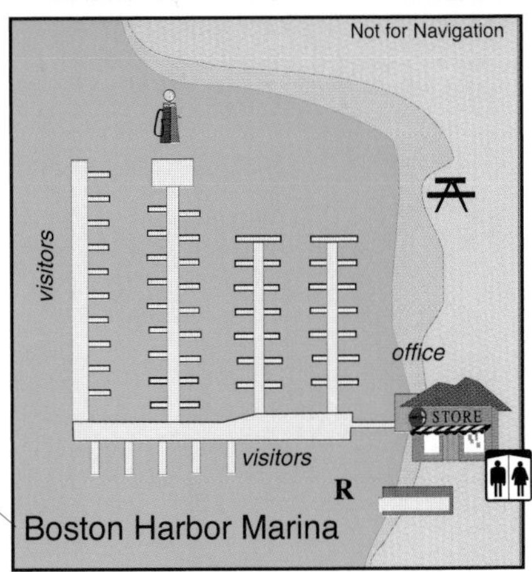

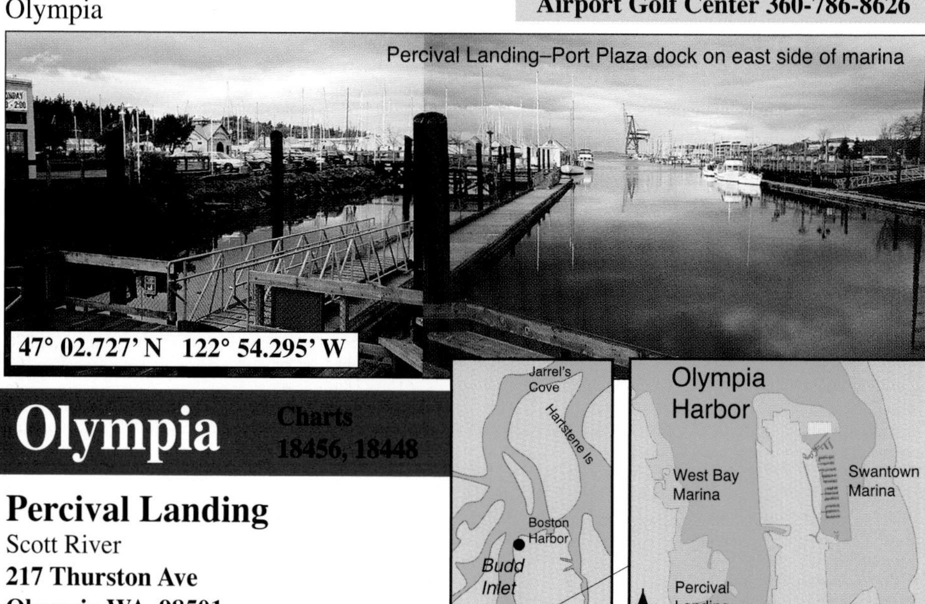

Olympia

Charts 18456, 18448

Percival Landing

Scott River
217 Thurston Ave
Olympia WA 98501
Ph: 360-753-8380 Fax: 360-753-8334
Charts 18456, 18448
olympiaparks@ci.olympia.wa.us
www.ci.olympia.wa.

Moorage east side Port Plaza dock–public. **Water. Power:** 30 amp. **Washrooms.**
Adjacent: Oyster Bar restaurant.
Nearby: Grocery store, uptown stores, restaurants and all facilities.
This facility is adjacent to the Olympia Yacht Club (west side). The marina extends down the east side of the harbor and along the south waterfront. It is literally a downtown feature of Olympia.

Swantown Marina

Bruce Marshall
1022 Marine Dr NE **VHF 65A**
Olympia WA 98501
Ph: 360-528-8049 Fax: 360-528-8094
marina@portolympia.com
www.portolympia.com

Moorage. Visitors. **Laundry. Washrooms. Showers. Pumpout. Power**: 20, 30 amp. Wi-fi Internet access. Restaurants, groceries, liquor store, PO, launch ramp. Chandlery, repairs, service. Market. Fuel 7 miles.

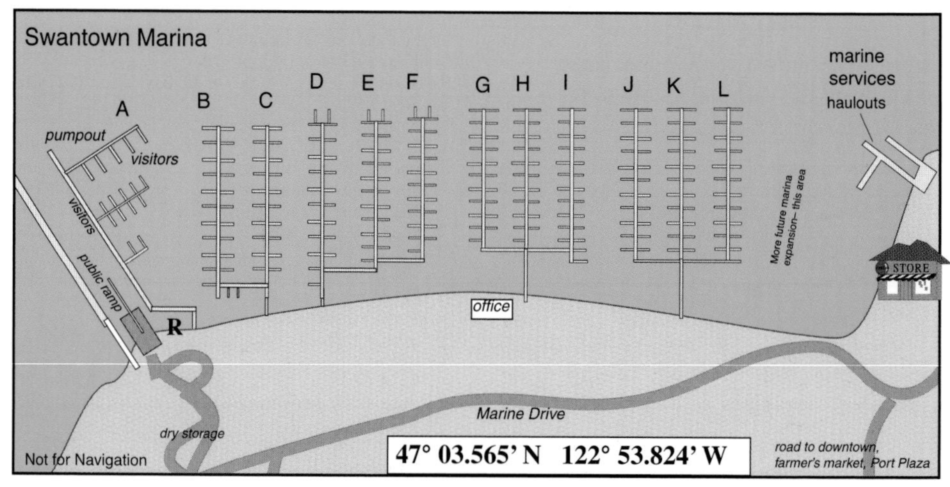

Index

For comprehensive information on coastal marine parks and anchorages see the companion guide to this book–*Anchorages and Marine Parks*.

Bibliography and recommended reading

A Guide to the Western Seashore. Rick M. Harbo. Hancock House, Surrey, BC. 1988.
Anchorages and Marine Parks. Guide to anchorages and marine parks in British Columbia and the San Juan Islands. Peter Vassilopoulos. Seagraphic Publications. 2000.
BC Cruising Guide Series–Desolation Sound, Gulf Islands, Sunshine Coast. Bill Wolferstan. Whitecap Books.
Best Anchorages of the Inside Passage. Bill Kelly and Anne Vipond. 2006
Canadian Tide and Current Tables. Pacific Coast all volumes. Ottawa-Department of Fisheries and Oceans. Annual.
Charlies Charts North to Alaska. Charles E. Wood. Margo Wood. Polymath Energy Consultants Ltd. Surrey B.C.
Cruising Atlas Queen Charlottes to Olympia, Evergreen Pacific, 1990
Exploring the Gulf Islands and Desolation Sound to Port Hardy and Blunden Harbour. A Cruising Guide. Don Douglas. Fine Edge Productions. Anacortes WA.
Exploring the Inside Passage to Alaska. A Cruising Guide. Don Douglas. Fine Edge Productions. Anacortes WA.
Exploring the South Coast of British Columbia. A Cruising Guide. Don Douglas. Fine Edge Productions. Anacortes WA.
Exploring Vancouver Island's West Coast. A Cruising Guide. Don Douglass. Fine Edge Productions. Anacortes WA.
Gulf Islands Cruising Guide. Peter Vassilopoulos. Pacific Marine Publishing. Delta BC. 2006.
Local Knowledge. Kevin Monahan. Fine Edge, Anacortes, WA, 2003
Marine Parks of British Columbia. An Explorer's Guide. Peter Chettleburgh. Special Interest Publications. Vancouver. BC. 1985.
Marine Weather Hazards Manual. A guide to local forecasts and conditions. Vancouver. Environment Canada. 1990.
North of Desolation Sound. Peter Vassilopoulos. Pacific Marine Publishing. Delta BC. 2005.
North to Alaska. Hugo Anderson. Anderson Publishing Co. 1993.
Oceanography of the British Columbia Coast. Richard E. Thomson. Department of Fisheries and Aquatic Sciences. 1981.
Radar Book (The), Kevin Monahan. Fine Edge, Anacortes, WA, 2003
Sailing Directions. British Columbia Coast. Ottawa. Department of Fisheries and Oceans.
Sea Kayak Series, (Around Vancouver Isl/Gulf Islands/Nootka Sound) Rocky Mountain Books, Surrey BC, 2004
Sea Kayaking Canada's West Coast. John Ince and Hedi Kottner. Raxas Books. Vancouver, BC. 1996.
The San Juan Islands. Afoot and Afloat. Marge and Ted Mueller. The Mountaineers. Seattle. 1988.
Waggoner. Robert Hale. Robert Hale Publishing. Seattle. Annual. *This is an excellent cruising publication with up-to-date information about marinas and other facilities. It includes planning and piloting information.* Ph: 800-733-5330.
Weatherly Waypoint Guides for GPS and Loran Navigation. Robert Hale. Robert Hale Publishing. Volumes 1–3: Puget Sound, San Juan Islands, Strait of Juan de Fuca. Gulf of Georgia, including Gulf Islands, Jervis Inlet. Desolation Sound to Port Hardy.
West Coast of Vancouver Island. Don Watmough. Evergreen Pacific. Shoreline WA.

My wife Carla and I have cruised the area this guide covers for more than thirty years. We have visited all areas described in the book and have stopped at and moored at most moorages included in the foregoing pages. Mariners who adventure beyond the known routes and popular areas will enjoy discovering for themselves others I may have omitted. There are numerous books on cruising the coast and these along with your charts and reference books should enable you to extend your cruising range substantially and safely. Happy boating. –Peter Vassilopoulos.

By the same author

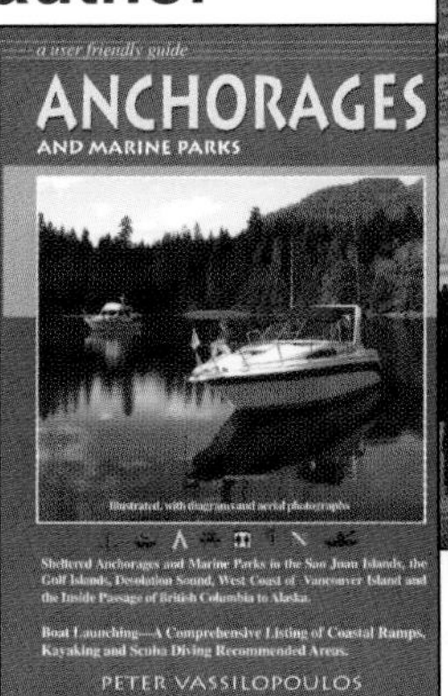

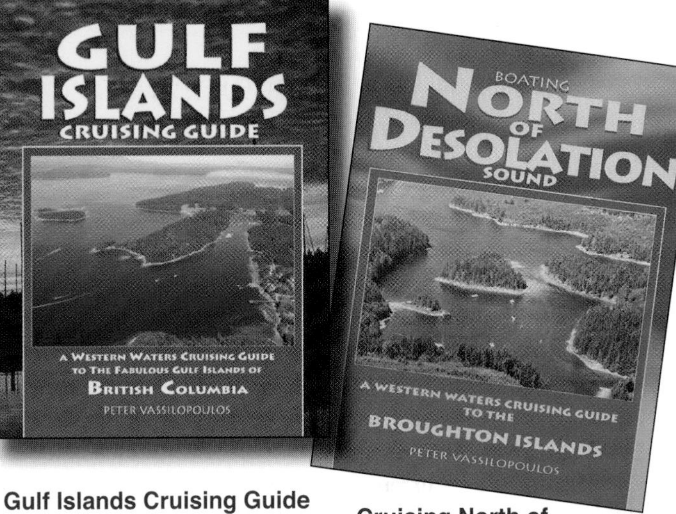

Anchorages and Marine Parks Guide to parks and anchorages in the Pacific NW. $19.95

Gulf Islands Cruising Guide Full colour aerial and ambient photos with directions and recommendations. $46.95

Cruising North of Desolation Sound A guide to the Broughtons– In full colour. $46.95

Gulf Islands Cruising Guide–a coffee table styled full colour, Illustrated guidebook– ***Peter Vassilopoulos $46.95.*** Packed with information and loaded with colourful diagrams and photographs of the area. See the most popular cruising area, the Gulf Islands, from the air and from a mariner's perspective.

North of Desolation Sound– a coffee table styled full colour, Illustrated guidebook– ***Peter Vassilopoulos $46.95.*** This is a comprehensive reference book/guide to the Broughton Islands area and routes from Stuart Island to Seymour Inlet. Filled with full colour photos, aerial pictures and diagrams. A must for serious mariners cruising the BC inland coast.

Anchorages and Marine Parks–*Peter Vassilopoulos $19.95*

A companion guide to **Docks and Destinations** providing information on places to find sheltered anchorage overnight and to facilities and features of marine parks. It covers, in a south to north progression, the San Juan Islands and all of BC coastal waters including the west coast of Vancouver Island.

These books are available at marine stores or you may order direct:

Pacific Marine Publishing 604-943-4618
PO Box 1312 Stn A, Delta BC V4M 3Y8
or PO Box 984, Point Roberts WA 98281-0984

Sgt Ken Burton, RCMP marine division, carries the author's books aboard for reference.

Docks and Destinations

Comments about this and other cruising guides by the same author

My wife and I have sailed this area for the past three summer vacations and despite the distance from England we keep coming back. We have found your guides essential reading and enormously useful and our holidays have been all the more enjoyable as a result. *–David D. Cotterell, England*

We often refer to our copy of **Docks and Destinations** while out on the water. We ALWAYS refer to your book when we are working in our store. What a great book!
–Dan and Leah Lee, Thrifty Foods, Salt Spring Island.

I have been to a number of places mentioned in your two books and found your information to be very accurate and extremely useful. I have pointed them out to boating friends and clients and gained points with them for doing so.
–Robert McMurray, artist, accountant, mariner.

Our best and most informative cruising guide. Always our first recommendation to our customers looking for a cruising guide on the coast. (We use it on our own boat.)
–Brad Mah, Nikka Industries, Vancouver/Steveston.

Mariners have commented on the clarity of your book. It is well designed—succinct yet containing enough information to enable the boater to make wise cruising decisions. *–Ann Taylor, Greenway Sound.*

This guide is updated when reprinted. Major updates and changes will be made periodically when new editions are published. Please write to me if you have any information or suggestions for inclusion in future editions. Your comments are welcome.
–Peter Vassilopoulos.

We cruise this incredible coast in our little boats and are reminded of our insignificance by the magnitude of the tumbling waterfalls, deep fjords and tall coastal mountains.

Canada: PO Box 1312 Stn A, Delta, British Columbia, Canada V4M 3Y8
USA: PO Box 984, Point Roberts, WA 98281-0984
Ph: 604-943-4618 Fax: 604-604-943-4689
boating@dccnet.com Please contact us for updating information.